GAMBIT

Guide to the Bogo-Indian

Steffen Pedersen

First published in the UK by Gambit Publications Ltd 1998

A copy of the British Library Cataloguing in Publication data is available from the British Library

ISBN 1 901983 04 8

DISTRIBUTION:
Worldwide (except USA): Biblios Distribution Services, Star Rd, Partridge Green, West Sussex, RH13 8LD, England.
USA: BHB International, Inc., 41 Monroe Turnpike, Trumbull, CT 06611, USA.

For all other enquiries (including a full list of all Gambit Chess titles) please contact the publishers, Gambit Publications Ltd, 69 Masbro Rd, Kensington, London W14 0LS.
Fax +44 (0)171 371 1477. E-mail 100561.3121@compuserve.com.

Edited by Graham Burgess and Chris Baker
Typeset by Petra Nunn
Printed in Great Britain by Redwood Books, Trowbridge, Wilts.

10 9 8 7 6 5 4 3 2 1

Contents

Symbols

+	check
#	checkmate
!!	brilliant move
!	good move
!?	interesting move
?!	dubious move
?	bad move
??	blunder
+–	White is winning
±	White is much better
⩲	White is slightly better
=	equal position
⩱	Black is slightly better
∓	Black is much better
–+	Black is winning
Ch	championship
Cht	team championship
tt	team tournament
Wch	world championship
Ech	European championship
Wcht	World Team Championship
ECC	European Clubs Cup
Ct	candidates event
IZ	interzonal event
Z	zonal event
OL	olympiad
jr	junior event
wom	women's event
mem	memorial event
rpd	rapidplay game
corr	correspondence game
1-0	the game ends in a win for White
½-½	the game ends in a draw
0-1	the game ends in a win for Black
(*n*)	*n*th match game
(D)	see next diagram

Bibliography

Books
Hooper & Whyld: *The Oxford Companion to Chess* (OUP, 1996)
Taulbut: *The New Bogo-Indian* (Cadogan, 1994)
Matanović et al.: *ECO E* (Šahovski Informator, 1991)

Periodicals
Informator
New in Chess

Electronic
ChessBase MegaBase '98
The Week in Chess
Sosonko: Catalan/Bogo-Indian (CD-ROM, New in Chess, 1997)

Introduction

The Bogo-Indian or, as it is occasionally called, the Bogoljubow Defence (after Efim Bogoljubow, who played it regularly in the 1920s), is initiated by the moves 1 d4 ♘f6 2 c4 e6 3 ♘f3 ♗b4+. It is a sound alternative to the Queen's Indian. Black embarks on rapid development, but compared to a Queen's Indian often has to surrender the bishop-pair and contrary to the Nimzo-Indian apparently gets no weaknesses in return to play against. However, Black's pieces acquit themselves quite well, provided Black knows how to use his pawns to provide good squares for them. It is worth noting that the Bogo-Indian has the practical advantage over the Queen's Indian that Black can also employ it against the Catalan, rather than having to learn a whole new opening.

I do not think that the Bogo-Indian is a difficult opening to learn. Black's development is fast and healthy, and does not commit him to a do-or-die strategy. Very few precise variations have to be memorized and in most cases one can get by with a general understanding of the strategic principles.

In each chapter there are the following sections:

- Typical Pawn Formations
- Planning for White
- Planning for Black
- Quick Summary
- The Theory of ...

For the average club player I think that the first few sections will be the most useful, while the more experienced player will want to investigate the theoretical material in greater detail.

Chapter 8, on 4 ♘c3, needs a little explanation, as this is in fact a line of the Nimzo-Indian. Most Bogo-Indian players also play the Nimzo-Indian, and so will already have a line prepared against this system – and if not, they may well have a book covering the Nimzo-Indian. However, I have not adopted the 'see another book' approach, because some players use the Bogo via the move-order 1 d4 ♘f6 2 ♘f3 e6 3 c4 ♗b4+, and meet 2 c4 not with 2...e6, but with the Benko, Budapest, or some other opening, and are therefore not regular Nimzo players. This chapter will also be useful for some players of the white side who wish to meet the Queen's Indian with 4 ♘c3, as it equips them to face the transposition to the Nimzo-Indian that occurs after 4...♗b4.

During the process of writing this book a number of people have been very helpful. Peter Heine Nielsen, Lars Bo Hansen, Graham Burgess, John Nunn and Mona Andersen deserve special thanks.

Odense, July 1998
Steffen Pedersen

1 The Ambitious 4 ♘bd2

1 d4 ♘f6 2 c4 e6 3 ♘f3 ♗b4+ 4 ♘bd2 *(D)*

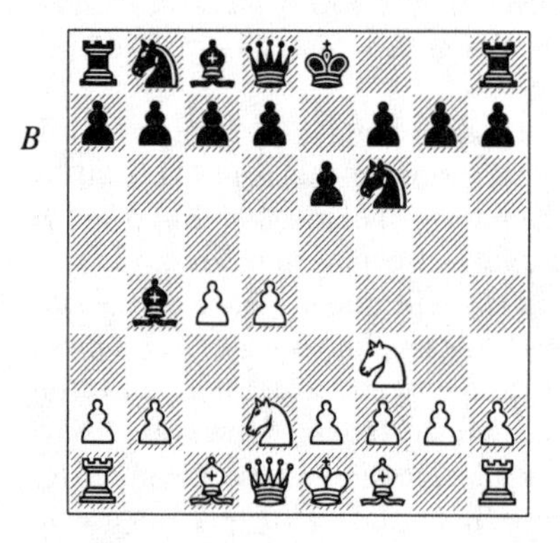

In many respects 4 ♘bd2 is White's most ambitious reply to the Bogo-Indian. Rather than offering an exchange of dark-squared bishops by 4 ♗d2, White seeks to obtain the bishop-pair by a subsequent a3, but without suffering the structural damage typical in the Nimzo-Indian. On the other hand, the move is a little slow, and Black may well be able to secure enough activity to offset the bishop-pair, or may avoid the exchange on d2 altogether, dropping his bishop back along the a3-f8 diagonal when challenged, justifying the loss of time by claiming that the knight is poorly placed on d2.

4 ♘bd2 was the recommendation against the Bogo-Indian in *Beating the Indian Defences* (Burgess/Pedersen), which provided a repertoire for White. I was responsible for the Bogo chapter in *BTID*, and believe that my recommendations and assessments there were valid, and therefore you may notice some overlap. However, the material here is updated and expanded considerably, and covers all lines for both White and Black.

Typical Pawn Structures

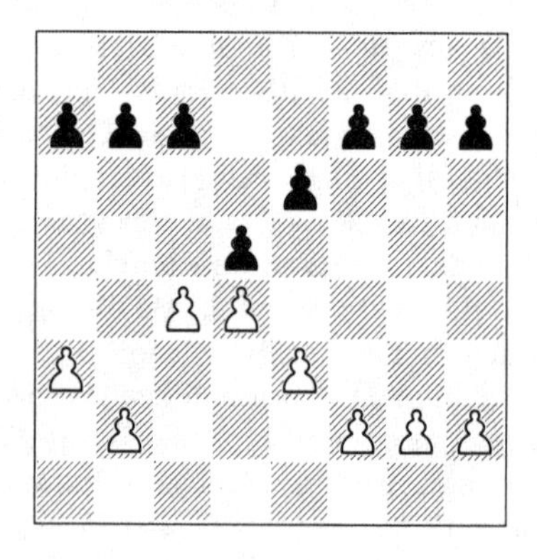

The above structure is often seen when Black decides to meet 4 ♘bd2 with 4...d5. Black will then have good control of the e4-square, while White might aim for active play on the queenside. Black often avoids the exchange on d2, by dropping the bishop back to e7.

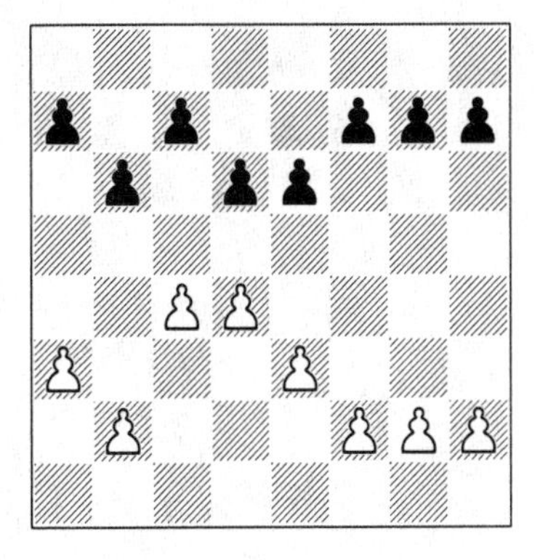

Here Black has gone for a queenside fianchetto. Normally Black has had to concede the bishop-pair and this may show up as a serious disadvantage if Black makes any further advances with his centre pawns. Therefore it is advisable for Black to leave those pawns alone for the time being, and instead he often starts a kingside attack by advancing his g- and h-pawns (assuming White has relocated his queen's bishop to g5).

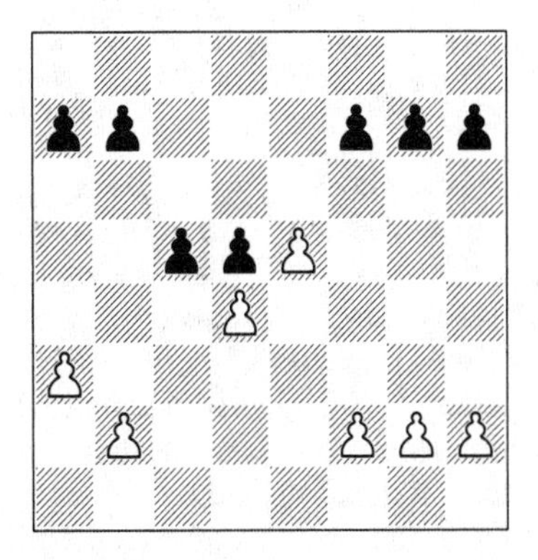

This structure, though rather unusual for the Bogo-Indian, is often seen in this chapter. White has managed to build up a broad centre. This is possible because Black has attempted to keep his dark-squared bishop after being threatened by a3. Black has in turn counter-attacked in the centre with ...d5 and ...c5. It is important now that White does not panic. Usually he should not worry about Black capturing on d4, as this pawn is easily won back. It is more important that White reinforces the e5-pawn, which is the spearhead of his attacking plans on the kingside.

Planning for White

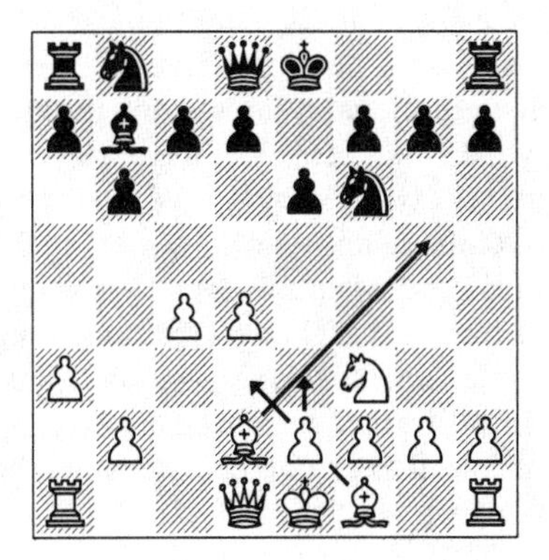

An important part of White's plan consists of gaining the bishop-pair. Black's position is still very solid but often he will feel the absence of his dark-squared bishop. In the above diagram White can try to emphasize this by moving the bishop to g5 (this also avoids having it harassed by ...♘e4 at some stage) followed by smooth development with e3, ♗d3, etc.

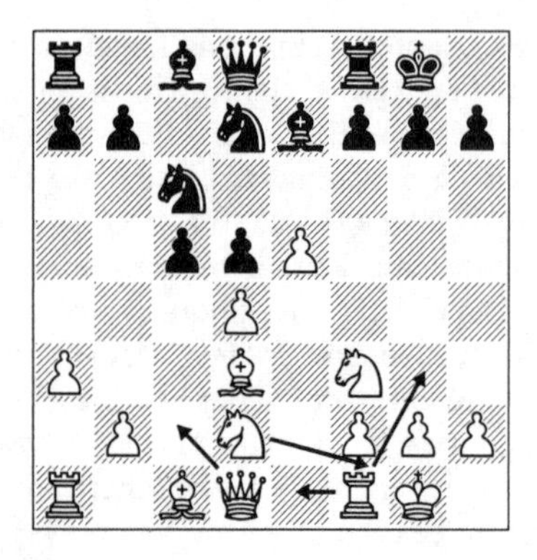

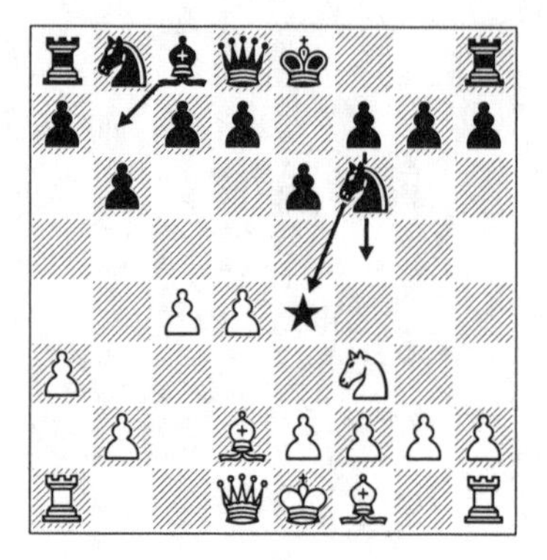

White may have the opportunity to construct a broad pawn-centre if Black decides to retreat his dark-squared bishop rather than exchanging it for White's knight on d2. This centre does not come free of charge since Black can start a counter-attack by ...d5 and ...c5, as in the above diagram. A typical plan for White is now to reinforce his e-pawn by moving the rook to e1, often followed by a knight manoeuvre via f1 to g3, thus obtaining a promising attacking position, which can be further improved by moving the queen to c2, thereby attacking the h7-pawn.

Planning for Black

The next diagram is very similar to one already examined in the 'Planning for White' section. There Black had played his bishop to b7, allowing White to play ♗g5. Often Black finds the bishop quite irritating on g5 and so takes measures to prevent this. One way is to play ...h6, while another is simply to use a different move-order and start with ...♘e4 followed by ...♗b7 and ...f5.

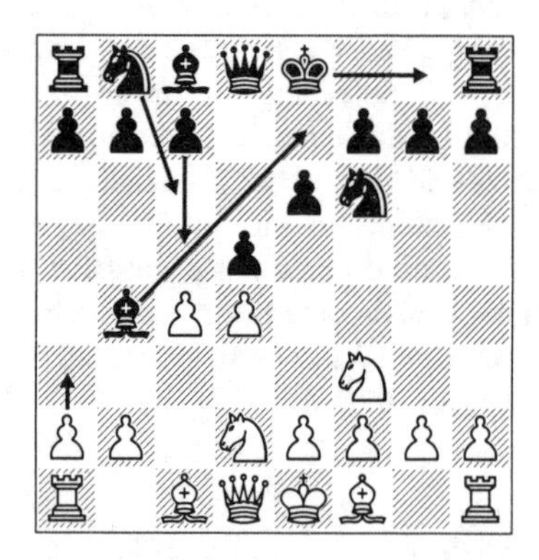

If Black does not want to surrender the bishop-pair then a solid way to avoid this is 4...d5. When White plays a3 Black can safely retreat the bishop. This may seem like a loss of tempo but compared to a Queen's Gambit the white knight on d2 is slightly misplaced. Black is also ready to strike at White's centre with ...c5. Often White finds this so annoying that he hurries to give a queen check on a4, forcing Black's knight to c6.

Quick Summary

4 ♘bd2 is one of the sharpest options for White against the Bogo. Black has four main replies.

4...c5 (Line A) is an attempt to exploit the unnatural position of White's knight on d2 but the continuation 5 a3 ♗xd2+ 6 ♕xd2 cxd4 7 ♘xd4 looks slightly in White's favour.

4...d5 (Line B) is a safe approach, which has the advantage that Black can retreat his dark-squared bishop without worrying about an intimidating white centre. White has a choice between 5 ♕a4+ (Line B1), which forces the black knight to c6, where it is somewhat misplaced, and the stereotyped 5 e3 (Line B2). I like 5 ♕a4+ best, and particularly the line 5...♘c6 6 a3 ♗xd2+ 7 ♗xd2 ♘e4 8 ♕c2, which is considered in Line B12, leads to fascinating complications. The safer 8 ♖d1 is treated under Line B11.

4...0-0 is dealt with in Line C. There is a split in the variations after 5 a3 ♗e7 6 e4 d5. White can try to maintain the central tension with 7 ♕c2 (Line C1) or go for the more aggressive 7 e5 (Line C2).

4...b6 (Line D) is currently considered the soundest option but in my opinion Black has still not found a clear way to equality after 5 a3 ♗xd2+ 6 ♗xd2 ♗b7 7 ♗g5 d6 8 e3 ♘bd7 9 ♗d3. His best plan is to start chasing White's bishop by 9...h6 10 ♗h4 g5 11 ♗g3 h5!?. This is quite tricky and White probably has to offer a pawn with 12 h4 g4 13 ♘g5 ♗xg2 14 ♖g1.

The Theory of 4 ♘bd2

1 d4 ♘f6 2 c4 e6 3 ♘f3 ♗b4+ 4 ♘bd2

We shall examine the following possibilities:

A)

4...c5 *(D)*

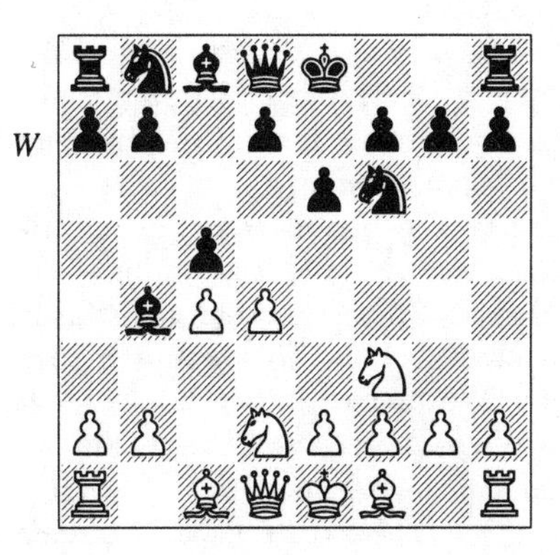

This is a very active reply, but compared to the other options, Black is generally forced to concede the bishop-pair here.

5 a3

5 e3 often transposes to the main lines but there are a few independent variations:

a) 5...0-0 6 a3 ♗xd2+ 7 ♕xd2 cxd4 (7...b6 is line 'c11' in the note to Black's 6th move) 8 ♘xd4 (8 exd4!? transposes to 'c12' in the note to Black's 6th move) 8...♘c6 9 ♗e2 e5 10 ♘xc6 dxc6 11 f3 ♕e7 12 b3 e4! 13 ♗b2 ♖d8 14 ♕b4 c5 15 ♕c3 exf3 16 gxf3 ♘h5 (16...♗h3!?) 17 h4 ♗f5 18 ♔f2 with a slight advantage for White, Browne-Timman, Tilburg 1982.

b) Black may also try to keep the dark-squared bishop by 5...cxd4 6 exd4 b6 7 ♗d3 0-0 8 a3 ♗e7 but White's slightly superior control of the centre should promise him an advantage, e.g. 9 0-0 ♗b7 10 b3 d5 11 ♖e1 dxc4 12 bxc4 ♘c6 13 ♗b2 ♕d6 14 ♕e2 ♖fd8 15 ♖ad1 ± Browne-Alburt, USA Ch 1981.

5...♗xd2+ 6 ♕xd2

This was my suggestion in *BTID*, but it is not clear that it is better than 6 ♗xd2. Here are some variations after the bishop capture:

a) 6...d6 7 dxc5 dxc5. I am a little uncertain what Black is aiming for in this line. The pawn structure is fairly symmetrical, the position quite open and White has the bishop-pair. If White plays accurately he should obtain the better game:

a1) 8 ♗f4 ♕xd1+ 9 ♖xd1 b6 10 e3 ♗b7 11 ♗e2 ♘c6 12 0-0 0-0 13 b4! cxb4 14 axb4 ♖fd8 15 b5 and White has the advantage, Efimov-Spiridonov, Prague 1985.

a2) 8 ♕c2 ♘bd7 9 0-0-0!? ♕c7 10 g3!? (White plays very aggressively, but Black defends well) 10...♘g4! 11 ♗f4!? (11 ♗e1 is more passive) 11...e5 12 ♗h3 h5! (not 12...♘xf2? 13 ♗xd7+ ♗xd7 14 ♘xe5 ♗c6 15 ♘g6!) 13 ♗xg4 hxg4 14 ♘xe5 ♘xe5 15 ♖d5 ♖h5!, Seirawan-Smyslov, Tilburg 1994, and now Smyslov thinks that White should play 16 ♖hd1 ♗e6 17 ♖xe5 ♖xe5 18 ♕h7 ♖d8 19 ♖xd8+ ♕xd8 20 ♗xe5 g6! =.

a3) 8 ♗c3 ♕xd1+ 9 ♖xd1 b6 10 g3 ♗b7 11 ♗g2 ♘bd7 12 0-0 ♔e7 13 ♖d3 (13 ♘e5) 13...♗e4 14 ♖d2 ♗c6 15 ♖d3 ♗e4 16 ♖e3! ♖ac8 17 ♗h3 h6 18 ♘h4 ± I.Sokolov-Short, Pärnu 1996.

b) 6...b6 7 ♗g5 ♗b7 8 e3 ♕e7 9 ♗e2 d6 10 dxc5 bxc5 11 ♕d2 ♘c6?! (Ftačnik suggests 11...0-0 12 ♖d1 ♖d8 13 0-0 h6 14 ♗h4 g5 15 ♗g3 ♘e4 with unclear play) 12 b4! 0-0 13 b5 ♘b8 14 0-0 ♘bd7 15 ♖fd1 and White is better, Ftačnik-Podzielny, Bundesliga 1993/4.

c) 6...cxd4 7 ♘xd4 and now:

c1) 7...♘c6 8 ♘xc6 dxc6 9 g3 e5 10 ♗c3 ♕e7 11 ♗g2 ♗g4 12 0-0 ♕e6 13 f3 ♗f5 14 e4 ♗g6 15 b3 with a slight advantage to White, Van der Sterren-Lalev, Albena 1983.

c2) 7...♘e4 8 ♗e3 0-0 9 g3 b6 10 ♗g2 ♗b7 11 0-0 ♘d6 12 ♗xb7 ♘xb7 13 ♕c2 ♕c8 14 ♖fd1 ♘c6 15 ♖ac1 ± Cebalo-Djurić, Yugoslav Ch 1986.

c3) 7...d6 8 g3 0-0 9 ♗g2 a6 10 ♗b4!? (Smyslov has drifted into a rather passive position, and with this move Yusupov tries to maximize the pressure) 10...♘e8 11 ♕d2 ♖a7! 12 0-0 b6 13 ♖fd1 ♖c7 14 b3 ♗b7 15 ♗xb7 (15 e4!? ±) 15...♖xb7 16 a4 with a substantial advantage to White, Yusupov-Smyslov, USSR Ch (Moscow) 1988.

c4) 7...d5 gives White a choice:

c41) 8 e3 e5 9 ♘f3 ♘c6 10 ♗c3 ♗g4 (10...e4 11 ♘e5 ± Ruban) 11 ♗e2! dxc4 12 ♘xe5 ♘xe5 13 ♗xe5 ± Ruban-Gorelov, Uzhgorod 1988.

c42) 8 cxd5 ♕xd5 9 e3 0-0 10 ♗b4 ♖d8 (with 10...♖e8 Black can avoid having his f-pawns doubled but White still has a very pleasant position, for example 11 ♘b5 ♘a6 12 ♕xd5 ♘xd5 13 ♗d6 ♗d7 14 e4 ♖ed8 15 ♗g3 ♗xb5 16 ♗xb5 ± Ruban-Vitolinš, Uzhgorod 1988) 11 ♗e7 ♖d7 12 ♗xf6 gxf6 13 ♕g4+ ♔f8 14 ♗e2 ♘c6 15 ♗f3 and White is better, Lobron-Korchnoi, Biel 1986.

Returning to the position after 6 ♕xd2 *(D)*:

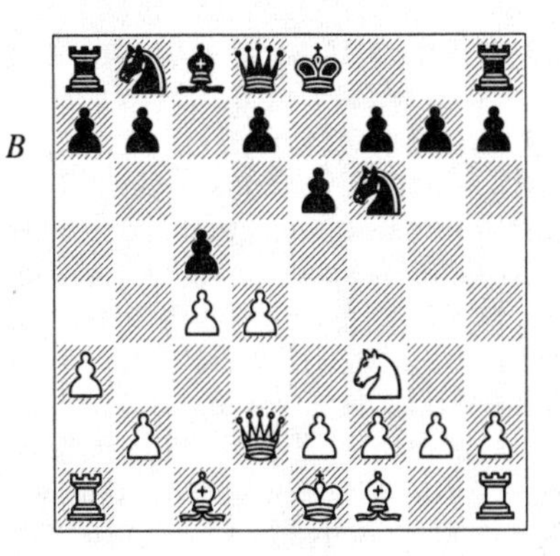

6...cxd4

There are a number of alternatives:

a) 6...0-0?! 7 dxc5 a5 8 g3 (8 ♕f4! is perhaps stronger; in Begovac-Trepp, Swiss Ch 1993 White simply kept his pawn after 8...♘a6 9 ♗e3 a4 10 0-0-0 ♘e8 11 g4 ♕e7 12 ♕d4 ±) 8...a4 9 ♕c2 ♘c6 10 ♗g2 ♕a5+ 11 ♗d2 ♕xc5 12 ♖c1 b5 13 cxb5 ♕xb5 14 0-0 ♗b7 15 e4 ♖ac8 16 ♗c3 ♘e7 with unclear play, Hertneck-Christiansen, Munich 1991.

b) 6...♘e4 7 ♕c2 f5 and now 8 b4 b6 9 e3 ♗b7 10 bxc5 bxc5 11 ♖b1 ♗c6 12 ♗e2 ♕a5+ 13 ♗d2 ♕xa3 14 0-0 ♗a4 was unclear in the game A.Petrosian-Vitolinš, Jurmala 1983 but White should play 8 dxc5.

c) 6...b6 (please note that this may be a simple blunder in view of line 'c3') and now:

c1) 7 e3 with a further branch:

c11) 7...0-0 8 ♗e2 a5 (it is seriously worth considering 8...cxd4!? with the idea of transposing to line 'c12'; White probably cannot get any advantage by recapturing with the knight or the queen but recapturing with the pawn does not seem too inspiring either) 9 b3 ♗b7 10 0-0 d6 11 ♖d1 ♘bd7 12 ♗b2 ♘e4 13 ♕e1 ♕e7 14 ♘d2 ♘xd2 15 ♕xd2 ♖fd8 16 ♕c3 with a pleasant game for White, Portisch-Andersson, London 1982.

c12) 7...cxd4 8 exd4 0-0 9 ♗e2?! (this is too casual; 9 b4!? is better, intending to meet 9...d5 with 10 c5 – Timman) 9...d5 10 b3 ♗a6 11 ♕b2 dxc4 12 bxc4 ♘c6 13 ♗g5 ♖c8 and Black has the better game already, Kasparov-Timman, Brussels 1987.

c13) 7...♗b7 8 ♗e2 ♘c6 9 0-0 0-0 10 b3 ♘e4 11 ♕c2 f5 12 ♖d1 (12 ♗b2 intending ♘d2 is probably better) 12...♘e7 13 dxc5 bxc5 14 ♗b2 d6 15 ♘d2 ♘g6 16 ♗f3? ♘h4 ∓ Dahlberg-Korchnoi, Lone Pine 1981.

c2) 7 b4 ♗b7 8 ♗b2 0-0 9 e3 ♕e7 (Epishin also analysed 9...cxb4 10 axb4 ♕e7 11 c5 ♘e4 12 ♕c2 d6 13 ♗d3 f5 14 0-0 with a small advantage to White) 10 ♗d3 ♘a6 11 dxc5 bxc5 12 b5 ♘c7 13 0-0 d5 14 ♘e5 with an advantage to White, Epishin-Christiansen, Vienna 1991.

c3) 7 dxc5 bxc5 8 ♕g5 is an impudent way of winning a pawn but may in fact be very strong. However, in practice White often rejects this possibility because Black gets a lead in development, while White has spent some time moving his queen around. Black has tried:

c31) 8...d6? 9 ♕xg7 ♖g8 10 ♕h6 ♘bd7 11 g3 ♗a6 12 ♕d2 ♕b6 13 ♕c2 ♗b7 14 ♗g2 a5 15 0-0 and Black has nothing to show for his lost pawn, P.Cramling-Spassky, London Women vs Veterans 1996.

c32) 8...0-0 9 ♕xc5 ♘e4 (Black has no real compensation after 9...♘c6 10 b4 ♗b7 11 ♗b2 a5 12 b5 ♘e4 13 ♕h5 ♘e7 14 ♘g5 ♘xg5 15 ♕xg5 ± Wells-Rossiter, Oakham 1994) 10 ♕d4 (10 ♕e3!?) 10...f5 11 e3 ♗b7 12 ♗e2 a5 13 0-0 ♖f6 with some compensation for Black, Vilela-Lebredo, Cienfuegos 1983.

Returning to the position after 6...cxd4 *(D)*:

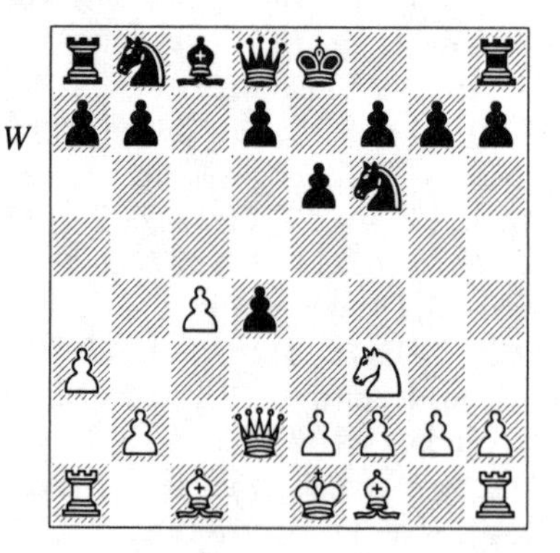

7 ♘xd4

Other options are no less interesting:

a) 7 ♕xd4 ♘c6 8 ♕d6!? (after 8 ♕d1 0-0 9 e3 e5! 10 b4 d6 11 ♗e2 a5 12 b5 ♘e7 Black was doing well in the game I.Sokolov-Dorfman, Burgas 1992) 8...♘e4 9 ♕d3 d5 10 e3 0-0 11 ♕c2 ♕a5+ 12 ♘d2 and then:

a1) 12...♖d8 13 ♖b1 ♘e5!? (very optimistic) 14 b4 ♕c7 15 ♘xe4 dxe4 16 ♕xe4 f5 17 ♕c2 b5 18 c5 ♗b7 with compensation for Black, M.Gurevich-Miezis, Vlissingen 1997.

a2) 12...♘d6!? is M.Gurevich's idea, when Black seems to have good play in all lines he analyses: 13 ♖b1 dxc4 14 ♗xc4 ♘xc4 15 ♕xc4 ♘e5; 13 ♗d3 dxc4 14 ♗xh7+ ♔h8 15 ♗e4 ♘xe4 16 ♕xe4 c3 17 bxc3 ♕xc3; or 13 cxd5 ♕xd5 14 b3 e5.

b) 7 b4!? (White postpones the decision of how to recapture and instead starts gaining space on the queenside) 7...0-0 (7...a5 8 b5 is a little better for White) 8 ♗b2 d5 9 cxd5 ♕xd5 10 ♕xd4 ♕xd4 11 ♘xd4 ♗d7 12 e3 ♖c8 13 ♗d3 ♘c6 14 ♘b3 and the bishop-pair ensures White the advantage, Kožul-Christiansen, Novi Sad OL 1990.

7...0-0

It is clear that Black must act in the centre, and so first takes his king out of the battle zone. Some other, more direct attempts have also been seen:

a) 7...d5 8 cxd5 ♕xd5 9 e3 0-0 10 ♘b5 ♕c6?! (10...♘c6 ±) 11 b4 a6 12 ♘d4 ♕b6 13 ♗b2 ± Salov-Vitolinš, Borzhomi 1984.

b) 7...♘c6 8 e3 d5 9 cxd5 exd5 10 ♘xc6 (10 b4!?) 10...bxc6 11 b4 0-0 12 ♗b2 a5 = Browne-Djurić, New York 1986.

8 e3

8 g3 d5 9 cxd5 ♕xd5 was fine for Black in Alburt-Dvoretsky, Vilnius Z 1975.

8...d5

It is also feasible to fianchetto the bishop before pushing this pawn, for example 8...b6 9 ♗e2 ♗b7 10 0-0 d5 11 b4 ♘c6 12 ♗b2 ♘e4 13 ♕d1 dxc4 14 ♗xc4 ♘xd4 15 ♗xd4 ♕g5 with counterplay, Miles-Sharif, Metz 1985.

9 b4 ♕e7

This is more solid than 9...a5 10 b5! b6 11 ♗b2 ♗b7?! (Gulko suggests 11...♖a7 with the idea of ...♖c7) 12 ♖c1 dxc4 13 ♗xc4 ♗xg2 14 ♖g1 ♗e4 15 ♗xe6!, when White has a big advantage, since the bishop cannot be taken due to 15...fxe6 16 ♖xg7+ ♔h8 17 ♘xe6 ♕e8 18 ♕d6, Gulko-Romero, Leon 1992.

10 ♗b2 ♖d8 11 cxd5 ♘xd5 12 ♖d1

It was preferable to get the queen away from the d-file, e.g. 12 ♕c2 ±.

12...e5 13 ♘f3 ♘c6 14 b5 e4 15 bxc6 exf3 16 gxf3 bxc6 17 ♖g1 f6

The position is unclear, Miles-S.Agdestein, Gjøvik 1983.

B)

4...d5 *(D)*

This is the other way of striking in the centre, and compared to 4...c5 Black is not obliged to concede the bishop-pair here. Now White must make a choice:

Some lesser alternatives:

a) 5 g3 dxc4 6 ♕c2 ♘c6 7 ♗g2 b5 8 a4 ♗b7 9 e3 a6 10 0-0 ♗e7 11 b3 ♘b4 12 ♕b2 with an unclear position, Alburt-Christiansen, USA Ch 1990.

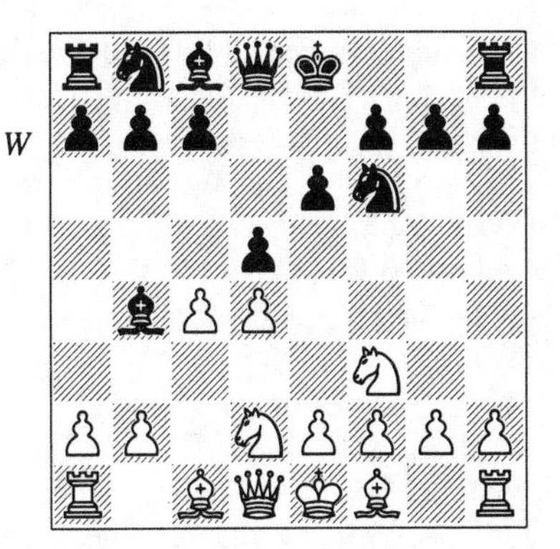

b) 5 a3 ♗e7 and now:

b1) 6 e3 0-0 transposes to Line B2.

b2) 6 g3 is Cebalo's speciality and leads to a kind of Catalan position. White has gained the move a3 for free if Black continues with normal moves like ...0-0, ...♘bd7, ...c6, etc. This might enable White to try a more active plan. For example, White can attempt to advance his b-pawn two steps, which is a lot more difficult in a regular Catalan. Therefore Black has usually chosen some alternative ways to play this position:

b21) 6...dxc4 7 ♘xc4 c5 8 ♗f4!? (White attempts to exploit the weaknesses created by Black's previous move, particularly the d6-square; instead White got nothing from 8 ♗g2 ♘c6 9 dxc5 ♕xd1+ 10 ♔xd1 ♘e4 = in Cebalo-Kurajica, Yugoslavia 1987) 8...b5?! (very risky, but Black is perhaps already in some trouble; 8...0-0 9 dxc5 ♗xc5 10 b4 ♗e7 11 ♕b3 also looks promising for White, but 8...♘d5 is worth a try) 9 ♘ce5 ♗b7 10 dxc5! ♕xd1+ 11 ♖xd1 ♗xc5 12 ♗g2 ♘bd7 13 ♘xd7 ♘xd7 14 0-0 and White is better, since Black will find it difficult to get castled, Cebalo-A.Grosar, Maribor 1994.

b22) 6...a5!? 7 ♗g2 0-0 8 0-0 ♘bd7 9 b3 c5! 10 ♗b2 b6 11 cxd5 ♘xd5 12 e4 ♘5f6 13 ♖e1 ♗b7 14 e5 ♘d5 15 ♘e4 b5!? with equality, Cebalo-Trepp, Biel 1989.

b23) 6...c5 7 cxd5 exd5 8 ♗g2 ♘c6 9 dxc5 ♗xc5 10 0-0 ♔f8 (10...a5!? – Ruban) 11 b4! ♗b6 12 ♗b2 with an edge for White, Ruban-Rohde, Tilburg 1992.

b24) 6...0-0 7 ♗g2 and then:

b241) 7...c5 8 dxc5 ♗xc5 9 b4 ♗e7 10 ♗b2 a5 11 b5 a4 12 ♕c2 ♘bd7 13 0-0 b6 14 ♘d4 ♗b7 15 cxd5 exd5 16 ♘f5 with a huge positional plus, Brinck-Claussen – Ortega, Havana OL 1966.

b242) 7...b6!? 8 0-0 ♗b7 9 b4 c5! (White would enjoy a nice space advantage after 9...♘bd7 10 c5!) 10 bxc5 bxc5 11 ♖b1 (Yudasin thinks that 11 ♕b3! is more accurate, and gives 11...♕b6! 12 ♖b1 ♘bd7 =) 11...♕c8! 12 dxc5 ♘bd7! 13 ♗b2 ♘xc5?! (according to Yudasin, 13...♖b8! is better, with the idea 14 ♕c2 ♕xc5) 14 ♕c2! ♘ce4 15 ♘xe4?! (15 ♖fc1 is a better try for an advantage) 15...♘xe4 16 ♖fc1 dxc4! 17 ♘e5 ♘d6! with an equal position, Lputian-Yudasin, Philadelphia 1994.

b3) 6 ♕c2 and now:

b31) 6...♘bd7 7 e3 transposes to Line B2.

b32) After 6...0-0, 7 e3 also transposes to Line B2, whilst 7 e4 is Line C1, while 7 g3 was seen in Grivas-Angelis, Katerini 1993, when Black did not manage to equalize: 7...a5!? (7...b6) 8 ♗g2 ♘c6 9 0-0 dxc4 10 ♕xc4 a4 11 ♖d1 ♗d7 12 ♕d3! ±.

b33) 6...b6 7 e4 dxe4 (7...0-0 8 ♗d3 g6 9 0-0 ♗b7 10 ♖d1 a5 11 cxd5 exd5 12 e5 was very good for White in Mirallès-Spassky, Cannes 1989) 8 ♘xe4 ♗b7 9 ♗d3 ♘c6! 10 ♗e3 ♘g4 11 0-0 f5 and Black has already equalized, Yusupov-Spassky, Barcelona 1989, but since the game continued in very entertaining fashion I will give a few more moves: 12 ♘c3 0-0 13 ♖ad1 (13 h3 and 13 d5 are possible improvements) 13...♘xd4!? (this is the beginning of a series of spectacular sacrifices, whose soundness is not easy to judge; 13...♗d6 is a safe alternative) 14 ♘xd4 (14 ♗xd4 is perhaps a better test, e.g. 14...♗xf3 15 gxf3 ♘xh2! 16 ♔xh2 ♕xd4 17 ♔g2 ♕f6 18 ♖h1 ♗d6 gives Black some compensation, but I do not think it is quite enough) 14...♗d6 15 g3 (or 15 h3 ♕h4! 16 ♖fe1 f4 with an attack) 15...♘xh2! 16 ♗e2 ♘xf1 17 ♗xf1 ♕f6 18 ♗g2 ♗xg2 19 ♔xg2 f4 20 gxf4 ♗xf4 with the better game for Black.

B1)

5 ♕a4+ *(D)*

This early queen check forces Black to put his knight on the less attractive c6-square.

5...♘c6 6 a3

An interesting alternative is 6 ♘e5!? ♗d7 7 ♘xc6 ♗xd2+ 8 ♗xd2 ♗xc6 9 ♕c2 and then:

a) 9...0-0!? 10 f3 ♖e8! with a completely satisfactory position for Black, Ftačnik-Rashkovsky, Belgrade 1988.

B

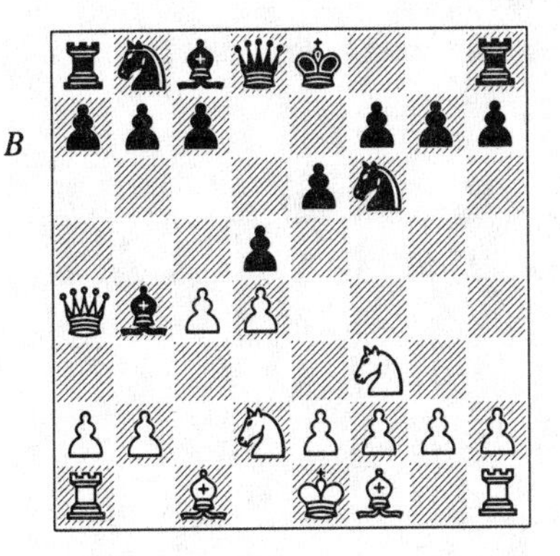

b) 9...dxc4 10 ♕xc4 0-0 11 f3 a6! 12 e4 ♗b5 13 ♕c3 ♗xf1 14 ♖xf1 ♘d7 15 0-0-0 ♕e7 16 ♔b1 ♖fc8 (16...c5!? – Mirković) 17 ♗e3 and White is slightly better, Mirković-Novaković, Bela Crkva 1988.

6...♗xd2+

Another quite important option is to retreat the bishop, viz. 6...♗e7:

a) 7 g3 0-0 8 ♗g2 ♘e4 9 ♕c2 ♗f6 (worse is 9...f5 10 0-0 ♗f6 11 e3 ♔h8 12 b4 ♗d7 13 ♗b2 ♕e8 14 ♖ac1 ♖c8 15 ♖fe1 ♘e7 16 ♘e5 c6 17 ♘d3 ♖c7 18 ♘f3 a6 19 ♘fe5 ± Vaganian-Ljubojević, Barcelona 1989) 10 e3 ♘xd2 11 ♗xd2 dxc4 12 ♕xc4 e5 and Black has equalized, H.Olafsson-Petursson, Akureyri 1988.

b) 7 e3 0-0 and then:

b1) 8 ♗d3 a6 (Ftačnik prefers 8...a5! with the idea 9 ♕c2 a4 10 cxd5 exd5 11 ♗b5 ♗d7 12 ♗xa4 ♘xd4) 9 ♕c2 (9 0-0 dxc4 10 ♕xc4 ♗d6 11 e4?! e5 12 d5 ♘e7 13 ♕c3 ♖e8! 14 ♖e1 c6 15 dxc6 ♘xc6 was fine for Black in Ligterink-Larsen, Reykjavik 1986) 9...♖e8 10 0-0 g6 11 b4 ♗f8 12 ♗b2 ♗g7 13 ♖ad1 ♘e7 (13...♘h5 is probably better, intending ...f5, and if White continues 14 e4 then there is 14...♘f4) 14 e4 c6 15 e5 ♘h5 16 ♖fe1 ♘f4 17 ♗f1 dxc4 18 ♘xc4 ± Ftačnik-Hulak, Bundesliga 1989/90.

b2) 8 ♕c2 with a choice for Black:

b21) 8...♖e8 9 b3 (9 b4 is also good; then the game Savon-Veresov, USSR 1969 continued 9...♗f8 10 ♗b2 g6 11 ♗e2 ♗g7 12 0-0 ♘e7 13 ♖fc1 c6 14 a4 a6 15 ♗a3 ♘f5 16 b5! with the better game for White) 9...♗f8 (9...a5 transposes to 'b232') 10 ♗b2 g6 11 ♗d3 ♗g7 12 0-0 ♘e7 13 ♖ad1 c6 14 e4 ± M.Gurevich-Andruet, Marseilles 1988.

b22) 8...♘b8 9 ♗d3 b6 10 e4 dxe4 11 ♘xe4 ♘bd7 12 ♗e3 ♗b7 13 ♘xf6+ ♘xf6 14 0-0-0 ♕c8 (M.Gurevich-Gunawan, Jakarta 1996) and now White should continue 15 ♖he1 c5 with a choice between playing for the initiative with 16 d5 exd5 17 cxd5 or going for a more direct attack by 16 ♘e5 ♖d8 17 dxc5 bxc5 18 g4 – M.Gurevich.

b23) 8...a5 9 b3 and Black has been unable to solve all his problems:

b231) 9...♘b8 10 ♗b2 c6 11 ♗d3 ♘bd7 12 0-0 b6 13 cxd5 cxd5 14 ♘e5 ♗b7 15 ♘c6 ± Karpov-Adams, Roquebrune rpd 1992.

b232) 9...♖e8 10 ♗d3 ♗f8 11 0-0 g6 12 ♗b2 ♗g7 13 ♖ad1 ♗d7 14 ♖fe1 ♘e7 15 ♘e5 c6 16 ♘df3 ♖f8 17 e4 and White has the better game, M.Gurevich-Gipslis, Moscow 1992.

b233) 9...♗d7 (this position also frequently arises from the move-order 7...♗d7 8 ♕c2 a5 9 b3 0-0) gives White two choices:

b2331) 10 ♗d3 and now:

b23311) 10...g6 11 0-0 ♘h5!? 12 e4 ♗f6 13 e5 ♗e7 14 ♖e1 ♘g7 15 ♗f1 a4 with counterplay, Ftačnik-Averbakh, Palma de Mallorca 1989.

b23312) 10...♘a7 11 0-0 a4 12 b4 dxc4 13 ♘xc4 ♗b5?! (according to Nepomniashchy 13...h6 is better) 14 e4 g6 15 ♗b2 ♘h5 16 ♖fe1 ♗f6 17 ♖ad1 ♗g7 18 ♘e3 c6 19 d5! with a clear advantage for White, Nepomniashchy-Taimanov, Russia 1996.

b2332) 10 ♗b2 ♖c8 (after 10...♘a7 11 ♗d3 h6?! Black soon runs into trouble; in Wilder-Kogan, USA Ch 1987 White continued very energetically: 12 ♖g1! c5 13 dxc5 ♗xc5 14 g4 dxc4 15 ♗xc4 ♖c8 16 g5 hxg5 17 ♘xg5 with a winning attack) 11 ♗d3 ♘a7 12 ♘e5!? h6?! (Black should go for complications after 12...c5!? 13 dxc5 dxc4 14 bxc4 ♗xc5 15 ♘xd7 ♕xd7 16 ♗xf6 gxf6 17 ♗xh7+, when White has a pawn more but Black has active counterplay – Gelfand and Kapengut) 13 g4!? c5 14 h4 with a dangerous attack, Gelfand-Yusupov, Munich 1992.

7 ♗xd2 ♘e4 *(D)*

Black has conceded his dark-squared bishop and thus it is a good idea to avoid being pinned by ♗g5.

Some lesser alternatives are:

a) 7...0-0 8 ♗g5 ±.

b) 7...♗d7 8 ♕c2 a5 9 ♗g5 (9 ♖d1!?) 9...h6 10 ♗xf6 ♕xf6 11 e3 0-0 12 ♗e2 ♖fc8 13 cxd5 exd5 14 0-0 a4 15 ♖ac1 ♖a5 16 ♕d2 b6 17 ♖c3 ♕d6 18 ♖fc1 with a big advantage to White, Petursson-Spassky, Reykjavik 1988.

We shall now consider two main continuations for White, which are both directed against Black's threat of ...♘xd2:

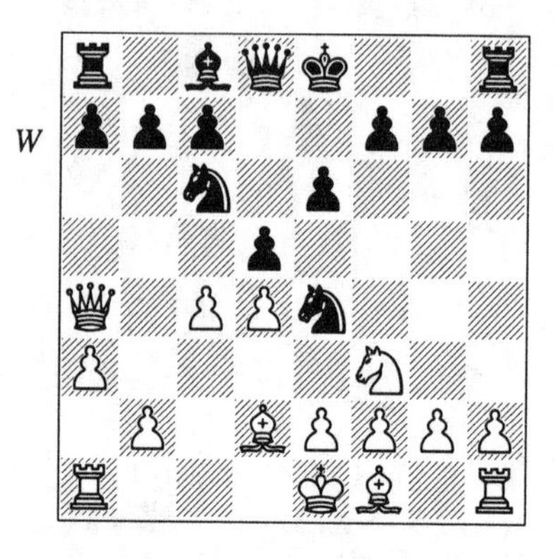
W

B11: 8 ♖d1 17
B12: 8 ♕c2 18

White in fact has quite a wide choice at this point:

a) 8 ♗f4 0-0 (an aggressive option is 8...g5!? 9 ♗e3 f5 10 ♘e5 ♗d7 11 ♘xd7 ♕xd7 12 f3 f4 13 ♗g1 ♘d6, when in spite of his many weaknesses Black has a quite active position, Malaniuk-Salov, USSR Ch 1987) 9 e3 ♗d7 10 ♕c2 ♗e8 11 h4!? f5 12 h5 ♘d6 13 cxd5 exd5 14 ♗d3 ♘e4 15 0-0-0 with unclear play, Grabliauskas-S.Pedersen, Danish open jr Ch 1992.

b) 8 ♗e3 0-0 9 g3 ♕e8 10 cxd5 exd5 11 ♗g2 with roughly equal play, Browne-Rohde, Philadelphia 1988.

c) 8 e3 ♘xd2 (8...0-0 is probably safer; then 9 ♖d1 will transpose to Line B11, while 9 ♕c2 is Line B12) 9 ♘xd2 e5!? (a subtle move but certainly not without drawbacks; 9...0-0 is safer but after 10 ♘f3 ♘e7 11 ♗d3 ♗d7 12 ♕c2 h6 13 0-0 White stands better, Agdestein-Salov, Manila IZ

1990) 10 ♘f3! (10 dxe5 d4! is probably OK for Black) 10...0-0! 11 ♘xe5 ♘xe5 12 dxe5 d4 13 ♖d1 (13 0-0-0) 13...c5 14 exd4 cxd4 15 ♗e2 (15 c5! – Rashkovsky) 15...♗d7 16 ♕b3 ♕a5+ 17 ♖d2 ♗c6 18 ♕g3 f6! 19 e6! ♖ae8 20 b4 and White is better, Savchenko-Rashkovsky, Gausdal 1993.

B11)

8 ♖d1 0-0 *(D)*

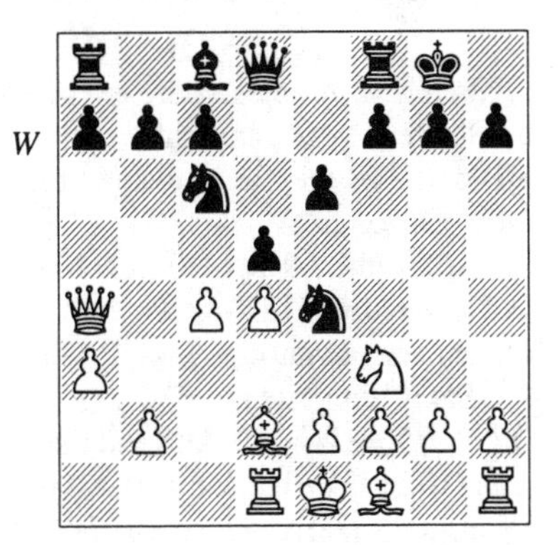

Black's two most popular plans in this position are:

1) To activate the bishop via the manoeuvre ...♗d7-e8 followed by ...f6 or ...f5.

2) To play ...♘d6 in order to make White resolve the tension in the centre. White must reply with either the anti-positional c5 or cxd5, which solves Black's problems with the development of the bishop.

Which plan to adopt of course depends on the specific situation but is in most cases primarily a matter of taste.

9 e3

Some alternatives are:

a) 9 g3 and then:

a1) 9...♗d7 10 ♕c2 a5 11 ♗g2 f5 12 0-0 ♗e8 13 ♗e3 a4 14 ♘e5 ♖a6!? 15 f3 ♘d6 16 ♗f2 ± Piket-Bosch, Dutch Ch 1996.

a2) 9...♘d6 10 c5 ♘f5 11 ♗c3 ♗d7 12 ♕c2 a5 13 ♗g2 a4 14 h4 f6 15 0-0 ♕e8 16 e4 ♘fe7 17 ♘e1 ♔h8 18 ♘d3 dxe4 19 ♗xe4 ♘d5 = Ftačnik-Seul, Dortmund 1992.

b) 9 ♗c1 and now:

b1) 9...♗d7 10 ♕c2 a5 11 g3 ♘d6 12 c5 ♘e8 =/± ½-½ Sapis-Grabarczyk, Polish Ch 1997.

b2) 9...♕e7 10 g3 ♖d8 11 ♗g2 ♘d6 12 c5 ♘e4 13 0-0 ♗d7 14 ♕c2 a5 15 b3 b6 with unclear play, Anderton-S.Pedersen, Gausdal 1992.

9...♗d7!?

Other options are:

a) 9...♘d6 10 ♕c2 dxc4 11 ♗xc4 ♘xc4 12 ♕xc4 ♕d5 13 ♖c1 ± Lputian.

b) 9...♘e7 10 ♗d3 (or 10 ♕c2 b6 11 ♗d3 ♗b7 12 0-0 ♘g6 13 b4 f5 14 ♘e5 dxc4 15 ♗xc4 ♕d6 ½-½ A.Petrosian-Spassky, Sarajevo 1986) 10...b6 11 0-0 ♗b7 12 c5?! (Greenfeld claims a small advantage for White after 12 ♗c1!) 12...a5! 13 cxb6 cxb6 14 ♖c1 ♘f5 15 ♖c2 ♘fd6 16 ♖fc1 f6 with a good position for Black, Greenfeld-Korchnoi, Beersheba (2) 1995.

c) 9...♕f6 10 ♗d3 ♕g6!? (this move leads to some fascinating complications; instead Lputian-Kurajica, Sarajevo 1985 continued 10...♘d6 11 0-0 dxc4 12 ♗xc4 ♗d7 13 ♗d3 with the better game for White) 11 0-0 ♘c5! 12 ♕xc6! (12 dxc5 ♕xd3 13 ♗a5 ♕xc4 14 ♕xc4 dxc4 15 ♗xc7 f6!

16 ♖c1 ♖f7 17 ♗d6 ♘a5 18 ♘d2 ♗d7 = Gelfand and Khuzman) 12...♘xd3 13 ♕xc7 ♘xb2 14 ♗b4 (Dautov thinks that this move only helps Black and instead suggests 14 ♘e5! ♕f6 15 ♖c1 ♘xc4 16 ♘xc4 dxc4 17 ♖xc4 with a clear advantage after either 17...b6 18 ♖a4 ♕d8 19 ♖xa7 or 17...♕d8 18 ♖fc1 b6 19 ♗b4 ♖e8 20 ♕xd8 ♖xd8 21 ♗e7 ♖e8 22 ♖c7 f6 23 e4) 14...♖e8 15 ♘e5 ♕f6 16 cxd5! (16 ♖c1 ♘xc4 17 ♘xc4 dxc4 18 ♖xc4 b6 only leads to equality) 16...♘xd1 17 d6 ♘b2 18 d7 ♗xd7 19 ♕xd7 with compensation, Gelfand-Timman, Linares 1993.

10 ♕c2 ♗e8! 11 ♗e2

The reason why White develops his bishop modestly on e2 is that after 11 ♗d3 Black plays 11...f5 followed by ...♗h5.

11...f6!?

11...f5 is a perfectly viable alternative. Then Aseev-Stangl, Berlin 1992 continued 12 0-0 ♗h5 13 ♗e1! ♔h8 14 ♔h1 ♖f6 (14...♘d6!?) 15 ♘e5 ♗xe2 16 ♕xe2 ♕e8 17 f3 ♘d6 18 ♗g3 with the better game for White.

12 0-0

12 b4 a6 13 0-0 ♔h8 14 ♔h1 ♘e7 15 ♗e1 c6 16 ♖c1 b5 was unclear in Tukmakov-Rashkovsky, Kuibyshev 1986.

12...♗h5 13 ♖c1 ♔h8?!

According to Ruban Black should play 13...♘xd2 14 ♕xd2 ♘e7 =.

14 ♖fd1 g5 15 ♗c3

White is slightly better, Ruban-Adler, Balassagyarmat 1989.

B12)

8 ♕c2 *(D)*

8...e5!?

B

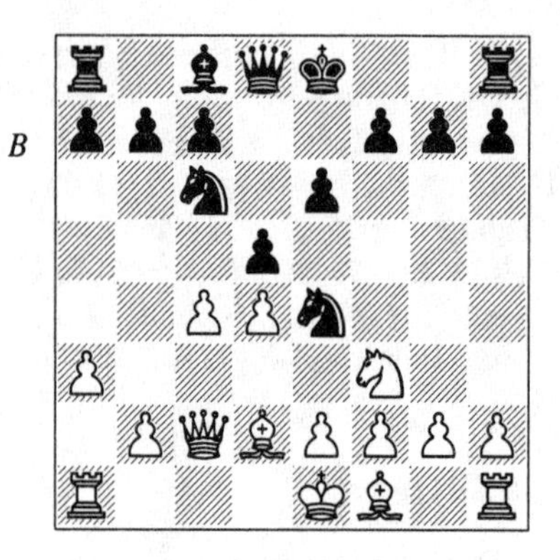

This move initiates some exciting play. There are of course safer options for Black, but they tend to lead to a better position for White:

a) 8...♘xd2!? 9 ♕xd2 dxc4 10 e4 0-0 11 ♗xc4 b6 12 0-0 ♗b7 13 b4 with a space advantage, Inkiov-Polaczek, Saint John 1988.

b) 8...a5 9 e3 0-0 10 ♗d3 and then:

b1) 10...f5?! (this kind of Stonewall set-up is rarely very good) 11 0-0 a4 12 ♗b4! ♖f6 13 ♘e5 ♗d7 14 f3 ♘g5 15 ♖ac1 ♘f7 16 f4 ± Timman-Salov, Saint John Ct (6) 1988.

b2) 10...♘xd2 11 ♘xd2 h6 (or 11...♕h4 12 g3 ♕h5 13 ♗e2 ♕h6 14 ♗f3 ♖d8 15 0-0 a4 16 ♖fd1 b6 17 cxd5 exd5 18 ♖ac1 ♗b7 19 ♘b1 ± Van der Wijk-Etmans, corr. 1989) 12 0-0 a4 13 ♖ac1 ♗d7 14 ♘f3 ♕f6 15 ♕c3 and White has a slight advantage, Dautov-Savchenko, Leningrad 1989.

9 dxe5

9 ♘xe5? is bad in view of 9...♘xd4 10 ♕d3 ♘xd2 11 ♕xd4 ♘b3.

9...♗f5 10 ♖d1

Black has nothing to fear after 10 ♕a4 ♘xd2 11 ♘xd2 0-0 12 ♘f3 ♖e8, but 10 e3!? is an interesting idea, when White is ready to play 11 ♗d3, so Black must enter the complications following 10...♘g3 11 ♕b3 ♘xf1 (the greedy 11...♘xh1 leads to trouble after 12 cxd5 ♘e7 13 e4 ♗g4 14 e6! 0-0 15 exf7+ ♖xf7 16 ♘e5 ±) 12 ♖xf1 dxc4 13 ♕xb7 ♗e4 14 ♘d4! (14 ♕a6 ♕d5 15 ♗c3 ♖d8 is dangerous for White) 14...♖b8 15 ♕xc6+!? (Yakovich also considers the line 15 ♘xc6 ♕xd2+! 16 ♔xd2 ♖xb7 17 ♘b4 c5 18 f3 ♗g6 19 ♘c2 ♗d3 20 ♖fb1 ♔e7 21 b4 ♖hb8 with an unclear game that is very likely to end up in a drawn rook ending) 15...♗xc6 16 ♘xc6 ♕d5!? (more active than 16...♕c8 17 ♘xb8 ♕xb8 18 0-0-0 0-0 19 ♗c3 ♖d8 20 ♖xd8+ ♕xd8 21 ♖d1 ♕e7, when White has a better ending – Yakovich) 17 ♘xb8 0-0 18 ♘a6 ♕b5 19 0-0-0 (playing it safe; 19 ♘b4 a5 20 0-0-0 ♖b8! is a bit awkward for White) 19...♕xa6 20 ♗c3 ♕h6 21 h3 ♕g5 22 ♖g1 h6 23 ♖d4 ♖d8 ½-½ Yakovich-Lugovoi, Novgorod 1995.

10...0-0!?

10...♘g3?! 11 ♕b3 ♘xh1 12 cxd5 ♘e7 13 e4! ♗c8 14 ♗c4 gives White good compensation.

11 ♕c1 d4

There is no way back for Black. 11...♘xd2 12 ♖xd2 ♕e7 13 cxd5 ♘xe5 14 ♘xe5 ♕xe5 15 ♕c3 just gives White an extra pawn.

12 ♗c3!

The game Chekhov-Goldin, USSR 1987 continued with the inferior 12 ♗f4? f6! 13 e6 (White should probably aim for the unclear position after 13 e3 fxe5 14 ♘xe5 ♘xe5 15 ♗xe5 c5!?) 13...♘c5 14 b4 ♘xe6 15 b5 ♘e7 16 g3 c6 17 bxc6 ♘xc6 and Black was better.

12...dxc3

Otherwise White simply wins the d4-pawn.

13 ♖xd8 ♖axd8 14 bxc3 ♖d7 15 ♘d4!

Goldin and Khasin only considered 15 e3 ♘c5 16 ♗e2 ♘d3+, which they assessed as unclear.

15...♘xd4

15...♖fd8 is also insufficient, e.g. 16 e3 ♘xe5 17 ♘xf5 ♖d1+ 18 ♕xd1 ♖xd1+ 19 ♔xd1 ♘xf2+ 20 ♔e1 ♘xh1 21 ♗e2 and White wins because the knight never emerges from h1.

16 cxd4 ♖xd4 17 e3 ♖d7 18 ♗e2

White is better. Next he will castle.

B2)

5 e3 *(D)*

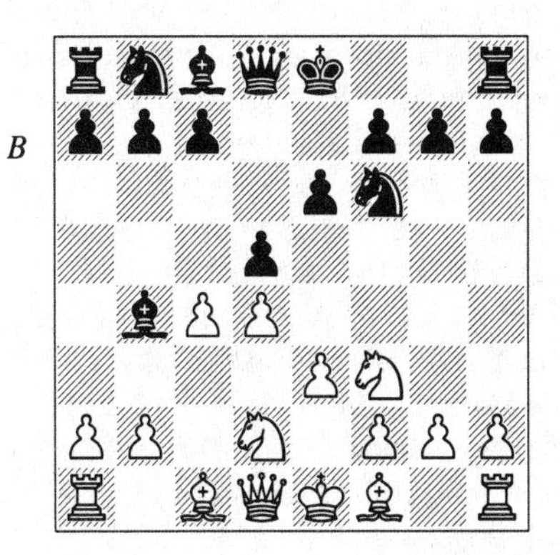

A very solid approach. White simply wants to complete his development, and does not permit Black to complicate the game.

5...0-0

5...c5 is a more aggressive option, but has never attracted many followers. 6 a3 ♗xd2+ 7 ♗xd2 (7 ♕xd2 cxd4 8 ♘xd4 e5 9 ♘f3 e4 10 ♘d4 0-0 11 b4 ♘bd7 12 ♗b2 ♘e5 13 cxd5 ♕xd5 = Novikov-Rashkovsky, USSR 1985) 7...cxd4 8 exd4 0-0 9 c5!? (White expands on the queenside and hopes that this will result in a strong passed pawn, but 9 ♗g5 is possibly a better try for advantage, when Rashkovsky analyses 9...dxc4 10 ♗xc4 b5 11 ♗d3 ♗b7 12 0-0 a6 and thinks that White is somewhat better) 9...b6 10 b4 bxc5 11 bxc5 ♘e4 12 ♗b5?! (12 ♗d3 is better) 12...♗d7 13 a4 ♕e8 14 ♗xd7 ♕xd7 15 ♗f4 f6 and Black has equalized, Yailian-Rashkovsky, Aktiubinsk 1985.

6 a3

Chasing the bishop away before proceeding the development gives White the additional possibility of capturing on c4 with the knight if Black exchanges pawns. 6 ♗d3 is an alternative, but after 6...dxc4 7 ♗xc4 Black has two reasonable replies:

a) 7...c5 8 a3 ♗xd2+ 9 ♗xd2 cxd4 10 exd4 h6 (better than 10...♘c6 11 ♗g5 b6 12 0-0 ♗b7 13 ♖c1 ♘e7 14 ♘e5 ♘f5 15 ♘g4 with the better game for White, Dreev-Rashkovsky, Palma de Mallorca 1989) 11 0-0 ♘c6 12 ♖c1, Dreev-Dolmatov, New York 1989, and now rather than the passive 12...♘e7?! Black should play 12...♘xd4! 13 ♗b4 ♘xf3+ 14 ♕xf3 ♖e8 15 ♖fd1 ♘d5 16 ♗xd5 exd5 17 ♖xd5 ♕h4 = Dreev.

b) 7...♘c6 8 0-0 ♕e7 9 a3 ♗d6 10 ♗b5 ♗d7 11 ♘c4 a6 12 ♗a4 b5 13 ♘xd6 cxd6 14 ♗c2 e5 = Uhlmann-Larsen, Halle 1963.

6...♗e7 *(D)*

6...♗xd2+ is quite rare in this particular position, but nevertheless a solid alternative:

a) 7 ♗xd2 b6 8 ♗d3 (8 ♗e2 is worth considering) 8...♗a6 9 ♕e2 ♘bd7 10 0-0 c5 11 cxd5 ♗xd3 12 ♕xd3 exd5 13 dxc5 bxc5 with approximately equal play, Pytel-Plachetka, Zemun 1980.

b) 7 ♕xd2!? b6 8 b3 ♘bd7 9 ♗d3 ♗b7 10 0-0 c5 11 ♗b2 ♖c8 12 ♖ac1 ♕e7 13 ♕e2 ♖fd8 = Franco-Gallardo, Cordoba 1990.

W

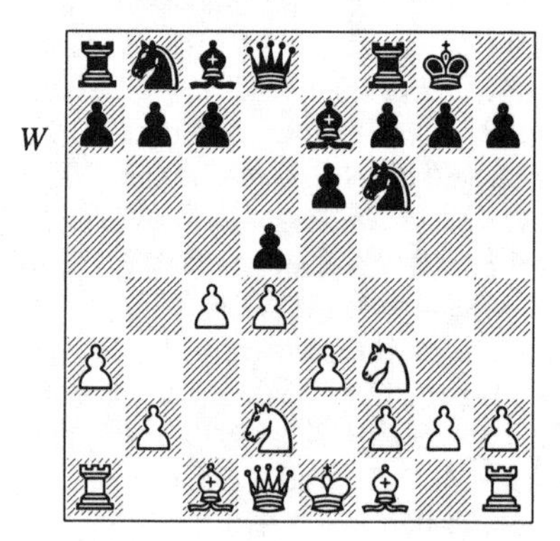

7 ♗d3

Comparing with 6 ♗d3, the reply ...dxc4 does not make much sense here, since White can recapture with the knight, thus obtaining firm control of the e5-square. 7 ♗d3 is a sensible developing move, preparing to castle, and retaining options whether to advance on the queenside or in the centre. However, the alternatives are also interesting:

a) 7 b4 a5 (A.Petrosian-Rashkovsky, USSR 1981 continued 7...b6 8 c5 a5 9 ♗b2 bxc5 10 dxc5 c6 11 ♘b3 ♘e4 12 ♗d3 ♗a6 13 ♗xa6 ♖xa6 14 0-0 ♗f6 15 ♗xf6 ♕xf6 16 ♘xa5 ♘xc5 17 ♕d4 ♘e4 with unclear play) 8 b5 (8 ♖b1 axb4 9 axb4 dxc4 10 ♘xc4 ♗d7!? is fine for Black) 8...c5 and now:

a1) 9 bxc6 bxc6 10 c5!? ♕e8?! (10...♕c7 11 ♕c2 ♘bd7 12 ♗b2 ♗a6 looks more sensible) 11 ♕c2 ♘fd7 12 ♗b2 f5 13 ♗e2 ♗a6 14 ♗xa6 ± A.Petrosian-Ivanović, Belgrade 1988.

a2) 9 ♗b2 ♘bd7 10 ♗d3 cxd4 11 exd4 b6 12 0-0 ♗b7 13 ♖e1 ♖c8 14 ♖c1 ♖c7!? intending ...♕a8 with unclear play, Rukavina-Toth, Budva 1981.

a3) 9 ♗d3 b6 10 cxd5, Voronkov-Zakharov, corr. 1968, 10...♘xd5! =.

b) 7 ♕c2!? ♘bd7 8 b4 a5 9 ♖b1 axb4 10 axb4 b6 11 ♗d3 c5 12 dxc5 bxc5 13 b5 ♗b7 14 0-0 ♗d6 15 ♗b2 with chances for both sides, I.Sokolov-Hraček, Pärnu 1996.

7...c5

This is the most aggressive continuation for Black, but others do not seem much worse:

a) 7...♘bd7 8 b4 a5 9 b5 (this kind of position usually gives Black few problems, so here when Black's knight has gone to d7 it is worth considering 9 ♖b1!?) 9...c5 10 bxc6 bxc6 11 0-0 ♗a6 12 ♗b2 c5 13 ♘e5 ♖c8 = Filip-Smyslov, Havana 1967.

b) 7...b6 and then:

b1) 8 e4 dxe4 9 ♘xe4 ♗b7 10 ♕c2 ♘bd7 11 0-0 c5 12 ♖d1 ♕c7 (or 12...♘xe4!? 13 ♗xe4 ♗xe4 14 ♕xe4 ♘f6 15 ♕e2 ♕c7 =) 13 ♗g5 h6 14 ♗h4 ♖fe8 15 ♗g3 ♕c6 16 d5 exd5 17 cxd5 ♕c8 18 ♘xf6+ ♗xf6 19 ♗f5 was pleasant for White in Gufeld-Gipslis, Tbilisi 1967.

b2) 8 b3 ♗b7 9 ♗b2 and then:

b21) 9...c5 10 0-0 cxd4 11 exd4 ♘bd7 12 ♖e1 ♖e8 13 ♘f1 (instead Ivkov-Korchnoi, Sousse IZ 1967 continued 13 ♘e5 dxc4 14 bxc4 ♘xe5 15 ♖xe5 ♗f8 16 a4 g6 17 a5 ±) 13...♗f8 14 ♘g3 dxc4 15 bxc4 g6 16 ♕e2 ♗g7 (Malaniuk suggests 16...♕c7) 17 ♘e5! intending f4, with the better game for White, Malaniuk-Ciolac, Montecatini 1994.

b22) 9...♘bd7 10 0-0 c5 11 ♕e2 cxd4 12 exd4 ♖c8 13 ♖ac1 ♖c7!? (13...♖e8 14 ♖fd1 ♗f8 15 ♘e5 dxc4 16 bxc4 ♘xe5 17 ♕xe5 ± Bobotsov-Ivkov, Beverwijk 1968) 14 ♘e5 dxc4 15 bxc4 ♘xe5 16 ♕xe5 ♖d7 17 ♖fe1 ♗c5 18 ♘b3 ♗d6 = Ivkov-Fuchs, Havana OL 1966.

b23) 9...♘e4!? 10 0-0 ♘d7 11 ♖c1 c5 12 ♕e2 ♘xd2! 13 ♘xd2 cxd4 14 exd4 ♗f6 15 ♘f3 dxc4 16 ♗xc4 ♖c8 with equality, Yusupov-Speelman, Belfort 1988.

b3) 8 0-0 c5 9 dxc5 (9 cxd5 exd5 10 dxc5 bxc5 11 e4 ♘c6 12 ♕c2 g6 13 exd5 ♕xd5 14 ♖e1 ♗b7 15 ♗c4, Yermolinsky-Nasybullin, USSR 1987, and now after 15...♕h5 16 ♘f1 ♗d6!? Black could have got some attacking chances as compensation for his inferior pawn structure – Nasybullin) 9...bxc5 10 b3 a5 (10...♗b7 11 ♗b2 ♘bd7 is perhaps better) 11 ♗b2 a4 12 bxa4 ♗d7 13 ♗c2 ♕a5 14 cxd5 exd5 15 ♘b3 ♕a7 16 ♖c1 ± Antoshin-Gipslis, USSR 1970.

Returning to the position after 7...c5 *(D)*:

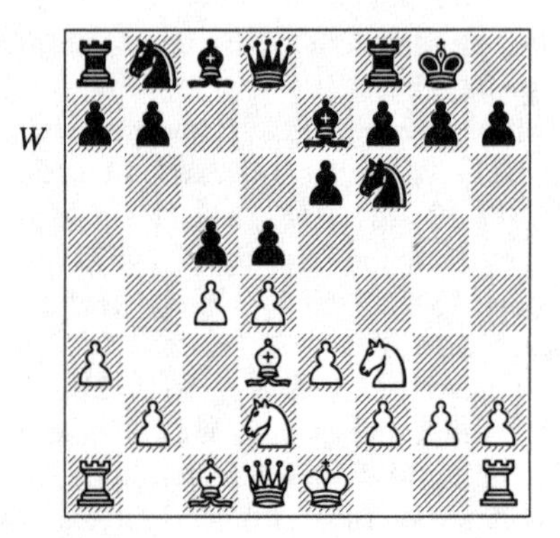

8 dxc5

White can hardly avoid the central pawns being exchanged off and therefore goes for a slight initiative. The alternatives give Black better chances:

a) 8 0-0 dxc4 9 ♘xc4 b5!? 10 ♘ce5 c4 11 ♗e2 ♗b7 12 a4 a6 13 axb5 axb5 14 ♖xa8 ♗xa8 (Black's aggressive play has given him a two pawns vs one scenario on the queenside, and good control of the e4-square; therefore White now decides to attack Black's queenside pawns) 15 b3 ♘e4 16 bxc4 f6 17 ♘d3 bxc4 18 ♘f4 ♘c3 19 ♕c2 ♘xe2+ 20 ♕xe2 ♕c8 = Inkiov-P.Nikolić, Zagreb IZ 1987.

b) 8 b3 cxd4 9 exd4 dxc4 10 ♘xc4 (in Sorin-Korchnoi, Oviedo rpd 1992 White accepted the hanging pawns in the centre, but after 10 bxc4 b6 11 ♗b2 ♗b7 12 0-0 ♘bd7 13 ♕e2 ♖e8 14 ♖ad1 ♕c7 15 ♖fe1 ♖ad8 16 h3 ♘f8 Black was doing well) 10...b5 11 ♘ce5 ♗b7 12 0-0 ♕d5 13 ♗g5 ♘c6 14 ♘xc6 ♗xc6 ∓ Inkiov-P.Nikolić, Thessaloniki OL 1988.

8...a5!

8...♗xc5 9 0-0 a5 10 b3 ♘c6 11 ♗b2 ± Toran-O'Kelly, Palma de Mallorca 1967.

9 cxd5

Black has few problems against other moves:

a) 9 ♖b1 ♘a6!? (Black simply allows White to play b4, but is ready to confuse matters with ...b6 afterwards) 10 b4 axb4 11 axb4 b6!, and in Yusupov-P.Nikolić, Tilburg 1987 White did not find anything: 12 cxb6 ♘xb4 13 ♗e2 ♕xb6 14 0-0 ♗d7 15 ♕b3 ♖fb8 16 ♗b2 ♗a4 17 ♕c3 ♕c7 ½-½.

b) 9 0-0 ♘bd7! (here we see why Black's last move was important: while 9...♗xc5 transposes to Toran-O'Kelly above, now Black is able to take on c5 with the knight, thereby increasing his control of the e4-square) 10 b3 ♘xc5 11 ♗c2 b6 12 ♗b2 ♗b7 (12...♗a6 13 ♘e5 ♖c8 is also fine for Black, P.Cramling-Cu.Hansen, Malmö 1996) 13 ♕e2 dxc4 14 ♘xc4 b5 15 ♖fd1 ♗d5 16 ♘ce5 ♕b6 = Adianto-Goldin, New York Open 1993.

9...exd5!?

9...♕xd5 leads to an almost symmetrical pawn structure but with White having a slight initiative, for example 10 ♕e2 ♖d8 11 ♗c4 ♕xc5 12 0-0 a4 13 e4 ♕h5 14 e5 ♘fd7 15 ♗b5 b6 16 ♘c4 ♗b7 17 ♖d1 ♗c6 18 ♗xc6 ♘xc6 19 ♗f4 ± Timman-Kurajica, Sarajevo 1984.

10 b3!?

White has tried a variety of plans in this position, but surprisingly this quiet move seems to be the most promising. Let us have a brief look at the others:

a) 10 ♘d4 ♗xc5 11 0-0 ♗g4 12 ♗e2 ♗xd4 13 ♗xg4 ♗b6 14 ♗e2 ♘c6 15 ♘f3 ♘e4 16 ♕d3 ♘c5 17 ♕c2 ♖c8 18 ♗d2 ♘e4 19 ♗c3 ♕e7 20 ♕d3 ♖fd8 = Polugaevsky-Korchnoi, Roquebrune rpd 1992.

b) 10 ♘b3 ♘bd7 11 a4 ♘xc5 12 ♘xc5 ♗xc5 13 0-0 ♘e4 = Evdokimov-L.B.Hansen, Gistrup 1990.

c) 10 0-0 ♘bd7 11 ♘b3 a4 12 ♘bd4 ♘xc5 13 ♗c2 ♘fe4 14 ♗d2 ♗f6 15 ♗b4 b6 = Portisch-Salov, Rotterdam 1989.

10...♘bd7 11 ♗b2 ♘xc5 12 ♗e2 ♗g4 13 0-0 ♘e6

In all variations in the previous note Black was able to utilize the e4-square, but here White has played the opening with great subtlety, as he has not yet revealed which piece he intends to play to d4. For instance 13...♕b6 might be met by 14 ♗d4!?.

14 ♘d4 ♗xe2 15 ♕xe2 ♘xd4 16 ♗xd4 ♕d7 17 ♕d3 ♖fc8 18 ♗b2! ♖a6 19 ♖ad1

White is slightly better, Kantsler-Balashov, USSR Ch (Moscow) 1991.

C)

4...0-0 *(D)*

5 a3

Other options are:

a) 5 e3 d6 (5...d5 is Line B, whilst 5...b6 transposes to Line D) with two possibilities:

a1) 6 ♗e2 ♘bd7 7 0-0 ♗xd2 8 ♘xd2!? e5 9 b3 exd4 10 exd4 d5 11 ♗f3 ♖e8 12 cxd5 ♘b6 13 d6! ♕xd6 14 ♘c4 ♕e6 15 ♘xb6 axb6 16 d5 ♕e5 17 ♗e3 ± Miles-Short, Manchester 1982.

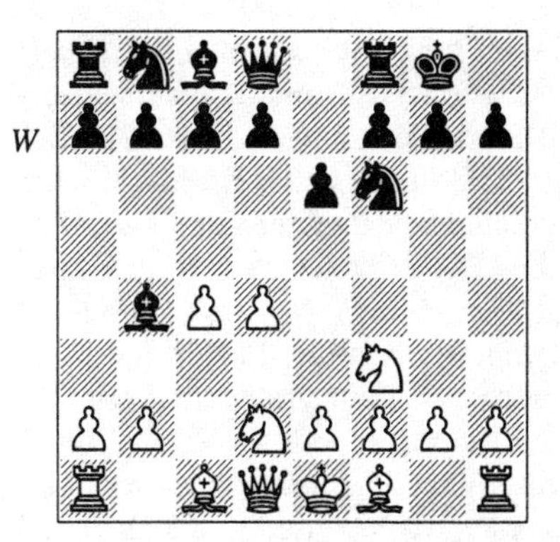

W

a2) 6 ♕c2 ♘c6 (6...♕e7 7 ♗d3 e5 8 0-0 ♗xd2 9 ♘xd2 exd4 10 exd4 ♘c6 = Yermolinsky) 7 a3 (also interesting is 7 ♗d3!? e5 8 d5 ♘e7 9 0-0 ♗xd2 10 ♘xd2 followed by f4, with an advantage to White – Malaniuk) 7...♗xd2+ 8 ♗xd2 e5 9 ♗c3 ♕e7 10 d5 ♘b8 11 ♘d2!? c6 12 e4 cxd5 (12...♘h5!?) 13 cxd5 ♘h5 14 ♘c4! ♘a6 15 ♘e3 and White is better, Malaniuk-Yermolinsky, Lucerne Wcht 1993.

b) 5 g3 and then:

b1) 5...b6 6 ♗g2 ♗b7 (this position frequently arises from the Queen's Indian, viz. 1 d4 ♘f6 2 c4 e6 3 ♘f3 b6 4 g3 ♗b7 5 ♗g2 ♗b4+ 6 ♘bd2 0-0) 7 0-0 c5!? (more solid is 7...♗e7 or 7...d5) 8 a3 ♗xd2 9 ♗xd2 cxd4 10 ♗b4 ♖e8 11 ♗d6! ♗xf3 (11...♘c6 12 ♘xd4 ♘a5! is stronger according to Poluliakhov, whilst 11...♘e4 12 ♕xd4 ♘a6 13 b4 ♖c8 14 ♖ac1 ♘xd6 15 ♕xd6 ♘c7 16 ♖fd1 was substantially better for White in Karpov-Andersson, Madrid 1973) 12 exf3! (12 ♗xf3!? ♘c6 13 ♗xc6 dxc6 14 ♕xd4 ♘e4 15 ♖fd1 is probably also a little better for White, although 15...♘xd6 16 ♕xd6 ♕f6! might solve some of Black's problems) 12...♘c6 13 f4 ♖c8 14 b3?! (much better is 14 ♖c1, when Poluliakhov gives the line 14...♘e7 15 ♗b7 ♖c6 16 ♗xc6 dxc6 17 c5 ♘f5 18 ♗e5 ±) 14...♘e7! 15 g4! (White attempts to restrict Black's pieces as much as possible, rather than winning the exchange with 15 ♗b7 ♖c6! 16 ♗xc6 dxc6 17 ♗xe7 ♖xe7, when Black has some compensation) 15...h6 16 h3 b5 17 c5! ♘c6 18 ♖e1 ♘d5 19 ♕d3 a6 20 ♗xd5 exd5 21 ♕f5 ♖e6! 22 ♕xd5 with compensation, Poluliakhov-Kruszynski, Poland 1991.

b2) 5...d6 6 ♗g2 ♘c6 7 0-0 e5 (7...♗xd2 8 ♕xd2 ♘e4 9 ♕e3 f5 10 b3 a5 11 ♗a3 ♕f6 12 ♖fd1 ♖e8 13 ♘e1 ♕g6 14 ♘d3 ♘f6 15 ♗b2 ± Polugaevsky-Razuvaev, Moscow 1967) 8 ♘b3 (8 d5 ♘b8 9 ♘b3 also looks good for White, for example 9...♘bd7 10 a3 ♗c5 11 ♘xc5 ♘xc5 12 b4 ±) 8...exd4 9 ♘fxd4 ♘xd4 10 ♕xd4 ♘d7! 11 ♗d2 a5 12 ♗xb4 axb4 13 ♖fd1 ♕e7 14 ♕d2 ♘b6 15 ♕xb4 ♖a4 16 ♕c3 ♖xc4 17 ♕d3 ♖a4 18 ♘d4 ± D.Gurevich-Yermolinsky, USA 1995.

5...♗e7

Retreating the bishop allows White to set up a broad pawn-centre, but Black is able to counter this by a ...d5 break.

5...♗xd2+ leads to quieter play:

a) 6 ♕xd2 and now:

a1) 6...b6 most likely transposes to Line D, note to White's 6th move.

a2) 6...d6 with a further branch:

a21) 7 b3 ♘bd7 8 ♗b2 ♘e4 9 ♕c2 f5 10 g3 ♘df6 11 ♗g2 ♕e8 12 ♘d2 ♗d7 13 ♘f1!? ♕h5 14 f3 ♘g5 15 h4 ♘f7 16 f4 d5! 17 ♗f3 ♕h6 18 cxd5 ♘xd5 with a messy position, Ftačnik-Benjamin, Los Angeles 1991.

a22) 7 b4 ♘bd7 8 e3 e5 9 dxe5 dxe5 10 ♗b2 ♕e7 11 ♕c3 (Vukić suggests 11 c5 e4 12 ♘d4 ♘e5 13 ♖c1 with a slight advantage) 11...e4 12 ♘e5 a5 13 ♘xd7 ♗xd7 14 ♗e2 axb4 15 axb4 ♖xa1+ 16 ♗xa1 c5 = Browne-Larsen, Mar del Plata 1981.

b) 6 ♗xd2 *(D)* with a choice for Black:

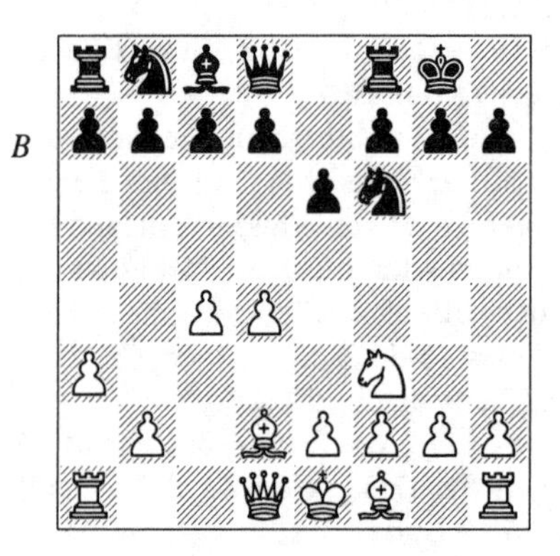

b1) 6...d6 and now:

b11) 7 ♕c2 ♕e7 8 ♗c3 ♘bd7 9 e3 e5 10 ♗e2 (10 dxe5!?) 10...exd4! 11 ♘xd4 ♘c5 12 0-0 ♘ce4 13 ♗e1 c5! 14 ♘b5 ♗f5 15 ♗d3 ♗g6 = Chernin-Oll, Pamplona 1991/2.

b12) 7 g3 ♘c6 (another way to prepare ...e5 is 7...♕e7, while 7...♘e4 transposes to 'b34') 8 ♗c3 ♘e4 9 ♖c1 e5 10 ♗g2 ♗g4!? (10...exd4 11 ♘xd4 ♖e8 12 0-0 ♘xc3 13 ♖xc3 ♘xd4 14 ♕xd4 ♖xe2 15 c5 ♗e6 is also fine for Black) 11 d5 ♘e7 12 0-0 f5 13 ♘d2 ♘xd2 14 ♕xd2 f4 = J.Watson-Yermolinsky, Reno 1994.

b13) 7 ♗g5 ♘bd7 8 e3 ♖e8 (8...e5 9 ♗e2 b6 10 0-0 a5?! {10...♗b7 is better} 11 ♕c2! ♗b7 12 dxe5!? dxe5 13 ♖fd1 ♕e8 14 ♗xf6 ♘xf6 15 c5 ± Lputian-Larsen, Hastings 1986/7) 9 ♗e2 e5 10 0-0 ♕e7 11 ♖c1 ♘f8 12 c5 h6 13 cxd6 cxd6 14 ♗xf6 ♕xf6 15 dxe5 dxe5 16 ♕a4 ♖e7 17 ♕b4 ± Savchenko-Gostiša, Erevan OL 1996.

b2) 6...b6 (when Black embarks on a queenside fianchetto, there is a close resemblance to Line D, and so I recommended a comparison between these two lines) 7 ♗g5 ♗b7 8 e3 d6 9 ♗e2 ♘bd7 10 0-0 h6 (10...♕e8 11 ♘d2 ♘e4 12 ♘xe4 ♗xe4 13 f3 ♗b7 14 b4 with a space advantage, P.Cramling-Tempone, Buenos Aires 1994) 11 ♗h4 c5 12 ♗g3 d5 13 cxd5 exd5 14 dxc5 bxc5 15 b4 ♘e4 with unclear play, Khalifman-Anand, Groningen FIDE KO Wch 1997.

b3) 6...♘e4 is Black's best move, denying White the possibility of moving the bishop to g5. There is now a wide choice for White:

b31) 7 ♗e3 d5 8 ♖c1 dxc4 9 ♖xc4 ♕d5 10 ♕c2 ♗d7 11 g3 ♗b5 12 ♖b4 ♗c6 13 ♗g2 ♘a6 14 ♖c4 ♗b5 (the alternative 14...♘d6!? is better, with unclear play) 15 ♘d2 ± Cebalo-Korchnoi, Biel 1986.

b32) 7 ♗f4 d6 (7...b6 8 e3 ♗b7 9 ♗d3 d6 10 0-0 ♘d7 transposes to Line D, note 'b1' to Black's 6th move) 8 ♕c2 f5 9 ♖d1 ♕e7 10 g3 ♘d7 11 ♗g2 e5 12 ♗c1 ± Yusupov.

b33) 7 ♕c2 ♘xd2 8 ♕xd2 ♕e7 9 e4 d6 10 e5 dxe5 11 dxe5 b6 12 ♗e2 ♗b7 13 ♖d1 c5 = P.Nikolić-Christiansen, Reggio Emilia 1987/8.

b34) 7 g3 d6 8 ♗g2 and now:

b341) 8...f5 9 0-0 (9 ♗e3!?) 9...♘d7 10 ♖c1 ♘df6 11 ♕b3 a5?! (according to Bareev 11...b6! equalizes) 12 ♖fd1 ♗d7 13 ♘g5! and White is better, Bareev-Raaste, Saltsjöbaden 1987.

b342) 8...♘xd2 9 ♕xd2 ♕e7 10 0-0 e5 11 ♖ac1 ♖e8 12 ♖c3 ♘d7 13 ♖e3 ♕f8 14 dxe5 dxe5 15 ♕c3 f6 16 ♖d1 a5 17 ♘h4 c6 18 b4 ± Vilela-Rivas, Bayamo 1983.

b343) 8...♘d7 9 ♗e3! (this is not only to avoid the exchange of the bishop but more importantly also to prepare ♘d2; another option is 9 0-0 ♕e7 10 ♖c1 f5 11 c5!? ♘df6 12 ♘g5! ♘xd2 13 ♕xd2 e5 14 cxd6 cxd6 15 dxe5 dxe5 16 ♗d5+!? ♔h8 17 ♗b3 h6 18 ♘f3 e4 19 ♘d4 ± Lputian-Psakhis, USSR Ch 1987) 9...f5 10 ♕c2 ♘df6 11 ♘d2 ♘xd2 12 ♗xd2 ♕e8 (12...e5!? – Benjamin) 13 c5! dxc5 14 dxc5 (better is 14 ♕xc5 ±) 14...c6 15 f4 e5 16 fxe5 ♕xe5 17 ♗f4 ♕e6 18 0-0 ♖e8 19 ♖fe1 ♕f7 20 ♖ad1 ♗e6 = Lutz-Benjamin, Horgen 1994.

6 e4

White is setting up an impressive pawn-centre, and of course Black must seek to challenge this pawn phalanx immediately. White can also embark on the safer 6 e3, but then Black should have no problems, for example 6...c5 (6...d5 transposes to Line B2) 7 dxc5 a5! 8 b3 ♘a6 (again, control of the e4-square is essential, and thus 8...♗xc5?! 9 ♗b2 ♘c6 10 ♕c2 b6 11 ♘g5 g6 12 ♘de4 ♘xe4 13 ♘xe4 ♗e7 14 ♕c3 e5 15 ♕d2 d6 16 ♗e2 ♗b7 17 ♘c3 was clearly better for White in the game Kindermann-Makarychev,

Bayern-CSKA ECC 1988) 9 ♗b2 ♘xc5 10 ♕c2 (or 10 ♗e2 b6 11 0-0 ♗b7 12 ♘d4 ♕b8 13 ♗f3 d5 = Miles-Yusupov, Linares 1997) 10...b6 11 ♘g5 g6 12 ♗e2 ♗b7 13 0-0 ♖c8 14 b4 ♘a6 15 b5 ♘c5 16 ♖ad1 ♕c7 17 ♘gf3 ♘fe4 18 ♗a1 f5 = M.Gurevich-P.Nikolić, Leningrad 1987.

6...d5 *(D)*

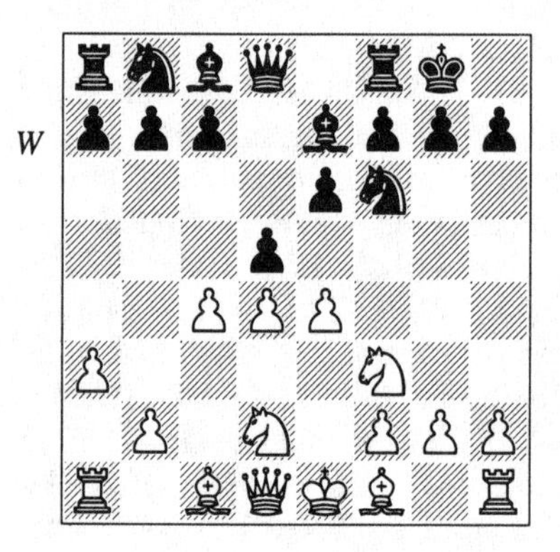

Now we shall look at:

Some alternatives are:

a) 7 ♗d3!? c5! (7...dxe4 8 ♘xe4 ♘c6 9 ♗e3 ♘g4 10 0-0 ♘xe3 11 fxe3 f5 12 ♘c3 ± Seirawan-Adams, Roquebrune rpd 1992) 8 dxc5 (8 e5 ♘fd7 9 cxd5 exd5 transposes to Line C2) 8...dxe4 9 ♘xe4 ♘xe4 10 ♗xe4 ♕xd1+ 11 ♔xd1 ♗xc5 12 b4! ♗e7 (the greedy 12...♗xf2?! 13 c5 f5 14 ♗b1! gives White splendid compensation) 13 ♔e2 f5 14 ♗c2 ♗f6 15 ♖b1 e5! = Yakovich-Makarov, Novgorod 1995.

b) 7 cxd5 exd5 8 e5 and now 8...♘fd7 transposes to Line C2, but Black has the additional possibility 8...♘e4!? 9 ♗d3 f5 10 0-0 c5 11 dxc5 a5!:

b1) 12 ♘b3?! ♘c6 13 ♗b5 f4! 14 ♘bd4 ♘xd4 15 ♘xd4 ♗xc5 16 ♘b3, A.Petrosian-Ulybin, Pavlodar 1987, and now 16...♗a7! looks good for Black, with the idea of 17 ♗e2 ♘xf2 18 ♖xf2 ♕b6 –+.

b2) 12 ♕c2!? ♘c6 13 ♗b5 ♘xc5 14 ♘b3 ♘e4 15 ♗xc6 bxc6 16 ♕xc6 ♗a6 17 ♖d1 ♗c4 18 ♘bd4 a4 19 ♘e6 ♕c8 20 ♕xc8 ♖fxc8 21 ♘fd4 g6 22 f3 and White is better, Ruban-Ulybin, USSR 1986.

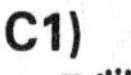

C1)

7 ♕c2 *(D)*

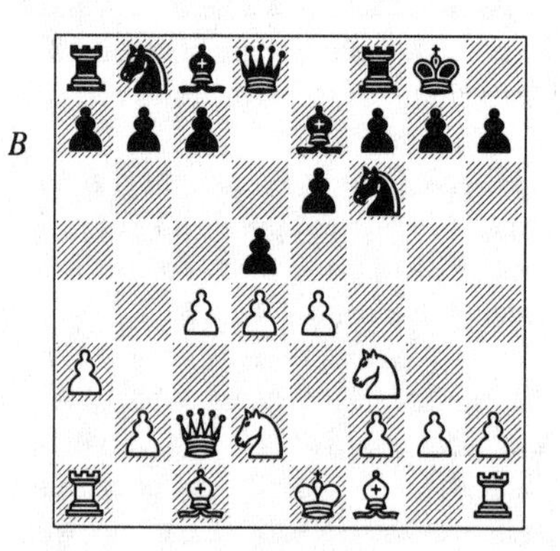

With this move White tries to keep the tension in the centre, but Black is well developed and his chances do not seem worse.

7...dxe4

Black may also strike directly at the centre: 7...c5 8 dxc5 a5!? (8...dxe4 9 ♘xe4 ♘xe4 10 ♕xe4 f5 11 ♕e3 a5 12 ♗e2 ♕c7 13 ♕f4 ♕xf4 14 ♗xf4 ♗xc5

15 0-0 ♘c6 16 ♖fd1 was better for White in Portisch-Wahls, Biel 1995) 9 cxd5 exd5 10 ♗d3 h6 11 0-0 (there is no reason to force Black to fix the queenside after 11 ♖b1 a4; Miles-P.Nikolić, Lugano 1989 continued 12 0-0 ♘c6 13 h3 ♗e6 14 ♖e1 dxe4 15 ♘xe4 ♗a2 16 ♖a1 ♗b3 17 ♕e2 ♖e8 with an unclear position) 11...♘c6 12 h3 ♗e6 13 b3 ♘d7 14 exd5 ♗xd5 15 ♘e4 ♗xe4 16 ♗xe4 ♘xc5 17 ♗xc6 (keeping the bishop-pair with 17 ♖d1! ♕b6 18 ♗d5 would have given White an advantage) 17...bxc6 18 ♗e3 ♕d3 and Black is close to equality, Dreev-Oll, Tbilisi 1989.

8 ♘xe4 ♘c6

The counter-attack against d4 is currently the most popular, but Black might also consider fighting for control over e4, by 8...♘bd7 9 ♗d3 (an interesting but rather unexplored idea is 9 ♘eg5 h6 10 h4 c5 11 ♗e3 ♕c7 12 0-0-0 b6 13 ♗d3 ♗b7 14 ♖h3 with unclear play, Cebalo-Kruszynski, Caorle 1991) 9...♘xe4 10 ♗xe4 ♘f6 11 ♗d3 b6 12 ♗e3 and now:

a) 12...c5!? 13 0-0-0 ♕c7 14 ♘g5?! (better is 14 ♘e5! cxd4 15 ♗xd4 ♖d8 16 ♗c3 ♗b7 17 ♖he1 with an advantage) 14...h6 15 ♘h7 ♖d8 16 ♘xf6+ ♗xf6 and Black has the better game, Gausel-Mokry, Gausdal 1989.

b) 12...♗b7 13 0-0-0 ♕c8 14 ♖he1! c5 (14...♖e8 15 ♘e5 c5 16 g4 gave White a dangerous attack in M.Gurevich-J.Horvath, Budapest 1987) 15 ♘e5 cxd4 16 ♗xd4 ♖d8 17 ♗c3 ♗xg2?! (this is quite risky, but White also has a promising position after 17...g6 18 g4) 18 ♖e3! (a major improvement on 18 ♖g1? ♕b7 19 f3 ♗xf3 20 ♖df1 ♖xd3! 21 ♕xd3 ♗e4 with the better game for Black, Gelfand-Dimitrov, Adelaide jr Wch 1988) 18...♕b7 19 ♖g1 threatening 20 ♖g3 with a very dangerous attack, Gelfand-Delchev, Arnhem jr Ech 1988/9.

9 ♗e3

This is not a new move, but has had a revival lately. 9 ♗d3 used to be more popular:

a) 9...♘xe4 10 ♗xe4 ♘xd4 11 ♘xd4 ♕xd4 12 ♗e3 ♕e5 13 ♗xh7+ ♔h8 14 ♗d3 ♕a5+ (14...♗c5 15 0-0 ♗xe3 16 fxe3 ♕xe3+ 17 ♔h1 with compensation) 15 ♗d2 ♕e5+ 16 ♗e2 ♕f5 17 ♗d3 ♕e5+ ½-½ Dreev-Vaganian, Reggio Emilia 1995/6.

b) 9...♘xd4!? 10 ♘xd4 ♕xd4 11 ♘xf6+ ♗xf6 12 ♗xh7+ ♔h8 13 ♗e4 ♗d7!? 14 ♖b1 (14 ♗xb7 ♖ab8 15 ♗f3 ♕e5+ is unclear) 14...♗c6 15 ♗xc6 bxc6 16 ♗e3 ± Cu.Hansen-Yusupov, Munich 1992.

c) 9...h6 10 ♗e3 (10 ♕c3 is another attempt, but 10...♘xd4! 11 ♘xd4 ♘xe4 12 ♗xe4 ♗f6 13 ♗e3 c5 looks like an effective equalizer) 10...♘g4 11 ♖d1 f5 12 ♘c3 ♗f6 13 0-0 ♗xd4 14 ♗xf5 ♖xf5 15 ♗xd4 ♖xf3 16 gxf3 ♘xh2 17 ♔xh2 ♕h4+ 18 ♔g2 ♕g5+ 19 ♔h1 ♕h5+ 20 ♔g2 ♕g5+ = Epishin-Arnason, New York Open 1989.

9...♘xe4 10 ♕xe4 f5!? 11 ♕d3 f4

Black must continue actively. Instead 11...♗f6 12 0-0-0 e5 13 dxe5 ♕xd3 14 ♗xd3 ♘xe5 15 ♘xe5 ♗xe5 16 ♖he1 was slightly better for White in the game Wedberg-Ziska, Torshavn 1987.

12 ♗d2 e5!? 13 dxe5 ♗g4

13...♕e8 14 ♗e2 ♗f5 15 ♕b3 ♕g6 16 ♗xf4 ♕xg2 17 ♖g1 ♕h3 18 ♖g3 ♕h5 19 0-0-0 was very good for White in P.Cramling-Timman, Malmö 1997.

14 ♗c3

Tisdall suggests 14 ♕e4!?.

14...♗c5!?

Or 14...♕e8 15 ♗e2 ♗f5 16 ♕d5+ ♔h8, Gunawan-Adianto, Jakarta 1996, and now Tisdall recommends 17 0-0.

15 b4

15 ♕d5+? ♕xd5 16 cxd5 ♗xf3 17 gxf3 ♘xe5! is good for Black, but Tisdall's idea 15 ♕e4!? might still be worth a try.

15...♕xd3 16 ♗xd3 ♖ad8 17 ♗e4 ♗xf3 18 gxf3

18 ♗xf3!? is suggested by Tisdall, and his analysis goes 18...♗d4 (or 18...♖d3 19 ♗d5+ ♔h8 20 bxc5 ♖xc3 21 ♔d2 ±) 19 ♗xd4 ♘xd4 (19...♖xd4 20 ♗d5+ ♔h8 21 ♖d1 and White is better) and now either 20 ♗e4 or 20 0-0-0 with the better position for White.

18...♗d4 19 ♗xd4 ♖xd4 20 ♗d5+ ♔h8 21 e6 ♘e7 22 ♗xb7 g6!

Black intends to continue ...♔g7-f6, with some compensation, I.Sokolov-Hellsten, Malmö 1997.

C2)

7 e5 *(D)*

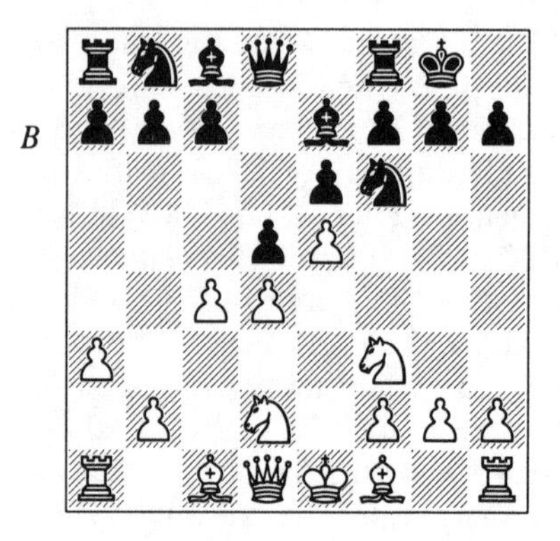

7...♘fd7 8 cxd5

The direct 8 b4!? is also interesting. There is no way Black can exploit the fact that White has not exchanged on d5. Lputian-Yusupov, Baden-Baden 1996 continued 8...a5 (8...b6!?) 9 b5 c5 10 ♗b2!? b6? (better is 10...♖e8) 11 cxd5 exd5 12 ♗d3 ♖e8 13 0-0 ♘f8 14 ♘e1! intending f4 with a clear advantage.

8...exd5 9 ♗d3

9 b4 is also interesting:

a) 9...b6 10 ♕b3! ♗b7 11 ♗d3 ♖e8 12 0-0 ♘f8 13 ♖e1 c6 14 ♘f1 ♘e6 15 ♘e3 g6 16 ♗b2 a6 (if 16...♘d7, then 17 b5 is strong – Chuchelov) 17 ♗f1 ♘d7 18 a4 ♘df8 19 ♖ed1 ± Chuchelov-Makarov, Novosibirsk 1989.

b) 9...a5 10 b5 c5 11 ♗d3 cxd4 12 ♘b3 (12 ♕c2?! ♔h8! 13 ♘b3, Dautov-Orlov, USSR 1988, 13...a4 14 ♘bxd4 ♘c5 15 0-0 ♘xd3 16 ♕xd3 ♘d7 =) 12...a4 13 ♘bxd4 ♘c5 14 0-0 (14 ♗c2 ♗g4 15 h3 ♗h5 16 ♘f5 ± Dautov) 14...♘bd7 15 ♘f5 ♘xd3 16 ♕xd3 ♘c5 17 ♘xe7+ ♕xe7 18 ♕xd5 ♘b3 19 ♗g5 ♕e6 20 ♖ad1 ± Lputian-Gulko, Erevan OL 1996.

9...c5 10 0-0

Launching a direct attack with 10 h4 is also possible but Black probably has nothing to fear after 10...h6 11 ♗b1 ♖e8! 12 ♕c2 (12 ♘b3 cxd4 13 ♕c2 ♘f8 14 ♘bxd4 ♗g4 was quite good for Black in the game Sapis-P.Stempin, Polish Ch 1989) 12...♘f8

13 dxc5 ♘c6 with good compensation – Sapis.

10...♘c6 11 ♖e1 *(D)*

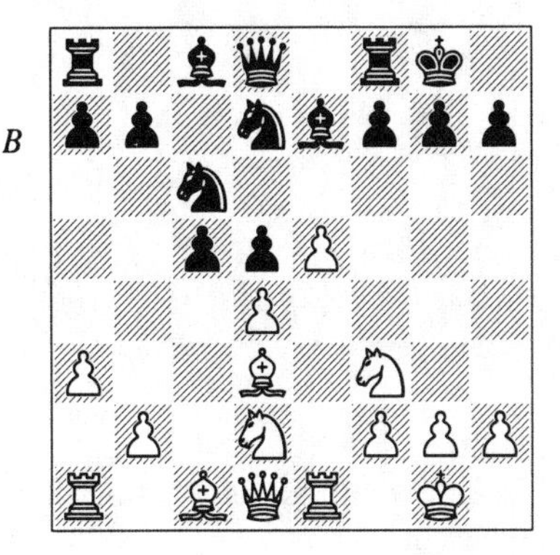

11...a5

It is important that Black interpolates this move before capturing on d4 as after 11...cxd4?!, White continues 12 b4 and Black does not have time for 12...♕c7 due to 13 ♕c2!.

However, 11...♖e8!? is a perfectly viable alternative:

a) 12 ♕c2 h6 13 ♘f1 (13 dxc5 is probably better, transposing to 'c' in the next note) 13...♗f8 14 ♗f4?! ♘xd4 15 ♘xd4 cxd4 16 b4 a5 17 ♖ab1 axb4 18 axb4 g5 19 ♗g3 ♗g7 ∓ Portisch-P.Nikolić, Tilburg 1988.

b) 12 h3 ♘f8 (12...♗f8?! turned out to be inaccurate in Yusupov-Petursson, Reykjavik 1988: 13 ♘f1 g6 {13...cxd4 14 ♗xh7+!} 14 ♗g5 ♗e7 15 ♗xe7 ♖xe7 16 ♘e3 cxd4 17 ♘xd5 ♖e8 18 ♗c4 ♘dxe5 19 ♘xe5 ♖xe5 20 ♖xe5 ♘xe5 21 ♕xd4 ♕g5 22 ♔h2! intending f4, and White was clearly better) 13 dxc5 ♗xc5 14 ♘b3 ♗b6 15 ♗g5 ♕c7 16 ♖c1 with a pleasant position for White, Browne-Barle, Reykjavik 1988.

12 h3!?

An interesting waiting move, which in the future might serve the purpose of preventing ...♗g4 or simply provide an escape for the king. Alternatives:

a) 12 ♗c2?! ♖e8! (Black rightly waits before taking on d4 until White has moved his knight to f1; the game Hellsten-L.V.Jakobsen, Gistrup 1997 continued 12...cxd4?! 13 ♘b3 ♖e8 14 ♘bxd4 ♘c5 15 h3 ♗f8?, when Black succumbed to a deadly attack after 16 ♗xh7+! ♔xh7 17 ♘g5+ ♔g6 18 ♘df3!, intending ♘h4+) 13 ♘f1 cxd4 14 ♗f4 (14 ♘g3 ♘f8 15 ♘xd4 ♗c5 16 ♘xc6 bxc6 17 ♗e3 ♗b6 18 ♗xb6 ♕xb6 19 ♖b1 ♖a7 was unclear in Hertneck-Hecht, Munich 1988) 14...♘f8 15 ♘xd4 ♗c5 16 ♘xc6 bxc6 17 ♗g3 ♕b6 18 ♘d2!? ♘e6 = Yusupov-Ehlvest, Saint John Ct (3) 1988.

b) 12 ♘f1 cxd4 13 ♗c2 f6!? 14 exf6 ♗xf6 15 ♘g3 ♘c5 ∓ G.Flear-Chandler, British Ch (Blackpool) 1988.

c) 12 dxc5!? ♘xc5 (12...♖e8?! 13 ♕c2 h6 14 ♘b3 a4 15 ♘bd4 and now Black should prefer 15...♘xc5 = Ivkov-Polugaevsky, Belgrade-Moscow 1974 over 15...♗xc5? 16 e6! ♘xd4 17 ♘xd4 fxe6 18 ♘xe6 ♕f6 19 ♗g5!, which was very good for White in Schüssler-L.B.Hansen, Copenhagen 1988) 13 ♘b3 ♘xd3 14 ♕xd3 ♗g4 15 ♘bd4 ♕d7 = Schandorff-Kindermann, Thessaloniki OL 1988.

d) 12 ♕c2!? h6 (12...g6!?) 13 ♗f5! (13 ♘f1 cxd4 14 ♘g3 ♘c5 15 ♗f5?! a4!? 16 ♗f4 d3! 17 ♗xd3 ♗g4 18

♖ad1?! {18 ♗e2! is the only move} 18...♘e6! was very good for Black in Browne-Makarychev, Saint John 1988) 13...cxd4 14 ♘b3 ♕b6 (14...a4 15 ♘bxd4 ♘c5 16 ♗e3 ♘xd4 17 ♘xd4 ± Burmakin-Mozaliov, St Petersburg 1996) 15 e6 ♘c5 (15...♘f6 16 exf7+ ♖xf7, Piket-Brenninkmeijer, Groningen 1988, 17 ♗g6 ♖f8 18 ♘bxd4! ± Piket) 16 exf7+ ♖xf7 17 ♘bxd4 ♘xd4 18 ♘xd4 ♕f6 19 ♗h7+ ♔h8 20 ♗e3 ♗d7 21 ♖ac1 ♖c8 22 ♕g6 ± Piket-Dimitrov, Adelaide jr Wch 1988.

12...♖e8 13 ♘f1

13 ♗c2 ♕c7 14 ♘f1 cxd4 15 ♗f4 ♘c5 16 ♘xd4 ♘xd4 17 ♕xd4 ♘e6 18 ♕d3 g6 19 ♗g3 d4 was unclear in Browne-Ivanović, New York Open 1988.

13...cxd4 14 ♘g3 ♘f8

Not, of course, 14...♗f8?? due to the thematic sacrifice 15 ♗xh7+! +–, but 14...g6!? is interesting, with the idea of ...♗f8-g7.

15 b3!

As we shall see, this move not only serves the purpose of preventing Black from playing ...a4 but also introduces the rook manoeuvre ♖a2-e2.

15...f6!

More accurate than 15...♗d7 16 ♖a2! f6 17 ♖ae2 fxe5 18 ♘xe5 ♘xe5 19 ♖xe5 ± Yusupov-Kindermann, Munich 1988.

16 exf6 ♗xf6 17 ♖xe8 ♕xe8 18 ♗b2 ♕f7 19 ♕d2 ♗d7 20 ♖d1

White has compensation, P.Cramling-Yusupov, Novi Sad OL 1990.

D)

4...b6 *(D)*

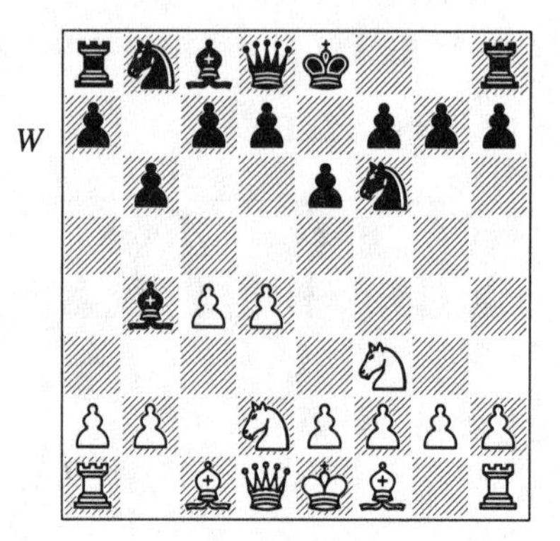

5 a3

The alternatives merely transpose to other lines:

a) 5 e3 ♗b7 6 a3 ♗xd2+ and then 7 ♕xd2 is 'c' in the next note while 7 ♗xd2 transposes to 'c' in the note to White's 7th move.

b) 5 g3 ♗b7 6 ♗g2 0-0 7 0-0 is Line C, note 'b1' to White's 5th move.

5...♗xd2+ 6 ♗xd2

6 ♕xd2 ♗b7 is a major alternative:

a) 7 b4 a5 8 ♗b2 ♘e4 9 ♕c2 axb4 10 axb4 ♖xa1+ 11 ♗xa1 ♕e7 12 c5 0-0 13 e3 f5 14 ♗e2 ♘g5 15 ♕d1 ♘xf3+ 16 ♗xf3 ♗xf3 17 ♕xf3 ♘c6 18 ♗c3 bxc5 19 bxc5 = Ree-Andersson, Wijk aan Zee 1984.

b) 7 g3 and now:

b1) 7...♗xf3!? (doubling White's pawns) 8 exf3 d5 9 b3 0-0 10 ♗e2 ♕e7 11 0-0 ♖d8 12 ♗b2 dxc4 13 ♗xc4 c5 14 ♕e3 cxd4 15 ♗xd4 ♘c6 16 ♗b2 ♘d5 17 ♕e4 ♘a5 18 ♖ac1 ♘xc4 19 ♖xc4 ♖ac8 with a minute advantage for Black, Salov-P.Nikolić, Wijk aan Zee 1997.

b2) 7...0-0 (more stereotyped) 8 ♗g2 d6 9 0-0 a5 10 b3 ♘bd7 11 ♗b2

♗e4 12 ♖fd1 ♕b8 13 ♖ac1 b5!? 14 c5 b4 15 a4 ♗d5 16 ♕e3 ♕b7 with equality, Sakaev-Rashkovsky, Russian Ch (Elista) 1996.

c) 7 e3 (we have reached a position that usually arises from the Queen's Indian, viz. 1 d4 ♘f6 2 c4 e6 3 ♘f3 b6 4 e3 ♗b4+ 5 ♘bd2 ♗b7 6 a3 ♗xd2+ 7 ♕xd2) with a choice for Black:

c1) 7...0-0 and then:

c11) 8 ♗e2 a5 9 b3 transposes to 'c2'.

c12) 8 b4 a5 9 ♗b2 axb4 10 axb4 ♘e4 11 ♕c2 ♖xa1+ 12 ♗xa1 f5 13 ♗d3 ♘c6 14 ♕b3 ♕e7 15 c5 ♘d8 16 ♗c4 ♘f7 17 ♗b2 ♖b8 with unclear play, Nogueiras-Andersson, Thessaloniki OL 1988.

c13) 8 b3 ♘e4 9 ♕c2 f5 10 ♗d3 d6 11 ♗b2 ♘d7 12 0-0 ♖f6 13 c5 ♗d5 14 cxd6 cxd6 = Smyslov-Seirawan, Montpellier Ct 1985.

c14) 8 ♗d3 ♘e4 9 ♕c2 f5 (it is interesting to note that compared to a similar line of the Nimzo-Indian, i.e. 1 d4 ♘f6 2 c4 e6 3 ♘c3 ♗b4 4 ♕c2 0-0 5 a3 ♗xc3+ 6 ♕xc3 ♘e4 7 ♕c2 f5 8 e3 b6 9 ♗d3 ♗b7, White is here a tempo ahead) 10 0-0 d6 11 ♘d2 ♕h4 12 f3 ♘xd2 13 ♗xd2 ♘d7 14 ♖ae1 ♖ae8 15 ♕a4 ♕e7 16 b4 a6 17 e4 ± Ftačnik-Kavalek, Prague 1990.

c2) 7...a5!? (this pre-emptive move is very typical in the Bogo-Indian) 8 b3 0-0 9 ♗e2 and now:

c21) 9...♘e4 (there is no need to rush to occupy this square and so it is perhaps better to complete queenside development) 10 ♕c2 f5 (10...♘g5 is interesting, despite Avrukh's condemnation of it: 11 0-0 ♘xf3+ 12 gxf3 and now either 12...f5!? or 12...♕g5+ 13 ♔h1 ♕h5 14 ♕d1 f5 with unclear play) 11 0-0 d6 12 ♘e1 ♘d7 13 f3 ♘ef6 14 ♘d3 c5 15 ♗b2 ♕e7 16 ♖ad1 and White is better, Yakovich-Liang Chong, Beijing 1997.

c22) 9...d5!? (a rather unusual idea in this type of position, but typical of Korchnoi's original style) 10 0-0 ♘bd7 11 ♗b2 c5 12 ♖fd1 ♕e7 13 ♘e5 ♖fd8 14 ♘xd7 ♘xd7 15 ♖ac1 a4! 16 bxa4 dxc4 17 ♗xc4 ♘e5 with counterplay, Gelfand-Korchnoi, Vienna 1996.

c23) 9...d6 10 0-0 ♘bd7 11 ♗b2 and now:

c231) 11...c5 12 ♖ad1 ♖c8 13 dxc5 ♘e4 14 ♕c2 bxc5 15 ♘d2 ± Franco-Kurajica, San Sebastian 1994.

c232) 11...♕e7!? (it is interesting to see that Adams elects simply to control the e4-square rather than possess it) 12 ♖ad1 ♖fd8 13 ♕c2 ♖ac8 14 b4 axb4 15 axb4 c5 16 ♕b3 d5 17 bxc5 dxc4 18 ♕xc4 bxc5 19 ♗a3 ♗d5 20 ♕c1 ½-½ Yakovich-Adams, Køge 1997.

c233) 11...♘e4 leads to a further branch:

c2331) 12 ♕d3 f5 13 ♘d2 e5 14 f3 ♘xd2 15 ♕xd2 ♕e7 16 ♖ac1 e4 17 d5 exf3 18 ♖xf3 ♘e5 19 ♖f4 ♘g6 = Miles-Seirawan, USA Ch 1988.

c2332) 12 ♕c2 f5 13 ♘e1 (13 ♖ad1 ♘g5!? 14 ♘d2 f4! 15 e4 ♖f6 16 c5 ♘f8 17 c6 ♗a6 18 ♗xa6 ♖xa6 was unclear in Munhbayar-Enkhbat, Mongolian Ch 1994) 13...♕g5! 14 ♗c1 ♕g6 15 f3 ♘g5 16 ♘d3 c5 17 ♕c3 ♘f7 18 ♘f2 ♖ae8 19 ♗b2 cxd4 20 exd4 e5 = Chevallier-Kosten, French Cht 1993.

c2333) 12 ♕c1!? f5 13 ♘e1 (we now see White's idea in dropping the queen back to c1 as opposed to c2: 13...♕g5 has no point here since the pawn on e3 is protected) 13...♕h4 (13...♕e7 14 f3 ♘ef6 15 ♘d3 e5 16 ♘f2!? ± Avrukh) 14 f3 ♘g5 15 ♘d3 ♖ae8 16 c5!? ♗a6 17 cxd6 cxd6 18 ♕c7 and White is better, Atalik-Mencinger, Ljubljana 1997.

Returning to the position after 6 ♗xd2 *(D)*:

B

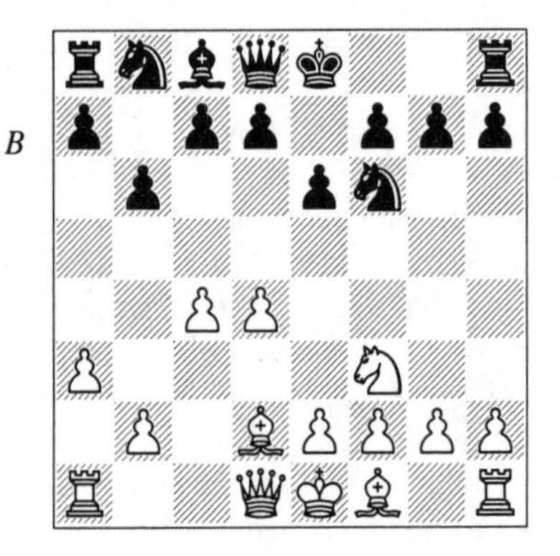

6...♗b7

The alternatives mainly involve Black denying White the possibility of pinning the knight by ♗g5:

a) 6...d6!? 7 ♗g5 h6 8 ♗h4 ♘bd7 9 e3 g5!? (the start of an unconventional plan: Black simply tries to manage without putting the bishop on b7; 9...♗b7 transposes to the main line) 10 ♗g3 ♘e4 11 d5 e5 12 ♗d3 ♘df6 13 ♕c2 ♘c5 14 ♗e2 a5 (14...♘ce4!?) 15 ♘d2 ♕e7? (15...a4 is essential, even though White seems to have a good position after 16 f4!) 16 b3! ♗d7 17 ♖c1 intending b4 with a clear advantage, Epishin-G.Kuzmin, Moscow 1992.

b) 6...♘e4 and then:

b1) 7 ♗f4 ♗b7 8 e3 d6 9 ♗d3 ♘d7 10 0-0 0-0 11 b4 a5 12 ♕c2 ♘ef6 13 e4 h6 14 ♗d2 axb4 15 axb4 c5 16 bxc5 bxc5 17 d5 ± Lputian-Agzamov, Sochi 1985.

b2) 7 ♗e3!? ♗b7 8 g3 0-0 9 ♗g2 f5 10 0-0 d6 11 ♘g5! ♕e8 12 ♘xe4 ♗xe4 13 ♗xe4 fxe4 14 ♕c2 ♕c6 15 b4 ± Krasenkow-Othman, Erevan OL 1996.

b3) 7 g3 ♗b7 8 ♗g2 ♘xd2 9 ♕xd2 d6 10 0-0 ♘d7 11 d5 e5 12 b4 0-0 13 ♘e1 ♕e7 14 ♘d3 ♖fc8! 15 c5 bxc5 16 bxc5 ♘xc5 17 ♘xc5 dxc5 18 ♖ab1 with unclear play, P.Nikolić-Andersson, Næstved 1985.

c) 6...h6 and then:

c1) 7 e3 ♗b7 8 ♗d3 d6 (or 8...♘e4 9 ♕c2 ♘xd2 10 ♕xd2 d6 11 d5 e5 12 0-0 a5 13 b4 ± Greenfeld-Rogers, Biel 1986) 9 ♕c2! c5 10 dxc5 bxc5 11 ♗c3 ♘bd7 12 0-0 a5 13 e4 0-0 14 ♖ad1 ♕c7 15 ♘h4! ± intending f4, Vaganian-Andersson, Næstved 1985.

c2) 7 ♗f4!? (this is a relatively new attempt by White, but so far Black has experienced few problems) 7...♗b7 8 e3 d6 with a varied choice for White:

c21) 9 ♖c1 ♘h5 10 ♗g3 ♘xg3 11 hxg3 ♘d7 12 ♗d3 c5 13 ♗c2!? ♕f6 14 ♗a4 0-0-0 with an equal position, Toloza-Garcia Palermo, Buenos Aires 1996.

c22) 9 ♗d3 ♘bd7 10 0-0 ♘h5 11 ♗g3 ♘xg3 12 fxg3 ♘f6 13 ♕e2 c5 14 dxc5 bxc5 15 e4 ♘g4 16 ♖ad1 0-0 17 ♗b1 ♕b6 = Izeta-Garcia Ilundain, Terres Catalanes 1997.

c23) 9 ♕c2 ♘bd7 10 0-0-0!? ♕e7 11 ♗g3 0-0-0 12 ♘d2 ♘h5 13 ♖g1 ♔b8 14 ♗e2 ♘xg3 15 hxg3 c5 16 ♗f3 cxd4 17 exd4 d5 with a satisfactory position for Black, Savchenko-Kurajica, Portorož ECC 1993.

c3) 7 g3 ♗b7 8 ♗g2 0-0 (Krasenkov-Shpilker, Norilsk 1987 saw Black immediately occupying e4 with his bishop: 8...♗e4 9 0-0 d6 10 b4 0-0 11 ♕b3 ♘bd7 12 ♖fd1 a6 13 ♖ac1 ♕b8 intending ...b5, with chances for both sides) 9 0-0 d6 *(D)* and then:

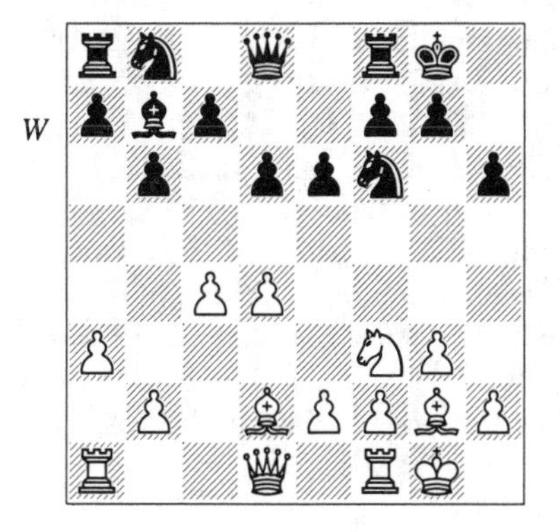

c31) 10 d5!?. Dydyshko, obviously very proud of this move, awarded it two exclamation marks in *Informator*. However, although it certainly is very dangerous for Black, it also has its drawbacks. 10...exd5 (10...e5 11 ♘h4 is very good for White) 11 ♘h4 and now practice has seen:

c311) 11...c6?! 12 cxd5 cxd5 (or 12...♘xd5 13 ♗xd5 cxd5 14 ♗c3 ±) 13 ♘f5 ♘c6 14 ♗c3 ♘e5 15 f4!? (15 ♘e3!? is a simpler way to an advantage, but White continues his aggressive play) 15...♘c4 (or 15...♘g6 16 ♕d4 {threatening ♘xh6} 16...♔h7 17 ♕b4 ♘e8 18 ♖ad1 ± Dydyshko) 16 ♕d4 ♖e8 17 e4! ♗c8 18 ♖ae1! ♗xf5 19 exf5 ± Dydyshko-Zagrebelny, Primorsko 1990.

c312) 11...♕c8!? 12 ♗c3!? ♘e4 (12...♕e6!?) 13 ♖c1 (13 cxd5 ♘xc3 14 bxc3 ♘d7 15 ♘f5 ± Dydyshko) 13...c5 14 ♗xe4! dxe4 15 ♕xd6 ♖e8 16 ♕f4 ♕e6 17 ♘f5 g5 18 ♕c7 ♕xf5 19 ♕xb7 ♘d7 20 ♖cd1 ± Riemersma-Bjarnason, Hafnarfjördur 1995.

c32) 10 b4 ♘bd7 11 ♗c3 ♕e7 and now:

c321) 12 ♕b3!? ♘e4 13 ♗b2 f5 14 ♖ad1 ♕f7 15 ♘e1 a5 16 b5 e5 = Granda-Kurajica, Groningen FIDE KO Wch 1997.

c322) 12 ♕c2 ♗e4. In positions like these we often see Black occupying the e4-square with the bishop rather than the knight. The reason for this is that White is not very happy with an exchange of the light-squared bishops, and therefore it is much more difficult to remove this piece from e4. 13 ♕b2 c6 14 ♖fc1! a5 (14...d5 15 ♗d2 ♖fc8 16 a4 was another possibility, again with an edge for White) 15 ♗f1 ♗g6 16 ♘d2 ± Hjartarson-Kurajica, Linares 1995.

7 ♗g5

Now that Black has conceded his dark-squared bishop, White takes the opportunity to pin Black's knight. Other approaches:

a) 7 ♗f4 also activates the bishop before proceeding with e3, but is less aggressive than the text-move and does not prevent it being chased by Black's kingside pawns. 7...d6 8 e3

♘bd7 9 ♗e2 ♕e7 10 h3 ♘e4 11 ♗h2 f5 12 ♖c1 a5 13 b3 0-0 14 0-0 e5 15 c5! ± Khalifman-Arkell, London 1991.

b) 7 g3 d6 8 ♗g2 ♘bd7 9 0-0 has occurred a couple of times in Bareev's games, and Black has not yet found a clear way to equalize:

b1) 9...a5!? 10 b4 axb4 11 axb4 0-0 12 b5! ♖xa1 13 ♕xa1 ♕a8 14 ♗b4 ± Bareev-Hjartarson, Munich 1993.

b2) 9...0-0 10 b4 ♗e4 11 ♖c1 ♕e7 12 ♕b3 ♖fc8?! (12...c5 is probably better) 13 c5! ± Bareev-Salov, Linares 1992.

c) 7 e3 (amazingly, Black has experienced a lot of problems after this quiet move) 7...0-0 8 ♗d3 d6 9 0-0 ♘bd7 10 b4 (Miles-Morović, Havana 1996 continued 10 ♗c3 ♘e4 11 ♗xe4 ♗xe4 12 ♕e2 ♕e7 13 ♘d2 ♗b7 14 e4 c5 15 ♖fd1 cxd4 16 ♗xd4 ♖fc8 17 ♖ac1 ♖c7 18 b3 ♖ac8 19 ♕e3 ±) 10...c5 11 ♗c3 ♕e7 12 ♘d2 ♖fc8 13 ♖c1 a6 (or 13...e5?! 14 dxe5 dxe5 15 ♗f5 with a substantial advantage for White) 14 ♕e2 d5!? 15 dxc5 bxc5 16 ♖fd1 cxb4 17 axb4! (17 ♗xb4 is also good) 17...dxc4 18 ♘xc4 ± Miles-Sunye Neto, Linares 1994.

7...d6 8 e3 *(D)*

It is not so easy to organize the lines around here, since Black can elect to flick in ...h6 here or at any of the following moves. However, since Black always follows up with ...d6 anyway and White invariably chooses a set-up with e3, I have decided to assume that these moves are played at this point.

8...♘bd7

Here it is an important option to start chasing the bishop: 8...h6 9 ♗h4

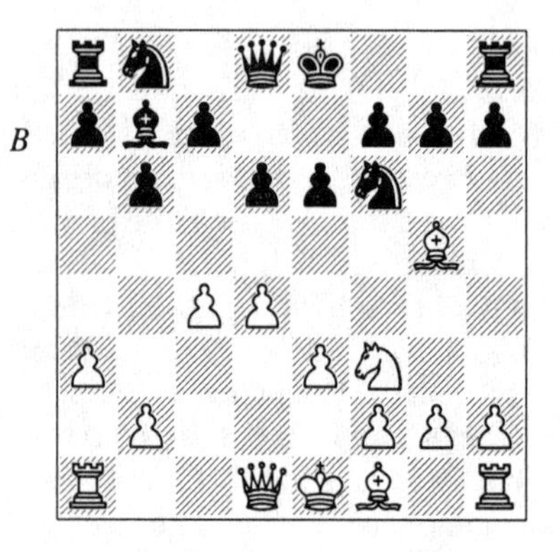
B

g5 10 ♗g3 ♘e4 11 ♘d2 (Karpov also analyses 11 ♗d3!? h5 12 h4 g4 {not 12...♘xg3?! 13 fxg3 g4 14 ♘g5 ♗xg2 15 ♖h2 ♗b7 16 ♖f2 ±} 13 ♗xe4 ♗xe4 14 ♘g5 ♗xg2 15 ♖h2 ♗b7 16 d5 with unclear play) 11...♘xg3 12 hxg3 ♘d7 13 g4 c5 14 ♘b1! (a very fine manoeuvre, as the knight is much better placed at c3) 14...cxd4 15 ♕xd4 ♕f6 16 ♘c3 ♕xd4 17 exd4 ♘f6 18 f3 ♔e7 19 b4 ± Karpov-Adams, Dos Hermanas 1995.

9 ♗d3

This is White's sharpest approach, though the game only becomes sharp when Black decides to chase White's bishop around to g3 by ...h6, ...g5 followed by ...h5. The consistent approach from White is then to reply h4, and after ...g4 to move the knight to g5 and sacrifice the g2-pawn for an active position. The same idea can occur when White develops the f1-bishop to another square, generally e2.

There are a number of alternatives for White at this junction, and most of them may look rather similar. Therefore it may be a little confusing to find one's way around in the following material, because there are a lot of transpositions. One general consideration, however, is that it is clear that Black gains nothing with the above-mentioned ...g5, ...h5 idea when White's bishop is still on f1 defending g2 – quite the contrary.

a) 9 ♗e2 and now:

a1) 9...0-0 (White usually obtains an easy game when Black castles kingside) 10 0-0 ♕e8 (10...♖e8 11 b4 c5 12 ♕b3 ♕c7 and now 13 ♖fd1 ♘e4 14 ♗h4 ♘f8 15 dxc5 dxc5 16 ♗g3 ♘xg3 17 hxg3 ♖ed8 was equal in Lerner-M.Gurevich, USSR Ch 1985, but afterwards Lerner recommended 13 ♘d2 with an edge) 11 ♘d2! ♘e4 12 ♘xe4 ♗xe4 13 f3 ♗b7 14 b4 f5 15 ♗h4 e5 16 ♖c1 ± P.Cramling-Tempone, Buenos Aires 1994.

a2) 9...h6 10 ♗h4 with a further branch:

a21) 10...g5 11 ♗g3 h5 12 h4 (12 h3!?) 12...g4 13 ♘g5 ♗xg2 14 ♖g1 ♗b7 15 f3!? (15 ♕a4?! ♔f8!? 16 ♕c2 ♕e7 17 e4 e5 18 d5 ♘h7 19 ♘xh7+ ♖xh7 20 f3 ♘f6 ∓ Komljenović-Ubilava, Zaragoza 1996) 15...♕e7 16 ♖f1 ♘h7 17 ♘xh7 ♖xh7 18 ♕a4 with compensation, Nowak-Makarychev, Frunze 1985.

a22) 10...♕e7 11 ♘d2!? e5 and now:

a221) 12 d5 a5 13 e4 a4 14 f3 ♘c5 15 ♕c2 ♗c8 (15...c6!?) 16 0-0 g5 17 ♗f2 ♗d7 18 ♖ae1! with an edge, Hjartarson-Cebalo, Linares 1996.

a222) 12 ♗f3 (hoping to provoke ...e4) 12...♗xf3 13 ♕xf3 0-0 14 0-0 e4 15 ♕e2 a5 16 b4 ♕e6 with roughly equal play, M.Muse-Kosten, Berlin 1996.

b) 9 ♗h4!? has little independent value if Black plays 9...h6, but there are some other options:

b1) 9...0-0 10 ♗e2 c5 11 0-0 ♕e7 (11...♕c7!?) 12 ♖c1 ♖fd8 13 ♖e1 ♖ac8?! (a common mistake in such positions; White is well prepared for an opening of the centre, hence the rook is just misplaced here; better is 13...♘f8!?) 14 ♗d3 ♘f8 (14...cxd4 15 exd4 d5 16 cxd5 ♗xd5 17 ♘e5 ± Lputian) 15 d5! h6 (not 15...exd5 16 ♗f5!) 16 dxe6 ♘xe6 (Lputian-Olafsson, Tilburg 1994) and now Lputian suggests 17 ♘d2 with the better game for White.

b2) 9...c5 10 ♗d3 0-0 11 0-0 cxd4 12 exd4 d5 is a position that has occurred twice in games between Karpov and Andersson:

b21) 13 ♖e1 dxc4 14 ♗xc4 ♕c7 15 ♖c1 ♖fc8! (if 15...♖ac8 then White plays 16 ♗g3 ♕d8 17 ♕d3 with an edge since there is no connection between Black's rooks) 16 ♖c3 ♕d6 17 ♗g3 ♕f8 18 ♕d3 a6 19 ♘g5 b5 20 ♗a2 ♖xc3 21 ♕xc3 ♗d5 22 ♗b1 ♖c8 = Karpov-Andersson, Skellefteå 1989.

b22) 13 cxd5 (not a very terrifying novelty) 13...♗xd5 14 ♘e5 ♕c7 15 ♕e2 ♖ac8 16 ♖fe1 ♗b7 17 ♖ad1 ♘d5 18 ♕h5 ♘7f6 19 ♕g5 ♘e7 20 f3 ♘g6 21 ♗f2 ♘d5 22 ♕d2 ♕e7 23 ♗g3 ♖fd8 = Karpov-Andersson, Biel 1990.

c) 9 ♖c1 h6 10 ♗h4 ♕e7 11 b4 0-0 12 ♗e2 a5 13 0-0 axb4 14 axb4 ♖a3 15 d5!? ♖fa8 16 ♘d4 ♘e5 with an unclear position, Gofshtein-Maksimović, Iraklion 1992.

d) 9 ♘d2!? h6 10 ♗h4 c5 (10...♕e7 11 ♗e2 transposes to 'a22') 11 ♗e2! 0-0 12 0-0 ♖c8 13 b4 ♖e8 (Lev-Alterman, Kfar-Saba 1996) and now 14 ♕b3 gives White an edge.

e) 9 ♕c2 *(D)* and then:

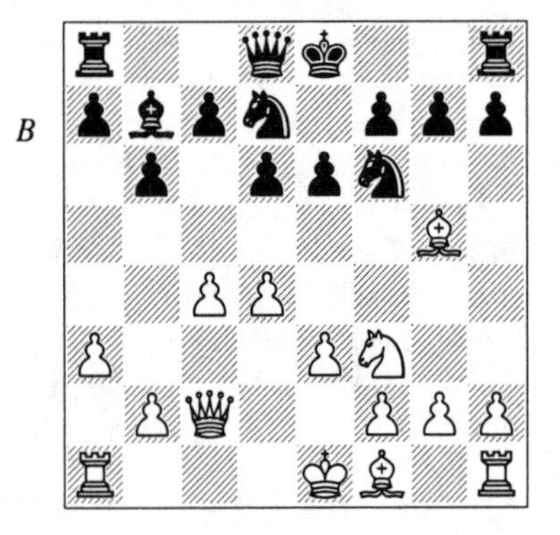

e1) 9...♕e7 10 ♖d1 is a useful waiting move, which eschews the decision of where to put the light-squared bishop until Black has shown his cards.

e11) 10...♗e4!? 11 ♕a4 (or 11 ♕c3 ♗xf3! 12 gxf3 ♘e4 13 fxe4 ♕xg5 = Epishin) 11...0-0 12 ♗h4 a6 13 ♗d3 ♗xd3 14 ♖xd3 e5 15 ♖d1 exd4 16 ♖xd4 ♘e5 = Epishin-Kosten, Geneva 1993.

e12) 10...h6 11 ♗h4 and then:

e121) 11...a5 12 b3 ♖c8 13 ♗e2 g5?! 14 ♗g3 h5 15 h4 g4 16 ♘g5 ♗xg2 17 ♖g1 ♗b7 18 b4 axb4 19 axb4 with compensation, Krasenkow-Bogdanovski, Erevan OL 1996.

e122) 11...0-0 12 ♗d3 c5 13 0-0 ♖fd8 14 ♘d2 ♖ac8 15 ♕b1 ♘f8 (White would also be a little better after 15...cxd4 16 exd4 d5 17 cxd5 ♗xd5 18 ♗a6) 16 b4 ♗a8 17 ♖fe1 g5 18 ♗g3 ♘h5 19 ♘f1 and White is better, Yusupov-Hort, Reykjavik 1985.

e123) 11...♗e4 12 ♕c3! g5?! (better is 12...c5 or 12...♗xf3 13 gxf3 ♘e4 14 fxe4 ♕xh4 – the latter is a common idea, but note that it is better for Black without the moves ...h6 and ♗h4 inserted, since here White can continue 15 ♗g2 followed by 0-0 and f4) 13 ♗g3 ♗g6 14 ♘d2 ♘h5 15 c5! 0-0 16 cxd6 cxd6 17 ♗a6 f5 18 f3 ♘df6 19 ♗f2 ± Epishin-Hort, San Bernardino 1992.

e124) 11...g5 12 ♗g3 ♘e4 (12...♗e4 13 ♕c3 is 'e123' above, while Anand-Illescas, Leon (1) 1997 varied with 13 ♗d3 ♗xd3 14 ♕xd3 ♘h5 15 d5 e5 16 ♘d2 0-0 17 ♕e2 ♘g7 18 e4 f5 =) 13 ♘d2 (another game by Krasenkow went 13 d5 ♘df6 14 ♘d4 h5 15 f3 ♘xg3 16 hxg3 ♖g8 17 e4 g4 18 ♔f2 0-0-0 with unclear play, Krasenkow-Ru.Gunawan, Jakarta 1996) 13...♘xg3 14 hxg3 h5 15 b4 h4!? 16 gxh4 ♖xh4 17 ♖xh4 gxh4 18 c5 bxc5 19 dxc5 dxc5 20 ♘e4 ♗c6 21 ♘xc5 ♘xc5 22 ♖c1 ♗d5 23 ♕xc5 ♕xc5 24 ♖xc5 0-0-0! and because of the lasting weakness on g2, White is not able to show any advantage in this endgame, Krasenkow-Macieja, Polish Ch (Warsaw) 1997.

e2) 9...c5 and now:

e21) 10 ♖d1 ♕c7 11 ♗e2 0-0 12 0-0 ♖ac8 13 ♗h4 ♗e4 14 ♕d2 ♖fe8 15 ♗g3 e5 16 dxe5 dxe5 17 ♘h4! ± Epishin-Andersson, Malmö 1994.

e22) 10 ♗d3 ♖c8 11 d5! exd5 12 cxd5 h6 13 ♗h4 ♗xd5 14 0-0-0 g5 15 ♗g3 c4?! 16 ♗f5 ♘c5 17 ♖xd5!

♘xd5 18 ♖d1 ♘e7 19 ♗xc8 ♕xc8 20 ♗xd6 ♘d3+ 21 ♔b1 ± Timman-Hellsten, Malmö 1997.

e3) 9...h6 10 ♗h4 ♕e7 11 ♗e2 g5 12 ♗g3 h5 13 h4 g4 14 ♘g5 ♗xg2 15 ♖g1 ♗b7 16 0-0-0 (this position is similar to the one reached in the main line, the only difference being that the bishop is on e2 rather than on d3; here White should try utilizing this to carry out a f3-break) 16...0-0-0 17 ♔b1 e5 18 d5 ♔b8 19 ♖d2 ♘e8?! (19...♘f8 is better – Kholmov) 20 f3! gxf3 21 ♗xf3 ♘g7 22 ♖dg2 with compensation, Shulman-Kholmov, Karaganda 1994.

Returning to the position after 9 ♗d3 *(D)*:

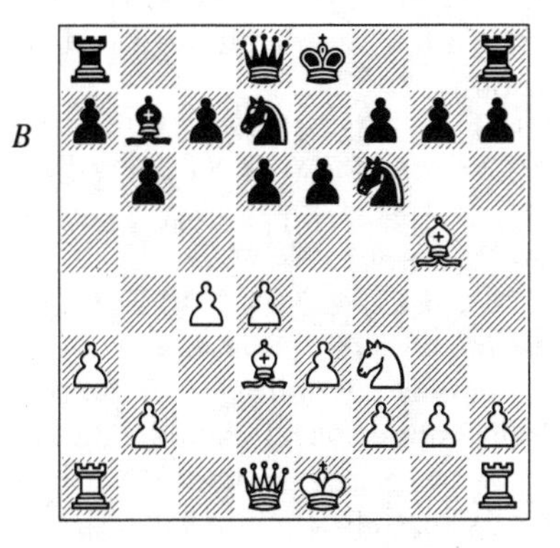

9...h6

Another option is 9...♕e7 10 0-0 c5:

a) 11 ♖e1 0-0 12 e4 cxd4 13 ♘xd4 h6 14 ♗h4 ♘e5 15 b3 ♖fd8 16 a4 ♘g6 17 ♗g3 a6 18 ♖a2 ♕c7 19 ♖d2 ♕c5 20 ♗b1 ♘h5 = Lputian-Andersson, Sarajevo 1985.

b) 11 b4!? 0-0 12 ♘d2 ♖ac8 13 ♕a4 ♖c7 14 ♖ae1 ♖fc8 15 f4 h6 16 ♗h4 d5?! (more prudent is 16...♕f8 17 f5 e5 18 d5 with only a small advantage for White) 17 cxd5 exd5 18 ♗f5 ± Timman-Andersson, Reykjavik 1988.

10 ♗h4 g5

10...♕e7 is again possible:

a) 11 b4!? a5 12 0-0 axb4 13 axb4 0-0 14 ♕e2 (14 ♘d2! is stronger – Korchnoi) 14...c5 15 e4 e5 16 bxc5 bxc5 17 d5 with an edge for White, Korchnoi-Andersson, Wijk aan Zee 1983.

b) 11 ♕c2 e5! (this has a more solid reputation than 11...g5 12 ♗g3 h5, transposing to the main line) 12 dxe5 (12 ♗f5!? still needs a practical test) 12...♘xe5 13 ♘xe5 dxe5 14 ♗xf6 ♕xf6 15 ♗e4 ♗xe4 16 ♕xe4 0-0 = Lukov-Kholmov, Erevan 1984.

11 ♗g3 *(D)*

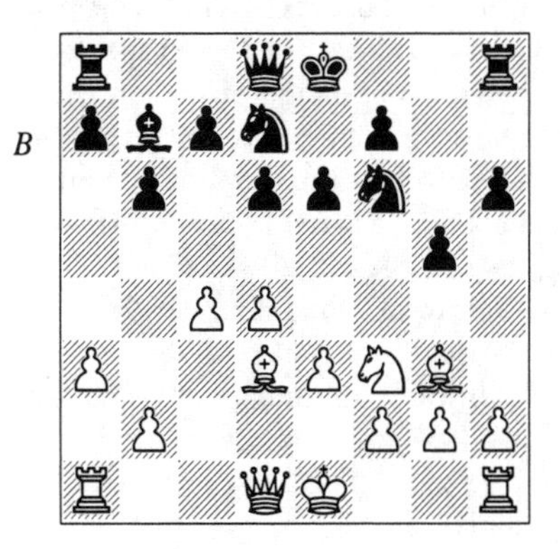

11...h5!?

The most direct approach. Alternatives are:

a) 11...♘e4 12 0-0 ♘xg3 (12...h5 13 ♗xe4 ♗xe4 14 h4 g4 15 ♘g5 is better for White – Psakhis) 13 fxg3!

(13 hxg3 is maybe also better for White but this creates possible threats along the f-file) 13...♕e7 14 b4 c5 15 ♘d2 h5 16 ♗e4 ♗xe4 17 ♘xe4 f5 18 dxc5! fxe4 19 cxd6 ♕g7 20 ♕a4 ♖c8 21 c5! with a strong attack, Psakhis-Vyzhmanavin, USSR Ch 1984.

b) 11...♕e7 12 ♕c2 h5 13 h3! (13 h4 g4 14 ♘g5 ♗xg2 15 ♖g1 ♗b7 transposes to the main line, but here, when Black has not got access to e4, the text-move turns out to be best) 13...h4 14 ♗h2 g4 (very consistent, but 14...♖g8 is more circumspect) 15 hxg4 h3 (this position was initially given as '∓' by Hort, but either Nikolić did not know about this or did he not agree with it) 16 ♗g1! (to understand this move, one has to analyse the line 16 ♗g3 0-0-0! with the idea 17 g5?! hxg2 18 ♖xh8 ♖xh8 19 gxf6? ♗xf3 –+) 16...♘xg4 (if Black now plays 16...0-0-0, 17 g5! is strong as the g-pawn is not dangerous when Black takes on g2, so Black must respond 17...♘g4 but then White is much better after 18 ♗e4) 17 ♗e4 d5 18 cxd5 f5 19 ♗d3 ♗xd5 20 ♕xc7 ± P.Nikolić-Seirawan, Wijk aan Zee 1986.

12 h4

Definitely the most consistent approach. White is ready to sacrifice a pawn for a very strong initiative. Alternatives:

a) Lputian analyses 12 ♘xg5?! but more or less refutes it with 12...h4 13 ♗f4 e5 (but not 13...h3 14 ♘f3 hxg2 15 ♖g1 e5 16 dxe5 dxe5 17 ♘xe5 ♘xe5 18 ♗xe5 ♕e7 19 ♕a4+ ♔f8 20 ♕b4 ±) 14 0-0 ♕e7 15 ♕a4 0-0-0! (15...exf4 16 exf4 0-0-0 17 ♖fe1 is less clear) 16 ♕xa7 exf4 17 exf4 ♘b8! ∓.

b) 12 h3 is more cautious but hands over the initiative to Black:

b1) 12...♖g8 13 ♕e2 (13 ♖c1!? a5 14 b4 axb4 15 axb4 ♖a3 16 c5! bxc5 17 dxc5 dxc5 18 bxc5 h4 19 c6 ♗xc6 with an unclear position, Shirov-Ulybin, Tbilisi 1989) 13...♕e7 (13...♘e4!?) 14 e4 h4 15 ♗h2 ♘h5 16 ♘xh4? (it is tempting to win a pawn with this, but nevertheless White should have preferred 16 ♘d2! ♘f4 and then either 17 ♕f3!? or 17 ♗xf4 gxf4 18 ♖g1 =) 16...gxh4 17 ♕xh5 ♕f6! 18 e5 dxe5 19 dxe5 (Hjartarson-Korchnoi, Reykjavik 1987) and now Black should play 19...♕e7! 20 ♗f1 0-0-0 21 0-0-0 ♘c5 with a large advantage – Hjartarson.

b2) 12...♘e4 13 ♕c2 f5 14 0-0-0 ♕f6 15 ♔b1 0-0-0 16 h4 g4 17 ♘g5 with an unclear position, Lputian-Lukov, Erevan 1984.

12...g4 13 ♘g5 ♗xg2 14 ♖g1 ♗b7 15 ♕c2 ♕e7 16 0-0-0 0-0-0

Another possibility is to prevent White from advancing on the queenside with 16...a5 but this also weakens the shelter in front of the king, should Black later decide to castle long: 17 ♔b1 a4 18 ♔a1 ♔d8 19 c5!? bxc5 20 ♗b5 ♗d5! 21 ♗xa4, Mikhalevski-Loginov, Budapest 1993, 21...cxd4 22 ♖xd4 ♘c5 23 e4 e5! 24 ♖b4 ♗b7 with unclear play – Mikhalevski.

17 b4 ♔b8 18 ♔b2 e5

With chances for both sides, Gelfand-Cu.Hansen, Wijk aan Zee 1993.

2 4 ♗d2: The Solid 4...♗e7

1 d4 ♘f6 2 c4 e6 3 ♘f3 ♗b4+ 4 ♗d2 ♗e7 *(D)*

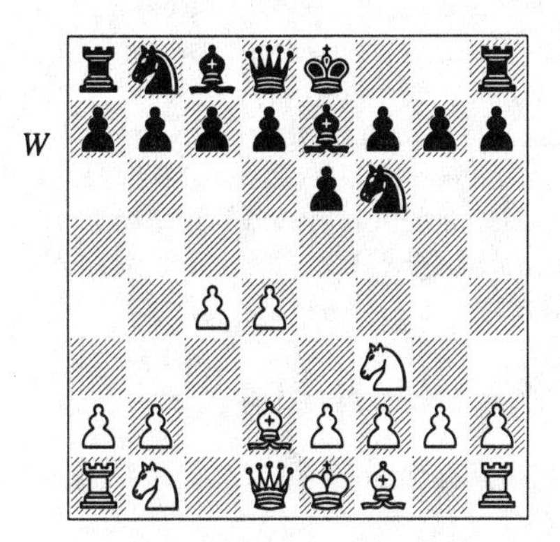

This retreat is a little passive but has a reputation of being very solid. It often transposes into positions arising from the Catalan, but Black must also be prepared to play a normal Orthodox Queen's Gambit if White continues 5 ♘c3. Then 5...d5 is almost obligatory, when White can play 6 ♗g5 or 6 ♗f4. However, the most popular continuation for White is 5 g3, and after 5...d5 a normal Catalan position has arisen with the only difference that White's dark-squared bishop is on d2.

Typical Pawn Structures

The most common pawn structure arising after 4...♗e7 is the one shown below:

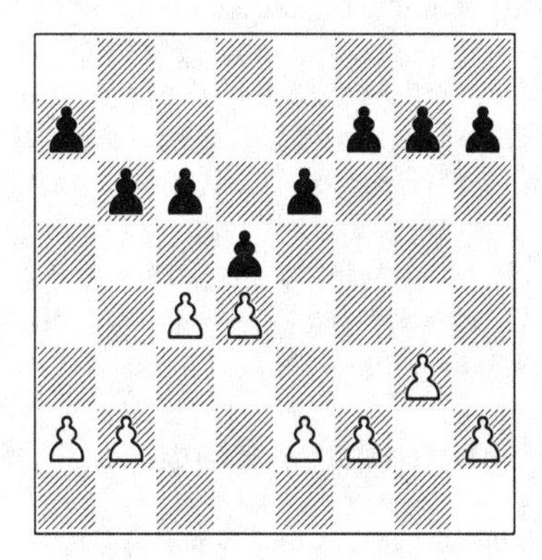

Black's set-up looks a little passive, but Black will manoeuvre patiently behind this fortress and at a timely moment he will hope to burst out with ...c5.

Planning for White

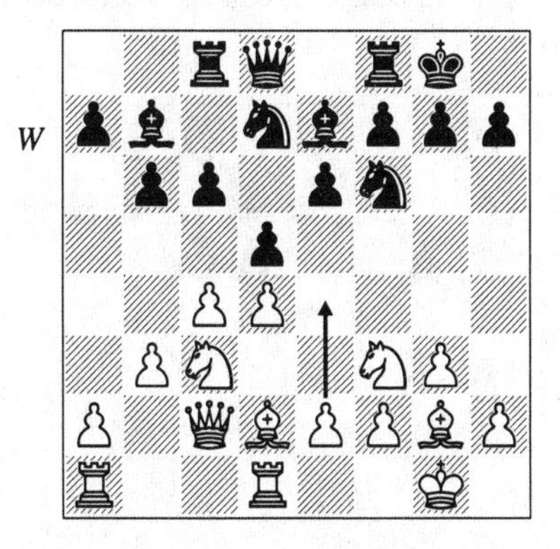

The most convincing plan in positions like this is to play for the e2-e4

advance. It does involve a lot of preparation, however, and White will of course always have to look out for a ...c5 break. However, if e4 can be played successfully it often brings with it a nice positional plus, owing to White's space advantage and greater piece activity. In the above position White has moved his pawn to b3 in order to defend c4. Only then can the knight be brought out on c3. The move ♖d1 is not a direct preparation of e4, but it does its best to discourage Black from playing ...c5.

Planning for Black

It should not come as a surprise that ...c5 is the break Black should put his money on. Below Black has even placed his bishop on a6, so White is unable to develop his knight to c3. On a6, the bishop does not actively support Black's centre but does a good job of hindering White's plan. In the meantime Black is ready to break out with ...c5.

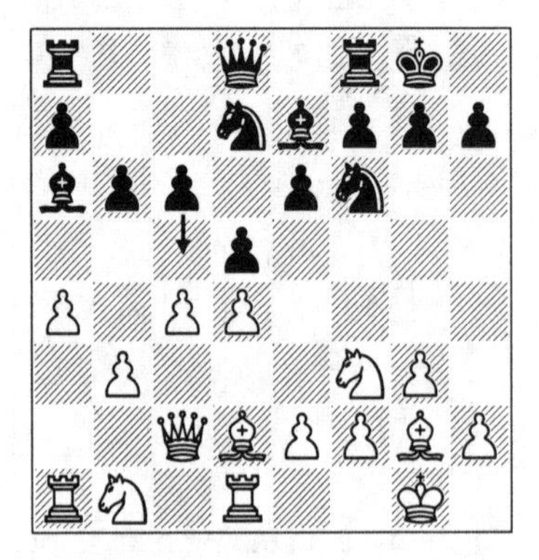

Quick Summary

A standard position arises after 4...♗e7 5 g3 d5 6 ♗g2 0-0 7 0-0 c6. White has tried a variety of moves, but the two most important are 8 ♕b3 (Line A) and 8 ♕c2 (Line B). With 8 ♕b3 White can hardly expect to achieve the e4 advance but on the other hand it leaves the c-file vacant for the rooks, and so a normal plan would be to exchange pawns on d5 and try doubling on the c-file. 8 ♕c2 supports the e4-break, and if permitted White will prepare this by b3, ♘c3 and possibly ♖d1.

The Theory of 4 ♗d2 ♗e7

1 d4 ♘f6 2 c4 e6 3 ♘f3 ♗b4+ 4 ♗d2 ♗e7

With this move Black aims to transpose into a kind of Closed Catalan. This is a little passive but extremely solid.

5 g3

Apart from being a little passive, 4...♗e7 has a further disadvantage, namely if White plays 5 ♘c3. Black must then be prepared to play a Queen's Gambit after 5...d5 6 ♗g5, or 6 ♗f4. 6 ♕c2 is also interesting. Compared to the Orthodox Queen's Gambit with 5 ♕c2, White has been given the move ♗d2 for free, which is definitely not a disadvantage. Arduman-Daly, Pula Echt 1997 continued 6...0-0 7 e4 dxe4 8 ♘xe4 ♘c6 9 ♗c3 ♗d7 10 ♘xf6+ ♗xf6 11 ♗d3 g6 12 0-0-0 a5 13 a3 a4 14 h4 with a promising attack for White.

5...d5 6 ♗g2 0-0

Black has also experimented with delaying castling:

a) 6...c6!? (intending to grab the pawn on c4) 7 ♕c2 b6!? 8 0-0 ♗b7 (8...♘bd7!? intending ...♗a6 was suggested by Tiviakov, and tried out in Adianto-M.Gurevich, Jakarta 1996: 9 cxd5 cxd5 10 ♘c3 ♗b7 11 ♖fc1 0-0 12 ♗f4 ♖c8 13 ♕b3 a6 14 ♘e5 ♘xe5 15 ♗xe5 ♘d7 16 ♗f4 ♖c4! with the idea of ...♕a8 =) 9 ♖d1 0-0 (9...♘bd7!? = Tiviakov) and now:

a1) 10 ♗f4 with a further branch:

a11) 10...♘bd7 11 ♘e5 ♖c8 12 ♘c3 ♘h5 13 ♗d2 ♘hf6 (Black shows that he is satisfied with a draw; if he wants more, then 13...f5 is the move to try) 14 e4 dxc4 15 ♘xc4 b5 16 ♘e3 ♕b6 17 ♘e2 ½-½ Khalifman-Tiviakov, Elista 1998.

a12) 10...♘a6 gives White two promising choices:

a121) 11 ♘bd2 ♖c8 12 e4 c5 13 exd5 exd5 14 a3 ♗d6 15 ♗e5 is slightly better for White, Khalifman-Chandler, Reykjavik 1991.

a122) 11 ♘e5 c5?! (premature – this advance should be prepared by 11...♖c8; also 11...♘d7 is a viable alternative) 12 dxc5! ♗xc5 13 cxd5 exd5 14 ♘c3 ♕e7 15 ♕f5! ± Gulko-Chandler, Hastings 1988/9.

a2) 10 ♘e5 ♘fd7 (in such positions Black often has to retreat this knight; if 10...♘bd7?! White gains a positional plus with 11 cxd5 cxd5 12 ♘c6) 11 ♘d3!? (going for complications; 11 ♘xd7 ♘xd7 12 cxd5 cxd5 13 ♘c3 =) 11...♘a6!? 12 a3 ♖c8 13 ♗e3 ♗f6 14 ♘d2 ♕e7 15 ♖ac1 c5!? 16 dxc5 bxc5!? (Black certainly does not give ground either; 16...♘dxc5 17 ♘xc5 ♘xc5 18 cxd5 exd5 is a safer approach) 17 ♘b3 ♘b6! with a complicated game, Skembris-Tiviakov, Gausdal 1993.

b) 6...b6 7 ♘c3 and then:

b1) 7...♗b7 8 cxd5 ♘xd5 9 0-0 0-0 10 ♖c1 (10 ♘xd5 ♗xd5 11 ♕c2! is more precise) 10...♘d7 11 ♕c2 c5 12 ♖fd1 ♘xc3! 13 ♗xc3 ♕e8! 14 ♕b1 ♖c8 15 b3 h6 16 ♕b2 ♘f6 17 dxc5 ♖xc5 18 ♗d4 ♖xc1 19 ♖xc1 ♕a8! and with some strong moves Black has completely equalized, Pinter-Karpov, France 1993.

b2) 7...c6 8 ♘e5 ♘fd7 9 ♗f4 ♘xe5 10 ♗xe5 0-0 11 cxd5 cxd5 12 e4 ♗b7 13 exd5 ♗b4! (were it not for this move, Black would simply be worse) 14 ♕g4 f6! 15 ♗f4 ♗xd5 16 0-0 ♗xc3 17 bxc3 ♘c6 18 ♖fe1 ♖e8 19 ♗f1!? ♘a5 20 ♗d3 ♕d7 with an unclear position, Krasenkow-Jaracz, Polish Ch 1997.

7 0-0 *(D)*

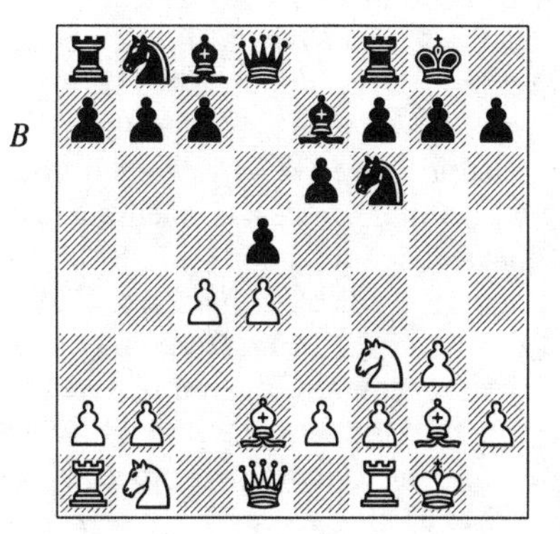

7...c6

Black reinforces his centre and may even be thinking about capturing the pawn on c4. Alternatives are:

a) 7...♘bd7 will normally transpose to one of the lines below (e.g. after 8 ♕c2), though 8 ♕b3 ♘b6!? has some independent value:

a1) 9 c5!? ♘c4 10 ♕c2 (10 ♗f4 b6 11 c6 a5 12 ♕c2 ♗a6 is unclear – Romanishin) 10...b6 11 ♗e1 bxc5 12 dxc5 ♘d7 (Dautov recommends 12...♘e4! 13 b3 ♗f6 14 ♘c3 ♘a3 15 ♕c1 a5!? =) 13 b3 ♘ce5 14 ♘xe5 ♘xe5 15 ♗c3 ♗f6 (better is 15...♘c6) 16 ♕b2! ♘g4 17 h3 ♗xc3 18 ♘xc3 ♘f6 19 c6! intending b3-b4-b5, with the better game for White, Romanishin-Lputian, Helsinki 1992.

a2) 9 cxd5 exd5 10 ♘e5 c6 11 ♘c3 ♗f5 12 a4! (White can only hope for an advantage if he succeeds in provoking weaknesses on the queenside; 12 ♖ad1 h6 13 ♗f4 ♗d6 14 a4 a5 15 ♘d3?! ♗xd3! 16 ♗xd6?! ♗c4 17 ♕a3 ♖e8 was better for Black in Yusupov-Spassky, Reykjavik 1988) 12...a5 13 ♖ad1 ♗b4 14 ♗f4 ♘fd7 15 ♘d3 ♕e7 16 ♖fe1 ♖fe8 17 ♔h1!? (Black's position looks very attractive but it is not easy to find a plan, and after this prophylactic move White intends to follow up with f3 and e4 – something that Black can hardly ignore) 17...h5 18 f3 ♗xd3 19 ♖xd3 c5 20 ♕c2 cxd4?! 21 ♖xd4 ♘c5 22 ♗d2 ♖ad8 23 f4 ± P.Nikolić-Eingorn, Zagreb IZ 1987.

b) 7...b6 retains the possibility of moving the c-pawn two squares. 8 cxd5 exd5 9 ♘c3 ♗b7 10 ♕c2 (10 ♖c1 c5 11 ♗f4 ♘a6 12 dxc5 bxc5 13 ♘e5 ♘c7 14 ♘c4 ♖b8! 15 ♗xc7 ♕xc7 16 ♘xd5 ♗xd5 17 ♗xd5 ♖bd8 18 e4 ♘xe4 = Timoshchenko-Psakhis, USSR Ch 1981) 10...c5 11 ♖ad1 ♘a6 (11...♘c6?! 12 ♗g5! is annoying, but a feasible alternative is 11...♘bd7 12 ♗f4 ♖c8 13 ♕b1 ♖e8 14 dxc5 bxc5 15 ♘g5 ♘f8 16 ♘ge4 ♕b6 17 ♘xf6+ ♗xf6 18 ♘xd5 ♗xd5 19 ♗xd5 ♖xe2 with counterplay, Khalifman-Ljubojević, Linares 1995) 12 ♗f4! (White is already better, due to his firm control of the centre, and Yusupov follows this with a series of powerful moves leading to a promising attack) 12...♕c8 13 ♗e5 ♖d8 14 ♘g5 h6 15 ♗h3 ♕c6 16 ♗xf6 ♗xf6 17 ♕h7+ ♔f8 18 ♘f3 ♘c7 19 ♖fe1! with the idea of e4, Yusupov-Yudasin, Minsk 1982.

Returning to the position after 7...c6 *(D)*:

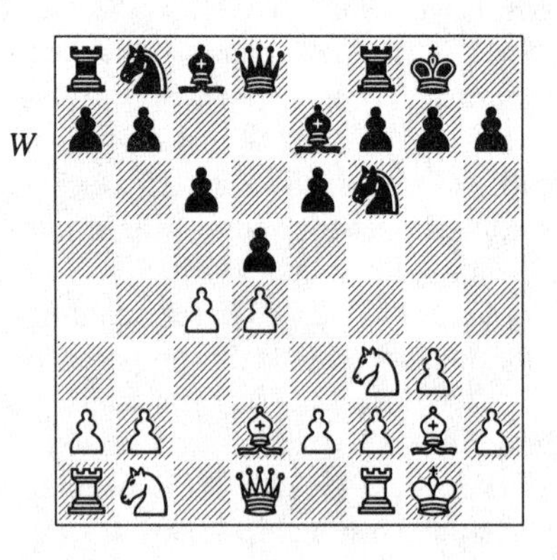

White now has two main options:

Others:

a) 8 ♗g5 ♘bd7 9 ♘bd2 b6 10 ♖c1 ♗b7 11 cxd5 exd5 12 ♘e1 ♖e8 13

♘d3 ♘e4 14 ♗xe7 ♕xe7 15 ♖e1 ♖ad8 = Kuligowski-Browne, Wijk aan Zee 1983.

b) 8 ♗f4 b6 (8...♘bd7 9 ♕c2 is Line B) 9 ♘e5 and now:

b1) 9...♘fd7 10 cxd5 cxd5 11 e4 ♘xe5 12 exd5! ♘g6!? (or 12...♗b7 13 dxe5 ♗xd5 14 ♗xd5 exd5 15 ♘c3 d4 16 ♘b5 ♘c6 17 ♖c1 ♕d7 18 ♖e1 ♖ad8 19 ♕b3! and White is better, Beliavsky-Vyzhmanavin, USSR Ch 1990) 13 d6 ♗f6! (13...♘xf4 14 dxe7 ♘h3+ 15 ♔h1 ♕xe7 16 ♗xa8 is insufficient for Black) 14 ♗e3 (14 ♗xa8!? ♘xf4 15 gxf4 ♕xd6 with reasonable compensation) 14...♗a6 15 ♗xa8! ♗xf1 16 ♔xf1 ♕xd6 17 ♗g2 ♘e7 18 ♘c3 ♘f5 19 ♘e4, Tukmakov-Dorfman, Aix-les-Bains 1991, and now 19...♕d8 20 ♘xf6+ ♕xf6 is about equal.

b2) 9...♗b7 10 ♘c3 ♘fd7 (Black could try 10...♘bd7!?) 11 e4! (trying to break open the centre before Black is properly developed; 11 cxd5 cxd5 12 e4 ♘xe5 13 ♗xe5 dxe4 14 ♘xe4 ♘c6 = Vyzhmanavin) 11...♘xe5 12 ♗xe5 dxc4 13 ♕g4 g6 14 ♖ad1 ♘d7 15 ♗f4 ♘f6?! (the knight does better to stay on d7, so Black should choose 15...b5!?) 16 ♕e2 b5 17 h4! ♖e8 18 ♗g5 ♘d7 19 ♗xe7 ♕xe7 20 e5 and White has excellent compensation, Epishin-Vyzhmanavin, USSR Ch 1990.

c) 8 b3 ♘bd7 9 ♗c3!? (9 ♕c2 transposes to Line B) 9...♘e4 10 ♗b2 f5. It is not surprising that Yusupov turns the game into a kind of Stonewall, an opening in which he has a great deal of experience. In fact, this position is a normal Stonewall but with White a tempo down. This can quickly be calculated: Black has lost one tempo on ...♗b4-e7, whilst White has lost two on ♗d2-c3-b2, instead of ♗b2 straight away. However, the only difference is that White's queen would usually be on c2 and this does not seem to matter very much. 11 ♘bd2 ♕e8 12 e3 (12 ♘e1!? intending f3 and ♘d3 is a standard idea) 12...♕h5 (12...g5 13 ♘xe4 dxe4 14 ♘d2 g4 is unclear – Yusupov) 13 ♘xe4 fxe4 14 ♘d2 ♕xd1 15 ♖axd1 a5! = Hertneck-Yusupov, Bundesliga 1995/6.

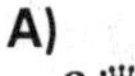

A)

8 ♕b3 *(D)*

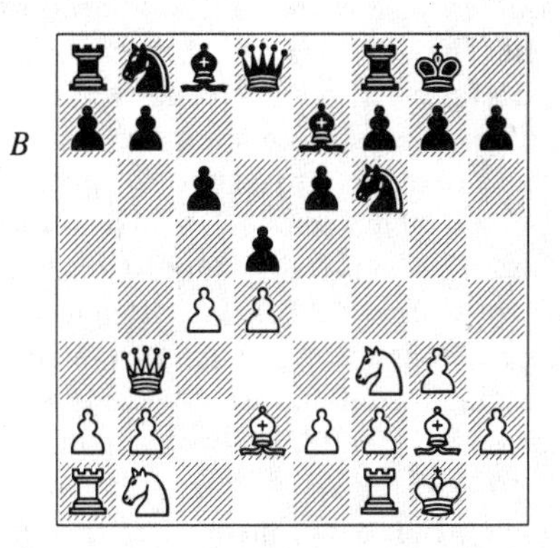

The main point behind this move, compared to 8 ♕c2, is that it leaves the c-file open for the rooks, and White is also able to develop the knight to c3 without releasing the tension in the centre.

8...b6

This is the most common plan for Black, who intends to develop the bishop to a6 threatening the c4-pawn and so forcing White to clarify the central tension. Then the knight can be brought to d7 and normally a fight for the c-file arises. Other options:

a) 8...♘e4 9 ♘e5 dxc4 10 ♕xc4 ♘xd2 11 ♘xd2 ♘d7 12 ♖fd1 ♕c7 13 ♘d3 ♖d8 14 ♕c2 ♘f6 15 e3 ♗d7 16 b4 ± P.Nikolić-Van der Wiel, Amsterdam 1988.

b) 8...a5. With this move Black intends to disrupt White's queenside somewhat; if permitted he will advance the pawn all the way to a3. It does, however, have some dark sides too. Black creates weaknesses in his own camp, and if White simply keeps the tension in the centre, the light-squared bishop can become a problem. The usual liberating manoeuvre ...b6 followed by ...♗b7/a6 is now a little suspect as White exchanges on d5, forcing Black to take back with the c-pawn, which gives White play down the c-file and a nice outpost on b5. Thus the best for Black is often to go into a Stonewall formation by moving the knight from f6 (usually to e4) followed by ...f5. 9 ♖c1 ♘bd7 and then:

b1) 10 ♘c3?! a4! is a common theme. Black will meet 11 ♘xa4 by 11...dxc4, with a satisfactory position.

b2) 10 ♗e1 b6?! (10...♘e4! 11 ♘bd2 f5 is preferable) 11 cxd5! cxd5 12 ♘c3 ♗a6 13 ♘b5 and White is better, Ruban-Makarov, USSR 1991.

b3) 10 ♗f4 should be met by 10...♘h5 followed by ...f5.

b4) 10 a4 ♘e4 11 ♗e1 f5 12 ♘c3 ♔h8 13 e3 ♕e8! 14 ♘e2 g5 15 ♘d2 ♕h5 16 f3 (16 ♕d1!?) 16...♘d6 17 ♕d1 ♘f6 18 b3 ♗d7 19 ♘f1 ± Salov-Short, Rotterdam 1989.

c) 8...♘bd7 and now:

c1) 9 ♘c3 ♘b6! 10 c5 (10 cxd5 exd5 11 ♘e5 transposes to 'a2' in the note to Black's 7th move) 10...♘c4 11 ♗f4 b6 12 cxb6 axb6 13 ♖fd1 ♗a6 was fine for Black in Flear-Tiviakov, Bastia rpd 1997.

c2) 9 ♗f4 should be answered by 9...♘h5. Then Nikolaidis-Nenashev, Porto Carras 1998 continued 10 ♘c3 (if 10 ♗c1, Black should reactivate the knight by 10...♘hf6 permitting a draw by repetition after 11 ♗f4, but of course White can change strategy and, for instance, play 11 ♘c3) 10...♘xf4 11 gxf4 ♕b6 12 ♖ab1 ♘f6 13 e3 ♖d8 14 ♕c2 dxc4 15 ♘e5 ♕a6 16 ♕e2 c5 17 dxc5 ♗xc5 18 ♘xc4 ♗b4 with a draw.

c3) 9 ♖c1 ♘e4 (9...♘b6 10 c5 ♘c4 11 ♗f4 b6 12 ♘a3 ♘xa3 13 ♕xa3 bxc5 14 dxc5 a5 15 ♗d6!? ± San Segundo-Salov, Madrid 1992) 10 ♗b4 ♗xb4 11 ♕xb4 a5 (or 11...♕b6 12 ♕b3 ♘df6 13 ♘c3 ♖d8 14 e3 dxc4 15 ♕c2 ♘d6 16 e4 ♘d7 17 ♖d1 ♘f8 18 ♕e2 ♕a6 19 e5 ♘f5 20 ♘e4 with compensation, Romanishin-Kharitonov, Lvov Z 1990) 12 ♕a3 b5!? 13 ♘e5!? (13 c5 and 13 cxb5 are of course both viable alternatives but White could not hope for any advantage then) 13...♘xe5 14 dxe5 f5! 15 f3?! (15 ♗xe4!? is probably better) 15...b4 16 ♕d3 ♕b6+ 17 e3 dxc4 18 ♕d4 c5 19 ♕d1! (not 19 ♕xc4? ♗a6 20 ♕c2 c4 21 fxe4 ♕xe3+ 22 ♔h1 ♖ad8 –+ Yusupov) 19...c3!? 20 bxc3 ♖d8 21 ♕e1 ♘g5 with unclear play, Ljubojević-Yusupov, Rotterdam 1989.

c4) 9 ♗g5 b6 10 ♖d1 (or 10 ♖e1 ♗b7 11 ♘c3 ♘e4!? 12 ♗xe7 ♕xe7 13

♘xe4 dxe4 14 ♘d2 c5 with counterplay, Krasenkow-Short, Groningen FIDE KO Wch 1997) 10...♗b7 11 ♘c3 a5 (11...h6 12 ♗xf6 ♘xf6 13 ♘e5 ♘d7 and now Krasenkov-Ruban, Russian Ch 1995 ended in a draw after 14 ♘xd7 ♕xd7 15 e4 ♖fd8 16 ♖ac1 ♗f6 17 cxd5 cxd5 18 e5 ♗e7 19 ♗f1 ♖dc8 20 h4 h5 21 ♗b5 ♕d8, but 14 ♘d3!? is a possible improvement for White) 12 cxd5 cxd5 13 ♖ac1 (13 a4!?) 13...♘e4 14 ♗xe7 ♕xe7 15 ♘d2 ♘ef6 16 e3 ♖fc8 17 a3 ♗a6 18 ♘b5 ½-½ Tukmakov-Chernin, Lvov Z 1990.

9 ♘c3 *(D)*

Some alternatives:

a) 9 ♗b4 dxc4! 10 ♕xc4 ♗a6 11 ♗xe7 ♗xc4 12 ♗xd8 ♖xd8 13 ♘c3 ♘d5 =.

b) 9 ♗f4 ♗a6 10 ♘bd2 ♘bd7 11 ♖fd1 ♘h5 12 e4!? looks tempting, but after 12...♘xf4 13 gxf4 ♗b7 14 ♖ac1 ♖c8 15 ♕e3 ♘f6 16 ♘e5 ♖c7 17 a3 c5! Black is doing quite well, Kasparov-Hübner, Hamburg (6) 1985.

c) 9 ♗g5 is stronger, but not a move that should frighten Black. The same idea again, i.e. 9...♗a6 10 ♘bd2 ♘bd7 followed by a timely ...c5, is satisfactory.

d) 9 cxd5 cxd5 10 ♖c1 ♗b7 11 a4 and then:

d1) 11...♘c6 12 a5 ♖c8 13 ♘c3 (13 a6 ♗a8 14 ♘a3 ♘e4 15 ♗e1 ♘d6 16 ♕d3 ♕e8 17 e3 ♖b8! = Bareev-Polugaevsky, Sochi 1988) 13...♗a6 14 ♕a4 bxa5!? 15 ♘xd5 ♘xd5 16 ♖xc6 ♖xc6 17 ♕xc6 ♗xe2 18 ♗xa5 ♕b8 19 ♕c2 ♗xf3 20 ♗xf3 ½-½ Gulko-Lerner, USSR Ch 1985.

d2) 11...♘e4 12 ♗e1 (12 ♗f4 looks better) 12...♘d6 (Black should bring out his other knight: 12...♘c6! 13 a5 ♖c8 =) 13 ♘e5 ♘d7 14 ♘c6 ♗xc6 15 ♖xc6 and White is better, Bareev-Chernin, Pula 1988.

B

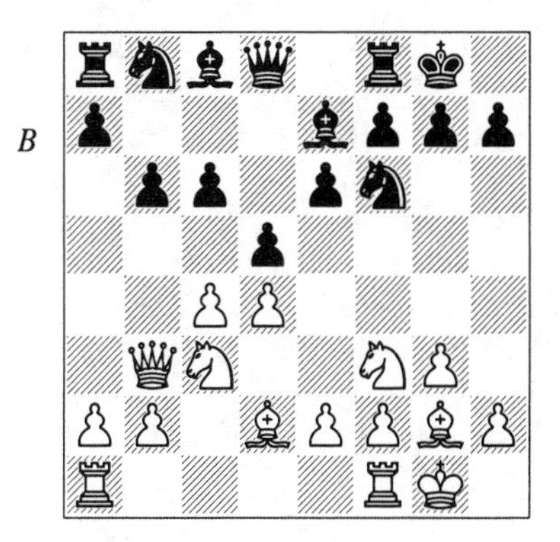

9...♗a6

Black appears to lose a tempo with this bishop manoeuvre but it is convenient to have the tension in the centre clarified. Nevertheless, 9...♗b7 is an equally important option. Then after 10 ♖ac1 ♘bd7 11 cxd5 cxd5 White has two possibilities:

a) 12 ♖c2 ♖c8 13 ♖fc1 ♖c4 (13...a6 to take away the b5-square from White's knight is probably better, e.g. 14 a4 ♗d6 15 ♘a2 ♖xc2 16 ♖xc2 ♕b8 followed by ...♖c8 =) 14 a4 ♕a8 15 ♘b5! ♖xc2 16 ♖xc2 a6 17 ♘c7 ♕b8 18 ♗f4 ♕a7 19 ♗h3! ♖c8 20 ♘xe6! fxe6 21 ♗xe6+ ♔f8 22 ♘g5 with a strong attack, Andersson-Polugaevsky, Bugojno 1982.

b) 12 ♗f4 ♘h5 13 ♗e5 f6 14 ♗c7!? (having provoked the weakness on e6 Romanishin suggests another way to exploit it: 14 ♗f4!? with the idea 14...♘xf4 15 gxf4 f5 {this seems logical but White can now begin a series of powerful moves} 16 ♘b5! ♖f6 17 ♖c7 ♖b8 18 ♖fc1 a6 19 ♘a7 ♘f8 20 ♘e5 ♗d6 21 ♖xb7 ♖xb7 22 ♖c8 ♕e7 23 ♘ac6 +–) 14...♕xc7 15 ♘xd5 ♕d6 16 ♘xe7+ ♕xe7 17 ♖c7 ♗d5 18 ♕b5 ♖fd8 19 e4 with compensation, Romanishin-Ribli, Polanica Zdroj 1993.

10 cxd5 cxd5 11 ♘e5

11 ♖fc1, as in Diachkov-Tiviakov, Russian Ch 1995, permits Black to develop the knight conveniently: 11...♘c6 12 ♘b5 ♕d7 13 a4 ♖fc8 14 ♗f4 ♘e8 15 ♘e5 ♘xe5 16 dxe5 ♖c5 =.

11...♗b7

The only way to get the b8-knight out. If for example 11...♘fd7 then 12 ♘xd5! exd5 13 ♘xf7! ♖xf7 14 ♗xd5 is strong.

12 ♗f4!?

Alburt-Tal, Taxco IZ 1985 showed that White is not in time to utilize the c-file: 12 ♖fc1 ♘bd7 13 ♘d3 ♘b8!? (if permitted Black would rather have his knight on c6) 14 ♘e5 ♘bd7 15 ♗f4 ♘xe5 16 ♗xe5 ♘e8 17 ♘b5 ♘d6 18 ♗xd6 ♗xd6 19 ♖c2 a6 20 ♘c3 ♖c8 =.

12...♘fd7!? 13 ♘xd7

L.B.Hansen also analyses 13 e4 ♘xe5 14 dxe5!? d4 15 ♖fd1 ♘c6 16 ♘e2 with an unclear position, while he suggests that the interesting sacrifice 13 ♘xd5!? may be White's best, continuing 13...exd5 14 ♗xd5 ♗xd5 15 ♕xd5 ♘xe5 16 ♕xa8 ♕xd4! 17 ♕b7! ♕d7!? 18 ♕xd7 ♘bxd7 19 ♖ac1 with an edge for White.

13...♕xd7 14 ♖fd1 ♘c6

14...f5 would rule out any e4-break by White, but Black is positionally worse after 15 ♖ac1 ♔h8 (15...♘c6? 16 ♘xd5! exd5 17 ♕xd5+ and White wins) 16 ♗xb8 ♖axb8 17 e3.

15 e4!? ♘a5

White would have a slightly more active position after 15...dxe4 16 ♗xe4 ♘b4 17 d5 ♘xd5 18 ♘xd5 exd5 19 ♗xd5 ♗xd5 20 ♖xd5 – L.B.Hansen.

16 ♕c2 ♖ac8! 17 exd5 ♗xd5 18 ♗xd5 exd5 19 ♕e2

Now rather than 19...♗b4? 20 ♕b5!, when White was better in the game L.B.Hansen-M.Gurevich, Wijk aan Zee 1993, Black should continue 19...♖fd8!? 20 ♘xd5 ♕xd5 21 ♕xe7 ♘c6 22 ♕g5! ♕xg5 23 ♗xg5 ♖xd4 24 ♗e3 with only a small advantage for White – L.B.Hansen.

B)

8 ♕c2 *(D)*

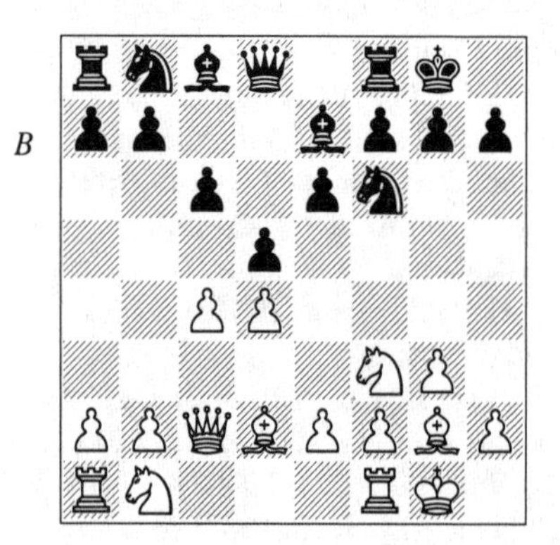

8...b6

8...♘bd7 is an alternative, with the following options for White:

a) 9 ♗f4 bears the clever idea that after 9...♘h5 10 ♗c1 ♘hf6 we are in normal Catalan waters (White's dark-squared bishop is suddenly on c1) and White can now continue 11 ♘bd2, but an interesting idea for Black is 9...b5!?, when Kengis-Garcia, Reykjavik 1994 continued 10 cxb5 cxb5 11 ♕c6 ♕b6 12 ♕xa8 ♗a6 13 ♕xf8+ ♗xf8 14 ♖c1 b4 15 e3 h6 with approximately equal play.

b) 9 ♗g5 h6 10 ♗xf6 ♗xf6 11 ♘c3!? b6 12 ♖fd1 ♗b7 13 ♕b3 ♗a6 14 cxd5 cxd5 15 e4 dxe4 16 ♘xe4 ♗b7 17 ♘e5 ♗d5 18 ♕b5 ♘xe5 and a draw was agreed, M.Hoffmann-Siegel, Bundesliga 1994/5.

c) 9 cxd5 cxd5 10 ♖c1 (White has full control of the c-file but can hardly use it for anything) 10...b6 11 ♕a4 ♗b7 12 ♘a3 a6 13 ♗b4 ♗xb4 14 ♕xb4 ♖c8 15 ♘e5 ♘xe5 16 dxe5 ♘d7 17 ♕d6 ♘c5 18 ♕xd8 ♖fxd8 and what seemed to be a small advantage for White has been neutralized, Smejkal-Polugaevsky, Moscow 1981.

d) 9 b3 b6 – see 8...b6.

e) 9 ♖d1 *(D)* and then:

B

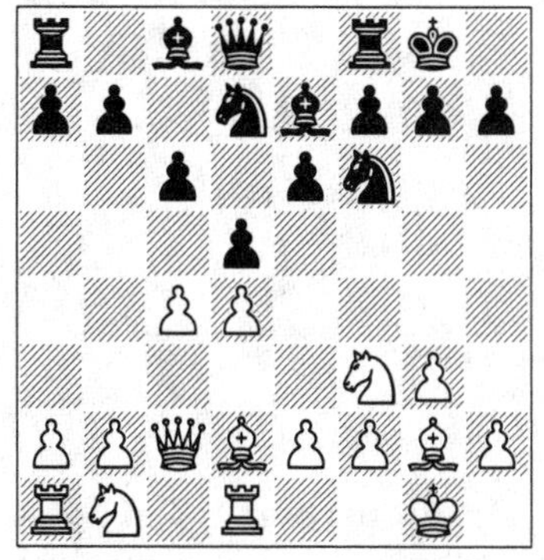

e1) 9...♘e4 10 ♘c3 f5 11 ♘xe4 (11 ♘e5 ♘xe5 12 dxe5 ♗d7 13 ♗e3 ♔h8 14 ♘xe4 fxe4 15 cxd5 cxd5 16 ♖ac1 ♕e8! = Schweber-Larsen, Buenos Aires 1983) 11...fxe4 12 ♘e1 (intending f3) 12...♘b6!? 13 b3 (or 13 c5 ♘d7 14 f3 b6! with counterplay – Salov) 13...♗f6! 14 ♗e3 (better is 14 ♗f4! – Salov) 14...♗d7 15 c5 ♘c8 16 f3 exf3 17 ♘xf3 (White has achieved what he wanted but it is nevertheless Black who now seizes the initiative) 17...♗e8 18 ♕d2 ♗g6 19 ♗g5 ♘e7 20 ♖f1 ♗e4 21 ♗xf6 gxf6 ∓ Andersson-Salov, Brussels 1988.

e2) 9...b6!? and now White has chosen between two ways of making room for the knight:

e21) 10 ♗c3!? a5!? 11 ♘e5 ♗b7 12 ♘d2 b5 13 b3 ♘xe5 14 dxe5 ♘d7 15 cxd5 cxd5 (the doubled e-pawns and difficulties in finding useful places for the pieces prompt White's next move) 16 e4 ♖c8 17 ♕d3 d4! (an excellent sacrifice) 18 ♕xd4 ♗c5 19 ♕d3 ♕b6 ∓ Burmakin-Sakaev, Russia Cup 1997.

e22) 10 ♗e1 ♗b7 11 ♘bd2 c5 12 cxd5 ♘xd5 13 ♖ac1 cxd4 14 ♘xd4 ♖c8 15 ♕b1 ♖xc1 16 ♖xc1 ♕a8 with equality – Black is ready for further exchanges along the c-file, Andersson-Polugaevsky, Bugojno 1981.

9 ♖d1

White is anticipating a ...c5 break by Black and therefore places his rook on the d-file opposite Black's queen. Other options:

a) 9 ♗g5 ♗b7 10 ♘bd2 ♘bd7 11 e4 dxe4 (11...c5!? is worth considering, for example 12 exd5 exd5 13

♖ad1 ♖c8 14 ♕f5 dxc4 15 ♘xc4 cxd4 16 ♖xd4 = Krasenkov-Kharitonov, Moscow 1992) 12 ♘xe4 c5 13 ♘c3 (13 ♘xf6+ ♗xf6 14 ♗xf6 ♕xf6 15 ♘g5 ♕xg5 16 ♗xb7 ♖ad8 17 h4 ♕g4 18 d5 exd5 19 ♗xd5 ± T.Sørensen-Dizdar, Reykjavik 1988) 13...♗xf3! (a courageous decision but Black seems to obtain excellent compensation) 14 ♗xf3 cxd4 15 ♗xa8 ♕xa8 16 ♗xf6 gxf6 17 ♘e4 f5 18 ♘d2 ♖d8 with counterplay, Dizdarević-Bareev, Erevan OL 1996.

b) 9 b3 ♘bd7 *(D)* and then:

b1) 10 ♗c3 ♗a6 11 ♘bd2 b5!? (according to Razuvaev, White obtains a good position after 11...♖c8, e.g. 12 e4 c5 13 exd5 exd5 14 ♖fd1 dxc4 15 ♘xc4 b5 16 ♗a5) 12 c5 b4 (otherwise Black will be stuck with a bad bishop) 13 ♗xb4 ♗xe2 14 ♖fe1 ♗xf3 15 ♗xf3 ♘e8 16 ♗c3 a5 17 ♗g4 ♘c7 18 ♘f3 ♖a7 19 h4! and White is better, Razuvaev-Eingorn, Moscow 1986. Black's 18th move was probably too passive and he should instead have played 18...f5 19 ♗h3 g5 with counterplay – Razuvaev.

b2) 10 a4 ♗b7 11 a5 c5 12 a6 ♗c6 13 cxd5 exd5 (13...♗xd5 14 ♘c3 ♗xf3 15 ♗xf3 cxd4 16 ♘b5 ♖c8 17 ♕b2 is very good for White) 14 ♘c3 ♖c8 15 ♖fd1 b5?! (Polugaevsky later preferred 15...♗d6! with the idea of protecting a7 by ...♗b8) 16 b4! cxb4 17 ♘a2 ♘e4 18 ♗e1 ♗a8 19 ♕b3 ♘b6 20 ♘xb4 ♘c4 ½-½ Speelman-Polugaevsky, Thessaloniki OL 1984.

b3) 10 ♖d1 ♗b7 (10...♗a6 transposes to the main line; the bishop is relatively safer on b7 but it is also less active; now Black has no pressure against c4 and White can proceed by developing the knight to c3) 11 ♘c3 ♖c8 (the immediate 11...c5 is also possible: 12 cxd5 exd5 13 ♗f4 ♕c8 {13...a6!?} 14 ♖ac1 ♖d8 15 ♘h4 g6 16 dxc5 ♘xc5 17 ♕b1 ± Burmakin-Shipov, Russian Ch (Elista) 1997) 12 e4 and now Black can either eliminate the pawn or start counterplay with ...c5:

b31) 12...dxe4 13 ♘g5! c5 14 dxc5 ♘xc5 15 ♘cxe4 ♘fxe4 16 ♘xe4 ♘xe4 17 ♗xe4 ♗xe4 18 ♕xe4 ♗f6 19 ♗c3 ♕e7 20 ♗xf6 ♕xf6 21 ♖d4 with a small advantage for White in the endgame, Beliavsky-Portisch, Frankfurt rpd 1998.

b32) 12...c5 13 exd5 exd5 14 ♗f4! ♖e8 15 dxc5! dxc4?! (15...♗xc5! 16 ♘d4! ♗a8! is better, with counterplay – Yudasin) 16 b4! bxc5 17 b5 ± Korchnoi-Yudasin, Pamplona 1994/5.

c) 9 ♘e5!? ♗b7 *(D)* with another branch:

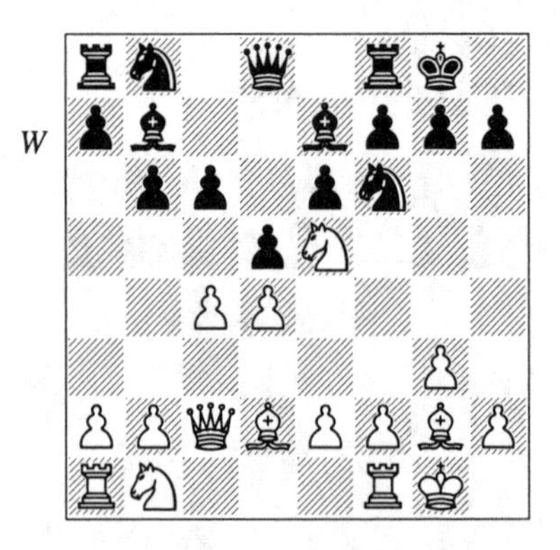

d1) 10 cxd5 cxd5 11 ♖c1 (White is controlling the c-file, but often, as also in this case, Black is able to neutralize this) 11...♗d6 12 ♗g5 h6 13 ♗xf6 ♕xf6 14 f4 ♕e7 15 ♘c3 ♘d7 16 ♘b5 ♖ac8 17 ♕a4 ♗xe5 18 dxe5 ♗c6 19 ♕a3 ♕xa3 20 ♘xa3 f6 21 exf6 ♘xf6 with equality, Chiburdanidze-Akhmylovskaya, Borzhomi wom Wch (3) 1986.

c2) 10 ♗f4 ♘bd7 11 ♘c3?! (probably better is 11 cxd5!? ♘xe5 12 d6!? ♘g6 13 dxe7 ♕xe7 14 ♗g5 with unclear play – Van Wely) 11...♘xe5 12 dxe5 ♘d7 13 h4 ♕b8 (13...h6!) 14 cxd5 cxd5 15 ♖fd1 ♘xe5 16 e4 d4 17 ♘b5 ♗f6 18 ♘xd4 ♖d8 = Van Wely-Salov, Wijk aan Zee 1992.

d3) 10 ♗c3 ♘a6 11 cxd5 ♘xd5 (11...cxd5 =) 12 ♖d1 ♕c7 13 e4 ♘xc3 14 ♘xc3 ♖ad8 with roughly equal chances, Hübner-Polugaevsky, Linares 1985.

d) 9 cxd5 cxd5 10 ♘c3 ♗b7 11 ♘e5 ♘fd7 12 ♘xd7 ♕xd7 13 ♖fc1 ♘c6 14 ♕a4 ♖fd8 15 e3 ♘a5 = Alburt-Short, Foxboro (2) 1985.

Returning to the position after 9 ♖d1 *(D)*:

B

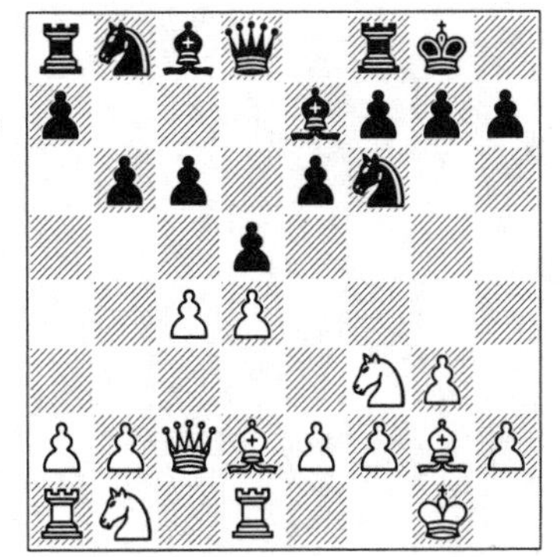

9...♗a6 10 b3 ♘bd7 11 a4 *(D)*

The plan a4-a5 is the most common for White, but Psakhis-Åkesson, Cap d'Agde 1994 saw another interesting idea: 11 ♗f4 ♖c8 12 ♘c3!? ♘h5 (or 12...dxc4!? 13 e4! with compensation) 13 ♗c1 f5 (13...♘hf6 14 e4 with a slight advantage for White) 14 e3 ♗d6 (14...dxc4 is now answered by 15 ♕e2!) 15 a4! ♕e7 16 a5 b5 (16...♗b7 is presumably better) 17 c5 ♗c7 18 ♘a2! with the better game for White.

B

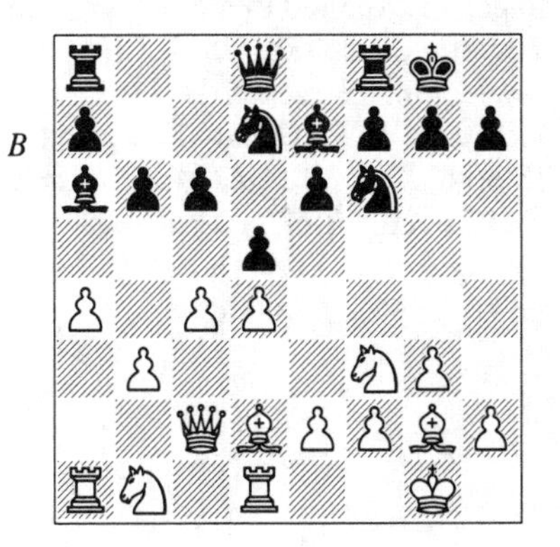

11...c5!

This seems to be the most reliable option for Black. Black prepares to break open the centre while maintaining the rook on the potentially useful a-file. This last point becomes apparent if White plays a4-a5xb6.

11...♖c8 12 a5 c5 (12...b5 13 c5 ±) 13 axb6 ♕xb6 is the other option for Black. Then after 14 ♕a2 there are two possibilities:

a) 14...♘b8 15 ♗a5 ♕d6 16 ♘bd2 cxd4 17 ♘xd4 ♗d8 (the critical line is 17...♕c5!? 18 ♕b2! dxc4 19 bxc4 ♕h5 with counterplay – Tisdall) 18 cxd5 ♘xd5 19 ♘c4 ± M.Marin-Kiselev, Bucharest 1997.

b) 14...♗b7!? 15 b4 (15 ♗a5!?) 15...cxb4 16 c5 ♘xc5 17 dxc5 ♗xc5 18 e3 ♕d6 with reasonable compensation, Danielsen-Galdunts, Erevan OL 1996.

12 ♘a3 ♗b7 13 ♕b2!?

White removes his queen from the potentially dangerous c-file, whilst also increasing his control of the e5-square, and helps prepare b4 at a later stage. 13 cxd5 led to a quick draw in Yusupov-Beliavsky, USSR Ch (Moscow) 1988: 13...♗xd5 14 ♘b5 a6 15 ♘c3 ♗xf3 16 ♗xf3 cxd4 17 ♗g5 dxc3 18 ♗xf6 ♖c8! 19 ♗xe7 ♕xe7 20 ♖d3 ♘e5 21 ♖xc3 ♘xf3+ 22 exf3 ½-½.

13...♖c8

This is a very logical move, but there are other sensible plans for Black:

a) Novikov-Tiviakov, USSR Ch (Moscow) 1991 featured 13...dxc4 14 ♘xc4 cxd4 15 ♘xd4 ♗xg2 16 ♔xg2 ♘c5 17 f3 ♕c8 18 a5 ½-½, but White may be a tiny bit better in the final position.

b) 13...♘e4 14 ♗e1 ♗f6 15 e3 cxd4 16 ♘xd4 ♕b8 17 ♖ac1 ♖d8 = Piket-Kramnik, Monaco rpd 1997.

14 ♖ac1 ♘e4

The game is equal. Black follows up with ...♗f6 and prepares to blow open the centre at a favourable moment, Yusupov-Kharitonov, USSR Ch (Moscow) 1988.

3 4 ♗d2: The Simplifying 4...♗xd2+

1 d4 ♘f6 2 c4 e6 3 ♘f3 ♗b4+ 4 ♗d2 ♗xd2+ *(D)*

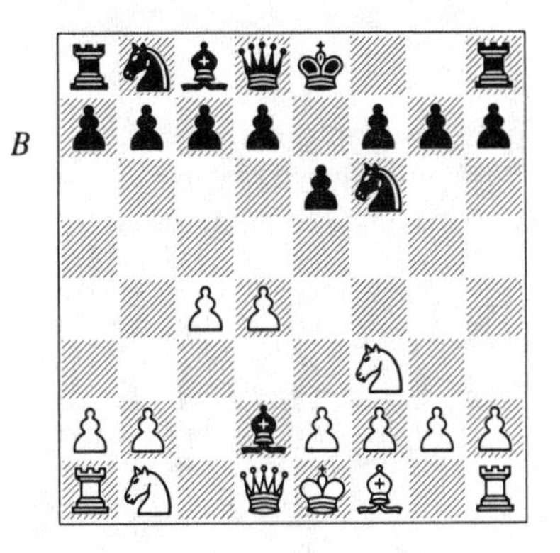

This variation has a rather dull reputation. White obtains quite good control of the centre, but if Black manages to exchange off the c- and d-pawns the game becomes extremely drawish. The line is a long-time favourite of Swedish grandmaster Ulf Andersson, and he has become famous for his immense number of draws in this line. I think he draws around 75% of his games, and as you will discover, this is not just in a few games, but in fact he has played this line in more than 50 games. All in all, 4...♗xd2+ is not a line to choose in a must-win situation, but it is often effective in blunting White's first-move advantage.

Typical Pawn Structures

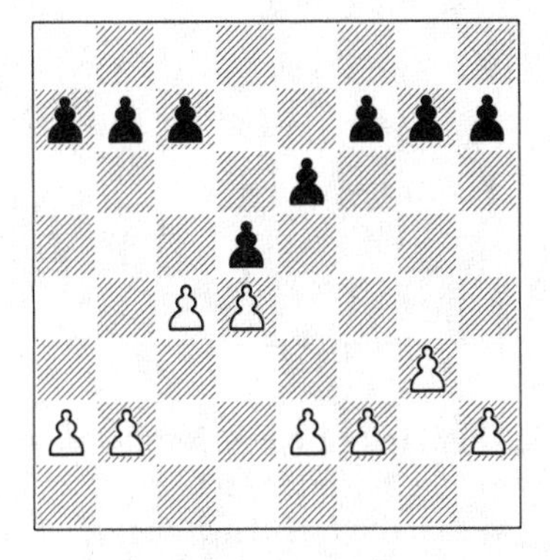

Here we have the most common pawn-structure in this chapter. Black has played ...d5, hoping to exchange the c- and d-pawns and obtain a rather symmetrical and drawish position.

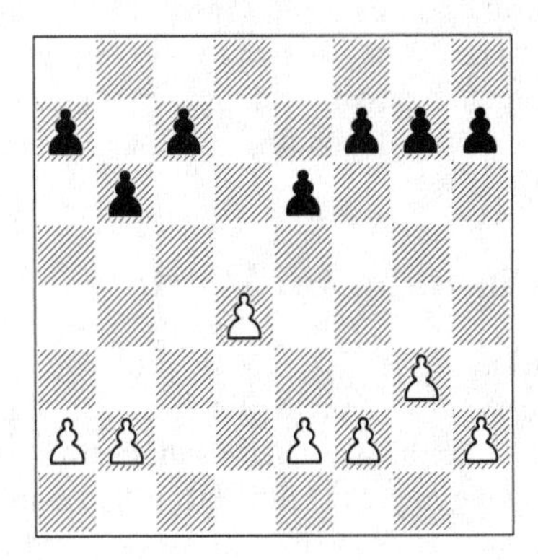

This structure can easily arise from the previous diagram, when White either takes on d5 or Black captures on c4. Black often follows up with either ...e5 or ...c5.

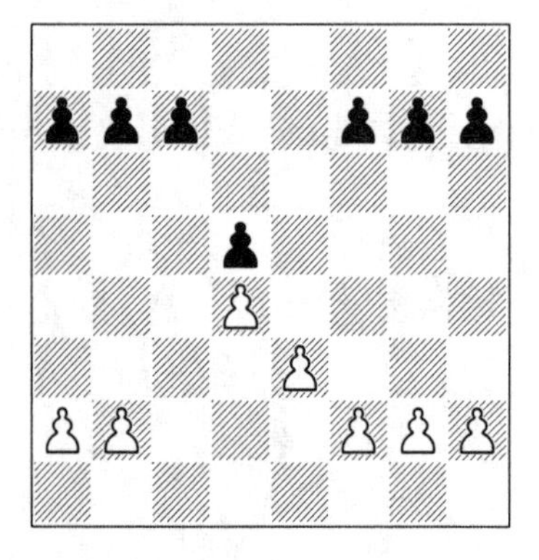

This kind of pawn formation will arise when White elects to exchange pawns on d5. It is sometimes referred to as the Karlsbad Pawn Formation (for convenience I shall also use this name), most frequently arising from a Queen's Gambit Declined or a Nimzo-Indian. White anticipates that Black will move his pawn to c6, and so usually chooses a plan involving an advance of the b-pawn to b5 in order to create a pawn weakness either on c6 or on d5, depending on Black's reaction.

Planning for White

Black intends ...dxc4 followed by ...c5, so a standard plan for White is to go into the Karlsbad Pawn Formation by playing cxd5 himself. When Black takes back with his pawn, White

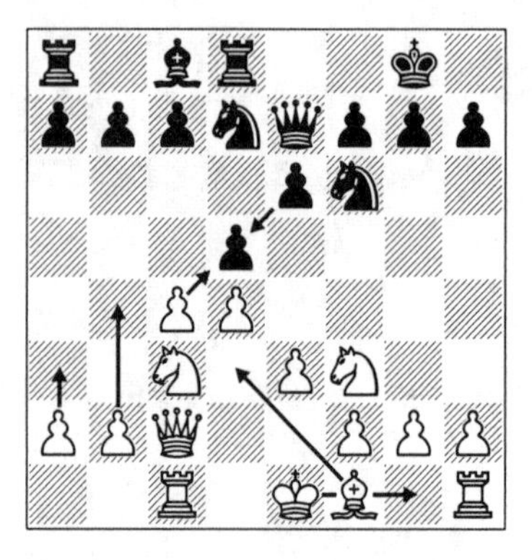

should develop quietly by ♗d3 and 0-0 followed by preparing his usual queenside advance with a3 and b4.

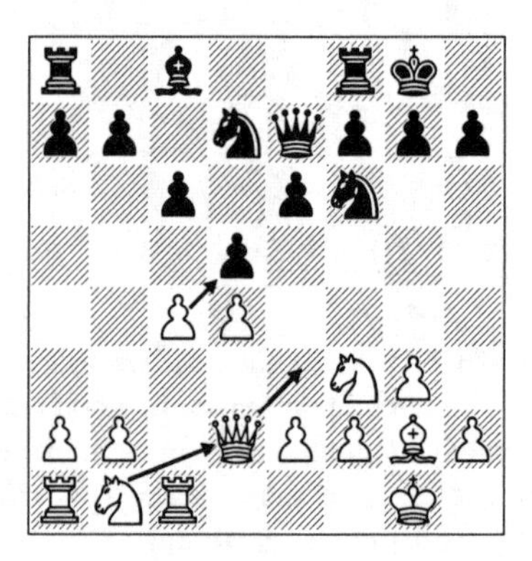

Here White has chosen a kingside fianchetto and Black has reacted calmly by simply developing and stabilizing his centre with ...c6. White has played his rook to c1 to protect the c-pawn, and also in the hope of generating pressure on the c-file. Often the queen is played to e3 making it more difficult for Black to open up with ...e5, and then the knight can be developed to d2.

Planning for Black

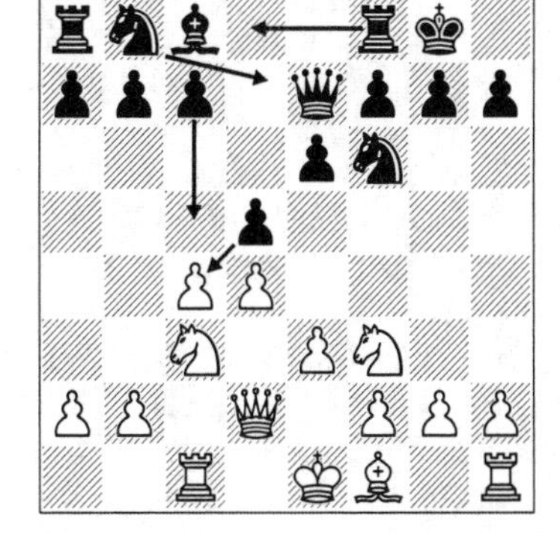

This is a fairly normal position and is actually just a couple of moves short of the first diagram in the section 'Planning for White'. A standard plan for Black is ...♖d8, ...♘bd7, take on c4 and follow up with ...c5, liquidating to a rather drawish position. Black can also try to take on c4 early on, and if ...c5 is feasible then play it and follow up with ...♘c6. White can at many points go into a Karlsbad Pawn Formation by exchanging on d5. Black would normally have to recapture with the e-pawn, and should then move his rook away from f8 and manoeuvre the knight from b8 around to g6. This is a very typical plan – and compared to a Queen's Gambit Declined, the absence of dark-squared bishops makes Black's life easier.

In the next diagram we are a couple of moves short of the second diagram in the section 'Planning for White'.

If Black does not wish to embark on the slightly passive set-up in that diagram, Black can try an idea involving

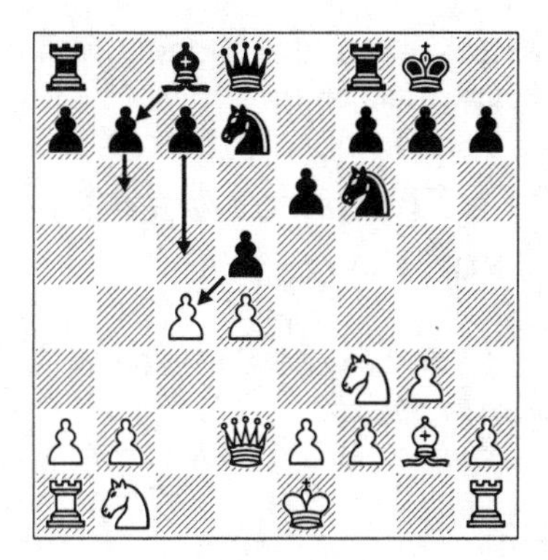

a queenside fianchetto followed by ...dxc4 and ...c5.

Quick Summary

In this chapter we distinguish between two set-ups from White. After 5 ♕xd2 0-0, which I have chosen as the main line, White can play either 6 ♘c3 (Line A) or 6 g3 (Line B). 6 g3 is generally considered the most promising for White and play often continues 6...d5 7 ♗g2 ♘bd7, when White can choose between 8 ♕c2 (Line B1) or 8 0-0 (Line B2). 8 ♕c2 is a refined move-order attempting to avoid the variation 8 0-0 dxc4 9 ♘a3 e5!, which seems to equalize for Black. The drawback is that White cannot obtain a set-up with ♖c1, ♕e3 and ♘bd2, as is possible after 8 0-0 c6 9 ♖c1. However, the 8 ♕c2 line is currently the most fashionable.

6 ♘c3 seems to give Black better chances of liquidating the pawns in the centre. The critical line runs 6...d5 7 e3 ♕e7 8 ♖c1 ♖d8 9 ♕c2, etc., although White can exchange on d5 at

various stages as well, as Black can choose to do on c4.

The Theory of 4 ♗d2 ♗xd2+

1 d4 ♘f6 2 c4 e6 3 ♘f3 ♗b4+ 4 ♗d2 ♗xd2+ 5 ♕xd2

After 5 ♘bxd2 Black can, with 5...d5 6 g3 0-0 7 ♗g2 ♕e7, transpose to Line D11 of Chapter 5. Note that 7...♘bd7 8 0-0 c6 9 ♕c2 is simply a tempo down for Black compared to the note to Black's 8th move in Line B1. However, 5...d6 is also feasible:

a) 6 e4 ♕e7!? (after 6...0-0 7 ♗d3 e5 8 dxe5 dxe5 9 ♘xe5 ♘c6 10 ♘xc6 ♕xd3 11 ♘e7+ ♔h8, Voronkov analysed 12 ♘xc8 ♖axc8, assessing the position as equal, but I think it slightly favours White; moreover White can play even better with 12 ♕f3) 7 ♗d3 (7 e5 dxe5 8 dxe5 ♘fd7 is not a problem for Black) 7...e5 8 0-0 0-0 9 ♕c2 ♘c6 10 ♕c3 exd4 11 ♘xd4 ♘xd4 12 ♕xd4 ♕e5 13 ♘f3 ♕xd4 14 ♘xd4 ♖e8 15 ♘b5 ♖e7 16 ♘c3 ♗e6 and Black is doing fine, Michel-Réti, Semmering 1926.

b) 6 g3 0-0 7 ♗g2 c5!? (a slightly unusual approach; 7...♕e7 transposes to Line D11 in Chapter 5) 8 0-0 ♘c6 9 ♘b3 ♕e7 10 ♕d2 ♗d7 11 ♖ad1 b6 = P.Nikolić-Andersson, Ter Apel 1994.

5...0-0 *(D)*

Alternatives are:

a) 5...d6 6 g3 0-0 7 ♗g2 ♕e7 8 0-0 transposes to Line D12 in Chapter 5.

b) 5...d5 6 g3 (6 ♘c3 0-0 7 e3 is Line A) 6...♘bd7 (Black can castle on this or the next move, transposing to Line B) 7 ♗g2 c6 8 ♘a3!? (8 ♕c2 0-0 9 ♘bd2 transposes to the note to Black's 8th move in Line B1) 8...♘e4 9 ♕d3 (if 9 ♕b4, then Black equalizes with 9...♕b6 10 ♕xb6 axb6) 9...♕a5+ 10 ♘d2 ♘xd2 11 ♕xd2 ♕xd2+ 12 ♔xd2 ♔e7 13 ♖hd1 ♘f6 14 ♖ac1 ♗d7 15 ♖c3 ± Karpov-Andersson, Brussels 1988.

c) 5...b6 6 ♘c3 ♗b7 7 ♕f4!? 0-0 8 e4 d6 9 0-0-0 ♘bd7 10 ♗e2 ♘h5 11 ♕e3 ♘hf6 12 h3 ♕e7 13 g4 with a promising attack for White, Piket-Danielsen, Leeuwarden 1993.

d) 5...♘e4 6 ♕c2 f5 transforms the game into a kind of Dutch, but with the dark-squared bishops traded off, White has the slightly better prospects, for example 7 g3 ♕e7 8 ♗g2 0-0 and now the most accurate for White appears to be 9 ♘bd2 rather than 9 0-0 d6 10 ♘c3 ♘xc3 11 ♕xc3 ♘d7 = Filip-Smyslov, Palma de Mallorca IZ 1970.

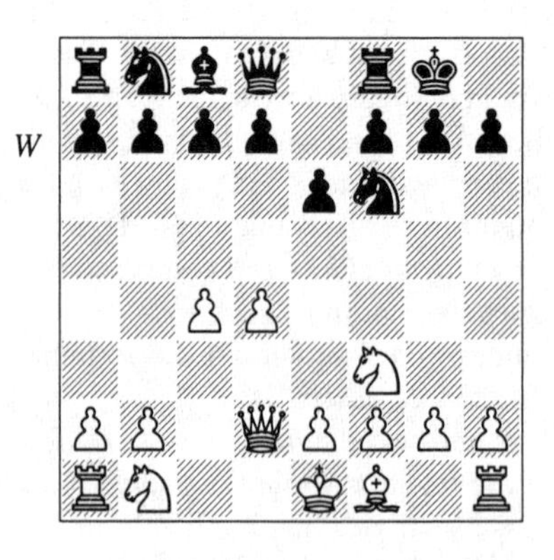

White now has the following main options:

A)

6 ♘c3 d5

Black can also play 6...d6, when 7 g3 transposes to Line B, whilst White might try 7 e4 as well, e.g. 7...♘c6 8 ♗e2 e5 9 d5 ♘e7 10 0-0 ♘g4 11 ♘e1 ♘g6 12 f3 ♘h6 13 ♘d3 f5, with unclear play, Rosetto-Safvat, Varna OL 1962.

7 e3 ♕e7 *(D)*

With this move Black introduces the idea of bringing a rook to d8, intending to clarify matters in the centre with a lot of exchanges. In this kind of position Black generally chooses between two plans:

1) play the rook to d8, take on c4 and following up with ...c5 and ...♘c6 to exert pressure on d4.

2) play ...♘bd7 intending to take on c4 and follow up with ...c5.

The text-move is quite logical in both respects, but Black can also play 7...♘bd7 immediately:

a) 8 cxd5 exd5 9 ♗d3 ♖e8 10 0-0 (this is very similar to an Exchange Queen's Gambit, but with the dark-squared bishops already exchanged off) 10...♘e4 11 ♕c2 ♘df6 12 b4 c6 13 ♘e5 ♗f5 14 ♘a4 ± Karpov-Andersson, USSR vs RoW (1), London 1984.

b) 8 ♖c1 dxc4 9 ♗xc4 c5 10 0-0 ♘b6 (or 10...cxd4 11 ♘xd4 ♕e7 12 ♖fd1 ♘b6 13 ♗b3 ♗d7 14 e4 ♖fd8 15 e5 ♘e8 16 ♕e3 ♖ac8 17 h3 and White is better, Portisch-Andersson, Tilburg 1982) 11 ♗e2 cxd4 12 ♖fd1 ♗d7 13 ♕xd4 ♕e7 14 ♘e5 ♖fd8 15 ♕h4 ♗e8 16 ♗f3 ♕c7 with roughly equal play, Yusupov-Kurajica, Indonesia 1983, but 11 ♗b3 and 13 ♘xd4 are possible improvements for White.

W

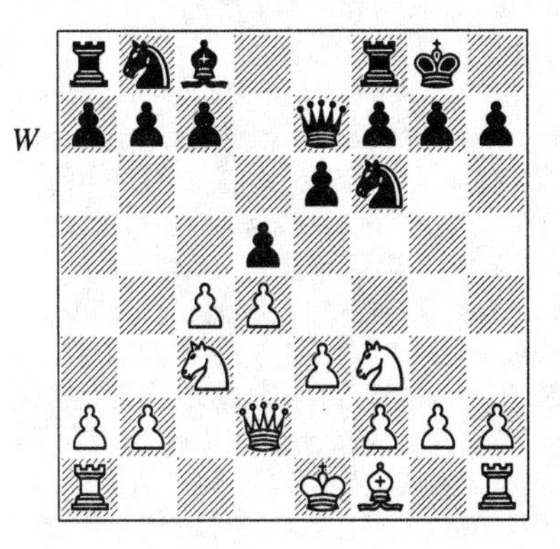

8 ♖c1

As Black's idea is to advance his c-pawn at some stage, this seems very logical, but White also has other options at his disposal:

a) 8 ♖d1 ♖d8 (8...b6 is a relatively unexplored idea, e.g. 9 cxd5 exd5 10 ♗e2 ♘bd7 11 0-0 ♗b7 12 ♕c2 c5 13 ♕f5 ♖fd8 14 ♘e5 ♘f8 15 ♖d2 ♘e6 16 ♘g4 ± Sisniega-Spassky, Thessaloniki OL 1988) 9 ♕c2 ♘bd7 (9...dxc4 is premature in view of 10 ♗xc4 c5 11 dxc5 ♖xd1+ 12 ♕xd1 ♕xc5 13 ♕d8+ ♕f8 14 ♕c7, and White has the initiative) and now:

a1) 10 ♗e2 dxc4 11 ♗xc4 c5 12 0-0 ♘b6 13 ♗e2 ♗d7 14 e4 cxd4 15 ♖xd4 e5 16 ♖d2 ♗c6 17 ♖fd1 ½-½ Kasparov-Andersson, Lucerne OL 1982.

a2) 10 cxd5 exd5 11 ♗d3 ♘f8 12 h3 (White intends to bring his knight to e5, and thus avoids 12 ♘e5 ♘g4 =)

12...♘g6 13 0-0 c6 14 ♖fe1 ♖e8 15 a3 ♗d7 16 b4 ♖ac8 17 e4!? dxe4 18 ♘xe4 ♘xe4 19 ♗xe4 ♗e6 20 ♕c5 ♘f8! 21 ♖e3 a6 with a level game, P.Nikolić-Andersson, Tilburg 1987.

b) 8 a3 and then:

b1) 8...♘bd7 9 ♕c2 dxc4 10 ♗xc4 c5 11 0-0 ♘b6 12 ♗a2 cxd4 13 exd4 ♗d7 14 ♖fe1 ♕d6 15 ♖ad1 ± P.Nikolić-Andersson, Wijk aan Zee 1984.

b2) 8...♖d8 9 ♖d1 dxc4 (possible is also 9...♘bd7 10 ♕c2 dxc4 11 ♗xc4 c5 12 0-0 ♘b6 13 ♗e2 ♗d7 14 ♖d2 cxd4 15 ♘xd4 ♖ac8 16 ♖fd1 ♘a4 = Yusupov-Andersson, Belfort 1988) 10 ♗xc4 c5 11 0-0 ♘c6 12 ♕e2 cxd4 13 exd4 ♗d7 14 ♖fe1 ♖ac8 15 ♗a2 ♕d6 16 ♗b1 ♘e7 17 ♘e5 ♗c6 18 f3 ± Salov-J.Horvath, Groningen 1983.

c) 8 cxd5 exd5 9 ♗d3 with the following options:

c1) 9...c5 10 0-0 ♘c6 11 dxc5 ♕xc5 12 ♖ac1 ♕e7 13 ♗b1 ♖d8 14 ♘d4 ♘e5 15 h3 ♗d7 16 ♖fd1 ♖ac8 17 a3 ± Mowsziszian-Kholmov, Budapest 1991.

c2) 9...c6 10 ♕c2 ♖e8 11 ♘e5 (maybe 11 0-0 ♘bd7 12 ♖ab1 ♘e4 13 b4 ♘df6 14 b5 c5 15 dxc5 ♘xc5 16 ♖bc1 ♘xd3 17 ♕xd3 ♗e6 18 ♘d4 is better, with a slight advantage for White, Gunawan-Trifunović, Vrnjačka Banja 1988) 11...♘bd7 12 ♘xd7 ♗xd7 13 0-0 ♕d6 14 h3 ♖e7 15 b4 ♖ae8 16 b5 c5 17 dxc5 ♕xc5 18 ♖fd1 ♖e5 with chances for both sides, Beliavsky-P.Nikolić, Belgrade 1987.

c3) 9...♘c6 (this is one advantage with 7...♕e7 as opposed to 7...♘bd7: Black can now develop his pieces more actively) 10 0-0 ♗g4 11 ♕d1 (or 11 a3 ♗xf3 12 gxf3 ♘d8 13 b4 ♘e6 14 ♔h1 a5 15 ♖ab1 axb4 16 axb4 c6 = Beliavsky-Makarov, Novosibirsk 1995) 11...♖fd8 12 ♗e2 ♖d6!? 13 ♘b5 ♖d7 14 ♖c1 ♘e4 15 ♘d2 ♗xe2 16 ♕xe2 ♘xd2 17 ♕xd2 ♘d8 18 ♖c2 ♘e6 19 ♖fc1 c6 = Seirawan-Andersson, Biel IZ 1985.

d) 8 ♗d3 dxc4!? 9 ♗xc4 c5 10 0-0 ♘c6 11 ♕e2 ♖d8 12 ♖ad1 ♗d7 13 a3!?, Notkin-Kholmov, Moscow 1995, and now Kholmov suggests 13...♖ac8! 14 d5 exd5 15 ♘xd5 ♘xd5 16 ♗xd5 ♗e6 =.

8...♖d8

This is more flexible than 8...dxc4, which was played in Yusupov-Andersson, Tilburg 1987, which continued 9 ♗xc4 c5 10 0-0 ♖d8 11 ♖fd1 ♘c6 12 ♕e2 cxd4 13 exd4 ♗d7! 14 a3 ♗e8 15 ♗a2 ±.

9 ♕c2 ♘bd7

A solid approach, but Black can also choose 9...dxc4, e.g. 10 ♗xc4 c5 11 0-0 and then:

a) 11...cxd4 12 ♘xd4 ♗d7 13 ♖fd1 ♘c6 and now Spassky has shown that Black is doing quite well after both 14 ♗b5 ♖ac8 and 14 ♘xc6 ♗xc6, in games against Andersson and Chernin respectively.

b) 11...♘c6 12 dxc5 ♕xc5 13 ♘e4 ♕e7 14 a3 ♗d7 15 ♗d3 h6 with equality, P.Nikolić-Andersson, Nikšić 1983.

10 cxd5

10 ♗e2 dxc4 11 ♗xc4 c5 12 0-0 cxd4 13 ♘xd4 should be no problem for Black. He can choose between:

a) 13...♘e5 14 ♗e2 ♗d7 15 ♘f3 ♘g6 16 ♕b3 ♗e8 17 ♖fd1 ½-½

Kharitonov-Kholmov, St Petersburg 1995.

b) 13...♘b6 14 ♗e2 ♗d7 15 ♗f3 e5 16 ♘b3 ♗g4 17 ♗xg4 ♘xg4 18 ♕f5 ♘f6 19 ♘e4 ♘bd5 = Danielsen-P.H.Nielsen, Aalborg 1993.

10...exd5 11 ♗d3 c6 12 0-0 ♘f8 13 a3

The most logical plan must be to prepare b4, but White may also choose between:

a) 13 ♘e2 ♘g6 14 ♘g3 ♖e8 15 ♕c5 ♕d8 16 ♘d2 ♘h4 and Black is doing fine, Andruet-Spassky, Bundesliga 1987/8. It is worth citing the entertaining conclusion to this game: 17 b4 a6 18 a4 ♗d7 19 ♖b1 ♘g4 20 ♕c2 g6 21 b5 axb5 22 axb5 h5 23 bxc6 bxc6 24 ♖fe1 ♕f6 25 ♘df1 ♖a3 26 ♖e2 c5 27 dxc5 ♘e5 28 ♗b5? ♕f3!! 0-1.

b) 13 h3 and now 13...♘e8 14 a3 ♘d6 15 b4 a6 16 ♘a4 ♕f6 17 ♘e5 left White slightly better in the game Djurić-Kveinys, Manila OL 1992, but Black should play 13...♘g6, when White probably can do nothing better than 14 a3, transposing to the main line.

13...♘g6 14 h3 ♖d6!? 15 ♖fe1 ♗d7 16 ♘d2 ♖e8 17 ♘f1 ♘e4

The game is level, Van der Sterren-Andersson, Wijk aan Zee 1988.

B)

6 g3 *(D)*

6...d5

This is the most common move. As mentioned in the section 'Typical Pawn Structures', Black would like to exchange off the c- and d-pawns to

B

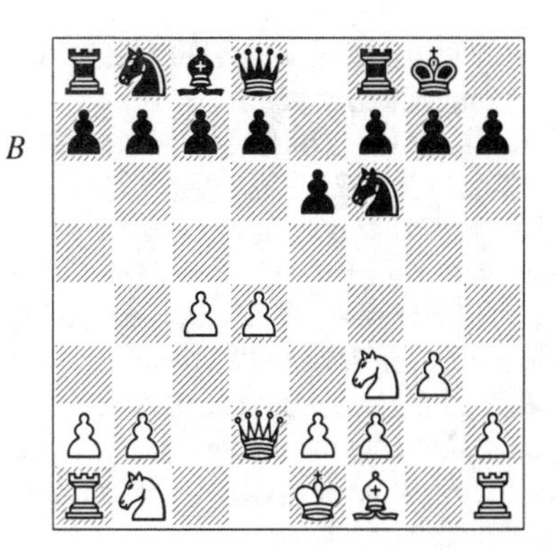

obtain a very drawish and technical position. What winning chances there are for either side, lie in outplaying the opponent in a simplified ending. For more combative souls there is 6...d6 7 ♗g2 *(D)* and then:

B

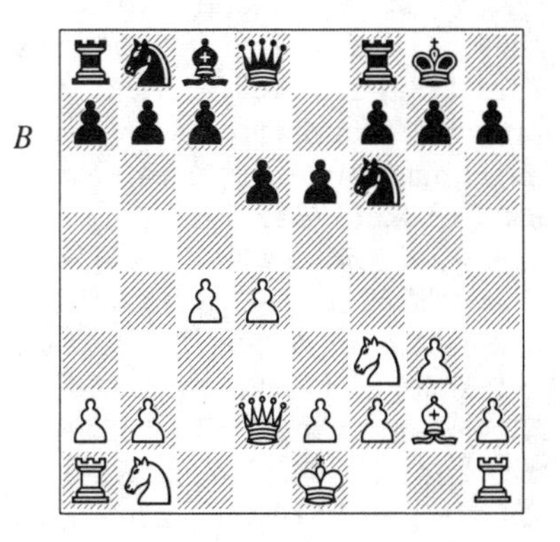

a) 7...♕e7 transposes to Line D12 of Chapter 5.

b) 7...♘bd7 8 ♘c3 e5 9 0-0 ♖e8 10 e4 a6 11 ♖fd1 ♖b8 (on 11...b6 Speelman analysed the very interesting and unclear variation 12 dxe5!? dxe5 13 ♘xe5!? ♖xe5 14 f4 ♖e8 15 e5 ♖b8 16 exf6 ♕xf6 17 ♘d5 and assessed the position as somewhere between unclear and clearly better for White, e.g. 17...♕d6 18 ♘b4!? ♕c5+ 19 ♔h1 ♘f6 20 ♘c6 ♗b7 21 ♘xb8 ♘e4! 22 ♖e1!) 12 b4 b6 (intending to exert pressure on e4 by 13...exd4 14 ♕xd4 ♗b7) 13 dxe5!? (13 d5 should be a little better for White) 13...dxe5 14 ♗h3 ♕e7 15 ♘d5 ♘xd5 16 cxd5 ♘f6 17 ♗xc8 ♖bxc8 with approximately equal chances, Van der Sterren-Speelman, Dutch Cht 1994.

c) 7...♘c6 8 ♘c3 (or 8 d5 ♘e7, when White has nothing better than 9 ♘c3 e5 10 0-0 with a transposition to 'c2') 8...e5 and now:

c1) 9 0-0 ♗g4 10 e3 (10 d5 ♘e7 transposes to 'c2', while 10...♗xf3 11 ♗xf3 ♘e7 12 ♗g2 ♘d7 13 e3 f5 14 f4 ♘g6 15 ♗h3 is slightly better for White, Gonzales-Tempone, Buenos Aires 1982) 10...♕d7 11 ♘d5! (this forces Black into a rather inconvenient knight manoeuvre) 11...♘e4 12 ♕d3 ♗xf3 13 ♗xf3 ♘g5 14 ♗g2 f5 (the continuation 14...exd4 15 exd4 ♘e6 16 ♗e4 h6 17 ♗h7+ ♔h8 18 ♗f5 is a little better for White, but perhaps preferable) 15 f4! exf4 16 gxf4 ♘e6 17 b4 ♘cd8 18 ♕a3 ♘f7 19 b5 a6 20 ♕b3 ♘fd8 21 a4 and White is a little better, Van Wely-Ulybin, Leeuwarden 1997.

c2) 9 d5 ♘e7 (interesting is also 9...♘b8 10 0-0 a5, when compared to some lines of Chapter 5, Black has not committed his queen to e7, e.g. 11 ♘e1 ♘a6 12 ♘d3 ♘d7 13 f4 {better is 13 e4} 13...exf4 14 gxf4 f5 = Ulybin-Totsky, Ekaterinburg 1997) 10 0-0 and now:

c21) 10...a6 11 e4 b5 12 cxb5 axb5 13 b4 ♗b7 and White has two promising lines:

c211) 14 a3 c6 15 dxc6 ♗xc6 16 ♕d3 ♕b8 17 ♖fd1 ♖d8 18 ♘d2 ± Razuvaev-Makarychev, Moscow 1972.

c212) 14 ♖fd1 ♕b8 15 ♘h4 ♗c8 16 h3 ± Pinter-Barlov, Zagreb IZ 1987.

c22) 10...a5 11 e4 ♘d7 12 ♘h4 ♘g6 13 ♘xg6!? (White decides to go for an attack but he could also keep a small edge with 13 ♘f5 ♘c5 14 ♘e3) 13...hxg6 14 f4 ♘c5 15 f5 ♗d7 (Gulko also considered 15...g5 16 ♖f2 ♗d7 17 ♖af1 f6 18 ♗f3 ♗e8 19 h4 and White is better) 16 h4! ♕e7 17 ♖ae1! (a good prophylactic move, as Black was threatening 17...gxf5 18 exf5 e4! followed by ...♕e5, with counterplay) 17...♖fb8 18 ♘b5 ♗xb5 19 cxb5 a4 20 ♖f2 ± Gulko-Larsen, Hastings 1988/9.

c23) 10...♗g4 (a typical Bogo-Indian theme: Black intends to exchange on f3 leaving White with a 'bad' bishop) 11 ♘e1 (Wojtkiewicz-Raptis, Katerini 1992 stated that even if Black is allowed to exchange on f3, White is still somewhat better: 11 h3 ♗xf3 12 ♗xf3 ♘d7 13 e4 f5 {perhaps Black should prepare this advance by 13...g6!?} 14 exf5 ♘xf5 15 ♗g2 ♘d4 16 f4 and White is better) 11...c6 12 dxc6 bxc6 13 ♘d3 ♕c7 14 ♖ac1 ♗e6 15 b3 with an edge to White, Korchnoi-Larsen, Hastings 1988/9.

c24) 10...♘g6 11 ♘e1 ♘g4!? (preparing to advance the f-pawn) 12 f3 ♘h6 13 ♘d3 (13 e4 f5 14 exf5 ♘xf5 15 ♘d3 is maybe an improvement)

13...f5 14 f4 exf4 15 ♘xf4 ♘xf4 16 ♖xf4 ♗d7 17 e4 fxe4 18 ♖xf8+ ♕xf8 19 ♖f1 ♕e7 20 ♘xe4 ♘g4 = Skembris-Andersson, Bar 1997.

7 ♗g2 *(D)*

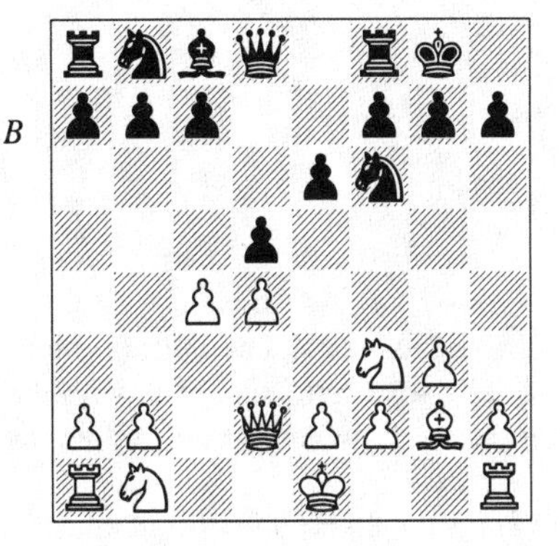

7...♘bd7

This is the most flexible. Black does not yet commit himself to ...c6 or ...♕e7, but simply develops a piece and introduces the idea of exchanging off the c- and d-pawns with ...c5. Alternatives:

a) 7...dxc4 8 ♘a3 ♗d7 9 ♘xc4 ♗c6 10 0-0 ♘bd7 11 ♖fc1 ♗d5 12 b4 ♕e7 13 ♕b2 ♖ac8 14 ♘a5 ± Portisch-P.Nikolić, Linares 1988.

b) 7...b6 8 cxd5 exd5 9 0-0 ♗b7 10 ♘c3 ♘bd7 11 b4! (with the idea of b5) 11...♘e4 12 ♕b2 ♖e8 13 e3 c6 14 ♖fd1 a5 15 a3 with a small advantage for White, Lautier-Yudasin, Lyons tt 1994.

c) 7...♕e7 8 0-0 and then:

c1) 8...dxc4 (although Black succeeds in eliminating the c- and d-pawns, this gives White an advantage) 9 ♘a3 c5 (9...♘e4!? deserves attention) 10 dxc5 ♕xc5 11 ♖ac1 (Black's problem is his slight lack in development and difficulties in getting the bishop out) 11...♘c6 12 ♘xc4 ♕e7? (12...♖d8! 13 ♕c2 ♗d7 14 ♕b3, with only a small advantage for White, was preferable) 13 ♘fe5! ♘xe5 14 ♘xe5 ♘d5 15 ♖fd1 ♘b6 16 ♕a5! ± Kasparov-T.Petrosian, Bugojno 1982.

c2) 8...♖d8 9 ♖c1 and now:

c21) 9...♘bd7 mixes two ideas, and if Black wishes to play like this then 7...♘bd7 is a better choice.

c22) 9...♘c6 (intending 10...dxc4 followed by ...e5) 10 ♕c3!? (10 ♘a3 is also possible) 10...♘e4 (Notkin recommends 10...dxc4 11 ♘a3 ♘d5 12 ♕xc4 with a slight advantage for White) 11 ♕e3 ♘d6 12 cxd5 ♘f5 13 ♕f4 exd5 14 ♘c3 ♗e6 15 e3 and White is better, Notkin-Jankovskis, Passau 1994.

c23) 9...c6 10 ♕e3 ♗d7 11 ♘bd2 ♗e8 is a rather passive but very solid deployment of the bishop. Black hopes to play ...c5 at some stage, when the bishop can join the game from c6. Another idea is to move the knight away from f6 and then follow up with ...f6 to bring the bishop out on the kingside. White has tried:

c231) 12 a3 a5 and now:

c2311) 13 ♕f4 (this is a little dubious because White cannot find a suitable moment to play e4 afterwards) 13...♘a6! 14 g4!? (14 e4 dxe4 15 ♘xe4 c5! is good for Black according to Timman) 14...c5! 15 g5 ♘e4 16 cxd5 (worse is 16 ♘xe4 dxe4 17 ♕xe4 cxd4 18 ♘xd4 ♕xg5 ∓) 16...exd5 17 e3 Timman-P.Nikolić, Tilburg 1988, and now Timman suggests 17...♘xd2 18 ♘xd2 ♖ac8 =.

c2312) 13 c5!? (this has some logic now that Black has weakened b6) 13...a4 14 ♘e5 ♘fd7 15 ♘d3 f6 (Black intends to bring the bishop out and/or carry out the central break ...e5; the next phase of the game centres around the e5-square) 16 ♗h3! ♗f7 17 f4 ♖e8 18 ♘f3 b6 (as Black can find no way to implement the ...e5 break, he decides to break up the queenside before White manages to open the b-file, but this results in a weak c-pawn) 19 cxb6 ♘xb6 20 ♘d2 ♖a5 21 ♖c3 and White is better, Timman-P.Nikolić, Reykjavik 1988.

c232) 12 ♘b3 leads to a final branch:

c2321) 12...♘bd7 13 ♘a5! ♖ab8 14 ♖ab1 ♖dc8 15 cxd5 ♘xd5 16 ♕d2 c5?! (Kasparov recommends the alternative 16...♘5b6! with the idea 17 e4 e5 =) 17 e4 with an edge for White, Kasparov-Timman, Belgrade 1989.

c2322) 12...♘a6 13 a3 ♖ac8 14 ♘e5?! (14 c5! is better for White – Kholmov) 14...dxc4! 15 ♖xc4 ♘d5 16 ♕c1 f6 and Black is doing fine, Razuvaev-Kholmov, Moscow 1991.

Returning to the position after 7...♘bd7 *(D)*:

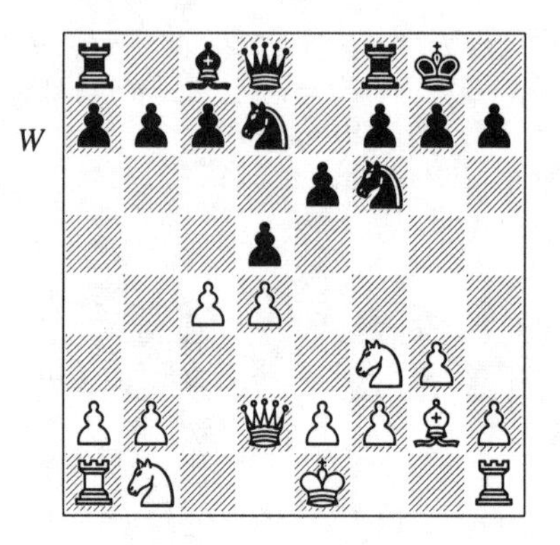

White can now choose between two lines:

B1)

8 ♕c2 b6!?

Black intends to play ...♗b7 and follow up with ...c5, before or after exchanging on c4. The only problem is that Black has to take back with the knight on d5 when White exchanges pawns.

The safe 8...c6 9 ♘bd2 is another option:

a) 9...♕e7!? 10 0-0 e5 (or 10...b6 11 e4 ♘xe4 12 ♘xe4 dxe4 13 ♕xe4 ♗b7 14 ♘e5 and White is a tiny bit better) 11 cxd5 ♘xd5 (11...cxd5 12 dxe5 is just good for White as Black will be left with an isolated pawn) 12 e4 ♘5f6 13 ♖fe1 ♖d8 (13...exd4 is of course a viable alternative, when Karpov mentions 14 e5 ♘d5, and then 15 ♘b3 with a slight advantage, but I am not sure that I trust this as Black can play 15...♘b4, but 15 ♘xd4 is interesting) 14 ♖ad1 exd4 15 ♘xd4 (Karpov also mentions 15 e5 ♘d5 16 ♘xd4 ♘7b6 17 ♘2b3 ♗g4 18 f3 ♗e6 19 f4 ♘b4! giving no assessment, but I would prefer White after 20 ♕c5!) 15...♘b6 16 ♘2b3 ♗g4 17 f3 ♗e6 18 ♕c5! ♕e8 19 e5 ♘fd7 20 ♕c1 ♘f8 21 f4 and White is better, Karpov-Andersson, Reykjavik 1991.

b) 9...b6 and now:

b1) 10 0-0 ♗b7 with a further branch:

b11) 11 e4 dxe4 12 ♘xe4 ♘xe4 13 ♕xe4 transposes to 'b2'.

b12) 11 ♖fd1 ♕e7 12 e4 dxe4 13 ♘xe4 c5 14 ♘xf6+ ♘xf6 15 ♕e2 cxd4 16 ♘xd4 ♗xg2 17 ♔xg2 a6 18 ♔g1 ♖ac8 19 b3 and White has a minute advantage with 3 vs 2 on the queenside, Ftačnik-Andersson, Manila OL 1992.

b13) 11 b4!? (White decides to keep the position of a more closed nature, and so advances his pawns on the queenside, hoping that Black will not be able to find a suitable way to open the game for his bishop) 11...a5 (11...c5?! 12 bxc5 bxc5 13 cxd5 is better for White) 12 a3 and now:

b131) 12...♕e7 (a recent try by Ulf Andersson and perhaps Black's best) 13 ♕b2 (13 c5 is interesting, when Black should probably play 13...bxc5 14 bxc5 e5 rather than activating the bishop immediately, e.g. 14...♗a6 and White can now play 15 ♖fe1 e5 16 e4! exd4 17 exd5 ♕xc5 18 ♕xc5 ♘xc5 19 dxc6 ±) 13...♖fb8 14 ♖fc1 c5! 15 bxc5 bxc5 16 dxc5 ♘xc5 17 cxd5 ♗xd5 18 ♕d4 ½-½ Psakhis-Andersson, Polanica Zdroj Rubinstein mem 1997.

b132) 12...axb4 13 axb4 dxc4 (worse is 13...♖xa1 14 ♖xa1 ♕c7 15 e4 dxe4 16 ♘xe4 c5 17 ♘xf6+ ♘xf6 18 dxc5 bxc5 19 b5 ♖a8 20 ♖xa8+ ♗xa8 21 ♘d2 ♗xg2 22 ♔xg2 h6 23 ♕d3 with a very good ending for White, although Black held the draw in Van Wely-Andersson, Ter Apel 1997) 14 ♘xc4 and now we have:

b1321) In Gavrikov-Wirthensohn, Arosa 1996, Black hesitated a little with 14...♕c7 and after 15 e4! ♖xa1 16 ♖xa1 ♖a8 17 ♖c1! h6 18 h3 ♖c8 19 e5 ♘e8 20 ♕b2 White had a pleasant position.

b1322) 14...c5! 15 dxc5 bxc5 16 b5 ♕c7 17 ♕b2 ♗d5 (this is a lot safer than 17...♖xa1 18 ♖xa1 ♖a8 19 ♖xa8+ ♗xa8, when White has more chances of pushing his passed pawn even further) 18 ♘fd2 ♗xg2 19 ♔xg2 ♘d5 and Black has almost equalized, Van Wely-Andersson, Ter Apel 1995.

b2) 10 e4!? (more forcing) 10...dxe4 11 ♘xe4 ♘xe4 12 ♕xe4 ♗b7 13 0-0 ♖b8 (if 13...♕c7, then Karpov suggests 14 ♘e5 with a slight advantage for White) 14 ♕e3 (Karpov also considered 14 ♕f4 and gave the following interesting line of play: 14...♕f6 15 ♕c7 c5 16 ♕xd7 ♖fd8 17 ♕c7 ♗xf3 18 ♗xf3 ♕xf3 19 dxc5 ♖bc8 20 ♕xa7 bxc5 and Black has good compensation as he controls the only open file and is ready to create even more counterplay by invading the 7th rank and/or pushing the e-pawn) 14...c5 15 dxc5 (15 ♖fd1!?) 15...♘xc5 16 ♖fd1 ♕c7 17 b4 ♘d7 18 ♖d4 ♘f6 19 ♕e5! ± Karpov-Serper, Dortmund 1993.

9 cxd5

This is the most consistent. Having weakened the c6-square with his previous move, Black would be reluctant to take back with the e-pawn. Instead after 9 0-0 ♗b7 10 ♖d1 Black can play:

a) 10...dxc4 11 ♘a3 (if 11 ♕xc4, then 11...♗xf3!? is interesting, e.g. 12 ♗xf3 ♘e5 13 ♕c3 ♘xf3+ 14 ♕xf3 ♕d5 =) 11...♕e7 12 ♘xc4 c5 =.

b) 10...♕e7 11 cxd5 ♘xd5 12 e4 ♘5f6 13 ♘c3 c5 14 d5 exd5 15 exd5 ±

Antonsen-P.H.Nielsen, Vejen jr Ech 1993.

9...♘xd5 10 0-0 c5! *(D)*

The slightest hesitation from Black could easily leave him with an inferior position, and so 10...♗b7 11 e4 ♘5f6 12 ♘c3 c5 13 ♖ad1 cxd4 14 ♘xd4 ♕e7 15 ♖fe1 is a little better for White, Karpov-Andersson, Österskärs (1) 1995.

W

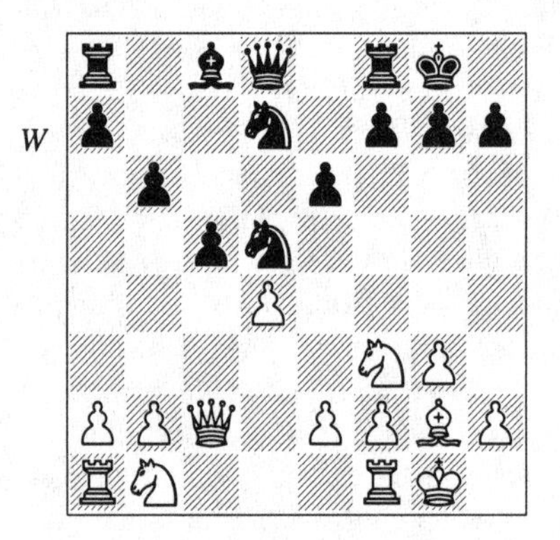

11 ♘c3

11 dxc5 ♘xc5 12 ♖d1 ♗b7 is about equal as 13 e4 is met by 13...♘b4.

11...♘xc3

Stohl recommends 11...♗b7 12 ♖fd1 ♖c8 =.

12 ♕xc3 ♗b7 13 ♖fd1 ♕e7 14 ♖ac1 ♖fc8 15 ♕e3

Stohl-Andersson, Prague 1996, and now, according to Stohl, Black should play 15...♔f8!? intending ...♗d5, ...♖c7 and ...♖ac8 with approximate equality.

B2)

8 0-0 *(D)*

8...c6

B

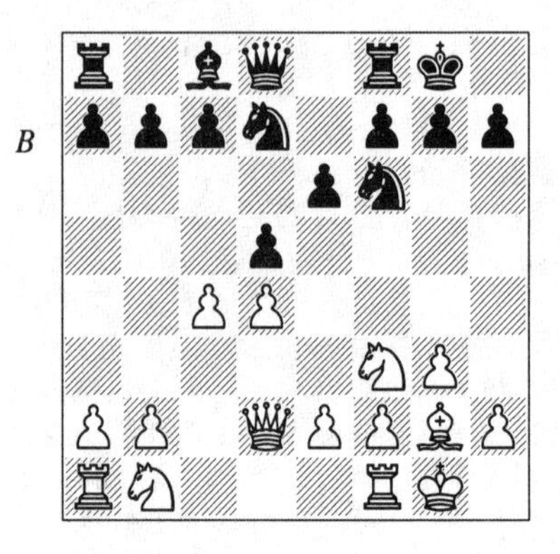

This is very solid but also not much fun. Black is going to free himself very slowly and in the majority of games, he ends up with a slightly inferior ending, but it should also be said that White is often really struggling to create genuine winning chances.

If Black is looking for a more interesting game, he should perhaps try taking on c4:

a) 8...b6!? 9 ♘c3 ♗b7 is suggested by Stohl, but I think White retains some advantage with 9 cxd5 ♘xd5 10 e4 ♘5f6 11 ♘c3.

b) 8...dxc4 9 ♘a3 e5! and now:

b1) 10 d5 c3!? 11 bxc3 ♕e7 is unclear according to Shipov.

b2) 10 dxe5 ♘xe5 (this is the real point: Black exploits the fact that the white queen will be *en prise* if White captures the knight) 11 ♕xd8 (11 ♕c3 ♘xf3+ 12 ♗xf3 ♗e6! 13 ♖fd1 ♕e7 14 ♘xc4 ♗xc4 15 ♕xc4 c6 with an equal position) 11...♘xf3+ 12 ♗xf3 ♖xd8 13 ♘xc4 ♗e6! 14 ♘a5 ♖d2 and Black has reasonable counterplay – Shipov.

b3) 10 ♘xc4 with a further branch:

b31) 10...exd4 11 ♘xd4 (11 ♕xd4 ♕e7 12 ♖fe1 is also a little better for White) 11...♘b6 12 ♘a5! c5 13 ♘db3 ♕xd2 14 ♘xd2 ♖e8 15 e3 ♘bd5 16 e4 ♘c7 17 e5 and now Black should play 17...♘fd5 18 ♖fe1 with only a small advantage for White, rather than 17...♖xe5?! 18 ♘dc4 ♖e8 19 ♘xb7 ♗xb7 20 ♗xb7 ♖ab8 21 ♗c6 ♖e6 22 ♗g2 ♖a6 23 ♖fc1 ♘e6 24 b3 ♘d4 25 ♗f1!, when White was clearly better in Shipov-V.I.Ivanov, Russia 1996.

b32) 10...e4!? 11 ♘g5 ♖e8 12 ♕f4 ♘b6 13 ♘xb6 axb6 14 ♘xe4 ♕xd4 15 ♘xf6+ ♕xf6 16 ♕xc7 ½-½ Lyrberg-Sjöberg, Stockholm 1997.

9 ♖c1

White protects his c-pawn and might be hoping to exploit the c-file at some stage. Compared to the lines where White places his queen on c2, it also increases the queen's flexibility.

Alternatives are:

a) 9 b3 b6 10 ♘c3 ♗a6 is in fact a position from the Queen's Indian and is classified as E15 in *ECO*. White can play:

a1) 11 ♘e5 ♘xe5 12 dxe5 ♘d7 13 f4 ♕e7 14 ♖fd1 ♖fd8 15 cxd5 cxd5 16 e4 (this looks quite good for White, but the following pawn sacrifice seems to give Black good compensation) 16...d4! 17 ♕xd4 ♖ac8 18 ♕e3 ♕b4 19 ♘e2 (19 ♘a4!?) 19...♘c5 20 ♖xd8+ ♖xd8 21 ♕c3 ♕xc3 22 ♘xc3 ♔f8 and even though White is a pawn up, Black's chances are to be preferred, due to his very active position, Tukmakov-Miles, Wijk aan Zee 1984.

a2) 11 ♕b2 dxc4 12 bxc4 ♗xc4 13 ♘d2 ♗a6 14 ♗xc6 ♖c8 15 ♗g2 ♘b8 16 ♘b3 ♕e7 17 ♖fe1 ♖c4 18 e4 ♖fc8 19 ♖ac1 ± Torre-Miles, Thessaloniki OL 1984.

b) 9 ♕c2 b6 and now:

b1) 10 ♘bd2 transposes to note 'b1' to Black's 8th in Line B1.

b2) 10 cxd5 cxd5 11 ♖c1 ♗b7 12 ♘bd2 (12 ♕c7 leads to some embarrassment after 12...♖c8) 12...♖c8 13 ♕b3 ♕e7 14 e3 ♘e4!? 15 ♘xe4 dxe4 16 ♘d2 f5 17 a4 ♗d5 with an equal position, Quinteros-Short, Dortmund 1986.

b3) 10 ♖d1 ♗b7 11 ♘c3 ♕e7 12 e4 dxe4 13 ♘e5 c5 14 ♘xd7 ♘xd7 15 ♗xe4 ♗xe4 16 ♕xe4 ♘f6 17 ♕e3 cxd4 18 ♖xd4 ♖ad8 = Shipov-P.H.Nielsen, Gistrup 1997.

9...♕e7

Black can also try:

a) 9...b6 (a standard set-up) 10 cxd5 cxd5 and then:

a1) 11 ♘c3 ♗a6 12 a4 ♗c4 13 ♘b5 ♕e7 14 ♘a3 ♘e4 15 ♕d1 ♗a6 16 ♘b5 ♗xb5 17 axb5 ♕b4 18 ♕a4 ♕xa4 19 ♖xa4 ♘d6 20 ♖c7 ♖fd8 21 ♖axa7 ♖xa7 22 ♖xa7 ♘xb5 23 ♖a1 ♔f8 = Portisch-Spassky, Reykjavik 1988.

a2) 11 ♘a3! (White does not want to block the c-file – the knight can rejoin the game later via c2) 11...♗a6 12 ♘e5 ♘xe5 13 dxe5 ♘d7 14 f4 ♖c8 15 ♖xc8 ♕xc8 16 ♖c1 ♕d8 17 ♘c2 ♘b8 18 ♘d4 ± Nogueiras-Andersson, Sarajevo 1985.

b) 9...♖e8!? (intending ...e5) and then:

b1) 10 ♘a3 ♕e7 11 ♕f4 e5 12 dxe5 ♘xe5 13 ♘xe5 ♕xe5 14 ♕xe5 ♖xe5 15 cxd5 ♘xd5 16 e4 ♘b6 17 b4 ♗d7

18 ♖ab1 a6 = Lukacs-P.H.Nielsen, Budapest 1993.

b2) 10 ♕e3 (this is White's standard neutralizing method but it does not seem to work here) 10...dxc4! 11 ♖xc4 (if 11 ♘a3, 11...b5 is feasible) 11...e5! 12 dxe5 (12 ♘xe5 ♘xe5 13 dxe5 ♖xe5! 14 ♕xe5 ♕d1+ 15 ♗f1 ♗h3 16 ♘d2 ♕xa1 is awkward for White) 12...♘xe5 13 ♖d4 ♕b6! 14 ♕c3 Dokhoian-Andersson, Wijk aan Zee 1990, and now Dokhoian analyses 14...♘eg4! 15 ♘bd2 c5 16 ♖d3 ♖xe2 17 ♘c4 ♕c7, when Black is a clear pawn up.

b3) 10 ♕d3 ♕e7 (10...dxc4 11 ♖xc4 ♕b6 12 ♕c2 e5 also looks interesting) 11 ♘bd2 e5 12 dxe5 ♘xe5 13 ♘xe5 ♕xe5 14 cxd5 cxd5 15 e3 ♕xb2 16 ♘b3 ♗d7 17 ♘d4 ♘e4 18 ♕f1 b6 19 ♖c7 ♖ed8 20 a4!? and White has some compensation, Van der Sterren-Andersson, Ter Apel 1994.

10 ♕e3 *(D)*

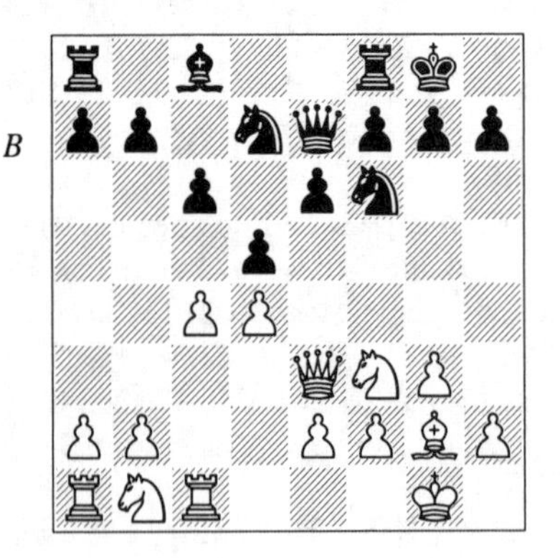

B

10...♖e8

Black puts yet more force behind the ...e5 break. Alternatives:

a) 10...♘e4!? could well be tried.

b) 10...b6 11 cxd5 ♘xd5 12 ♕g5 ♗b7 13 ♕xe7 ♘xe7 14 ♘bd2 ♖fd8 15 ♘c4 c5 16 ♘d6 ♗xf3 17 ♗xf3 ♖ab8 gave White a slightly better ending in Portisch-Andersson, Brussels 1988.

c) 10...dxc4!? 11 a4!? (this is an interesting idea: as Black seems to have few problems after 11 ♖xc4 ♖e8 intending ...e5, White wants to take on c4 with the knight) 11...♖e8 (11...♘d5 12 ♕d2 e5 is maybe better) 12 ♘a3 e5 13 ♘xc4 e4!? 14 ♘fe5 (14 ♘fd2!?) 14...♘xe5 15 dxe5 ♘g4 16 ♕xe4 ♘xe5 17 ♖d1! and White is better, Bacrot-Andersson, Pamplona 1997/8.

d) 10...♖d8 11 cxd5 ♘xd5 12 ♕a3. Andersson has had this position twice and has hung on both times, but few players relish the task of defending a slightly inferior position for a very long time and with no real winning chances:

d1) 12...h6 13 e3 (13 e4 ♕xa3 14 ♘xa3 ♘5f6 15 e5 is much more active) 13...♔f8 14 ♕xe7+ ♘xe7 15 ♘bd2 e5 16 ♘c4 exd4 17 ♘xd4 ♘f6 18 b4 ♖b8 19 ♘a5 ♗d7 20 a3 ♘fd5 and Black has solved most of his problems, Spassky-Andersson, Belfort 1988.

d2) 12...♔f8! 13 ♕d3 (perhaps 13 e4 ♘5f6 14 ♕xe7+ ♔xe7 15 ♘c3 is a better chance for White to gain an advantage) 13...♘5f6 14 ♖d1 ♔g8 15 ♘c3 b6 16 e4 ♗b7 17 e5 ♘e8 18 ♕e3 c5 and Black has equalized, Speelman-Andersson, Brussels 1988.

11 ♘bd2 e5

11...a5 was tried in Piket-Sunye Neto, Manila OL 1992 but seems to be inferior. The game continued 12 h3 a4 13 g4!? h6 14 ♖ab1 ♘f8?! (according to Piket, Black should play 14...♘h7 intending ...♘f8-g6) 15 ♕a3! and White was better.

12 dxe5 ♘xe5 13 ♘xe5 ♕xe5 14 ♕xe5 ♖xe5 15 cxd5 ♘xd5

White has a slightly better endgame after 15...♖xe2 16 dxc6 ♖xd2 17 cxb7 ♗xb7 18 ♗xb7.

16 e4 ♘b6

16...♘c7 17 ♘c4 ♖e7 18 ♘a5 ♔f8 19 b4 ♖b8 20 a4 ♗e6 21 ♖ab1 a6 22 f4 is also better for White, as in Karpov-Andersson, Belfort 1988.

17 f4 ♖e7 18 a4 a5 19 ♘b3! f6 20 ♖a3! *(D)*

This looks a little strange, but White intends ♘c5, when the rook can join the game by swinging across via the third rank.

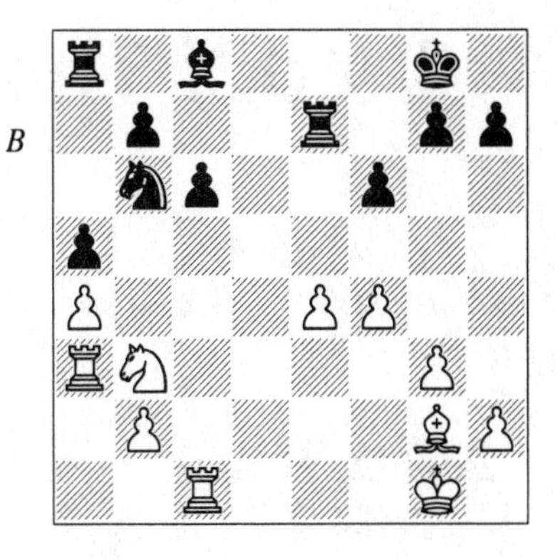

B

20...♗e6 21 ♘c5 ♗f7 22 ♖d3 ♖ae8 23 ♗h3

White is slightly better, Karpov-Andersson, Thessaloniki OL 1988.

4 4 ♗d2: The Flexible 4...a5

1 d4 ♘f6 2 c4 e6 3 ♘f3 ♗b4+ 4 ♗d2 a5 *(D)*

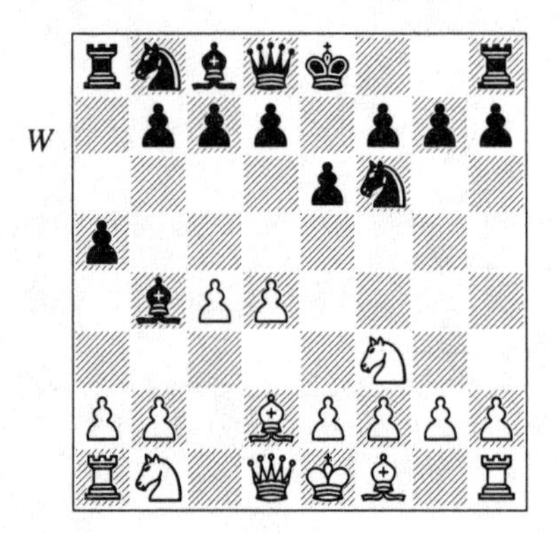

4...a5 is a solid alternative to the more common 4...♕e7. It is quite popular with a number of grandmasters, who seem to be attracted by its greater flexibility. Bronstein and Smyslov, players of quite different styles, were early practitioners. The only disadvantage appears to be the early commitment of the queenside structure.

The immediate strategic foundation of 4...a5 is that if White exchanges on b4, then Black will have useful pressure on the semi-open a-file, while the b4-pawn will be in no significant danger, and will frustrate the development of the b1-knight. Therefore Black is able to retain the tension, and can choose if and when to exchange off the 'Bogo' bishop.

Typical Pawn Structures

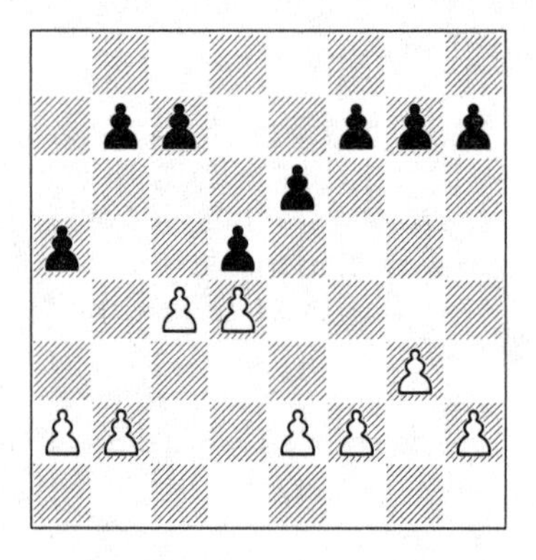

This diagram shows the basic pawn structure running through this chapter. It is quite rare in this line for Black to choose a set-up with ...d6 and ...e5.

An early exchange on d5 solves Black's opening problems since this would free his light-squared bishop. Normally White chooses to protect his pawn on c4 with his queen, but it is not uncommon for him to sacrifice the pawn instead. If White does protect his pawn by ♕c2, it is normal for Black to exert pressure on d4 with ...♘c6 followed by an exchange on c4.

Sometimes, however, White chooses not to fianchetto his light-squared bishop, and instead goes for a more traditional system of development with e3, ♗e2/d3, etc. Then we have a structure like this:

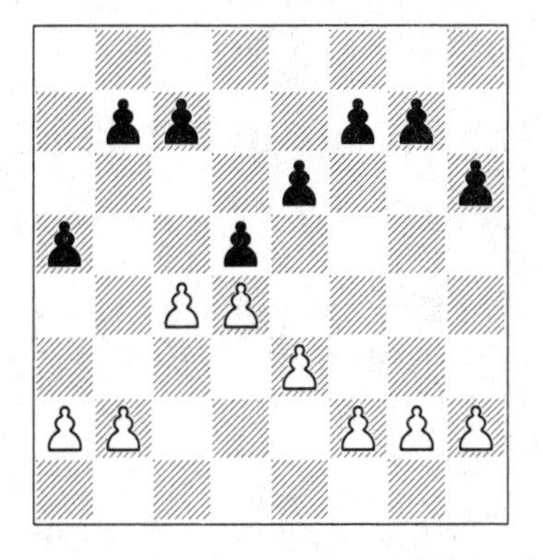

This solves the problem with the c4-pawn but on the other hand gives Black better prospects of carrying out exchanges in the centre.

Planning for White

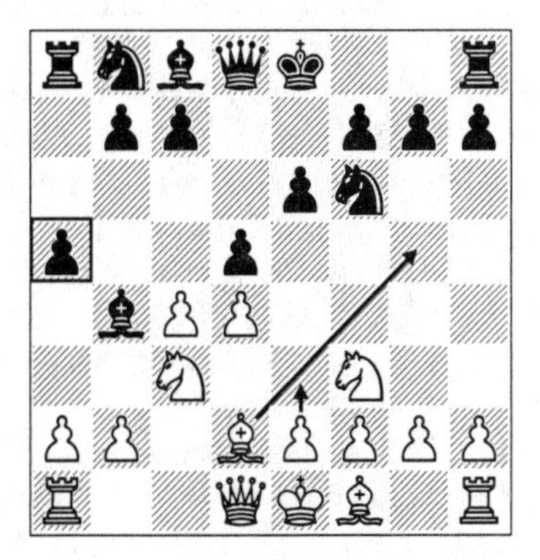

White can choose between a few different set-ups. One is simply to play ♘c3 and develop traditionally with e3, etc. After 5 ♘c3 d5, a quite new idea is to play ♗g5. This is a standard position from a Queen's Gambit except that Black's a-pawn is on a5 rather than a7. This may in some lines be a disadvantage for Black, but theory is still evolving.

A more common way for White to develop is with a kingside fianchetto. Black normally reacts by playing ...d5, when the following position arises:

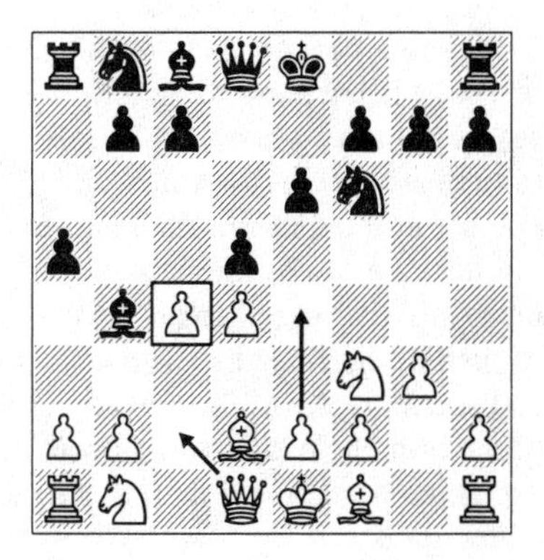

White will continue with ♗g2 and 0-0, but often protects his c4-pawn with ♕c2 first. At a later stage White hopes to carry out the central break e4, which would give a pleasant space advantage. And if Black takes on c4, White will recapture with the queen, play ♘c3 and follow up with e4.

Planning for Black

It is easiest to describe a general plan for Black if White chooses to fianchetto his light-squared bishop (this is also the most common).

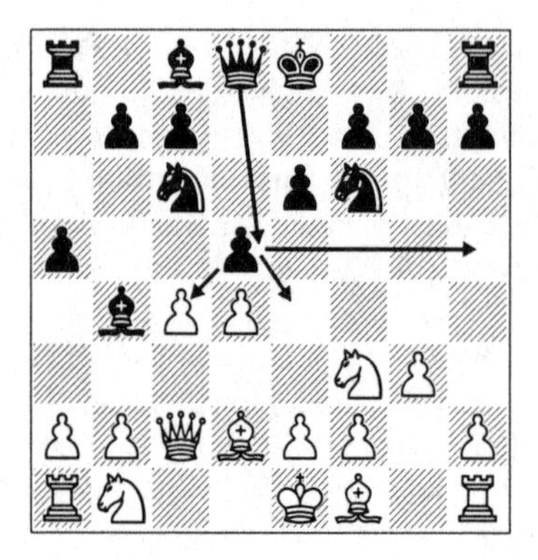

A normal reaction is to put a knight on c6, as in the above diagram. White seems to have a pleasant position, but in the early 1980s Smyslov and Taimanov invented the queen manoeuvre ...♕d5 (after a preliminary exchange on c4). If White exchanges queens on d5 then Black recaptures with the pawn and suddenly the c8-bishop comes to life. Normally White would avoid the exchange by ♕d3 but then Black can either pursue it by ...♕e4 or go for kingside play by ...♕h5.

Quick Summary

The variations 5 ♘c3 (Line A) and 5 g3 (Line B) are equally important. Particularly in the 5 ♘c3 line there have been developed some new ideas recently, mainly evolving around the move ♗d2-g5. White seems to lose a tempo, but play often merely transposes to another opening (the Nimzo-Indian or the Queen's Gambit) but with a black pawn on a5 instead of a7. It is not entirely clear which side this favours. The other main line is 5 g3. Black's most popular reply is then 5...d5, whereafter White can play the temporary pawn sacrifice 6 ♗g2 (Line B1) or the safer 6 ♕c2 (Line B2).

The Theory of 4 ♗d2 a5

1 d4 ♘f6 2 c4 e6 3 ♘f3 ♗b4+ 4 ♗d2 a5

We shall now look at the following main continuations for White:

There are quite a few alternatives for White:

a) 5 e3 0-0 6 ♗d3 b6 7 0-0 ♗b7 8 a3 ♗xd2 9 ♘bxd2 d6 10 ♕c2 ♕e7 11 ♘e4 ♘bd7 12 ♘xf6+ ♘xf6 13 ♘g5 h6 14 ♘h7 ♖fc8 15 ♘xf6+ ♕xf6 16 ♗e4 = Bachtiar-Christiansen, Surakarta/Denpasar 1982.

b) 5 a3 ♗xd2+ 6 ♕xd2 (6 ♘fxd2 has been played as well but does not look very logical) 6...d5 7 ♘c3 0-0 8 ♕f4!? ♕d6 (8...b6 9 e4 dxe4 10 ♘xe4 ♗b7 11 ♗d3 ♘bd7 12 0-0-0 ±) 9 ♕h4 (a safe alternative is 9 ♕xd6 cxd6 10 cxd5 exd5 11 e3 ±) 9...c5 10 dxc5 ♕xc5 11 e3 dxc4 12 ♗xc4 ♗d7 13 0-0 ♘c6 14 ♖ac1 ♘e5 15 ♘xe5 ♕xe5 16 ♖fd1 ± Zaitsev-Kholmov, Moscow 1992.

c) 5 ♕c2 gives Black a wide choice:

c1) 5...♘c6 6 e3 0-0 7 ♗d3 ♖e8 8 a3 ♗f8 9 ♘g5! g6 10 f4 d6 11 0-0 ♗g7 12 ♘c3 ♗d7 13 b3 and White is better, Quinteros-Panno, Mar del Plata 1969.

c2) 5...♗xd2+ 6 ♘bxd2 d6 7 e4 ♘c6 8 e5!? dxe5 9 dxe5 ♘d7 10 ♕c3

♕e7 11 a3 a4 12 ♗d3 ♘c5 13 ♗c2 f5 14 exf6 ♕xf6 15 ♘e4 ♘xe4 16 ♗xe4 ♕xc3+ 17 bxc3 ♘a5 = Korchnoi-Larsen, Las Palmas 1981.

c3) 5...d5 6 c5?! (6 e3 is better) 6...b6 7 ♗xb4 axb4 8 e3 bxc5 9 ♕xc5 ♕d6 and Black is doing well, Aseev-Rashkovsky, Moscow 1982.

c4) 5...d6 6 g3 0-0 7 ♗g2 ♖e8 8 0-0 e5 9 ♗g5 exd4 10 ♘xd4 h6 11 ♗xf6 ♕xf6 12 e3 c6 = Antunes-Taimanov, Lisbon 1985.

A)

5 ♘c3 *(D)*

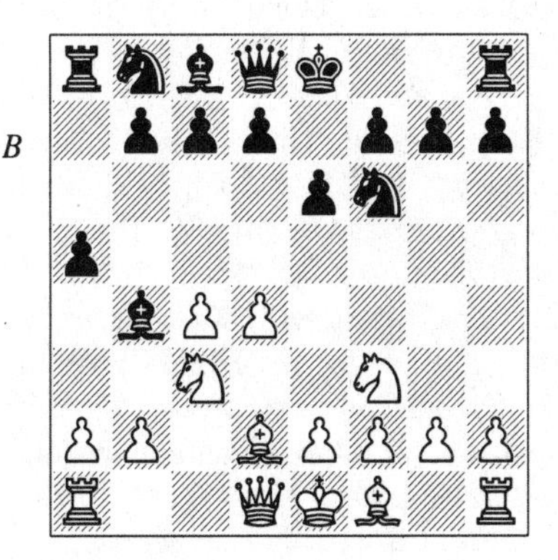

Now:

A1: 5...b6 70
A2: 5...d5 71

Lesser alternatives:

a) 5...0-0 and now:

a1) 6 ♕c2 d5 7 e3 b6 8 cxd5 exd5 9 ♗e2 ♗b7 10 0-0 ♗e7 11 ♖ac1 ♘bd7 12 ♖fd1 with an edge, Kempinski-Kovacs, Szombathely 1993.

a2) 6 a3 ♗xc3 7 ♗xc3 b6 8 e3 ♗b7 9 ♗e2 d6 10 0-0 ♘e4 11 ♘d2 ♘xc3 12 bxc3 f5 with an equal position, I.Ivanov-Polugaevsky, Toluca IZ 1982.

a3) 6 e3 b6 7 ♗d3 ♗b7 8 ♕c2 d5 9 cxd5 exd5 10 0-0 c5 11 a3 ♗xc3 12 bxc3 ♘bd7 13 a4! ♕c7 14 ♖fb1! with a substantial advantage for White, Morović-Gulko, Vina del Mar 1988.

a4) 6 ♗g5!?. This surprising change of plans has been quite popular recently. White aims for a Queen's Gambit type of position but with Black having already weakened his queenside. 6...d5 (the more passive 6...d6 gives White a pleasant position, e.g. 7 e3 ♘bd7 8 ♕c2 ♖e8 9 ♗d3 h6 10 ♗h4 e5 11 ♗h7+ ♔h8 12 ♗f5 exd4 13 ♘xd4 ± Savon-Kholmov, Volgograd 1994) 7 e3 ♘bd7 8 cxd5 exd5 9 ♗d3 ♖e8 10 0-0 c6 11 ♕c2 g6 12 h3 ♗e7 13 ♗f4 ♘f8 14 ♘e5 ♘h5 15 ♗h2 ♗d6 16 ♖ae1 ± I.Sokolov-Skembris, Portorož/Rogaška Slatina 1993.

b) 5...d6 6 ♗g5!? ♘bd7 and now:

b1) 7 ♕c2 h6 8 ♗h4 b6 9 e3 ♗b7 10 ♗d3 e5? (better is 10...c5 or 10...0-0) 11 dxe5 ♘xe5 12 ♘xe5 dxe5 13 0-0-0 ♗xc3 14 ♗e4! ♕c8 15 ♗xb7 ♕xb7 16 ♕xc3 ± Epishin-Smyslov, Biel IZ 1993.

b2) 7 e3 e5 8 ♗e2 0-0 9 0-0 ♗xc3?! (Black should probably insert an exchange on d4: 9...exd4 10 exd4 ♗xc3 11 bxc3 ♖e8 with the idea of ...♘f8) 10 bxc3 b6 11 ♘d2 h6 12 ♗h4 ♗b7 13 ♕c2 ♖e8 14 ♖ae1! ♕e7 15 ♗d1 ♕f8 16 ♕f5 (Christiansen considers 16 ♕b1! with the idea of ♗a4 even stronger) 16...♖e6 17 ♗a4 and White is better, Christiansen-Adams, Novi Sad OL 1990.

A1)

5...b6 *(D)*

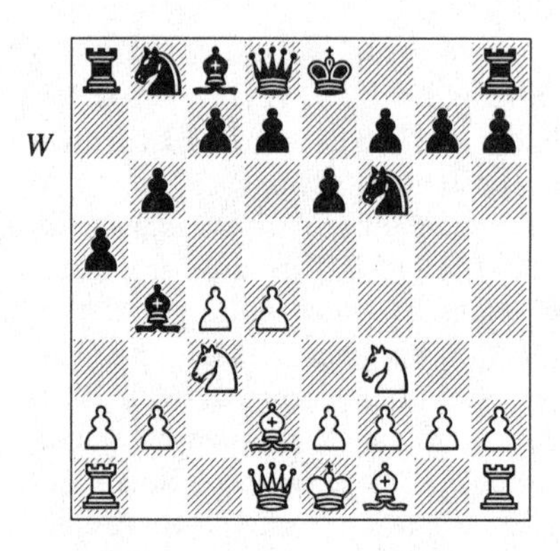

6 e3

This seems to be the most popular move, but recently White has also tried other ideas:

a) 6 g3 ♗a6 7 b3 with rather a pleasant choice for Black:

a1) 7...d5 8 cxd5 exd5 9 ♗g2 0-0 10 0-0 ♖e8 11 ♖e1 ♘bd7 12 ♖c1 c6 = Birbrager-Bronstein, USSR Cht 1967.

a2) 7...0-0 8 ♗g2 c6 9 a3 ♗e7 10 ♗g5 d5 11 ♗xf6 ♗xf6 12 cxd5 cxd5 13 0-0 ♘d7 14 ♕d2 ♗e7 15 ♖fc1 b5 = Karpov-Yusupov, Linares 1992.

b) 6 ♗g5. This idea has become quite popular in many branches of the ...a5 system. White simply plays a Nimzo-Indian but with Black having gained the move ...a5, which doesn't always seem to fit into his plans. It may be worth comparing this position with those that arise in Chapter 8. 6...♗b7 7 e3 d6 (another possibility is 7...h6 8 ♗h4 ♗xc3+ 9 bxc3 d6 10 ♘d2 with a normal Nimzo-Indian position except that Black has a pawn on a5) 8 ♗d3 ♘bd7 9 ♕c2 ♕e7 10 e4 (10 0-0-0!?) 10...c5 11 0-0 cxd4 12 ♘xd4 ♖c8 13 ♘db5 h6 14 ♗f4 ± Khalifman-Yusupov, Las Palmas 1993.

6...♗b7

6...♗xc3 7 ♗xc3 ♘e4 8 ♖c1 ♗b7 9 ♘d2 ♘xc3 10 ♖xc3 gave White a pleasant position in Vaiser-Taimanov, USSR 1982.

7 ♗d3 0-0

Black might also withhold this for a few moves, e.g. 7...d6, when White has a choice:

a) 8 a3 ♗xc3 9 ♗xc3 ♘e4 10 ♖c1 ♕e7 11 0-0 ♘xc3 12 ♖xc3 e5! and Black already stands well, Malich-Smyslov, Berlin 1979.

b) 8 ♕c2 ♘bd7 9 e4 e5 10 0-0 (Kasparov-Tal, Nikšić 1983 instead featured 10 ♘d5!? ♗xd2+ 11 ♕xd2 exd4 12 ♘xd4 ♘c5 13 0-0 0-0 14 ♖fe1 ♖e8 15 f3 c6 16 ♘c3 ♕c7 17 ♗f1 ♖ad8 and now 18 ♖ad1 permitted the central break 18...d5!; White should instead have played 18 ♘f5! with a substantial advantage, according to Kasparov) 10...0-0 and now:

b1) 11 ♖fe1 ♖e8 12 ♘d5 ♗xd2 13 ♕xd2 ♘f8 (13...c6 14 ♘c3 ♘f8 15 ♖ad1 ♘g6 16 ♗f1 ♕c7 17 d5 ± Van der Sterren-Rashkovsky, Baku 1983) 14 g3?! (this is a rather needless weakening of the kingside, and instead Taimanov recommends 14 ♗c2 with a small advantage) 14...♘6d7 15 ♗f1 ♘e6 16 b3 c6 17 ♘e3 ♘xd4 18 ♘xd4 exd4 19 ♕xd4 c5! 20 ♕xd6 ♘e5 with a good position for Black, Cvitan-Taimanov, Baku 1983.

b2) 11 ♘d5 ♗xd2 12 ♕xd2 c6 13 ♘c3 ♕e7 14 ♖fe1 ♖fd8 15 ♖ac1 ♘f8

16 d5! and White is better, A.Petrosian-Rashkovsky, USSR 1982.

8 0-0

Portisch-Karsa, Hungary 1985 saw a rather uncommon idea for Black (at least in this type of position); after 8 Qc2 Black continued 8...c5 9 d5 b5!? 10 Nxb5 (the question is whether Black has enough compensation after 10 dxe6 bxc4 11 exf7+ Rxf7 12 Bxc4 d5 13 Bb3!) 10...exd5 11 cxd5 Bxd5 12 Bxb4 cxb4 13 Nc7 Bxf3 14 gxf3 Ra7 15 Nb5 Ra6 16 Nd4 Rd6 17 Rg1 g6 with approximately equal play.

8...d6 9 Qe2

Other options:

a) 9 Re1 Nbd7 10 e4 e5 11 a3 exd4 12 Nxd4?! (12 axb4 dxc3 13 Bxc3 axb4 14 Bxb4 Ng4 =) 12...Ne5 13 Bg5 Bxc3 14 bxc3 h6 15 Bh4 Ng6 16 Bg3 Re8 and Black is better, Bobotsov-Najdorf, Lugano OL 1968.

b) 9 Qc2 Bxf3 (9...Nbd7 10 e4 e5 transposes to 'b' in the note to Black's 7th move) 10 gxf3 e5 was unclear in Van der Sterren-Taimanov, Baku 1983, but if White wants to have his queen on c2, then 8 Qc2 is more accurate.

9...Nbd7 10 e4

This is better than 10 a3, which permits Black to take control of e4 with 10...Bxc3 11 Bxc3 Ne4. Lein-Christiansen, Lone Pine 1981 continued 12 Nd2 f5 13 f3 Nxc3 14 bxc3 e5 15 Bc2 Bc6 16 f4 e4 with equality, but White might try 12 Be1 intending Nd2 and f3 to keep the bishop-pair.

10...e5 11 d5 Nh5 12 g3 Nc5 13 Bc2 Bxc3 14 Bxc3

White is slightly better, Lengyel-Lehmann, Solingen 1968.

A2)

5...d5 *(D)*

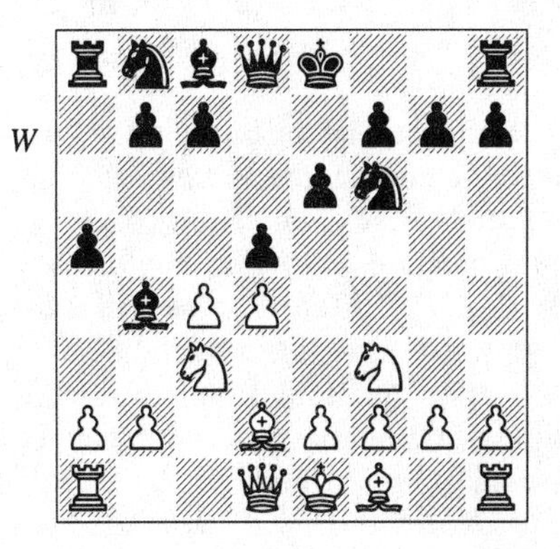

6 e3

6 Bg5 is also quite interesting. We have then arrived at a Ragozin Queen's Gambit (or a Vienna Variation if Black takes on c4) but with Black having gained the extra tempo ...a5. However, Nigel Short seems to think that this is actually a disadvantage for Black. Let us have a look at the following variations:

a) 6...dxc4 7 e4 c5 8 Bxc4 looks good for White, as ...a5 really turns out to be an unfortunate move here.

b) 6...h6 7 Bxf6 (Short recommends 7 Bh4 but I am not sure exactly what he has in mind, as after 7...dxc4 White's usual move would be 8 Qa4+, but this is rather ineffective here as the b4-bishop is defended) 7...Qxf6 8 e3 0-0 and now:

b1) 9 a3 Bxc3+ 10 bxc3 dxc4 11 Bxc4 b6 12 0-0 Bb7 13 Re1 Nd7 14 e4 Rfd8 15 Bb5 Qe7 16 Qb3 Rab8 17 Rab1 Ba8 18 a4 and White is better, Khalifman-Gofshtein, Ubeda 1997.

b2) 9 ♕c2 c5 (Short suggests 9...♖d8 10 a3 ♗f8 as better) 10 cxd5 exd5 11 a3 ♗xc3+ 12 bxc3 c4 (Lobron-Short, Dortmund 1995) 13 a4 ±.

6...0-0

Fianchettoing the queen's bishop is a very common idea in this variation, and thus Black can also try 6...b6 in this position. If White continues 7 ♗d3 ♗b7 8 0-0, the game will most likely transpose to our main line after 8...0-0 but in Osnos-Kholmov, Leningrad 1967 White instead exchanged pawns on d5 at move 7, i.e. 7 cxd5 exd5 8 ♘e5 0-0 9 ♗d3 ♗a6 10 ♗xa6 (10 ♕e2 deserves attention) 10...♘xa6 11 0-0 ♖e8 =. This kind of Exchange Queen's Gambit position is no real problem for Black, who quite easily exchanges the light-squared bishops, while White is less active than usual with his dark-squared bishop inside his own pawn chain.

7 ♗d3 b6

Other options are:

a) 7...c5 8 a3 ♗xc3 9 ♗xc3 ± Stohl.

b) 7...dxc4 8 ♗xc4 b6 9 0-0 ♗b7 (this seems to be a good way to avoid the type of positions where White exchanges on d5) 10 ♕e2 ♘bd7 11 ♖fd1 ♕e7 12 a3 ♗xc3 13 ♗xc3 ♘e4 14 ♗e1 ♘d6 15 ♗d3 c5 = Zviagintsev-Speelman, Lucerne Wcht 1997.

8 0-0 ♗b7

Again Black has a couple of other possibilities:

a) 8...dxc4 transposes to 'b' in the previous note.

b) 8...♗a6!? 9 b3 ♕e7 (9...♘bd7, intending ...c5, may be more accurate) 10 ♘e5! ♘fd7 (10...♘bd7 wouldn't be good in view of 11 ♘c6, but an idea is 10...♗b7 preparing ...♘bd7) 11 f4! c6 12 ♕c2 f5 13 ♘e2 and White is better, Ehlvest-Kveinys, Moscow OL 1994.

9 a3

9 cxd5 exd5 10 ♕c2 ♘bd7 11 ♘e2 ♗d6 12 ♘g3 has been suggested by Stohl, with a claim of ±, but this does not look entirely clear. Black might try 12...♗xg3 13 hxg3 ♗a6 14 ♗xa6 ♖xa6 15 ♖ac1 ♖a7, when he isn't much worse.

9...♗d6

Black should probably consider retreating the bishop all the way to e7.

10 ♕c2

The threat of ♘b5 makes the following exchange necessary...

10...dxc4 11 ♗xc4 ♘bd7

11...c5!? 12 dxc5 ♗xc5 13 ♖fd1, with only a slightly better game for White, is a more active way to play the position.

12 e4 e5 13 ♗e3 exd4 14 ♗xd4 ♕e7 15 ♖fe1

White has a substantial advantage, Nenashev-Moskalenko, Alushta 1994.

B)

5 g3 *(D)*

5...d5

This remains the most popular. Others:

a) 5...0-0 6 ♗g2 and now:

a1) 6...d5 7 ♕b3!? ♗e7 8 0-0 c6 9 ♖c1 ♘bd7 10 ♗e1, Ruban-Makarov, USSR 1991, and now Black should go into a kind of Stonewall position with 10...♘e4 11 ♘bd2 f5.

B

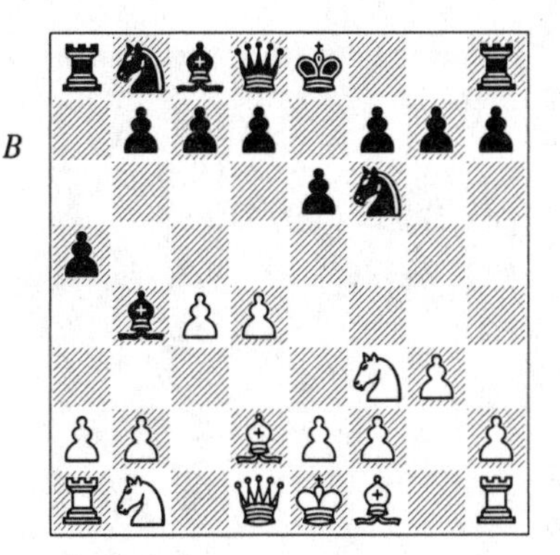

W

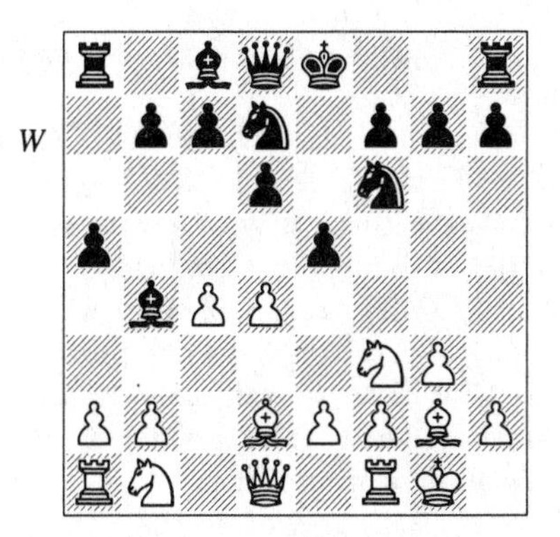

a2) 6...b6 7 0-0 ♗a6!? (7...♗b7 is a Queen's Indian but the text-move is a little sharper) and now:

a21) 8 ♕c2 c5 9 ♖d1!? d5?! (White is better placed for the forthcoming complications; better is 9...♖a7 or 9...♗xd2 with the idea of 10 ♘bxd2 ♘c6) 10 ♗g5! cxd4 11 cxd5 ♕c8!? 12 ♕xc8 ♖xc8 13 dxe6 ♗xe2 14 ♘xd4! ♗xd1 15 exf7+ ♔xf7 16 ♗xa8 ♘bd7 17 ♗g2 ♗c5 18 ♘c3 ♗xd4 19 ♖xd1! ♗xc3 20 bxc3 ♖xc3 21 ♗f1 ± Zakharevich-Makarychev, Russia 1995.

a22) 8 ♗g5 ♗e7 9 ♕c2 ♘c6 10 a3 h6 11 ♗xf6 ♗xf6 12 ♖d1 ♕e7 with approximately equal play, Kasparov-Yusupov, USSR Ch 1981.

b) 5...d6 6 ♗g2 ♘bd7 7 0-0 e5 *(D)* and now there are a number of moves that leave Black fighting for equality:

b1) 8 ♘c3 exd4 9 ♘xd4 0-0 10 ♕c2 ♘e5 11 ♗g5 h6 12 ♗xf6 ♕xf6 13 ♘d5 ♕d8 14 ♘xb4 axb4 15 c5 with an initiative, Polugaevsky-Smyslov, USSR Spartakiad 1979.

b2) 8 ♗g5 exd4 9 ♘xd4 0-0 10 a3 ♗c5 11 ♘c3 h6 12 ♗f4 ♘e5 13 ♘a4!? (typical of Shirov's original play, but 13 b3 is safer and maybe better) 13...♗a7 (the simple 13...♕e7 is worth considering) 14 ♘b5 ♗b8 15 c5 ♘g6 (15...♕e8!?) 16 ♗e3 d5 17 ♘bc3 c6 18 ♘b6 ♖a6 19 ♗d4 ♗f5 with equality, Shirov-Seul, Bundesliga 1992/3.

b3) 8 e3 ♗xd2 (8...0-0? 9 ♗c1!) 9 ♕xd2 0-0 10 ♘c3 and then:

b31) 10...♕e7 11 ♖fd1 ♖e8 12 ♘b5?! (Black's position is simply too solid to succumb to such an early attack; more prudent is 12 ♖ac1 or 12 e4) 12...♘f8 13 c5 e4 14 cxd6 cxd6 15 ♘e1 ♗g4 16 ♖dc1 ♘e6 = Adianto-Christiansen, San Francisco 1991.

b32) 10...♖e8 11 e4! c6 12 b3 b5!? 13 cxb5 cxb5 14 ♖fd1! ± Razuvaev-Christiansen, Bundesliga 1990/1.

b33) 10...c6 11 dxe5 (11 ♖fd1) 11...♘xe5 = I.Farago-P.Nikolić, Wijk aan Zee 1988.

b4) 8 ♗e3!? 0-0 9 ♕c2 exd4 10 ♗xd4 ♖e8 11 ♘c3 ♗xc3 12 ♗xc3 ♘e4 13 ♗d4 ♘g5 14 ♖ad1 ♘xf3+ 15 exf3 b6 16 f4 ♖b8 17 ♕c3 f6 18 ♗d5+ ♔h8 19 ♖fe1 ♗b7 = Gulko-Dzindzichashvili, USA Ch 1990.

b5) 8 ♕c2 0-0 9 ♘c3 ♖e8 and now:

b51) 10 ♖ad1 e4 11 ♘e1! (11 ♘g5 ♗xc3 12 bxc3?! ♕e7 13 f3 e3 14 ♗c1 ♘b6 gave Black a good position in P.Nikolić-Benjamin, Groningen PCA qual 1993) 11...♗xc3 12 ♕xc3 d5 13 b3 c6 14 ♘c2 b5?! (too optimistic; 14...h6 is better) 15 cxb5 cxb5 16 ♗f4 b4 17 ♕d2 and White is better, Piket-Benjamin, Amsterdam 1994.

b52) 10 dxe5 dxe5 11 ♖ad1 c6 12 ♗e3 ♕c7 13 ♘a4 (intending to trap the bishop with c5 and a3) 13...♗f8 14 ♘g5 h6 15 ♘e4 ♘g4 16 ♗c1 f5 17 ♘ec3 ♘c5 18 ♘xc5 ♗xc5 19 ♘a4 ♗f8 20 ♗h3! f4 with unclear play, Komljenović-B.Lalić, Benasque 1994.

b53) 10 e4 and now:

b531) 10...c6 11 ♖ad1 ♘f8?! (better is 11...♕c7!? intending ...b5) 12 dxe5 dxe5 13 ♗e3 ♕e7 14 ♘a4! (intending c5) 14...b5? (14...♗d6 is essential although White is clearly better after 15 h3 ♗e6 16 c5 ♗c7 17 b3) 15 cxb5 cxb5 16 ♘b6 ♖b8 17 a3! ♗d6 18 ♕c6 ♗c7 19 ♘xc8 ♖exc8 20 ♗h3 ♘e6 21 ♖c1! ± Piket-Christiansen, Groningen 1991.

b532) 10...♘f8 11 a3 exd4 12 axb4 dxc3 13 ♗xc3 ♘xe4 14 bxa5 ♘xc3 15 ♕xc3 c5 16 ♖fd1 b6 17 ♕d2 ♖xa5 18 ♖xa5 bxa5 19 ♕xd6 ♕xd6 20 ♖xd6 ♗d7 21 h4 a4 = Lobron-Christiansen, Munich 1992.

b533) 10...exd4 11 ♘xd4 ♘e5 12 b3 c6 13 ♔h1 ♕b6 14 ♘ce2 a4 15 ♖ab1 ♗xd2 16 ♕xd2 axb3 17 axb3 ♗d7 18 ♘c3 ♖ad8 19 f4 ♗c8 20 ♘c2 ♘ed7 21 b4 with a nice space advantage, Zsu.Polgar-Christiansen, Munich 1991.

Returning to the position after 5...d5 *(D)*:

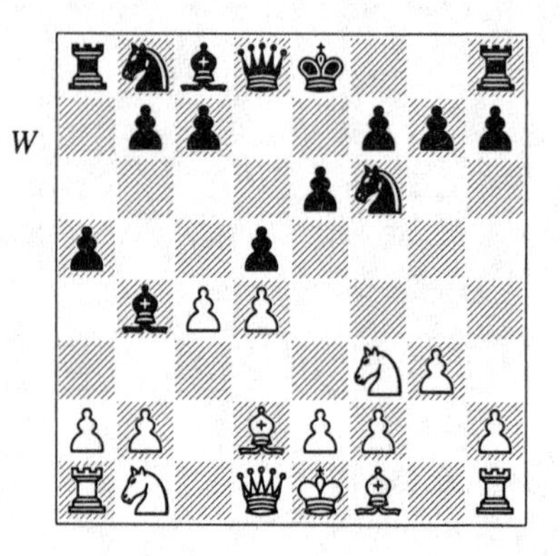

We shall now divide the analysis into:

B1)

6 ♗g2 dxc4

This capture is the critical test of 6 ♗g2, but there are other options too:

a) 6...0-0 transposes to note 'a1' to Black's 5th move.

b) 6...♘c6 7 a3 ♗xd2+ 8 ♘bxd2 0-0 9 0-0 ♕e7 10 ♕c2 ♖d8 11 ♖ad1 e5 12 dxe5 ♘xe5 13 ♘xe5 ♕xe5 14 ♘f3 is slightly better for White, Plaskett-Short, Hastings 1982/3.

c) 6...c6 7 ♕c2 b6 with a pleasant choice for White:

c1) 8 0-0 ♗a6 9 ♗xb4 axb4 10 ♘bd2 ♘bd7 11 a3 bxa3 12 ♖xa3 ♗b7 13 ♖fa1 ♖xa3 14 ♖xa3 0-0 15 b4 ± Gleizerov-Mochalov, Minsk 1997.

c2) 8 ♘e5! ♗d6 9 ♘c3 0-0 10 0-0 ♗a6 11 cxd5 cxd5 12 ♗g5 h6 13 ♗xf6 ♕xf6 14 f4 ♖c8 15 ♖f2! intending e4 with an edge, Oll-Aleksandrov, Minsk (2) 1993.

7 0-0

Other possibilities:

a) 7 ♕c2 is probably best met by 7...♕d5 but 7...b5 is also viable, e.g. 8 a4 bxa4 9 ♕xa4+ ♗d7 10 ♕c2 ♘c6 11 ♕xc4 ♖b8 12 0-0 0-0 13 ♘c3 ½-½ Rausis-Korchnoi, Enghien 1997.

b) 7 ♘a3!? ♗xa3 8 bxa3 0-0 9 ♕c2 b5 10 ♘e5 ♘d5 11 ♖b1 c6 12 0-0 f6 13 ♘f3 ♘d7 14 a4 with good compensation, P.Nikolić-Bistrić, Sarajevo 1983.

7...♘c6 8 ♗g5

8 ♕c2 transposes to Line B2, but an interesting idea, and perhaps better, is 8 e3 0-0 9 ♕c1 ♗d6 (9...b5!?) 10 ♕xc4 e5 11 ♘c3 exd4 12 exd4 ♗f5 (12...♘b4 is also better for White, e.g. 13 a3 ♗e6 14 ♕b5 ♗d7 15 ♕c4 ♗e6 16 ♕e2 ♘bd5 17 ♘g5 ♗g4 18 ♕d3 ±) 13 ♘h4 ♗d7 14 ♘b5 ♖e8 15 ♖fe1 ♖xe1+ 16 ♖xe1 ♕f8 17 ♘xd6 cxd6 18 d5 ♘e5 19 ♕d4 with a substantial advantage for White, Piket-Smyslov, Oviedo rpd 1992.

8...0-0

A solid alternative is 8...h6 9 ♗xf6 ♕xf6 10 a3 ♗d6 11 ♕a4 0-0 12 ♕xc4 e5 with a good position for Black, Borovikov-Aleksandrov, Sas van Gent jr Ech 1992.

9 e3

The alternatives do not look too bright:

a) 9 ♘c3 h6 10 ♗xf6 ♕xf6 11 e3 ♖d8 12 ♘d2 e5 and Black has the advantage, Sideif-Zade – Taimanov, Baku 1983.

b) 9 a3 ♗e7 10 ♘c3 ♖b8 11 a4 b6 12 e4 ♗a6 13 ♖e1 ♘b4 14 ♘e5 h6 15 ♗f4 ♘d7 and Black held on to his extra pawn in Gabaldon-Aleksandrov, Oviedo rpd 1992.

9...♖a6?!

This seems a little too creative. A more solid approach is 9...h6 10 ♗xf6 ♕xf6 11 a3 ♗d6 12 ♘bd2 e5 13 ♘xc4 exd4 =.

10 ♘bd2 h6 11 ♗xf6 ♕xf6 12 ♘xc4 b5 13 ♘ce5 ♘xe5 14 dxe5 ♕d8 15 ♕xd8 ♖xd8 16 ♖ac1

White is slightly better, Bates-Lehtivaara, Edinburgh 1997.

B2)

6 ♕c2 *(D)*

B

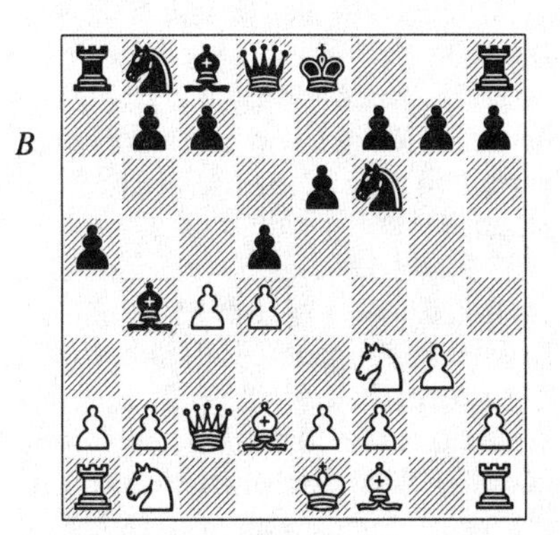

6...♘c6

The peculiar rook manoeuvre 6...♖a6 has, not surprisingly, never attracted a substantial following. White seems to have a relatively safe route to an advantage:

a) 7 ♗g2? allows Black to reveal the point of his last move: 7...dxc4 8 ♕xc4 ♖c6 9 ♕b5 ♗d7! 10 0-0 ♖b6 11 ♕d3 ♗b5 12 ♕e3 ♘c6 with a good game for Black – Adianto.

b) 7 a3 ♗e7 8 ♗g2 (8 ♘c3 ♘c6 9 e3 ♖a8 10 h3 0-0 11 g4 g6 12 0-0-0 might be even stronger, when White enjoys a promising attacking position, Agdestein-Nogueiras, Taxco IZ 1985) 8...♘c6 9 0-0 0-0 10 ♖d1 ♗d7 and now:

b1) 11 ♗f4 dxc4 12 ♕xc4 a4 13 ♘bd2 ♘d5 14 e4 ♘a5 15 ♕c2 ♖c6 16 ♕d3 ♘xf4 17 gxf4 ♖b6 with unclear play, Garcia Palermo-Garcia Gonzales, Havana 1985.

b2) 11 ♗e1 dxc4 12 ♕xc4 a4! 13 ♘c3 ♘a5 14 ♕d3 ♘b3 15 ♖ab1 c5 16 dxc5 ♕b8! = Adianto-Garcia Gonzales, Dubai OL 1986.

7 ♗g2

A major alternative is 7 a3, when Black has a choice between:

a) 7...♗xd2+ 8 ♘bxd2 is slightly better for White, who has simply been permitted to strengthen his centre, e.g. 8...dxc4 9 ♕xc4 ♕d5 10 ♗g2 ♘e4 11 ♕d3 ♘xd2 12 ♕xd2 0-0 13 ♖d1 ♖a6 14 0-0 ♖b6 15 ♕c1 ♕b5 16 ♖d2 ± Dokhoian-Taimanov, Belgrade 1988.

b) 7...♗d6 8 ♗g2 0-0 9 c5! (closing the position like this is only promising for White when Black has little prospect of getting in an ...e5 break) 9...♗e7 10 ♘c3 ♗d7 11 0-0 b6 12 cxb6 cxb6 13 ♖ac1 ♖c8 14 ♕d3! ♘e8?! 15 e4! ± Gheorghiu-Muse, Hamburg 1984.

c) 7...♗e7 8 ♗g2 dxc4 (an interesting manoeuvre, which often occurs in the Bogo-Indian, was seen in Tavadian-Chernin, Irkutsk 1983: 8...♘e4!? 9 ♗e3 ♘d6 {this forces White to release the central tension} 10 cxd5 exd5 11 ♘c3 ♗e6 12 ♖d1 ♘a7 13 ♗f4 and now 13...c6 intending ...♘ab5 is equal, according to Chernin) 9 ♕xc4 ♕d5 (this queen manoeuvre resembles that in the main line, but note that having the moves a3 and ...♗e7 inserted is an improvement for White) 10 ♕d3 and now Black has two choices:

c1) 10...♕e4?! (this is a standard idea as White cannot really escape a queen exchange, but at this particular point it seems to favour White) 11 ♕xe4 ♘xe4 12 ♗f4! ♗d6 13 e3 (13 ♘e5! ♗xe5 14 dxe5 ♘c5 15 ♘c3 ± Gheorghiu) 13...♖a6 14 ♘bd2 ♘xd2 15 ♘xd2 ♔e7 16 ♖c1 with a substantial advantage for White, Gheorghiu-Marasescu, Romanian Ch 1983.

c2) 10...0-0 11 ♘c3 ♕h5 12 0-0 ♖d8 13 ♕c4 ♗d7 14 ♖fe1! ♘d5 15 e4 ♘b6 16 ♕d3 a4, Ribli-Smyslov, London Ct (2) 1983, and now 17 ♗f4! is very good for White.

7...dxc4

Other possibilities:

a) 7...♘e4!? 8 0-0 and then:

a1) 8...f5 looks like a very good Stonewall for White if he simply continues 9 ♗xb4! ♘xb4 10 ♕c1. The game Rajković-Ivanović, Yugoslav Ch 1984 instead went 9 ♗f4 ♗e7 10 ♘c3 g5!? 11 ♗e5 0-0 12 ♖ac1 ♘xc3 13 bxc3 a4 14 cxd5 exd5 15 c4 ♗e6 16 cxd5 ♗xd5 17 ♘e1 ♘b4 18 ♗xd5+ ♘xd5 with an unclear position.

a2) 8...0-0 9 ♗e3 a4 10 ♘c3 ♗xc3 11 bxc3 ♘a5 12 cxd5 exd5 13 ♕xa4 ♘xc3 14 ♕b4 ♘e4 15 ♘e5 ♕d6 with approximately equal play, Borges-Lebredo, Santa Clara 1985.

b) 7...0-0 8 0-0 ♖e8 (8...dxc4 9 ♕xc4 ♕d5 would most likely transpose to the main line) 9 ♗c3!? dxc4 10

♘bd2 ♕d5 11 e4 ♕b5 12 ♖fe1 with compensation, Djurić-Rantanen, Järvenpää 1985.

8 ♕xc4 ♕d5 *(D)*

W

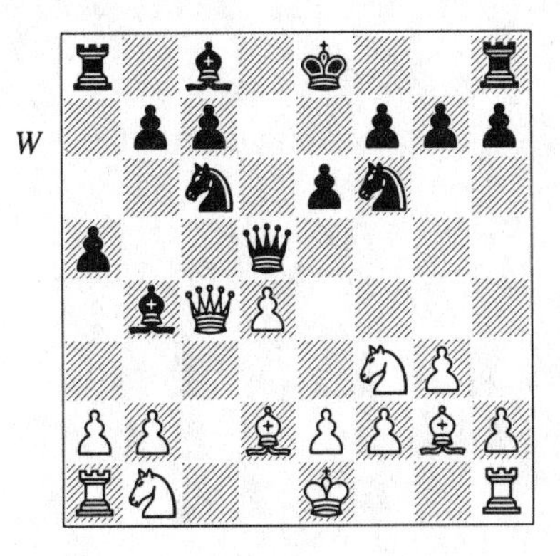

This queen manoeuvre was popularized in the early 1980s by Grandmasters Smyslov and Taimanov. By exchanging queens Black hopes to lessen White's control of the centre.

9 ♕d3

White cannot really avoid the queen exchange but he seeks to make it in the most favourable way.

9 ♕xd5 exd5 increases the scope of Black's light-squared bishop and thus causes Black fewer problems:

a) 10 ♘c3 and now:

a1) 10...♗e6 11 ♖c1 a4 12 ♘b5 ♗xd2+ 13 ♔xd2 ♔d8 14 ♘e5 ♖a5 15 ♘xc6+ bxc6 16 ♘c3 ♔e7 = Browne-Smyslov, Las Palmas IZ 1982.

a2) 10...♗f5 11 ♘b5 (this aggressive sortie doesn't seem to lead anywhere but on the other hand even after the stronger 11 0-0 White also obtains very little, for example 11...a4 12 ♖fd1 0-0 13 ♗e1 ♖fe8 14 e3 with equality, J.Horvath-Landenbergue, Mitropa Cup 1990) 11...0-0-0 12 ♖c1 (or 12 0-0 ♗xd2 13 ♘xd2 ♖he8 14 ♗f3 g5!? 15 ♖fe1 ♘b4 16 ♘a3 ♖d6 17 ♘f1 ♘e4 18 ♘e3 ♗d7 with roughly equal chances, Agzamov-Taimanov, USSR 1981) 12...♗xd2+ 13 ♘xd2 ♖he8 14 e3 ♖e7 15 ♘f3 = Sosonko-Taimanov, Wijk aan Zee 1981.

b) 10 0-0 ♗g4 11 ♗e3 and then:

b1) 11...a4 12 ♖c1 ♗a5 (on 12...♗d6 Cserna gives 13 ♘c3 ♖a5 14 ♗g5 a3 15 b3 with an edge for White) 13 ♘e5! ♗xe2 14 ♘xc6 bxc6 15 ♖xc6 ♖a6 16 ♖xa6 ♗xa6 17 ♘c3 a3 18 b4! ♗xb4 19 ♘xd5 ♘xd5 20 ♗xd5 0-0 21 ♖b1 ♗e7 22 ♖c1 ♗d6 23 ♖c3 ♖d8 24 ♗f3 ♖b8 25 ♗c1 ♔f8 26 ♔g2 ♖b1 and now rather than 27 ♗e4 ♖b4 ½-½ Cserna-Sunye Neto, Luanda 1983, Cserna suggests 27 h4!, when White has some winning chances after both 27...♖b4 28 ♖xa3 ♖c4 29 ♖xa6 ♖xc1 30 ♗d5! and 27...♗b7 28 ♗xb7 ♖xb7 29 ♗xa3 ♗xa3 30 ♖xa3.

b2) 11...♘e4 12 h3 ♗xf3 13 exf3!? (13 ♗xf3 f5 14 a3 ♗d6 15 ♘d2 ♘e7 = Taimanov) 13...♘f6 14 a3 ♗e7 15 ♘c3 ♘d8!? 16 f4 c6 17 f5! ± Burger-Taimanov, Budapest 1982.

9...0-0

Black intends to place his queen actively at h5, but permits White a broad centre. This is much more ambitious than the other option 9...♕e4, when after 10 ♕xe4 ♘xe4 White has a choice:

a) 11 ♗xb4 axb4 12 ♘bd2 ♘xd2 13 ♔xd2 ♗d7 14 ♖hc1 ♔e7 15 e3 ♖a7 16 ♘e1 ♖ha8 17 ♘d3 ♖xa2 18 ♖ab1 ♖2a4 19 ♘c5 ♖4a7 20 ♘xb7

♖xb7 21 ♗xc6 ♗xc6 22 ♖xc6 ♔d7 = Adamski-Sydor, Gdynia 1982.

b) 11 a3 with a further branch:

b1) 11...♗d6 and then:

b11) 12 ♗f4 a4! 13 ♘e5 ♘xd4! 14 ♗xe4 ♘b3 (14...f5 looks more accurate, as it avoids White's alternative on move 16) 15 ♖a2 f5!? 16 ♗d3 (16 ♗f3 is certainly worth investigating, e.g. 16...g5 17 ♗h5+ ♔f8 18 ♘f7 gxf4 19 ♘xh8 ♘c1 and now 20 ♖a1 ♘b3 is a repetition, but White might try 20 ♘c3, when Black would have to go for 20...♘xa2 21 ♘xa2 ♗e5 22 ♘f7 ♗xb2 with an unclear position) 16...g5 17 ♗b5+ c6 18 ♘xc6 gxf4 19 ♘e5+ ♔e7 20 gxf4 ♖g8 21 ♗c4 b5 with unclear play, Groszpeter-Barlov, Sochi 1984.

b12) 12 ♗e3! (intending ♘e5) 12...♘f6 13 ♘c3 a4 14 0-0 ♘d5 15 ♗d2 ♘a5 16 e4 ♘xc3 17 ♗xc3 ♘b3 18 ♖ad1 and White is better, Gligorić-Barlov, Yugoslav Ch 1986.

b2) 11...♘xd2 12 ♘bxd2 ♗e7 13 ♖c1 ♗d8!? (the beginning of a series of interesting manoeuvres; the game Portisch-Timman, Nikšić 1983 continued 13...a4 14 ♘c4 ♗d8 15 0-0 0-0 16 ♖fd1 ♘a5 17 ♘xa5 ♖xa5 18 ♘e5 c6 19 ♘c4 ♖a7 20 ♔f1 with just an edge for White) 14 ♘e4 ♘e7 15 ♘e5 ♘f5 16 e3 ♔e7 17 ♖c2 ♘d6 18 ♘c5 f6 19 ♘ed3 ♖a7! 20 ♔e2 b6 21 ♘e4 ♗a6 22 ♖hc1 ± Summerscale-Bell, British League (4NCL) 1996.

10 ♘c3 ♕h5 11 a3

Browne-Smyslov, Tilburg 1982 varied with 11 ♗f4 ♘d5 12 0-0 ♘xf4 13 gxf4 ♖d8 14 e3 f6 15 ♘e2 ♕f7 16 ♘g3 ♗f8 17 ♖ac1 ♘b4 18 ♕b1 c6 19 a3 ½-½.

11...♗xc3

Retreating the bishop is inferior:

a) 11...♗e7 transposes to note 'c2' to White's 7th move.

b) 11...♗d6 12 e4 ♖d8 13 ♕c4 e5 14 d5 ♘a7 15 h3 ♘e8 16 g4 ♕g6 17 ♘h4 ♕f6 18 ♘f5 ± De Boer-Van der Wiel, Arnhem/Amsterdam 1983.

12 ♗xc3 *(D)*

Dautov suggests 12 bxc3!? e5 13 e4 with a slight advantage for White.

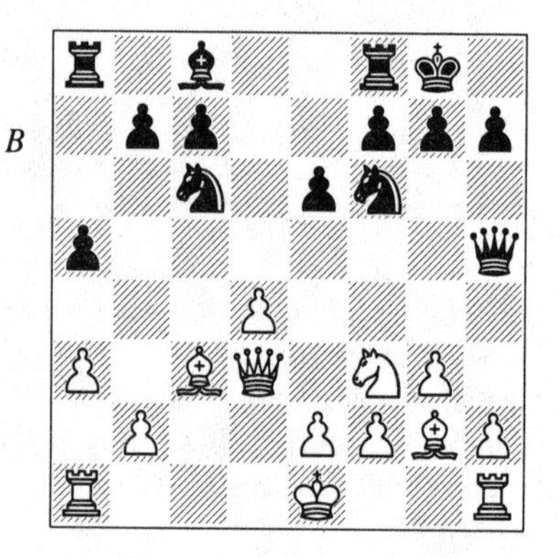

B

12...b6

Black might also try 12...♖d8 with the idea of ...e5, and after 13 ♕c2 we have:

a) 13...♘d5 14 ♖d1 f5 15 ♗d2 h6 16 e3 ♗d7 17 0-0 ♖ac8 18 ♘h4 ± Martin-Helmsen, corr. 1989-92.

b) 13...♕f5! resembles Romanishin's idea in the Nimzo-Indian (i.e. 1 d4 ♘f6 2 c4 e6 3 ♘c3 ♗b4 4 ♕c2 d5 5 cxd5 ♕xd5 6 ♘f3 ♕f5!?). If White exchanges queens and thus doubles Black's f-pawn, White will have a rather solid position with the bishop-pair but Black obtains very good control of the centre. 14 ♖c1 (14 ♕xf5 exf5 15 0-0 ♗e6 16 ♖ac1 ♗d5 = Dautov) 14...♕xc2 15 ♖xc2 ♗d7 16 0-0 ♘e7 17 ♘e5 ♗a4 18 ♖cc1 ♘fd5 19 ♗d2 ♘c6 20 ♘xc6 ♗xc6 21 ♖c5 a4 22 ♖fc1 ± Akopian-Smyslov, Moscow 1992.

13 0-0 ♗a6 14 ♕c2 ♘e7 15 ♖fe1

15 b4!? has been suggested by Tukmakov.

15...c5 16 ♕b3

16 e4 cxd4 17 ♗xd4 also leaves White with a pleasant advantage – Dautov.

16...♘ed5 17 e4 ♘xc3 18 bxc3 cxd4 19 cxd4 ♕b5 20 ♕e3!

White has a slight advantage, Tukmakov-Smyslov, Rostov-on-Don 1993.

5 4 ♗d2: The Popular 4...♕e7

1 d4 ♘f6 2 c4 e6 3 ♘f3 ♗b4+ 4 ♗d2 ♕e7 *(D)*

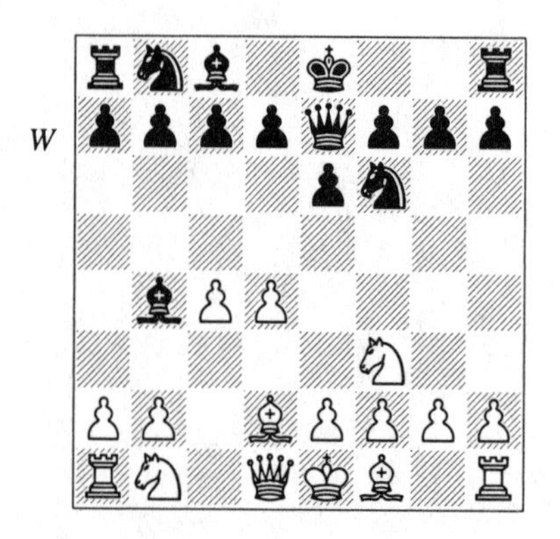

4...♕e7 has become Black's most popular option. Black doesn't yet commit himself to ...a5 and also postpones the exchange of the dark-squared bishops to a moment more favourable to him. Furthermore it prepares a set-up with pawns on d6 and e5.

Typical pawn structures

White has advanced his pawn all the way to f5 to create an attack on the kingside. Often Black has to play ...f6 to prevent White from breaking up Black's king's shelter. Then White can try to advance his g- and h-pawns, with quite a potent attack. Black should

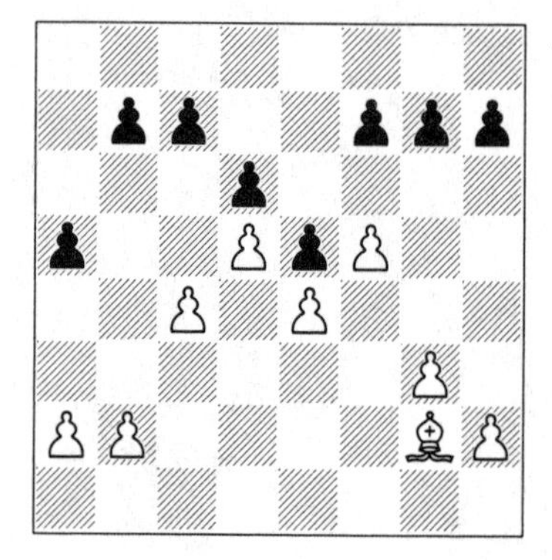

seek counterplay on the queenside involving the pawn-breaks ...c6 and/or ...b5. Black can also be quite content if he manages to obtain pawns on f6 and g5 with the white g-pawn on g4. White's light-squared bishop would then be a terrible piece in the ending and often Black can successfully defend the kingside.

In the next diagram White has settled for another strategy, namely a queenside advance, and Black has countered with the move ...c6. Black would then like to implement the pawn exchanges ...axb4, axb4 and ...cxd5, cxd5, when he then would play ...♘c7 and use the square b5 as a springboard to obtaining a nice outpost on d4. White on the other hand often exchanges on

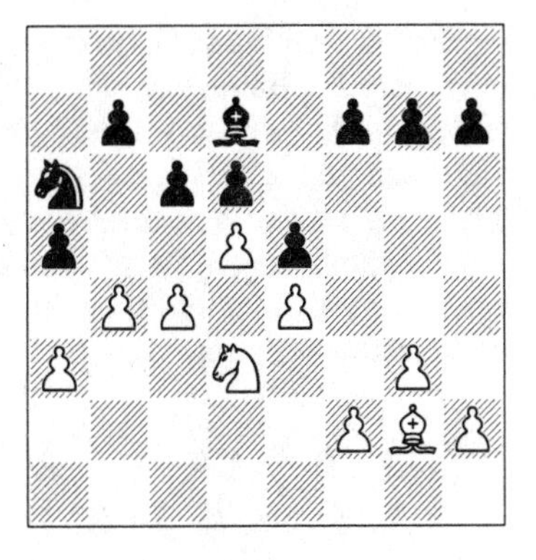

c6 (before Black is permitted the preceding sequence) or chooses to recapture on d5 with the e-pawn, which results in a set-up considered in the following diagram.

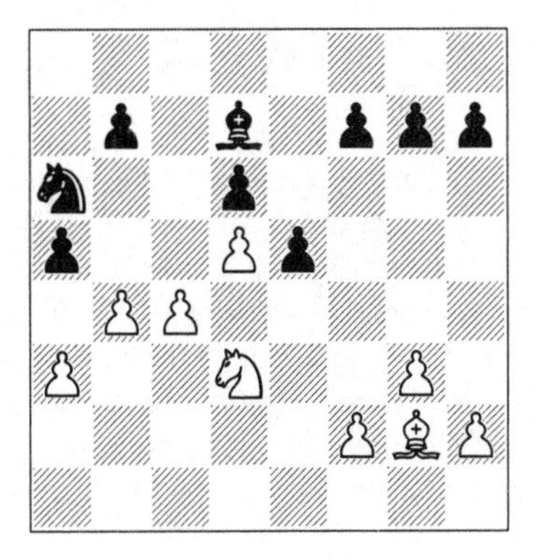

Here Black has better control of the centre, but White has good chances of creating a passed pawn with c5.

Planning for White

As the reader may have noticed from the pawn structures, White basically has two plans. White has a space advantage and thus a very logical plan is to advance the pawns on the queenside. The following position is a very typical result from this strategy:

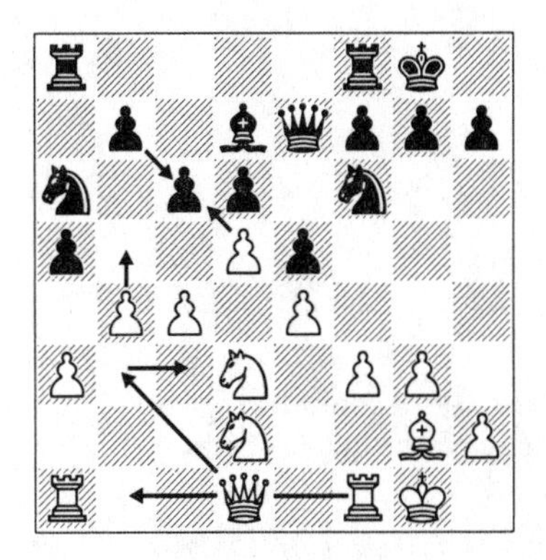

White would have liked to carry out the c5 advance, so Black has made this less attractive by countering with ...c6, and hopes to exchange pawns on b4 and on d5. If White takes back with the c-pawn on d5, then Black's knight is brought into play with ...♘c7-b5. Therefore a good plan for White is to exchange pawns on c6 and then transfer the queen to c3 via b3. White could then follow up with ♖fb1 preparing to get a passed pawn with b5.

Another very popular plan is to advance the f-pawn (*see diagram on the next page*). Very often all the way to f5, and if allowed even sacrificing it with f6 in order to disrupt the black kingside. Black would almost inevitably have to defend with ...f6, and then White can try to advance his g- and h-pawns to launch an attack. With his increased advantage in space, White can

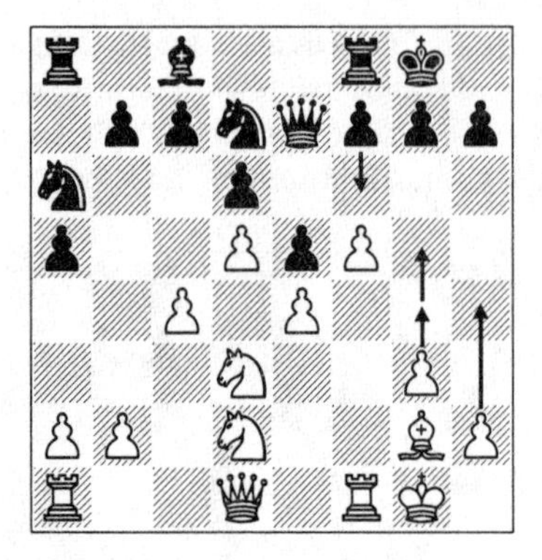

also try to combine the two plans and play on the queenside as well.

Planning for Black

Quite logically, Black's planning varies a little depending on what White aims for, but in general, when the centre has become closed, Black would like to break up with ...c6 and seek counterplay on the queenside.

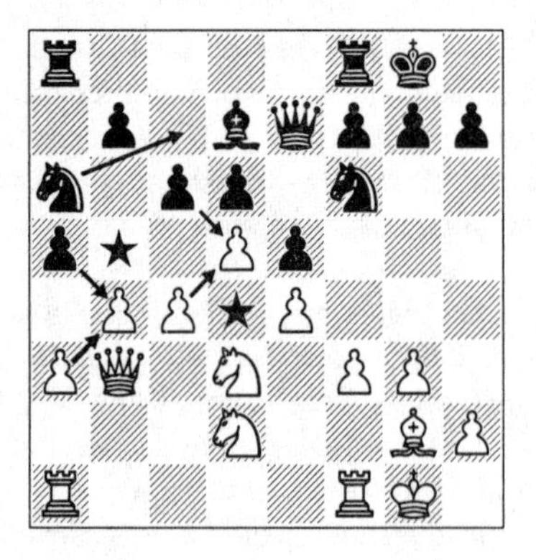

This is in fact a repetition of the first diagram in the section 'Planning for White', but with White having played ♕b3. This did in fact occur in a game Skembris-Beliavsky, Yugoslav Cht (Igalo) 1994, and now Black got a good game by exchanging on d5. White took back with the c-pawn, although taking with the e-pawn was probably preferable, and then Black exchanged on b4 followed by ...♘c7.

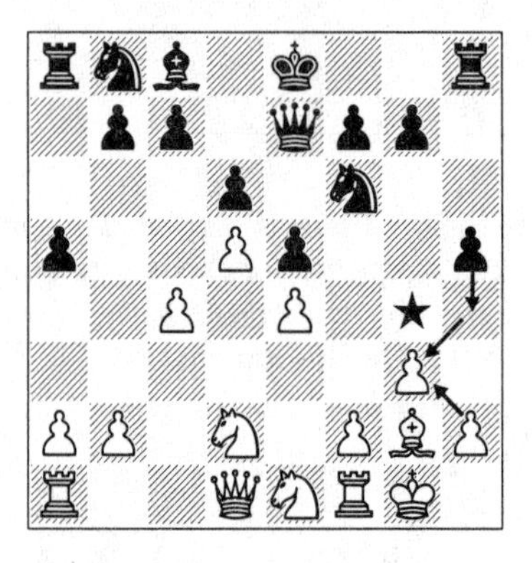

Another very interesting plan for Black when the centre is closed is to postpone castling and instead advance the h-pawn. If permitted Black can then play ...h5-h4xg3 to soften up White's king's shelter. Black would then have an open h-file and the g4-square is attractive to one of the minor pieces.

Quick Summary

As early as move 5 White has a number of alternatives, but most of them are rather innocuous. 5 a3 (Line A), 5 e3 (Line B) are rarely seen, and Black seems to equalize comfortably in both lines. 5 ♘c3 (Line C) is more logical and after 5...0-0 6 ♕c2 White starts fighting for control of the e4-square. White's main continuation is without doubt 5 g3 (Line D). Black has two main options, 5...0-0 (Line D1) and 5...♘c6 (Line D2). 5...0-0 is at first sight the most logical move, but allows White his favourite formation after 6 ♗g2 ♗xd2+ 7 ♕xd2 (Line D12) – 7 ♘bxd2 is Line D11. White would then be ready to put the knight on c3, and thus obtain good central control. 5...♘c6 seeks to avoid this, as after 6 ♗g2 ♗xd2+ 7 ♕xd2 Black can play 7...♘e4. Therefore White has to content himself with 7 ♘bxd2, and after 7...d6 8 0-0 Black again has two main continuations. He can either simply play 8...0-0 (Line D221) or first try to slow down White's queenside advance with 8...a5 (Line D222). The latter is in practice the most popular, and it seems to suit a wide variety of temperaments. The main line runs 9 e4 e5 10 d5 ♘b8 11 ♘e1, and here Black has a choice between the sharp 11...h5!? and the more conventional 11...0-0 leading to a very interesting strategic battle. White has a further option, after 5...♘c6, in 6 ♘c3 (Line D21). White aims to take advantage of the slightly unnatural placement of Black's knight on c6, either by threatening to play d5 at some stage or by gaining the bishop-pair. Black usually chooses between 6...d5 (Line D211) and 6...♗xc3 (Line D212). 6...♗xc3 seems the safest option for Black, and after 7 ♗xc3 ♘e4 White has a choice between 8 ♕c2 and 8 ♖c1. 8 ♕c2 allows Black to liquidate to a rather peaceful ending by 8...♘xc3 9 ♕xc3 ♕b4, and, although this should be a little better for White, it is not to everybody's taste. The main line after 8 ♖c1 continues 8...0-0 9 ♗g2 d6 10 d5, when Black can play 10...♘d8 or 10...♘b8 (or this same choice after a preliminary piece exchange on c3). The theoretical evaluation fluctuates between equality and a slight advantage for White.

The Theory of 4 ♗d2 ♕e7

1 d4 ♘f6 2 c4 e6 3 ♘f3 ♗b4+ 4 ♗d2 ♕e7

We shall now look at the following options for White:

5 ♕c2 (preparing e4) is also seen once in a while; Black can then choose between:

a) 5...0-0?! 6 e4 d5 (since Black does not have time to set up pawns on d6 and e5, he has to go for this; otherwise White would gain even more space by playing e5) 7 e5 ♘e4 8 ♗xb4 ♕xb4+ 9 ♘c3 (if White is allowed to develop quietly with ♗d3 followed by 0-0 he will clearly be better, so it is understandable that Black now tries something active) 9...c5 10 a3 ♕a5 11 dxc5 ♘c6 (11...♘xc3? would be desirable but White has the strong reply 12 b4!) 12 ♖c1 f5 13 exf6 ♘xf6 14 ♕d2! ♖d8?! (14...♕xc5 is perhaps better, but it is clear that White enjoys a large advantage after 15 cxd5 ♖d8

16 b4 ♕e7 17 d6! ♖xd6 18 ♕a2 due to Black's isolated e-pawn) 15 ♘b5! ♕xd2+ (or 15...dxc4 16 ♕xa5 ♘xa5 17 ♘e5 and White wins a pawn) 16 ♘xd2 ♗d7 17 ♗e2 and Black has no compensation for the sacrificed pawn, Shabalov-Nenashev, USSR 1988.

b) 5...♘c6 6 ♘c3 d5 7 e3 0-0 8 a3 ♗xc3 9 ♗xc3 with advantage to White, Petrosian-Agzamov, USSR Ch (Moscow) 1983.

c) 5...♗xd2+ (this is probably best; Black voluntarily exchanges on d2 now because White's queen is committed too early) 6 ♘bxd2 d6 7 e4 e5 8 d5 0-0 9 ♗e2 ♘h5 10 g3 ♗h3! 11 0-0-0 g6 12 ♔b1 a5 13 ♘h4 ♘g7 14 ♗f1 ♗d7 15 ♘g2 ♘a6 16 h4 c6 (it is now evident that Black's attack will become the more dangerous) 17 ♗e2 cxd5 18 cxd5 ♘b4 19 ♕b3 ♘f5! and now that Black's only badly placed piece has joined in, he has a promising game, Dzhandzhgava-Ulybin, Simferopol 1988.

A)

5 a3 *(D)*

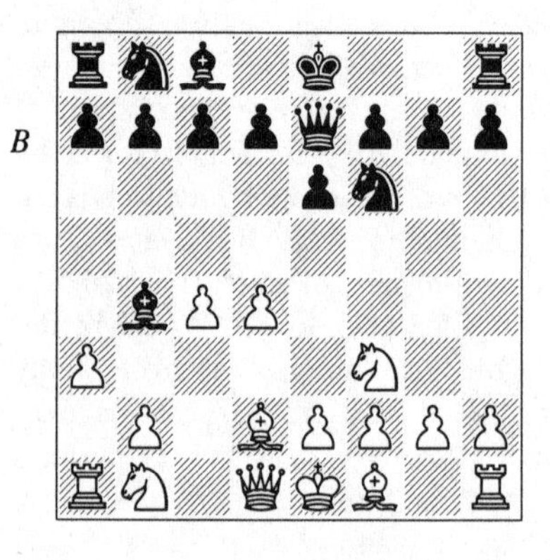

This can hardly be dangerous, given that Black often exchanges voluntarily on d2.

5...♗xd2+ 6 ♕xd2

6 ♘bxd2 is also possible, but is less consistent with White's strategy – particularly when he has wasted a move on a3. 6...d6 7 e4 (or 7 e3 0-0 8 ♕c2 e5 9 dxe5 dxe5 10 ♗e2 ♘c6 = Lichtenstein-Tartakower, Vienna 1928) 7...e5 8 d5 a5 (in Riazantsev-Osnos, St Petersburg 1997 Black castled straight away and White decided not to advance the pawns, but then Black had nothing to fear: 8...0-0 9 ♗d3 a5 10 b3 ♘a6 11 0-0 c6 12 ♕e2 g6 13 ♘e1 ♗d7 14 ♘c2 ♘h5 15 g3 ♘c5 =) 9 b4 0-0 10 g3 (comparing with Line D22, Black has practically won two tempi {he has not played ...♘c6 and ...♘b8}; still it is a rather closed position and Black can hardly exploit this advantage) 10...c6 11 ♗g2 cxd5 12 cxd5 ♗d7 13 0-0 axb4 14 axb4 ♖xa1 15 ♕xa1 ♘a6 16 ♖b1 ♗b5 17 ♗f1 ♗xf1 18 ♔xf1 ♕d7 19 ♕a5 ♖c8 = Lopez Colon-Vehi Bach, Spanish Cht (Oropesa del Mar) 1996.

6...d5

This seems to equalize right away.

The other option is 6...d6, which, though perfectly feasible, gives White more possibilities than the text-move: 7 ♘c3 0-0 8 e4 (worse is 8 g3 e5 9 dxe5 dxe5 10 ♗g2 ♖d8 11 ♕c2 ♘c6 12 e3 g6 13 0-0 ♗e6 14 b3 a5, when Black already has a comfortable position, M.Pytel-L.B.Hansen, Challes 1990) 8...e5 9 d5 a5 10 b3 ♘a6 11 ♗d3 ♗g4 12 ♕e3 ♘h5 13 0-0 ♘f4 14 ♗c2 ♔h8 15 ♘e1 (Black's pieces are occupying reasonably active squares but White is now ready to send them back) 15...g5 16 f3 ♗d7 17 g3 ♖g8 18 ♔h1 ♘h3 19 ♘d3 ♖af8 20 b4 with the better prospects for White, Osterman-Bönsch, Mitropa Cup (Bad Wörishofen) 1993.

7 e3 0-0 8 ♘c3 ♘bd7 9 ♗d3 dxc4 10 ♗xc4 e5

The game is equal, Fakhro-Valiente, Dubai OL 1986.

B)

5 e3 *(D)*

B

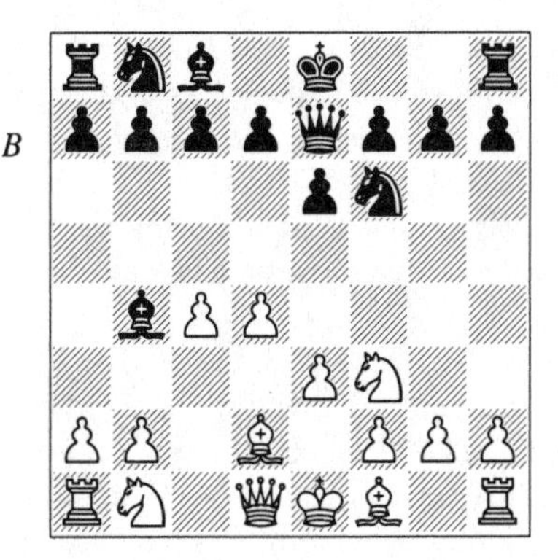

5...♗xd2+

This seems to be the easiest path to equality. Other possibilities:

a) 5...b6 and then:

a1) 6 ♗d3 ♗b7 7 ♕c2 ♗xd2+ 8 ♘bxd2 c5 9 0-0 ♘c6 10 a3 0-0 11 ♖ad1 g6 12 ♖fe1 ♖ac8 13 ♘e4 ♖fd8 (13...cxd4 14 exd4 d5 is probably also OK for Black) 14 d5 exd5 15 cxd5 ♘xe4 16 ♗xe4 ♘a5 = Marshall-Alekhine, New York (exhibition) 1929.

a2) 6 ♗xb4 (this is White's basic idea in playing 5 e3) 6...♕xb4+ 7 ♕d2 (this move is feasible now that the c4-pawn is defended) 7...♕xd2+ 8 ♘fxd2 (White wants to be able to play ♘c3; in Yuferov-Loginov, Kstovo 1994 White did not obtain any advantage after 8 ♘bxd2 ♗b7 9 ♗e2 d6 10 0-0 c5 11 ♖ac1 ½-½) 8...c5 9 dxc5 bxc5 10 ♘c3 ♔e7 (the careless 10...♗b7? would be a grave error in view of 11 ♘b5! winning material) 11 ♗e2 ♗b7 12 ♗f3 ♗xf3 13 ♘xf3 ♘c6 14 ♔e2 ♖hd8 15 ♖hd1 d6 16 b3 ♖d7 leading to equality, Spassky-Tal, USSR Ch (Moscow) 1973.

b) 5...0-0 6 ♗xb4 ♕xb4+ 7 ♕d2 ♕e7 (I suppose if Black wants to win it is not much fun playing 7...♕xd2+, although after 8 ♘bxd2 b6 9 ♗d3 ♗b7 10 e4 d6 11 0-0 ♘bd7 12 ♖fe1 e5 13 ♖ad1 ♖fe8 the position is about equal, Bönsch-Nikolac, Munich 1992) 8 ♘c3 d6 9 h3!? (Svidler-Antonio, Biel 1993 saw White develop more traditionally: 9 ♗e2 b6 10 0-0 ♗b7 11 ♕c2 e5 12 ♖fd1 ♘bd7 13 dxe5 dxe5 14 ♘d5 ♘xd5 15 cxd5 e4 16 ♘d4 ♘f6 17 d6 cxd6 18 ♘f5 ♕e5 19 ♘xd6 ♗d5 =) 9...e5 10 g4 exd4?! (perhaps Black should consider 10...♘c6!? with the idea of meeting 11 g5 by 11...exd4, when Black is fine after 12 ♘xd4 ♘xd4 13 ♕xd4 ♘d7, whilst 12 gxf6 dxc3 13 ♕xc3 ♕xf6 14 ♕xf6 gxf6 is certainly not a problem either) 11 ♘xd4 ♘a6 12 0-0-0 ♘c5 13 f3 (with this move White reinforces his control of the centre and restricts the scope of Black's pieces) 13...a6 14 ♖g1 ♔h8 15 g5 ♘g8 16 ♘d5 ♕d8 17 e4 with an advantage for White, Bönsch-Lutz, German Ch (Bad Neuenahr) 1991.

6 ♕xd2

6 ♘bxd2 d6 7 ♗e2 e5 8 0-0 0-0 9 ♖c1 c5!? 10 ♘b1 e4 11 ♘e1 b6 is fine for Black, Savon-Korchnoi, Tbilisi 1967.

6...0-0

In Mecking-Gipslis, Sousse IZ 1967, White obtained a good Benoni-type position after 6...c5 7 ♗e2 b6 8 ♘c3 0-0 9 0-0 ♗b7 10 d5 exd5 11 cxd5 d6 12 ♖ad1 a6 13 a4 ♘bd7 14 ♕c2 ♖fe8 15 ♖fe1 g6 16 e4, when Black was missing his dark-squared bishop.

7 ♘c3 d6 8 ♗e2 e5 9 d5 a5 10 0-0 ♘a6 11 b3 ♗f5 12 a3 ♘c5 13 ♕b2 ♘fe4

The position is equal, Tukmakov-Polugaevsky, USSR Ch 1969. White should try to advance on the queenside, but there is no real target, while Black has good control of the centre and the kingside.

C)

5 ♘c3 *(D)*

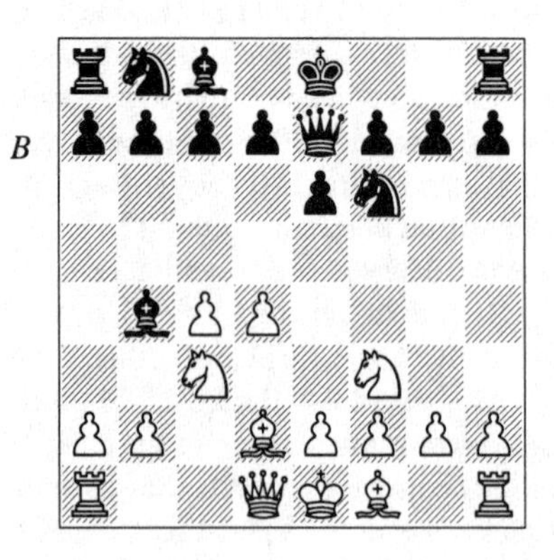

Black will, at some point, have to exchange his dark-squared bishop for this knight, thereby leaving White with an 'advantage' of having the bishop-pair. As compensation, Black should seek control of the central light squares, which is often accomplished by a queenside fianchetto.

5...0-0

5...b6 is seen less often but may in fact be the most accurate move-order, e.g. 6 e3 ♗b7 (6...♗xc3!? 7 ♗xc3 ♘e4 8 ♖c1 ♗b7 9 ♗d3 0-0 10 0-0 d6 11 ♘d2 ♘xc3 12 ♖xc3 c5 = Marshall-Capablanca, Berlin 1928) 7 ♗d3 0-0 8 0-0 c5 9 ♖c1 (9 a3 ♗xc3 10 ♗xc3 ♘e4 11 ♗xe4 ♗xe4 =) 9...d6 10 a3 ♗xc3 11 ♗xc3 ♘e4 12 b4 ♘xc3 13 ♖xc3 ♘d7 and Black has equalized, Browne-Weinstein, USA 1977.

6 ♕c2

White starts fighting for the e4-square. Other moves are less challenging:

a) 6 a3 ♗xc3 7 ♗xc3 b6 8 e3 ♘e4 9 ♕c2 ♗b7 10 ♗e2 d6 11 0-0 ♘d7 12 ♖fd1 a5 13 b4 ♘xc3 14 ♕xc3 ♖fe8?! (a 'mysterious' rook move; Larsen has been quite fond of moves like this, but he should have exchanged off into an endgame with 14...axb4 15 axb4 ♖xa1 16 ♖xa1 ♖a8 17 ♖xa8+ ♗xa8 18 ♕a1 ♕d8 19 ♕a7 ♕b8, or started operations on the kingside with 14...f5!?) 15 ♖ac1 gives White a small advantage since he is now ready to open the c-file with c5 at an appropriate moment, Dzindzichashvili-Larsen, Lone Pine 1980.

b) 6 g3 transposes to Line D1, note to White's 6th move.

c) 6 e3 d6 7 ♗e2 b6 8 0-0 ♗b7 9 ♕c2 ♘bd7 10 ♖ad1 ♗xc3 11 ♗xc3

♘e4 12 ♗e1 f5 = Vidmar-Nimzowitsch, New York 1927.

6...d6

A rather unusual but nonetheless interesting plan is 6...c5!? 7 a3 ♗xc3 8 ♗xc3 cxd4 9 ♘xd4 ♘a6 (worth considering is 9...♖d8!? intending to exchange off in the centre with ...d5) 10 g3 d5 11 cxd5 ♘xd5 12 ♗g2 e5! 13 ♘b3 and now rather than 13...♘xc3?! 14 ♕xc3 f6?! 15 ♘a5!, which left White clearly on top in Chernin-Klinger, San Bernardino 1991, Black should be able to keep the balance with 13...♖d8!, e.g. 14 0-0 ♗g4 15 h3 ♗h5 16 ♖fd1 ♘xc3 17 ♖xd8+ ♖xd8 18 ♕xc3 b6 =.

7 a3 ♗xc3 8 ♗xc3 ♘bd7

This is better than 8...♘c6 since in Podgaets-Kharitonov, USSR Ch 1983 the knight eventually had to go to d7 anyway, viz. 9 g3 a5 10 b3 e5 11 d5 ♘b8 12 ♗g2 ♘bd7 and then 13 ♘h4! ♘b6 14 ♗b2 ♘fd7 15 ♘f5 ♕f6 16 0-0 ♘c5 17 e4 ♗xf5 18 exf5 a4 19 b4 ♘b3 20 ♖ad1 ♘d7 21 f4 with a clear plus for White.

9 e3 b6 10 ♗d3 ♗b7 11 ♘g5 h6 12 ♘h7 ♘xh7 13 ♗xh7+ ♔h8 14 ♗e4 ♗xe4 15 ♕xe4 ♘f6 16 ♕f3

White has managed to exchange off the right minor pieces and is slightly better. The game Burmakin-V.Ikonnikov, Werfen 1996 continued 16...a5 17 0-0 d5 18 ♖ac1 c6 19 ♕e2 ♕d7 and now White should play 20 ♖c2!? intending ♖fc1, ♗e1 and f3 restricting Black's knight.

D)

5 g3 *(D)*

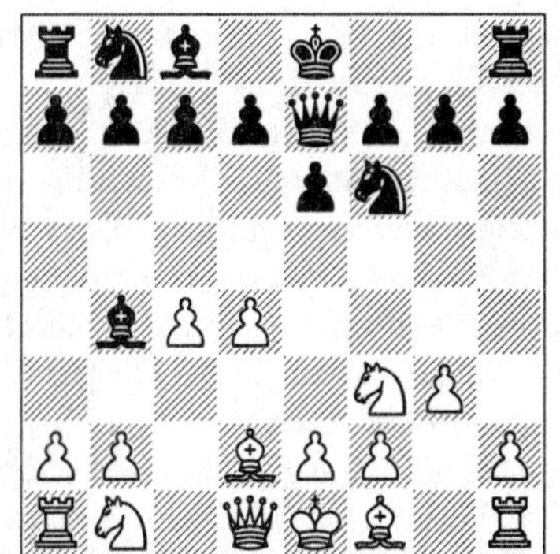
B

A standard plan for Black is to advance his centre pawns by ...d6 and ...e5, and so it is very logical to fianchetto the light-squared bishop in an attempt to control the central light squares. We shall now consider two main plans for Black. First we look at 5...0-0, which appears to be the most logical move. Black gets his king to safety before undertaking any action in the centre. 5...♘c6 is the other major option for Black. The knight does not seem to be very well placed on c6 but it helps to prepare the central advance and also has the point that Black is now ready to exchange on d2 without allowing White to recapture with the queen (for more explanation see Line D22).

Before we continue, let us take a look at some of the lesser variations:

a) 5...♗xd2+ 6 ♕xd2 may transpose to Chapter 3 after, for instance, 6...d5 or 6...0-0, while 6...♘e4 7 ♕c2 ♕b4+ 8 ♘bd2 ♘xd2 9 ♘xd2 ♕e7 10 ♗g2 d6 11 0-0 e5 12 e3 0-0 13 c5! is better for White, Gligorić-Wirthensohn, Lucerne OL 1982.

b) 5...♘e4 6 ♗g2 ♘xd2 7 ♘bxd2 c5 (7...d6 intending ...e5 is worth considering but quite complicated: 8 ♕a4+ ♘c6 9 d5 exd5 10 cxd5 is not winning directly as Black has 10...♕e4! threatening ...♗xd2+ but after 11 0-0 ♕xd5, Black must be ready for either 12 ♘e5 or 12 ♘g5!?) 8 a3 ♗xd2+ 9 ♕xd2 d6 10 0-0 0-0 11 ♖fd1 ♘c6 12 ♕e3 ♗d7 13 ♖ab1 ♖fd8 14 b4 cxd4 15 ♘xd4 ♘xd4 16 ♖xd4 ♗c6 17 ♖bd1 ♖d7 18 ♕b3 with a nice space advantage for White, Farago-Forintos, Hungarian Ch 1981.

D1)

5...0-0 *(D)*

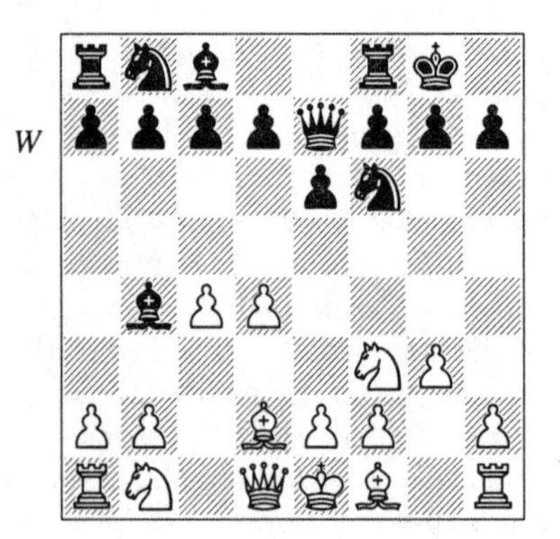

6 ♗g2

6 ♘c3 is a position that often arises from the move-order 5 ♘c3 0-0 6 g3. Black may now choose between:

a) 6...d5 7 a3 ♗xc3 8 ♗xc3 and then:

a1) 8...♘bd7 9 ♗g2 (9 ♗b4 c5 10 dxc5 a5! 11 ♗c3 ♘xc5 is satisfactory for Black) 9...dxc4 10 ♘d2 ♘d5 11 ♘xc4 ♘xc3 12 bxc3 e5 13 0-0 exd4?! (it does not seem right to open the c-file for White; 13...♖e8 or even 13...c5!? is better) 14 cxd4 ♘b6 15 ♘a5! with an edge for White, Rajković-Nikolac, Yugoslavia 1986.

a2) 8...♖d8!? 9 ♗g2 (9 ♖c1 is Rajković's suggestion) 9...a5 (9...dxc4 is perhaps an easier path to equality, e.g. 10 ♕a4 ♗d7 11 ♕xc4 ♗c6 12 ♖c1 ♘bd7 13 0-0 ♘b6 14 ♗b4! ♕e8 15 ♕c2 ♖ac8 = Vladimirov-Oll, Moscow 1989) 10 0-0 c6 11 ♕b3 ♘bd7 12 ♖fd1 ♘e4 13 ♗e1 ♘d6 (13...b6!? is a possible improvement) 14 c5 ♘c4 15 ♕c2 a4 16 e4 with the better game for White, Vyzhmanavin-Korchnoi, Moscow 1994.

b) 6...♗xc3 7 ♗xc3 ♘e4 8 ♖c1 ♘xc3 (or 8...d6 9 ♗g2 ♘d7 10 0-0 ♘xc3 11 ♖xc3 e5 12 dxe5 dxe5 13 ♕c2 ♘f6 14 ♘d2 c6 ½-½ Solozhenkin-Oll, St Petersburg 1993) 9 ♖xc3 d6 10 ♗g2 e5 11 0-0 e4!? (this is a new idea; previously Black kept the tension in the centre with 11...♖e8 or 11...♘c6) 12 ♘d2 f5 13 ♘b3 c6 14 f3 exf3 15 ♖cxf3!? ♖e8 16 ♖1f2 ♘a6 17 ♕f1! with the better prospects for White, D.Gurevich-Dzindzichashvili, USA Ch (Modesto) 1995.

6...♗xd2+

Black exchanges bishops before it is too late. This is an unavoidable preliminary action if Black wishes to set up pawns on d6 and e5. The alternatives are:

a) 6...d5 and now:

a1) 7 0-0 ♘c6 (7...♗xd2 8 ♕xd2 transposes to Line B of Chapter 3 but

White can also play 8 ♘bxd2 transposing to Line D11) 8 cxd5 (this is more accurate than 8 ♗g5 dxc4 9 ♘bd2 ♗xd2 10 ♘xd2 h6! 11 ♗xf6 ♕xf6 12 e3 e5 13 d5 ♘e7 14 ♘xc4 ♖d8 15 e4 c6 = T.Petrosian-Andersson, Tilburg 1982) 8...exd5 9 ♗g5 h6 10 ♗xf6 ♕xf6 11 a3 ♗a5 12 b4 ♗b6 13 e3 ♗g4 14 ♘bd2 ♖fd8 15 h3 ♗f5 16 ♘b3 with the better game for White, Gheorghiu-Andersson, Lucerne OL 1982.

a2) 7 ♕c2 ♘e4 (if 7...♘c6, White is able to keep Black away from e4 with 8 a3 ♗xd2+ 9 ♘bxd2; Lin Ta – Ma Hong-Ding, Chinese Ch 1986 continued 9...e5 10 dxe5 ♘xe5 11 cxd5 ♘xd5 12 ♘xe5 ♕xe5 13 0-0 c6 14 ♘c4 ♕h5 15 ♖fe1! ♗h3 16 e4 ♗xg2 17 ♔xg2 ♘c7 18 ♘d6 ♘e6 19 ♖ad1 ♖ab8 20 f4 ±) 8 a3 ♗xd2+ 9 ♘bxd2 ♘xd2 10 ♘xd2 ♖d8 11 0-0 a5 (Black could also try to solve his central problems with 11...dxc4 12 ♕xc4 c5!? but after 13 ♖ac1! ♘a6 14 ♘b3 cxd4 15 ♘xd4 e5 16 ♘b5 ♗e6 17 ♕e4 ♗d5 18 ♕e3 ♗xg2 19 ♔xg2 b6 White has a slightly more active position – Andersson) 12 e3 c6 13 ♕c3 a4 14 e4 with a small advantage to White, Andersson-Kurajica, Banja Luka 1979.

b) 6...♘c6 is dubious since White is able to recapture with the queen on d2 (compare with Line D22) thereby obtaining the ideal position of the pieces, for example 7 0-0 ♗xd2 8 ♕xd2 d6 9 ♘c3 e5 10 ♘d5! ♕d8 11 ♖ad1 ♖e8 12 dxe5 ♘xe5 13 ♘xe5 dxe5 14 ♕a5! ♘xd5 15 cxd5 ♕d6 16 ♖c1 and White's strong d-pawn combined with pressure down the c-file gives White a clear advantage, Pinter-De Guzman, Manila OL 1992.

Returning to the position after 6...♗xd2+ *(D)*:

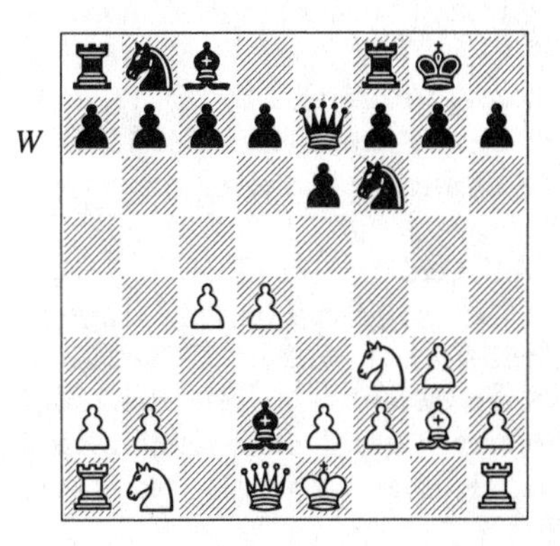

White has the following options:

D11)

7 ♘bxd2 d5

This is one of two respected strategies for Black. The other one involves putting his pawns on d6 and e5: 7...d6 8 0-0 (8 ♘f1 anticipates an advance of the e-pawn and for instance after 8...e5 9 ♘e3 White is ready to take advantage of the weaknesses on d5 and f5, but Black can change strategy and instead attempt to play for control of e4, for example 8...♘bd7 9 ♘e3 ♘e4 10 0-0 f5 11 ♘e1 ♘df6 12 f3 ♘g5 13 ♕d2 h6 14 ♖c1 c5 15 ♘1c2 b6 16 ♖fd1 ♗b7 = Korchnoi-Andersson, Hastings 1971/2) 8...e5 with the following options for White:

a) 9 e3 h6 (after 9...♘c6 Browne would probably have continued 10 d5

♘d8 11 b4 although White would rather have his pawn on e4 {compare with Line D22}) 10 ♕b3 (the careless 10 b4? loses material after 10...e4 11 ♘e1 ♗g4; this shows the point of 9...h6, preventing 11 ♘g5 in reply to 10...e4) 10...e4 11 ♘e1 c5 12 f3 exf3 13 ♘exf3 ♘c6 14 ♕c3 ♖e8 15 ♖ae1 ♗g4 ∓ Browne-Kurajica, Banja Luka 1979.

b) 9 ♕c2 c6 10 e4 ♗g4 11 h3 ♗xf3 12 ♘xf3 c5 13 d5 ♘bd7 14 ♘d2 g6 15 ♖ae1 ♘h5 16 ♕b3 b6 17 ♕e3 ♖ae8 18 ♕h6 ♔h8 19 ♘f3 ♕f6 20 h4 ♕g7 21 ♕xg7+ ♘xg7 with a roughly equal ending, Rogers-P.Nikolić, Manila OL 1992.

c) 9 e4 c5!? (this move forces White to close the centre because any exchange would give Black a nice outpost on d4; note that 9...♘c6 transposes to Line D22) 10 d5 ♗g4 (Black intends to exchange his bishop for a knight, hoping that the closed nature of the position will prove more comfortable for the knights but it is probably not enough for full equality) 11 ♕c2 (or 11 h3 ♗xf3 12 ♕xf3 ♘bd7 13 ♕e2 g6 14 ♖ae1 ♖ae8 15 h4 ♘h5 16 ♗h3 with an edge for White, Inkiov-Skembris, Athens 1983) 11...♗xf3 12 ♘xf3 ♘bd7 13 ♘d2 g6 14 f4 ♘h5 15 ♗h3?! (15 f5 maintains a slight advantage) 15...exf4 16 gxf4 f5 17 ♕c3 ♕h4! with good counterplay for Black, L.Spasov-Inkiov, Plovdiv 1984.

8 0-0 *(D)*

8...b6

8...c5 is an attempt to solve Black's central problems at once, but White develops a small initiative after, for

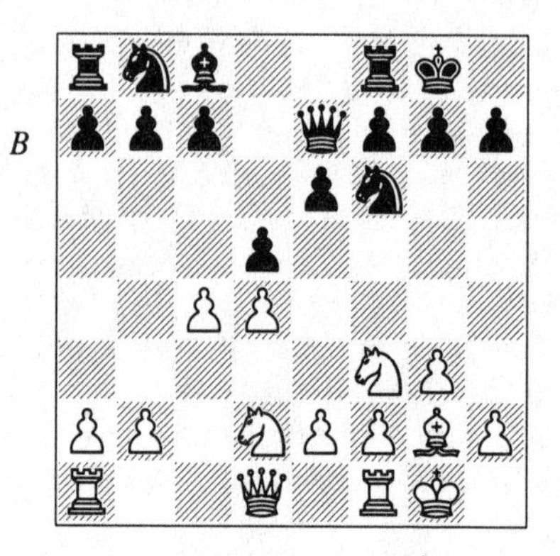

B

instance, 9 cxd5 ♘xd5 10 e4 ♘f6 11 dxc5 ♕xc5 12 ♖c1.

9 ♖c1 ♗b7 10 ♘e5

White activates his knight and increases the scope of his light-squared bishop.

10 cxd5 exd5 produces a more static pawn-centre and might also be sufficient for an advantage, for example 11 ♕a4 a5? (afterwards I.Sokolov suggested 11...♘a6 intending ...c5 as an improvement) 12 ♖fe1 c6? (this not only blocks the bishop's diagonal but also weakens the b6-pawn, better is 12...♖c8 intending ...♘bd7 or ...c5) 13 e4 ♘xe4 14 ♘xe4 dxe4 15 ♘e5 f6 16 ♕b3+ ♔h8 17 ♘d3 ♕d8 18 ♗xe4 a4 19 ♕c2 f5 20 ♗f3 ♕xd4 21 ♘f4 with a winning position for White, Salov-I.Sokolov, Amsterdam 1996. Although Black is a pawn ahead, he has too many weaknesses.

10...♘bd7?!

Black should not exchange this knight. Kramnik does not think that Black can equalize at this stage but anyway offers the following improvements for Black:

a) 10...c5 11 dxc5 bxc5 12 ♘b3 ±.

b) 10...♘a6! 11 cxd5 exd5 12 ♖e1 c5 13 e4! dxe4 14 ♘xe4 ♘xe4 15 ♗xe4 ♗xe4 16 ♖xe4 cxd4 17 ♕xd4 ♘c5 18 ♖e3 ±.

11 ♘xd7 ♕xd7 12 ♕c2 ♖ac8 13 c5!

This is the point. White's light-squared bishop is much stronger than its rather pathetic counterpart.

13...c6 14 ♕a4 ♗a8 15 e4

White has a clear advantage, Kramnik-J.Polgar, Dortmund 1997.

D12)

7 ♕xd2 *(D)*

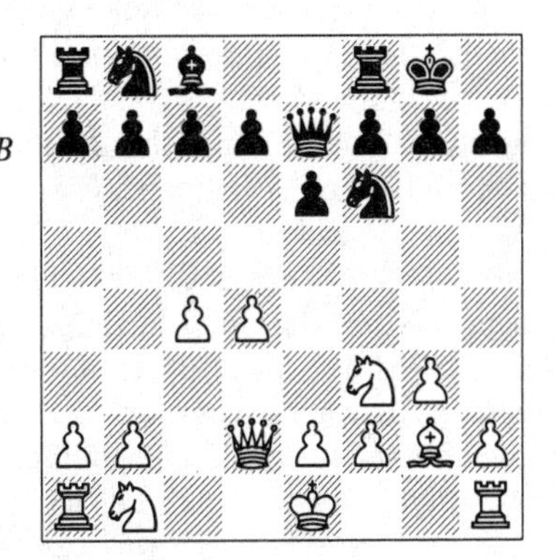

7...d6

Other possibilities:

a) 7...♘e4 8 ♕c2 f5 (with ...♘c6 played instead of ...0-0, Black could play 8...♕b4+ but here it is simply met by 9 ♘bd2 ♘xd2 10 ♘xd2 with a slight advantage for White) 9 0-0 d6 and now:

a1) 10 ♘c3 ♘xc3 11 ♕xc3 ♘c6 (11...♘d7 intending ...e5 is probably better) 12 d5 ♘d8 13 dxe6 ♘xe6 14 b4 ♗d7 15 ♘d2 ♗c6 16 e4. The possibility of a minority attack on the queen-side, as signalled by White's 14th move, promises him the better game. Vyzhmanavin-Balashov, USSR Ch (Lvov) 1984 continued 16...♕f6 17 ♕xf6 ♖xf6 18 f4 (White is building up a nice space advantage) 18...a5 19 b5 ♗xe4 20 ♘xe4 fxe4 21 ♗xe4 ♘c5 22 ♗d5+ ♔f8 23 ♖ae1 ±. Black has a well-posted knight on c5 but White's centralized bishop is even better.

a2) 10 ♘e1!? intends to bring the knight to d3 and also introduces the idea of chasing away Black's knight with f3 followed by a central action with e4.

a3) 10 ♘h4 g5 11 ♘f3 ♘d7 12 ♘e1 (in comparison with the suggestion in 'a2', Black has won a few tempi, but these have been used to make attacking gestures on the kingside – from White's point of view, it should of course be looked upon as a weakness, but I prefer Black) 12...♘ef6 13 ♘c3 ♘g4 14 ♘f3 (during the last four moves, the only thing White has managed is to develop his knight to c3; paradoxically, though, White is still ahead in development) 14...♕g7 15 e4 f4 16 ♘b5 fxg3 17 hxg3 ♘b8 18 e5 a6 19 ♘a3 (19 ♘c3? is wrong on account of 19...dxe5 20 ♕e4 exd4 21 ♘xd4 e5, when 22 ♕d5+ ♔h8 23 ♘e6 does not work because of 23...♕h6) 19...dxe5 20 ♕e4 h5 21 ♘xe5 ♘xe5 22 ♕xe5 ♕xe5 23 dxe5 ♘d7 with an approximately equal game, Polugaevsky-Ree, Amsterdam 1981.

b) 7...d5 8 0-0 ♘bd7 9 ♖c1 c6 10 ♕e3 ♖e8 transposes to Chapter 3.

8 ♘c3 e5

The alternatives do not look too bright:

a) 8...c6 9 0-0-0!? (a little unusual but quite interesting) 9...♖e8 10 e4 e5 11 h3! (White is playing to restrict the scope of Black's pieces) 11...♘a6 12 ♖he1 ♗d7 13 g4 ♖ad8 14 dxe5! dxe5 15 ♕d6 h6 16 ♖d2 ♕xd6 17 ♖xd6 ♖e7 18 ♖ed1 ♖de8 19 ♘h4 ± Lilienthal-Smyslov, USSR Ch 1940.

b) 8...c5 9 dxc5 dxc5 10 ♘e5! (a fine move, which assures that Black is not able to develop sensibly) 10...♕c7 11 ♕f4 ♘bd7 12 ♘g6! e5 13 ♘e7+ ♔h8 14 ♕f3 e4 15 ♕f4 ♕xf4 16 gxf4 ♘b6 17 ♘xc8 ♖axc8 18 b3 ♖ce8 19 e3 with a substantial advantage for White, Portisch-Parma, Portorož/Ljubljana 1985. Black is tied to the defence of the pawn on e4, while White can simply castle and centralize his rooks.

9 0-0 *(D)*

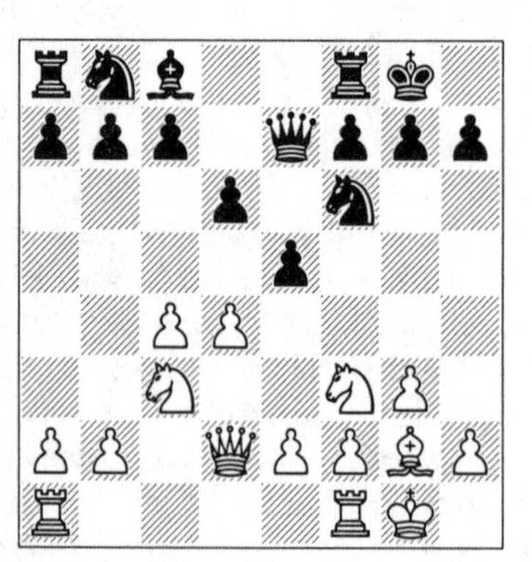

9...♖e8

This is a good waiting move, which intends to provoke White into playing e4, since Black may be planning to advance his e-pawn. Alternatives for Black are:

a) 9...♗g4 and then:

a1) 10 d5 (Black can be quite happy with this, as he often loses two tempi by playing ...♘c6 and ...♘b8) 10...a5 11 ♘e1 ♘a6 12 e4 c6 13 ♘d3 cxd5 14 cxd5 ♘d7 15 f3 ♗h5 16 ♘d1 ♘ac5 17 ♘xc5 ♘xc5 18 ♘e3 f6 19 ♖fc1 ♕d8 20 b3 b5 = L.B.Hansen-Korchnoi, Debrecen Echt 1992.

a2) 10 ♘e1 exd4 11 ♕xd4 ♘c6 12 ♕d2 ♖ae8 13 ♘c2 ♕d7 14 ♖fe1 ♗h3 15 ♗h1 with equality, I.Farago-P.Nikolić, Portorož/Rogaška 1993.

a3) 10 dxe5!? (without a pawn on e4, this exchange may be quite good, because the e4-square is accessible to White's minor pieces) 10...dxe5 11 ♘g5 ♖d8 12 ♕e3 c6 13 h3 ♗c8 14 ♖ad1 and White is better, P.Nikolić-Spiridonov, Sombor 1980.

b) 9...♘c6 10 d5 ♘b8 11 e4 (comparing this position with Line D22, we see that White's position is slightly improved; it is not so easy for White to play c5 here, but White's knight is much more active on c3) 11...a5 (or 11...♗g4 12 ♘e1! c6 13 ♘d3 cxd5 14 cxd5 ♘fd7 15 f3 ♗h5 16 ♖ac1 and White is better, Hebden-K.Kristensen, Copenhagen 1992) 12 ♘e1 and then:

b1) 12...♘a6 (playing for control of c5) 13 ♘d3 ♘d7 14 f4 ♘dc5 15 ♘xc5 ♘xc5 16 f5! f6 17 h4 ♗d7 and now 18 g4 ♖fb8 19 ♖f3 b5 20 cxb5 ♗xb5 21 g5 ♔h8 22 ♖g3 ♗a6 gave Black reasonable counterplay in the game Bates-Socko, Zagan jr Wch 1997, but a little accuracy from White's side would have made it more difficult for

Black, viz. 18 ♖f3! intending to meet either rook move to b8 with 19 ♗f1 and then to play g4 and ♖g3.

b2) 12...c6 (now Black shall decide when the queenside is to open up, rather than letting White play c5) 13 ♘d3 ♘a6 (13...cxd5!? 14 cxd5 ♘a6 has been suggested by Zagrebelny) 14 a3 (14 f4!? ♘b4 15 ♘f2! might be more accurate and if Black exchanges on d5 either on move 14 or 15 White can take back with the e-pawn) 14...cxd5 15 cxd5 ♗d7 16 ♖fc1 (or 16 b4!? axb4 17 axb4 ♖ac8 18 ♖fb1 ♘e8 19 b5 ♘c5 20 ♖a7 ♖b8 and Black is ready to create counterplay with ...f5) 16...a4 with approximate equality, Shipov-Zagrebelny, Moscow 1995.

c) 9...c6 10 e4 ♖e8 transposes to the note to Black's 10th move below.

10 e4 ♗g4 *(D)*

The centre is most likely to be closed, so Black intends to exchange his bishop for a knight, hoping that knights will prove better at manoeuvring in the resulting position. Furthermore, White's light-squared bishop is not too strong, as most of Black's pawns will be on dark squares and White's own pawns are restricting the scope of the bishop. Alternatives:

a) 10...a5 11 h3 c6 12 ♖fe1 ♘a6 13 ♖ad1 ♕c7 14 b3 ♗d7 15 ♕c1 exd4 16 ♘xd4 ♘c5 17 ♕c2 ♖e7 18 f4 ♖ae8 19 ♔h2 h6 20 ♖e3 with a nice space advantage for White, Yusupov-Kindermann, Lucerne OL 1982.

b) 10...c6 11 ♘h4!? a6 12 ♖ac1 b5 13 b3 ♕a7 14 dxe5 dxe5 15 cxb5 axb5 16 ♘f5 ♗xf5 17 exf5 ♕a5 18 ♖fd1 and White is better, Ehlvest-Rashkovsky, Moscow 1992.

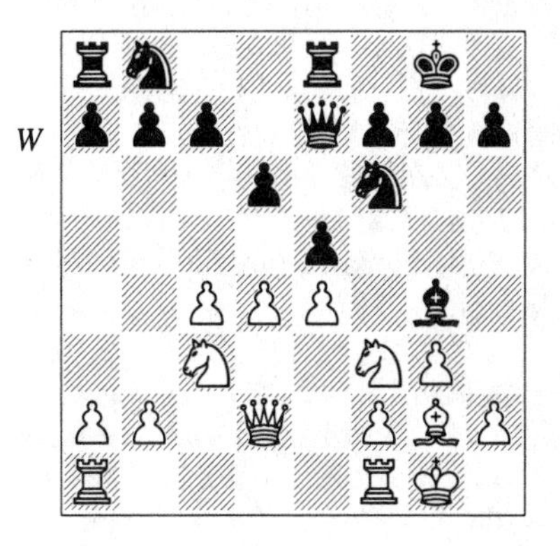

11 d5

White has, in two ways, tried to avoid the exchange of his knight, but neither should suffice for an advantage:

a) 11 ♘e1 ♘c6 (11...exd4 12 ♕xd4 ♘c6 13 ♕d2 a5 14 ♖c1 ± Manor-Adams, Adelaide jr Wch 1988) and now:

a1) 12 d5 ♘d4 13 f4 ♗d7 (otherwise Black's bishop will be locked out with f5) 14 ♘d3 c5 15 dxc6 ♗xc6 16 ♖ae1 ♘d7 17 ♘b4 ♕d8 18 ♔h1 ♘c5 19 ♘bd5 a5 20 ♖f2 b5 = Yusupov-Ivkov, Vrbas 1980.

a2) 12 f4!? ♗d7 (again Black's best is to retreat the bishop, since 12...exd4 13 ♘d5 ♘xd5 14 cxd5 ♘d8 15 ♕xd4 is very good for White, as in Nogueiras-Pinal, Havana 1985, and if 12...♘xd4, White simply plays 13 f5 and traps Black's bishop) 13 dxe5 (13 d5 ♘d4 transposes to 'a1') 13...dxe5 14 ♘d5 ♘xd5 15 cxd5 ♘b8 16 a4 (otherwise ...♗b5 is annoying) 16...♘a6 17

Nd3 Nc5 18 Nxc5 Qxc5+ 19 Kh1 Qd6 20 b3 c6 with a good game for Black, Kragelj-Kovačević, Pula 1994.

a3) 12 Nc2 with a choice for Black:

a31) 12...Nxd4 13 Nxd4 exd4 14 Qxd4 Qe5 15 Qd3 c6 16 h3 Be6 17 Rad1 Rad8 18 b3 a6 19 f4 Qa5 20 Rf2 h6 21 Rfd2 b5 22 cxb5 axb5 23 Kh2 ± Khenkin-Murdzia, Polish Cht (Krynica) 1997.

a32) 12...exd4 13 Nxd4 Ne5 14 Nd5 Qd8 15 Ne3 c5!? 16 Nxg4 cxd4 17 Nxf6+ Qxf6 18 b3 Nf3+ 19 Bxf3 Qxf3 20 Rfe1 (20 Qxd4 Rxe4 21 Qxd6 Rae8 gives Black reasonable counterplay) 20...Rxe4 21 Rxe4 Qxe4 22 Re1 Qg4 23 Qd3 b6 24 Re4 Qd7 25 Qxd4 with an edge for White, Dizdar-Kurajica, Erevan OL 1996.

b) 11 Nh4 Nc6 12 d5 Nd4 13 Nb5!? Nxb5 14 cxb5 Bd7 15 a4 a6 (this looks very natural but perhaps Black is better advised to play for the ...c6 thrust instead, for example 15...g6! 16 Rfc1 Rec8 17 Ra3 c6! 18 bxc6 bxc6 19 dxc6 Rxc6 20 Rxc6 Bxc6 = Zsu.Polgar-Ivkov, Monaco women vs veterans 1994) 16 bxa6 Rxa6 17 a5 (17 Rfc1!? ± Yusupov) 17...c6 18 dxc6 Rxc6! 19 Rfd1 Rec8? (it was necessary to hinder White's knight in coming to f5, e.g. 19...g6 with the idea of 20 b4 Rc4 =) 20 b4 Rc4 21 Nf5! Bxf5 22 exf5 d5 23 b5 and White is much better, Yusupov-Ro.Hernandez, Thessaloniki OL 1984.

11...Bxf3

This is clearly the most consistent approach. Others:

a) 11...a5 12 Ne1 (this is somewhat better for White now that the centre is closed and Black's knight is unable to come to d4) 12...Na6 13 Nd3 Nd7 (if 13...Bd7 White should play 14 f4 with advantage) 14 f3 Bh5 15 Nf2 Bg6 16 Nb5 b6 17 Bh3 Ndc5 18 Rae1 and White has the better prospects, Sorokin-Bielicki, La Plata 1997.

b) 11...c6 12 Ne1! (12 Rfd1 cxd5 13 Nxd5 Nxd5 14 Qxd5 Rd8 was fine for Black in Alterman-Dizdarević, Zagreb Z 1993, since White does not achieve anything with 15 c5, e.g. 15...Nc6 16 cxd6 Qf6 17 Qd3 Nd4 18 Nxd4 Bxd1 19 Nf5 Bg4 ∓ Dautov) 12...cxd5 13 cxd5 Na6 14 Nd3 Rac8 15 f4 and White is better, Podgaets-Lerner, USSR 1978.

12 Bxf3 *(D)*

B

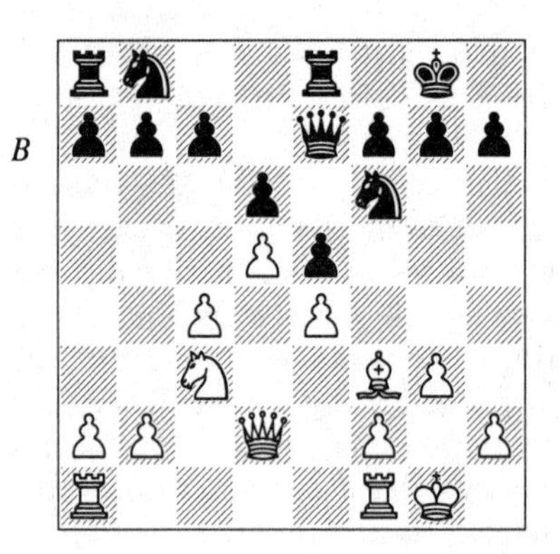

12...c5

With this move Black is consequently playing for a closed position in which he intends to place his pawns on dark squares, but I think White's space advantage is to be preferred. Alternatives:

a) 12...a5 13 a3 Na6 14 Rab1 c6 15 Rfe1 Rec8 (Meduna-Ivkov, Sochi

1983) and now White should play 16 ♘a4!? ♕c7 17 ♕e3 ± according to Yusupov in *ECO*.

b) 12...♘bd7?! gives White a free hand on the queenside: 13 b4 a5 14 a3 ♖a6 (Black should probably seek complications with 14...c5 15 dxc6 bxc6 16 ♖fd1 ♘b6!) 15 ♘b5! ♘b6 16 ♖ac1 axb4 17 axb4 ♕d7 18 ♕d3 ♖a4 19 ♕b3 ♖ea8 20 ♖fd1 and White is better, Beliavsky-Christiansen, Reggio Emilia 1987/8.

13 ♖ae1

Another good continuation is 13 a3 ♘bd7 14 ♗g2 a6 15 ♕e2 ♖ab8 16 ♖fc1 g6 17 b4 ♔g7 18 h4 ♕d8 19 ♗h3 and White was much better in Beliavsky-Balashov, Lvov 1978.

13...a6 14 b3 ♘bd7 15 ♗g2

Contrary to the Beliavsky-Balashov game above, White is here playing in the centre and on the kingside.

15...♖ab8 16 a4 ♕d8 17 ♕d1 ♖e7 18 ♖e3 ♕a5 19 ♖fe1 ♔h8 20 ♗h3

White has a small but quite clear advantage, Karpov-P.Nikolić, Skellefteå 1989.

D2)

5...♘c6 *(D)*

We shall now consider two main lines for White:

D21: 6 ♘c3 96
D22: 6 ♗g2 104

An alternative line for White is 6 ♕c2 but even though it has been played by some very strong players, it commits the queen rather early. Play might continue 6...♗xd2+ 7 ♘bxd2 d6 8 ♗g2 0-0 9 0-0 and then:

W

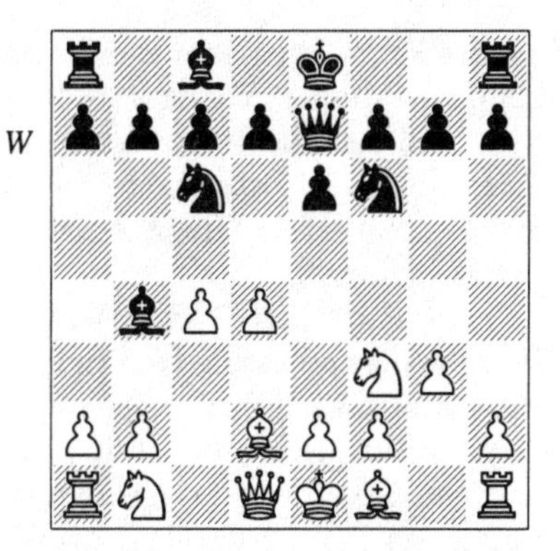

a) 9...e5 10 e3 (10 d5 is also possible but after 10...♘b8 White probably has nothing better than 11 e4, after which ♕c2 is not a particularly useful move compared to Line D221 and may indeed transpose to line 'b' below if Black continues 11...a5) 10...a5 11 b3 (White is playing the opening a little hesitantly) 11...♖e8 12 dxe5 (12 d5 ♘b4 13 ♕c3 e4 14 ♘g5 ♗f5 15 a3 ♘d3 is also very pleasant for Black) 12...dxe5 13 ♘g5 ♘b4! 14 ♕c3?! (14 ♕b1 is better but 14...♖d8 15 ♘de4 ♗f5 is good for Black anyway) 14...h6 15 ♘ge4 ♘xe4 16 ♘xe4 f5 17 a3 ♘c6 18 ♘d2 e4 with the better game for Black, Adianto-D.Johansen, Thessaloniki OL 1988.

b) 9...a5 10 e4 e5 11 d5 ♘b8 (11...♘b4 is not right, as after 12 ♕c3 White is ready to push Black's knight back with a3) with a choice for White:

b1) 12 ♕c3 ♘bd7 and now:

b11) 13 ♘e1 ♘c5 14 b3 ♗g4! 15 ♘c2 (if 15 f3 ♗d7 16 a3 Black should, according to Milos, start counterplay on the kingside with 16...h5!) 15...c6 16 ♖ae1 cxd5 17 exd5 ♕d7 18 f4 exf4

19 ♖xf4 ♖fe8 with a level game, Van Riemsdijk-Milos, Americana 1995.

b12) 13 ♘h4 ♘c5 14 ♖ae1 ♗d7 15 b3 c6 16 f4 ♖fe8 17 dxc6 bxc6 18 ♔h1 exf4 19 ♖xf4 ♕e5 = Timman-Speelman, London 1982.

b2) 12 ♖fc1 ♘a6 13 a3 ♗d7 14 b3 (White is now preparing ♕c3 and b4, which would leave Black's knight on a6 very badly placed) 14...c6 15 dxc6 (or 15 ♕c3 ♘c5 16 ♘e1 b5 with an unclear game) 15...bxc6 (15...♗xc6!? is maybe better, to keep up the pressure against e4 and retain the possibility of a pawn break with ...b5) 16 ♕c3 ♘c5 17 ♘h4 g6 18 b4 ♘e6 19 ♘hf3 and White is better, Barlov-Ivanović, Vršac 1987.

b3) 12 ♘e1 ♘a6 13 ♘d3 c6! (another way to prevent White from playing c5 is 13...♘d7 but then 14 a3 ♘dc5 15 ♘xc5 ♘xc5 16 b4 is better for White, as in I.Farago-Agzamov, Belgrade 1982) 14 ♕c3 cxd5 15 cxd5 ♗d7 16 ♖fc1 (note that 16 ♕xa5? is bad owing to 16...♘c5 17 ♕c3 ♗b5) 16...♖fc8 17 ♕a3 ♗b5 18 ♗h3 ♖xc1+ 19 ♖xc1 a4 20 ♘e1 ♕d8 with an equal position, I.Farago-Draško, Sarajevo 1983.

D21)

6 ♘c3 *(D)*

With this move White is trying to take advantage of the slightly unnatural placement of Black's knight on c6, in some variations by threatening to play d5, or hoping to gain the bishop-pair, as Black can hardly avoid exchanging his dark-squared bishop for White's knight.

B

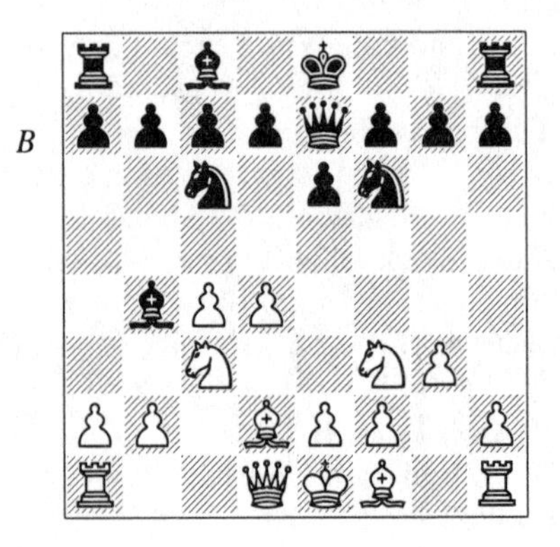

Thus Black tends to choose between:

Others are:

a) 6...0-0 7 ♗g2 and now:

a1) 7...d5 8 a3 ♗xc3 9 ♗xc3 transposes to Line D211.

a2) 7...♗xc3 8 ♗xc3 ♘e4 transposes to Line D212.

a3) 7...d6 (this is a rather imprecise move-order for Black) 8 0-0 ♗xc3 9 ♗xc3 ♘e4 (9...e5 10 ♕c2 a5 11 ♖ad1 ♖e8, Tal-T.Petrosian, Varese 1976, 12 d5 ±) 10 ♗e1! e5 11 d5 ♘d8 12 ♕c2 f5 13 ♘h4! ♘g5 14 f4 exf4 15 ♖xf4! g6 16 ♗c3 ♘df7 17 ♖af1 ♗d7 18 e4!. With strong active moves White has punished Black for his sloppy opening play, and is clearly better, Malaniuk-Macieja, Koszalin 1997.

b) 6...d6 and then:

b1) 7 ♗g2 ♗xc3 8 ♗xc3 ♘e4 9 ♖c1 transposes to Line D212.

b2) 7 d5! (exploiting Black's inaccurate move-order) 7...exd5 8 cxd5 (8 ♘xd5!? ♘xd5 9 cxd5 ♘e5 10 ♘xe5

♗xd2+ 11 ♕xd2 dxe5 12 ♗g2 0-0 13 0-0 is also better for White) 8...♘e5 9 ♘xe5 dxe5 10 ♗g2 a6 11 0-0 0-0 12 ♖c1 (12 ♕b3!?) 12...h6 13 ♕c2 and White has a small advantage, Korchnoi-Yusupov, Horgen 1995.

D211)

6...d5 *(D)*

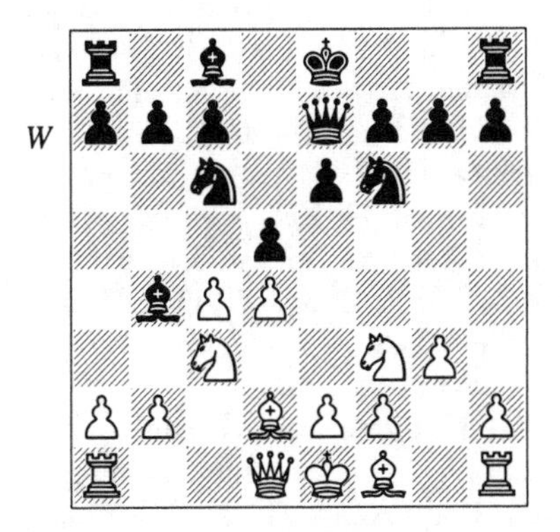

This leads to an unusual Queen's Gambit type of position, in which the black knight on c6 is not well placed but this is approximately balanced by White's slightly disharmonious development.

7 cxd5

This is probably best, even though it eases Black's play a little as he can increase the scope of his bishop by recapturing with the pawn. Other possibilities are:

a) 7 ♗g2 0-0 (7...dxc4 seems more testing: 8 0-0 0-0 9 ♗g5 h6 10 ♗xf6 ♕xf6 and now 11 ♘e4 ♕f5! 12 ♕c2 ♖d8 13 ♖fd1 ♗e7 14 ♖ac1 ♖b8! was good for Black in P.Nikolić-Bachler, Lugano 1987 but White should try 11 e3 intending ♕e2) 8 a3 ♗xc3 9 ♗xc3 and now:

a1) 9...♖d8 10 0-0 a5 11 ♘d2!? (an interesting way to try to force through e4, but 11 ♕c2 ♗d7 12 ♘e5 also looks good) 11...e5 12 dxe5 ♘xe5 13 cxd5 ♘xd5 14 ♗xe5 ♕xe5 15 ♘c4 ♕f6 16 ♗xd5 ♗h3? (16...♗e6 ± Van Wely) 17 ♖e1 c6 18 ♗xf7+ ♕xf7 19 ♕c2 and White is a clear pawn ahead, Van Wely-Gendler, Erevan OL 1996.

a2) 9...♘e4 10 ♖c1 (10 ♕c2 transposes to 'b31' below) 10...♖d8 11 ♕c2 a5 12 0-0 ♗d7 13 ♖fe1 ♗e8 14 cxd5 exd5 15 ♘d2! f5 16 e3 ♗g6 17 ♕b3 ♕d6 (Piket-Korchnoi, Nijmegen (4) 1993) and now 18 f4 a4 19 ♕c2 is slightly better for White according to Piket.

b) 7 a3 ♗xc3 8 ♗xc3 and now:

b1) 8...dxc4 9 ♕a4 0-0 10 ♕xc4 ♖b8 11 ♗g2 ♕d6 12 ♗d2 b5 13 ♕d3 b4 14 0-0 bxa3 15 bxa3 ♖b6 16 ♖fc1 and White is better, Dzhandzhgava-Dvoirys, Simferopol 1988.

b2) 8...a5 9 ♗g2 b6 10 ♘e5 (White should perhaps content himself with a slight advantage after 10 0-0 ♗b7 11 ♕c2) 10...♗b7 11 ♘xc6 ♗xc6 12 ♕c2 0-0!? (an interesting pawn sacrifice; safer is 12...♕d7) 13 cxd5 exd5 14 ♗xa5 ♗b5 15 ♗b4 c5 16 dxc5 ♖fc8 17 c6 ♖xc6 18 ♕d2 ♕e6 19 0-0 ♘e4 with good compensation, Eingorn-Kuligowski, Polanica Zdroj 1984.

b3) 8...♘e4 with the following options:

b31) 9 ♕c2 0-0 10 ♗g2 a5 11 b3 ♖d8 12 0-0 ♗d7 (this is a standard manoeuvre intending to bring the bishop out after ...♗e8 and ...f5;

another deployment of the bishop was seen in the game Kalinichev-Goldin, USSR 1987: 12...b6 13 ♗b2 ♗b7 14 ♖ac1 ♖ac8 15 ♖fd1 ♕f6 16 e3 with just an edge for White) 13 ♗b2 ♗e8 (13...f5 is perhaps more accurate) 14 ♘h4! (a strong move preventing a black set-up with 14...f5, due to 15 cxd5) 14...♘f6 15 ♖ad1 ♘a7 16 ♖fe1 a4 17 b4 ♗c6 18 e4! (18 c5 ♘b5 is more or less OK for Black because he can set up a light-square blockade) 18...dxc4 (Black cannot really take on e4, as shown by Razuvaev's analysis: 18...♘xe4? 19 cxd5 exd5 20 f3 +– and 18...dxe4 19 d5! exd5 20 ♘f5 ♕e6 21 ♗h3 ♔h8 22 b5 ♗e8 23 ♘xg7 ♕xh3 24 ♗xf6 +–) 19 d5 ♗d7 (19...♗e8 20 ♕xc4 ♘b5 21 ♕c1 is definitely not an improvement for Black – in Novikov-Maiwald, Cappelle la Grande 1998, Black found nothing better than 21...♗d7, when he was simply a tempo down on the main line) 20 ♕xc4 ♘b5 21 ♕c1! ♘e8 (21...exd5 22 e5 ±) 22 dxe6 ♗xe6 23 ♘f5 ♗xf5 24 exf5 ♖xd1 25 ♕xd1 ♖d8! 26 ♕c1 ♕d7 27 ♗xb7 ± Razuvaev-Goldin, Eupen ECC 1994.

b32) 9 ♕b3!? (with this move White exerts pressure on b7 and d5 but on the other hand the queen blocks the b-pawn) 9...0-0!? 10 ♗g2 (10 cxd5 exd5 11 ♕xd5 wins a pawn but is rather time-consuming – Black can obtain plenty of compensation with 11...♖e8 12 ♕c4 ♗g4 13 ♗g2 ♖ad8) 10...♖d8 11 0-0 a5 12 e3 b6 (the manoeuvre ...♗d7-e8 is not possible here with White's queen targeting b7) 13 ♖fc1 ♗b7 (13...♗a6!?) 14 ♗e1 with a slightly better position for White, Kaidanov-Goldin, Pleasantville 1993.

7...exd5 8 ♗g2 0-0

The immediate 8...♗g4 does not make any difference after 9 ♗g5 0-0 10 0-0 or 9 0-0 0-0. Note also that 9 e3? is a serious error as 9...♘xd4 wins a pawn.

However, in Gligorić-Christiansen, St John 1988, after 9 0-0, Black opted for 9...♗xf3 10 exf3 (10 ♗xf3 is inaccurate in view of 10...♘xd4 11 ♘xd5 ♘xd5 12 ♗xd5 0-0-0!) 10...0-0 (the greedy 10...♘xd4? is very dangerous because of 11 ♖e1 ♘e6 12 f4) 11 ♗g5! ♖ad8 12 f4! ♗xc3 13 bxc3 h6 14 ♖e1 ♕d6 15 ♗h4! ♖d7 16 f5 ±.

9 0-0 ♖e8

Other possibilities are:

a) 9...h6 (a very sensible move stopping White's bishop coming to g5) 10 a3 ♗xc3 11 ♗xc3 ♘e4 12 ♖c1 ♖d8 13 ♖e1 ½-½ Sosonko-Smyslov, Wijk aan Zee 1982.

b) 9...♖d8!? is a solid move well worth considering.

c) 9...♗g4 10 ♗g5 (or 10 a3 ♗xc3 11 ♗xc3 ♘e4 12 ♖c1 a5 = Timman-Petursson, Reykjavik 1988) 10...♖ad8 11 h3 ♗h5 12 g4 ♗g6 13 ♖c1 h6 14 ♗h4 ♗e4 15 a3 ♗d6 16 ♘b5 g5 17 ♘xd6 cxd6! (by doubling his own pawns Black obtains better control of the centre) 18 ♗g3 ♘e8 with an approximately equal position, Buturin-Rashkovsky, Lvov 1981.

10 e3

White will most likely be forced to move the e-pawn in order to defend d4, and so he can just as well do it here. The game Kasparov-Garcia Gonzalez,

Moscow IZ 1982 continued 10 ♕b3 ♗g4 and already here White saw nothing better than 11 e3 and after 11...a5 12 a3 ♗xf3 13 ♗xf3 a4, the queen was forced to retreat with an equal game to follow.

10...a6?!

It is not clear why Black plays this – in the following line of play it certainly turns out to be a loss of time. Relatively best is perhaps 10...♗xc3 11 ♗xc3 ♘e4 but Black can also play 10...♗g4 11 ♕c2 ♕d7 12 ♖fc1 ♖e7 (the pre-emptive 12...a5 is worth considering) 13 a3 ♗xc3 14 ♗xc3 ♘e4 15 b4 ± Gligorić-Am.Rodriguez, Lucerne OL 1982.

11 ♖c1 ♗f5 12 ♕b3 ♕d6

12...♘a5? is bad due to 13 ♘xd5! but maybe 12...♖ad8 is better.

13 ♘e5!

A very fine temporary pawn sacrifice.

13...♘xe5 14 dxe5 ♖xe5 15 e4!

This was the idea; White is threatening 16 ♗f4.

15...♗xc3 16 ♗xc3 d4 17 ♕xb7 ♖ae8 18 exf5 dxc3 19 ♖xc3

Vladimirov-Hecht, CSKA-Bayern ECC 1988. White is clearly better due to his strong bishop and pressure against Black's weak pawns on a6 and c7.

D212)

6...♗xc3 7 ♗xc3 *(D)*

7...♘e4 8 ♖c1

The alternative is 8 ♕c2 but then White must be prepared to exchange queens as well. 8...♘xc3 9 ♕xc3 and now:

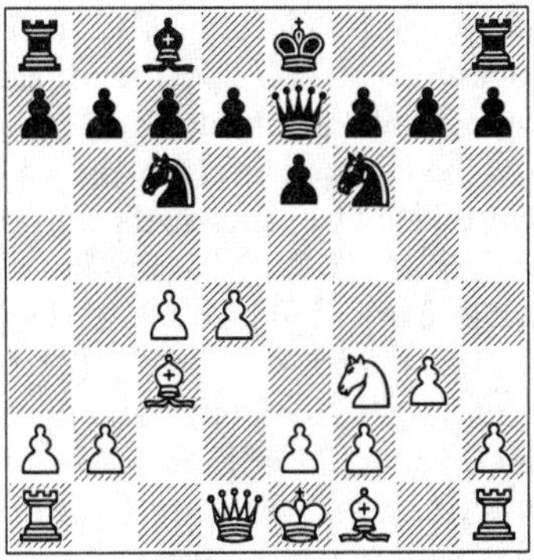

a) 9...0-0 10 ♗g2 d6 11 d5! (advancing the pawn before Black plays ...e5 gives White more opportunities). Black may now choose between:

a1) 11...♘d8 and here:

a11) 12 dxe6 is an important option, when 12...♘xe6 13 0-0 ♗d7 14 ♖fe1 ♗c6 15 e4 a5 16 b3 ♖fe8 17 ♖e3 ♘c5 18 ♘d4 ♗d7 19 ♖ae1 was very pleasant for White in Shipov-Khurtsidze, Cappelle la Grande 1998. Black could try 12...fxe6 although White probably still gets the better game – compare 'a22'.

a12) 12 0-0 e5 with a further split:

a121) 13 ♘d2 f5 14 f4!? ♘f7 15 e4!? fxe4 16 ♘xe4 ♗f5 17 ♖ae1 b6 18 ♘d2 ♖ae8 19 ♘f3 ♗g4 20 fxe5 ♘xe5 21 ♘xe5 ♖xf1+ 22 ♗xf1 dxe5 23 ♗g2 and White can claim an edge due to Black's isolated e-pawn, Gagarin-Zagrebelny, Vladivostok 1995.

a122) 13 e4 c5 (13...f5 14 exf5 ♗xf5 15 ♖ae1 ± Tal-B.Ivanović, Lucerne OL 1982) 14 ♘d2 ♗d7 15 a3 b6 (Black's strategy in this game is quite amusing: put all the pawns on dark squares and see if you can hold the position!) 16 f4 f6 17 ♖f2 ♘f7 18 ♖af1 a5 19 b3 ♖a7 20 a4 (eliminating any possible queenside counterplay – now the outcome of the game will be determined by events on the kingside) 20...g6 21 h3 ♔g7 22 f5 ♖h8 (was Black really afraid of 22...g5 23 ♗f3 intending ♗h5?) 23 ♕f3?! (23 fxg6 hxg6 24 g4!? looks like an improvement) 23...g5 24 ♕h5 ♗e8 25 h4 ♕f8 26 ♕e2 ♖g8 27 h5 ½-½ Khalifman-P.H.Nielsen, Århus 1997.

a123) 13 c5 (since Black's knight is not within reach of c5, this seems the most logical) 13...f5 14 ♖ac1 ♘f7 15 cxd6 (15 ♘d2?! ♗d7 16 ♕b4 b6 17 cxd6 cxd6 18 ♕a3 ♗b5 allowed Black to get out in Eingorn-Wahls, Berlin 1993) 15...cxd6 16 ♕e3! (much better than 16 ♕c7 ♕f6! with counterplay for Black) 16...♕d8 17 ♖c4 ♕a5 18 ♖fc1 ♕xa2 19 ♕d2 with excellent compensation for White, Novikov-Sedina, Saint Vincent 1998.

a2) 11...♘b8 *(D)* and White has a choice between keeping the structure closed or opening up the position by taking on e6:

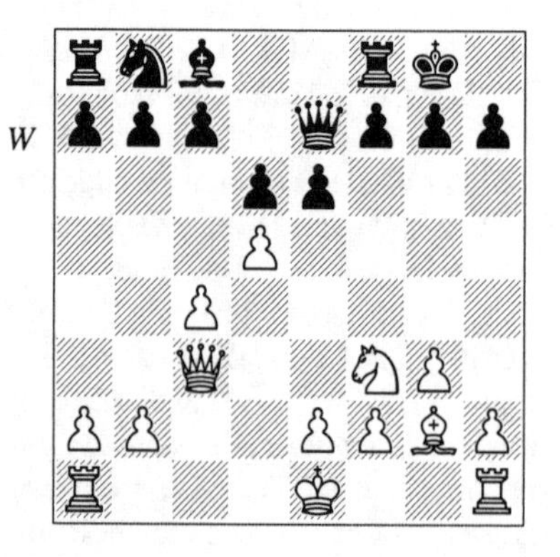

a21) 12 0-0 e5 13 e4 (this seems less convincing than against 11...♘d8, and when playing this kind of position White is better off with his rook on c3 instead of the queen {see 8 ♖c1}; note also that 13 c5 is worse here: 13...♘a6 14 b4 ♖e8! 15 ♖ac1 e4 16 ♘d4 ♕e5! with a good game for Black, Grabliauskas-Van der Sterren, Hamburg 1997) and now:

a211) 13...a5 14 c5 ♗g4 15 ♖fc1 ♘a6 16 cxd6 cxd6 17 ♘d2 ♕d8 18 ♕e3 b5 and Black is fine, Dautov-Benjamin, Cologne rpd 1997.

a212) 13...c5 14 ♘e1 ♘a6 15 ♘d3 ♗d7 16 f4 f6 17 a4!? (a rather committal decision, but probably quite good) 17...b6 18 ♔h1 ♘c7 19 f5 g6 20 g4 ♕g7 (20...g5!?) 21 ♖f3 gxf5?! (very surprising since the opening of the kingside is clearly favourable for White) 22 gxf5 ♔h8 23 ♕d2 ♖g8 24 ♖g3 ♕f7 25 ♗f3 ♖xg3 26 hxg3 ♖g8 27 ♔g2 ± Piket-Adams, London rpd 1995.

a22) 12 dxe6!? fxe6 13 0-0 a5 14 ♘d4 e5 15 ♘b3! a4 (on 15...♘c6, Shipov mentions the line 16 ♗xc6! bxc6 17 ♘xa5 ♗h3 18 ♖fe1 ♕f7 19 f3 e4!? 20 ♘xc6 exf3 21 exf3 ♕xf3 22 ♘e7+! ♔h8 23 ♕xf3 ♖xf3 24 ♘d5 ±) 16 ♘d2 ♘c6 17 e3 ♗e6 18 b4 axb3 19 axb3 ± Shipov-Draško, Belgrade 1994.

b) 9...♕b4 gives White a slightly better endgame, e.g. 10 ♕xb4 (probably better than 10 ♖c1 d6 11 ♗g2 ♔e7 12 0-0 ♕xc3 13 ♖xc3 e5 14 d5 ♘b8 15 ♘d2 ♘d7 16 b4 a5 17 a3 axb4 18 axb4 b6, when Black has equalized, Vyzhmanavin-Nadyrkhanov, Barnaul

1988) 10...♘xb4 11 ♔d2 d6 12 ♗g2 and then:

b1) 12...a5 13 a3 (or 13 ♘e1!?) 13...♘c6 14 d5 ♘e7 15 ♘d4 a4 16 ♖hc1 ♖a5 17 b4 axb3 18 ♘xb3 ♖a4 19 c5 e5 20 cxd6 cxd6 21 ♔e1 ± Savchenko-Loginov, St Petersburg 1996.

b2) 12...♔e7 13 ♘e1! (White is now prepared to exchange his bishop for Black's knight if it returns to c6) 13...c5?! 14 dxc5 dxc5 15 a3 and White is better, Eingorn-A.Petrosian, Manila OL 1992.

b3) Eingorn suggests 12...♘c6, with only an edge for White.

b4) 12...♗d7 13 a3 ♘c6 14 b4 ♖b8 15 e3 ♔e7 16 ♖hc1 promises White a tiny advantage, Van Wely-Ikonnikov, Vlissingen 1997.

Returning to the position after 8 ♖c1 *(D)*:

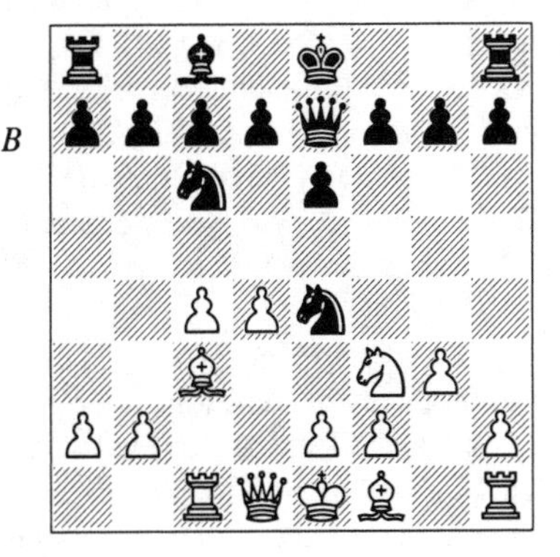

8...0-0

Alternatives:

a) 8...♘b4 attempts to create a little confusion in White's camp, but such an early knight sortie should not really be good. After the continuation 9 ♕a4 a5 10 ♗g2 0-0 White has rather a pleasant choice:

a1) 11 0-0 ♘xc3 and then:

a11) 12 ♖xc3 d6 13 a3 ♗d7 14 ♕b3 (more precise than 14 ♕d1 ♘a6 15 ♘e1 ♖ab8 16 c5 ♖fd8 17 ♕c2 ½-½ Gligorić-Rajković, Yugoslav Ch 1986) 14...♘c6 (here 14...♘a6 is met by 15 ♕xb7) 15 d5 a4 16 ♕c2 ♘d8 17 e4 ♖a5 18 e5!? (very aggressive, but it is not easy to spot another plan when c5 is practically ruled out) 18...exd5 19 cxd5 c6 (other moves are inferior, e.g. 19...dxe5 20 ♖xc7 ♕d6 21 ♘xe5! or 19...♖xd5 20 ♘g5 ♕xg5 21 ♗xd5 ♕xe5 22 ♖xc7) 20 exd6 ♕xd6 21 ♘g5 ♕g6 22 ♕xg6 hxg6 23 ♖d1 ± P.Nikolić-Rajković, Vršac 1983.

a12) 12 bxc3! ♘c6 13 c5 (White wishes to undouble his pawns) 13...d6 14 cxd6 cxd6 15 ♖b1 ♖b8 16 ♘d2 ♗d7 17 ♖b6 with a small advantage for White, Smejkal-Petursson, Thessaloniki OL 1984.

a2) 11 ♘d2 ♘xc3 12 bxc3! ♘c6 13 c5 d5 14 cxd6 cxd6 15 ♖b1! (the same idea as in 'a12' above, but more of a problem here, as a defence with ...♖b8 is not allowed) 15...♕c7 16 ♕b3 (intending ♕b6) 16...♖a6 17 0-0 a4 18 ♕b5 ♘a7 19 ♕d3 d5 20 c4 dxc4 21 ♕xc4! (21 ♘xc4 b5 22 ♘e5 ♗b7 23 ♖fc1 ♕e7 is also better for White, but the text-move is stronger) 21...♕xc4 22 ♘xc4 b5 23 ♘e5 f6 24 ♘d3 ± Tukmakov-Rashkovsky, USSR Ch (Minsk) 1987.

b) 8...d6 and then:

b1) 9 d5 ♘xc3 10 ♖xc3 transposes to various lines covered below after White's 10 d5 or 10 0-0 in our main line.

b2) 9 ♗g2 ♘xc3 10 ♖xc3 e5 11 d5 ♘b8 12 e4 0-0 13 ♘h4!? a5 14 0-0 ♘a6 15 ♕e1 (with the idea f4-f5) 15...g5! (surprisingly, this seems quite good) 16 ♘f5 (16 ♘f3 ♘c5 17 ♘d2 ♗d7 followed by ...♖ae8 and ...f5 is fine for Black) 16...♗xf5 17 exf5 ♘c5 18 ♗e4 ♕f6 19 f3 ♖fe8 20 ♕e3 ♔g7 21 ♔g2 h5 22 ♖h1 ♖g8 23 h3 h4 24 g4 ♖gb8 = Piket-Anand, Wijk aan Zee 1996.

9 ♗g2 *(D)*

9 d5 was an interesting new attempt in Gulko-Benjamin, USA Ch 1988 but has not attracted any followers. The game continued 9...♕c5 10 e3 ♘b4 11 ♕b3 ♘xc3 12 ♖xc3 a5 13 a3 ♘a6 14 ♗g2 ♕e7 with an approximately equal position.

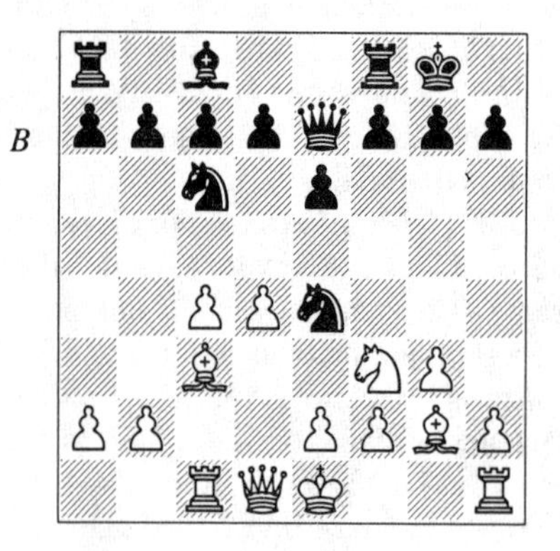

9...d6

The pre-emptive 9...a5 is a favourite of the Hungarian IM Emil Anka. After 10 0-0 (10 d5 is here well met by 10...♘b4) there is:

a) 10...d6 permits White to retain his bishop. 11 ♗e1 (11 ♘h4 f5 12 d5 ♘b4 13 ♗e1 ♗d7 14 a3 ♘a6 15 dxe6 ♗c6 16 b4 axb4 17 axb4 ♘g5 18 e4! fxe4 19 b5 +– was a neat little tactical turn that occurred in Rohde-Miles, San Francisco 1987 but Black can probably improve around move 13) 11...f5 12 d5 ♘d8 13 ♘d2 ♘c5 (afterwards Ivkov preferred 13...♘xd2 followed by ...e5) 14 ♘b3 b6 15 ♘xc5 bxc5 16 ♖c3 e5 17 f4! e4 18 ♖a3 ♘b7 19 ♕c2 ± Tatai-Ivkov, Praia da Rocha 1978.

b) 10...♘xc3 11 ♖xc3 d6 12 d5 ♘b4 13 a3 ♘a6 14 dxe6 fxe6 15 h4 e5 16 ♘g5 h6 17 ♘e4 ♗e6 18 ♖c1 ♔h8 19 b3 ± Cvitan-Anka, Geneva 1996.

10 d5 *(D)*

Another possibility is 10 0-0 ♘xc3 (10...a5 transposes to 'a' in the previous note) 11 ♖xc3 e5 12 d5 ♘b8 13 ♘d2, which for a long time was considered slightly better for White, but is now regarded as rather innocuous. Black has:

a) 13...♘d7 and then:

a1) 14 b4 f5 (14...a5 15 ♖a3) 15 c5! e4 16 f3 a5! 17 cxd6 cxd6 18 b5 exf3 19 exf3 ♕f6 with some counterplay, Vyzhmanavin-A.Petrosian, Moscow 1989.

a2) 14 e4 a5 15 ♕e2 (15 f4?! exf4 16 gxf4 f5! is a common defensive idea for Black) 15...♘c5 16 f4 ♗d7 17 f5 f6 18 b3 c6 19 h4 ♖fb8 20 a4! ♗e8 21 dxc6 bxc6 22 g4 with a promising attack for White, Polugaevsky-Beliavsky, Reggio Emilia 1991/2.

b) 13...a5! 14 c5 (14 e4 ♘a6 15 f4 exf4 16 gxf4 f5 gave Black few problems in Piket-Adams, Cannes 1992) 14...♘a6 (Black is playing for control of the dark squares) 15 cxd6 cxd6 16

♘c4 ♕d8 17 a3 b5 18 ♘d2 ♗d7 19 ♕b1 b4 20 axb4 axb4 21 ♖cc1 ♘c5 = Khalifman-Adams, Groningen 1990.

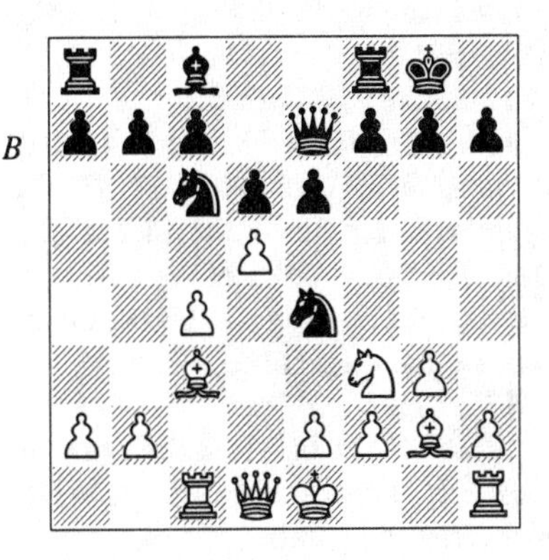

10...♘d8

This move has the best reputation, but Black may also decide to eliminate the bishop on c3 first and/or jump back to b8:

a) 10...♘xc3 11 ♖xc3 and then:

a1) 11...♘d8 12 dxe6 (or 12 ♕c2 e5 13 c5 dxc5 14 ♖xc5 c6 15 0-0 ♗f5 16 ♕c3 f6 17 ♖d1 ♕d6 18 ♘h4 ♗c8 19 ♖d2 ± Gulko-Kindermann, Biel 1988) 12...♘xe6 13 0-0 with a further branch:

a11) 13...a5 14 ♖e1 ♗d7 15 e4 ♗c6 16 b3 ♖ae8 17 ♖ce3 b6 18 ♕a1 ♕d8 19 a3 (19 h4!?) 19...♕a8 20 ♘h4 g6 = Bareev-Izeta, Erevan OL 1996.

a12) 13...♗d7 14 e4 (14 ♘h4 ♗c6 15 ♘f5 ♕f6 16 ♘e3 ♗xg2 17 ♔xg2 ♖fe8 = Polugaevsky-Korchnoi, Evian Ct (12) 1977) 14...♗c6 15 ♖e1 ♖fe8 16 ♖ce3 a5, Epishin-Ivanchuk, Tilburg 1993, and now Epishin suggests 17 ♕d2 b6 18 ♕c3 ♗b7 19 h4 with an advantage for White.

a2) 11...♘b8 12 dxe6 fxe6 13 ♘d4 e5 (13...♘d7? permits 14 ♘xe6 +–, while 13...c6 14 0-0 ♘d7 transposes to 'b2') 14 ♘c2 ♘d7 15 b4!? (15 ♘e3!?) 15...a5 16 a3 axb4 17 axb4 ♘f6 18 0-0 c6 19 e4 ♗e6 20 ♘e3 ± Tukmakov-Adams, Groningen PCA qual 1993.

b) 10...♘b8 11 dxe6! fxe6 12 0-0 (now White intends to keep his bishop with ♗e1) 12...♘xc3 13 ♖xc3 ♘d7 14 ♘d4 and now:

b1) 14...♘f6 15 c5 (15 ♕b3 is possibly better: 15...c5 16 ♘c2 ♖b8 17 ♖d1 b6 18 e4 ♗b7 19 f3 ♖bd8 20 ♖cd3 ± Pein-Jacobs, London 1988) 15...d5 16 c6 b6 17 f4 e5 18 fxe5 ♕xe5 19 ♕d2 ♗g4 = Dreev-Benjamin, Erevan OL 1996.

b2) 14...c6 (preparing ...e5 at some point, but this move also gives White a target) 15 b4 ♘f6 16 b5 e5 17 ♘c2 cxb5 18 cxb5 ♗e6 19 ♘e3 and White will keep an advantage if he can maintain control of d5, Karpov-Rogers, Spanish Cht (Oropesa del Mar) 1996.

11 ♗b4!? *(D)*

11 dxe6 is a major alternative:

a) 11...fxe6 12 0-0 ♗d7 (12...♘xc3 13 ♖xc3 transposes to 'a1' in the previous note) 13 ♗e1 ♘f6 14 ♘d4 e5 15 ♘c2 ♘e6 16 ♘e3 ♕f7 17 b4 ♗c6 18 ♘d5 and White is better, Korchnoi-T.Petrosian, Moscow Ct (4) 1971.

b) 11...♘xe6 12 ♗b4 and then:

b1) 12...♗d7 13 ♘e5!? ♘6c5? (after this mistake White obtains a nice position with the bishop-pair; instead Kramnik suggests 13...♕f6 14 ♗xe4 ♕xe5 15 ♗xb7 ♕xb2 16 ♖b1 ♕xa2 17 ♗xa8 ♖xa8 18 ♕b3 ♕a6, when White is only a little better) 14 ♘xd7

♘xd7 15 0-0 ± Kramnik-Ulybin, Khalkidhiki 1992.

b2) 12...a5 13 ♗a3 f5! (aware that passive play would give White the better game, Black seeks counterplay on the kingside) 14 0-0 ♔h8 15 b3 b6 16 ♗b2 ♗b7 with unclear play, Chetverik-Loginov, Zalakaros 1994.

b3) 12...♕f6 and now:

b31) 13 b3 a5 14 ♗a3 ♘6g5! 15 h4 ♘xf3+ 16 ♗xf3 ♖e8 =.

b32) 13 ♖c2 a5! 14 ♗a3 ♘6g5 15 h4 ♘xf3+ 16 exf3 ♘c5 17 0-0 = Zoler-Finkel, Israel 1993.

b33) 13 ♕c2 (avoiding ideas with ...♘6g5, as in the above variations) 13...♘6c5 (13...♘6g5 14 h4 ♘xf3+ 15 ♗xf3, as in Gavrikov-Wahls, Biel 1994, is better for White as Black cannot maintain his knight on e4) 14 0-0 ♖e8 15 ♗a3 a5 16 b3 ♕h6 17 ♖cd1 ± Chernin-Ulybin, Benidorm 1993.

B

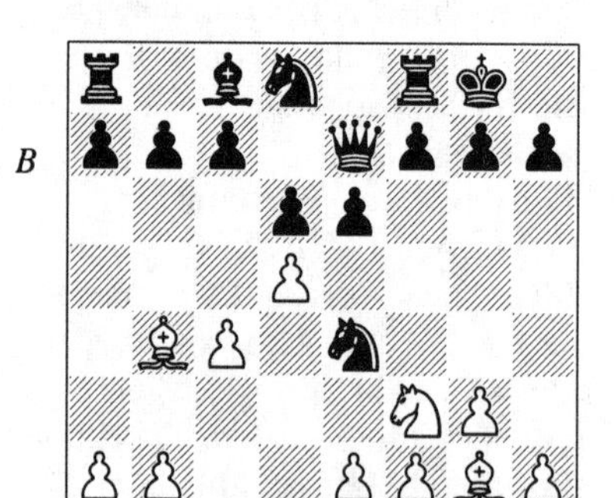

11...a5

It is important to insert this move as after the immediate 11...e5, White can play 12 ♘d2 and then 12...♘xd2 13 ♗xd2! with advantage, while 12...a5 13 ♘xe4 axb4 14 c5 f5 15 cxd6 cxd6 16 ♘d2 ♘f7 17 ♕b3 b5 18 ♕xb4 ♖xa2 19 0-0 ♕a7 20 ♘b1 was also better for White in the game Ehlvest-Wahls, Tilburg 1994.

12 ♗a3 e5 13 ♕c2

13 ♘d2 and now 13...♘c5 14 0-0 f5 15 f4 ♘f7 16 ♖c3 ♗d7 17 b3 was slightly better for White in Ftačnik-Hraček, Ostrava (5) 1997 but the simple 13...♘xd2 14 ♕xd2 b6 should be about equal – Ftačnik.

13...♘c5

13...f5 14 c5 b6! 15 cxb6 cxb6 16 ♘d2 ♘c5 17 ♘c4 is better for White according to Ftačnik.

14 ♗xc5 dxc5 15 0-0 f6

This is a little passive and afterwards Black has nothing to show for his slight lack in space and inferior pawn structure. Instead he might try to mix things up a little with 15...e4!? 16 ♘d2 e3.

16 e4 ♘f7 17 ♘e1!

The knight is directed to d3 from where it exerts pressure on Black's central pawns and assists the f-pawn's advance.

17...b6 18 ♘d3 ♗d7 19 f4 ♖ae8 20 ♖ce1

White is slightly better, Dautov-Hraček, Nussloch 1996.

D22)

6 ♗g2 *(D)*

6...♗xd2+ 7 ♘bxd2

The point of Black's 5th move comes to light if White chooses to recapture with the queen: after 7 ♕xd2 Black can proceed 7...♘e4 8 ♕c2 ♕b4+, when 9 ♘c3 ♘xc3 10 ♕xc3 ♕xc3+

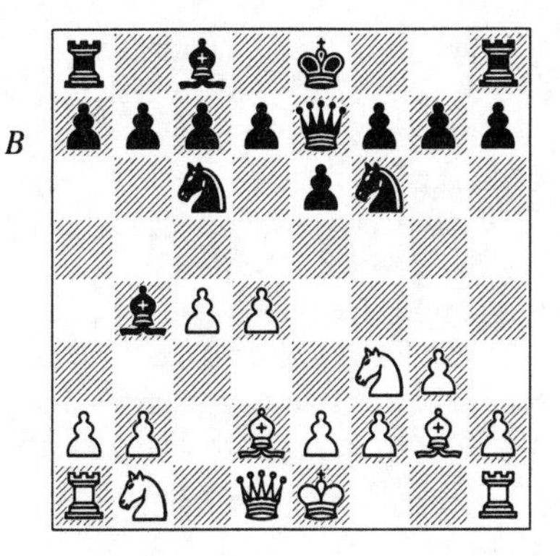

11 bxc3 leaves White with unpleasant doubled pawns and 9 ♘bd2 ♘xd2 10 ♕xd2 ♕xc4 nets a pawn for Black.

7...d6 8 0-0 *(D)*

Alternatives:

a) 8 e4 e5 9 d5 ♘b8 10 b4 0-0 11 0-0 transposes to Line D221.

b) 8 ♘f1 is an interesting idea. The knight is going to e3, from where it controls the central squares d5 and f5, and prevents a later ...♗g4. Black may choose between:

b1) 8...d5 9 a3 (avoiding a queen check on b4, which Black was allowed in Zysk-Hecht, Bundesliga 1988/9 after 9 ♘e3, the game went 9...♕b4+ 10 ♕d2 a5 11 ♖c1 0-0 12 a3 ♕xd2+ 13 ♔xd2 ♘e4+ 14 ♔e1 ♖d8 =) 9...0-0 10 ♘e3 ♖d8 11 0-0 (11 ♕b3!?) 11...dxc4 12 ♘xc4 e5 (12...♘xd4 13 ♘xd4 c5 appears good for Black) 13 ♘fxe5 ♘xd4 14 e3 ♘e6 15 ♕c2 a5 16 b3 ± Cifuentes-Dgebuadze, Malaga 1998.

b2) 8...e5 9 ♘e3 0-0 and now:

b21) 10 0-0 a5 11 ♖c1 ♖e8 12 b3 (12 d5) 12...e4! 13 ♘h4 g6 14 ♕d2 ♘b8 15 c5 d5 = Christiansen-Adams, Biel 1991.

b22) 10 ♖c1 (perhaps the most accurate) 10...♖e8 11 d5 ♘b8 12 b4 a5 13 a3 ♘g4 14 ♘xg4 ♗xg4 15 ♘d2 ♘a6 16 ♖b1 ± Gleizerov-Gasymov, St Petersburg 1994.

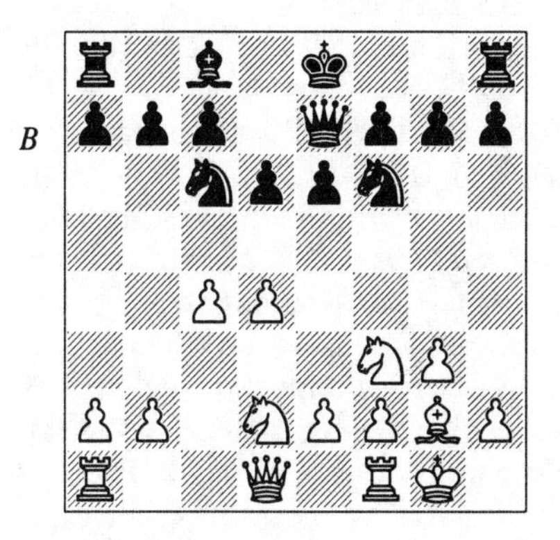

We have now come to a cross-roads for Black, who can choose between:

D221)

8...0-0 9 e4 e5

9...a5 is also possible. If White then wants to exploit Black's move-order, he could try 10 e5, but 10 d5 seems best:

a) 10...♘e5!? 11 ♘xe5 (11 ♘d4!?) 11...dxe5 12 ♕c2 exd5 13 cxd5 c6 14 ♘c4 ♕c5! 15 ♖ac1 ♖e8 16 ♖fe1 ± Hort-Seirawan, Lugano 1989.

b) 10...♘b8 11 dxe6 ♗xe6 12 ♘d4 ♘c6 13 ♘xc6 bxc6 14 ♕a4 ♖fb8 15 ♕a3 ♘d7 16 f4 and White is better, Lautier-Bologan, Erevan OL 1996.

10 d5 ♘b8 11 b4

This shows the drawback of 8...0-0 as opposed to the pre-emptive 8...a5.

White can expand on the queenside straight away.

11 ♘e1 a5 transposes into Line D222.

11...a5

Alternatives are:

a) 11...c6 12 ♖c1 (or 12 dxc6 ♘xc6 13 b5 ♘a5 14 ♕a4 b6 15 ♘e1 a6 16 ♘c2 axb5 17 ♕xb5 ♗a6 18 ♕b4 ♕c7 19 ♘e3 ♖ab8 20 ♖fc1 ♘c6 with an unclear position, Kurajica-Ivanović, Yugoslav Ch 1983) 12...cxd5 (this releases the tension prematurely; better is 12...a5 13 a3 ♗g4 14 ♕b3 axb4 15 axb4 ♘a6 with approximately equal play) 13 exd5! ♘a6 14 ♕b3 b6 15 ♖fe1 (intending ♘d4) 15...♕d8 16 ♘b1! ♘e8 17 ♘c3 with a distinct advantage to White, Popov-Sofrevski, Istanbul 1975.

b) 11...♗g4 12 ♕b3 ♗xf3 13 ♗xf3 a5?! (this does not seem right, but otherwise White simply has a nice space advantage) 14 bxa5 ♖a7 15 ♕c3 ♘bd7 16 ♘b3 ± Karpov-Seirawan, Mazatlan rpd 1988.

12 a3 ♘a6

12...♗g4 has also been played a few times, but the move seems premature here, and only appears to give White more options. An example is 13 h3 ♗xf3 (13...♗d7!?) 14 ♕xf3 ♘a6 15 ♖ab1 axb4 (after 15...c6 16 dxc6 bxc6 White has a pleasant choice between 17 ♕c3, as in the game, and 17 b5) 16 axb4 c5 17 dxc6 bxc6 18 ♕c3 ± Van der Sterren-Langeweg, Dutch Ch (Hilversum) 1984. In such positions Black tends to have better chances if his light-squared bishop is still alive.

13 ♕b3!

Presumably better than 13 ♘e1 ♗g4 14 f3 ♗d7 15 ♘d3, which transposes to Line D222.

13...♗g4

13...c6 is possible too, but after 14 dxc6 bxc6 15 ♕c3 White seems to enjoy a small advantage:

a) 15...♘c7?! 16 c5 dxc5 17 ♕xe5 ♕xe5 18 ♘xe5 is very good for White.

b) Seirawan suggests the preliminary 15...♖e8!? with the idea ...♘c7-e6.

c) 15...♗g4 16 ♘h4! ♖fb8 17 ♖fb1 (17 ♘f5 ♗xf5 18 exf5 axb4 19 axb4 d5 20 b5 with a small advantage for White, is probably better) 17...♘c7 18 h3! (18 ♘b3 axb4 19 axb4 ♖xa1 followed by ...d5 should be OK for Black) 18...♗d7 19 bxa5!? (or 19 ♘b3 axb4 20 axb4 ♖xa1 21 ♖xa1 ♕d8!? with an approximately equal position) 19...g6 Korchnoi-Seirawan, Brussels 1988, and now Korchnoi recommends 20 ♖xb8+ ♖xb8 21 ♖b1 ♖a8 22 ♖b6, when White is better.

14 ♖fb1

Alternatives:

a) 14 h3 should probably be met by 14...♗d7!?, when h3 is a slight weakness in White's position.

b) 14 ♖fc1 c6 15 ♘e1 axb4 16 axb4 c5! 17 b5 ♘b4 18 ♘f1 ♖fb8 = Psakhis-T.Petrosian, Kislovodsk tt 1982.

c) 14 ♘h4! was recommended by Petrosian, whereafter for instance 14...c6 15 dxc6 bxc6 16 ♕c3 transposes to note 'c' to the previous move.

14...c6 15 ♘e1 axb4 16 axb4 c5! *(D)*

17 ♘d3

White cannot hope for any advantage after 17 b5 ♘b4.

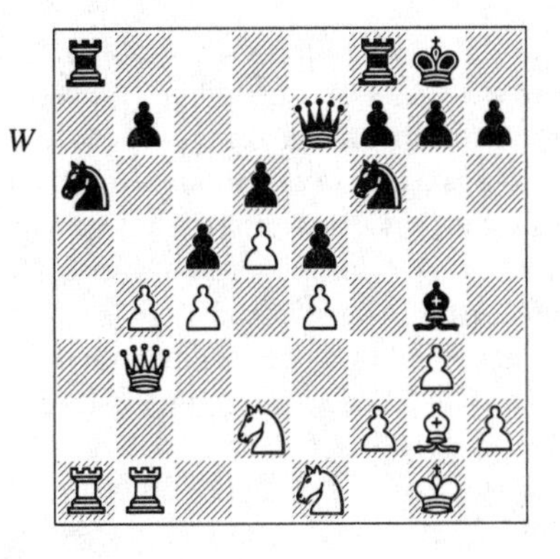

17...cxb4 18 ♘xb4 ♘c5 19 ♕e3 ♕c7 20 f4!?

20 h3!? ♗d7 21 f4 is maybe more accurate.

20...exf4! 21 gxf4 ♖ae8!

Black has good counterplay, Beliavsky-Salov, Brussels 1988.

D222)

8...a5 *(D)*

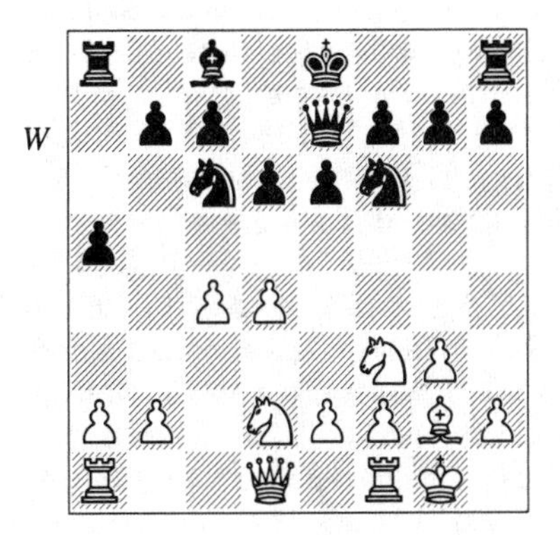

9 e4 e5

9...0-0 10 d5 transposes to Line D221.

10 d5 ♘b8 11 ♘e1

White wants to centralize his knight on d3, from where it supports the logical pawn advances c5, f4 and a3 followed by b4.

More direct queenside action beginning with 11 c5!? is also possible:

a) 11...dxc5 12 ♘c4 seems to give White pretty good compensation:

a1) 12...♘bd7 13 d6 ♕e6 14 ♖c1! b5 15 ♘cxe5! ♘xe5 16 ♘xe5 cxd6 (16...♕xe5 17 f4 ♕xd6 18 e5 ♕xd1 19 ♖fxd1 ♖b8 20 exf6 is also very good for White) 17 ♘c6 ♗b7 18 e5! dxe5 19 ♖xc5 ± Beliavsky-Dückstein, Vienna 1986.

a2) 12...0-0 13 ♖e1 (13 ♘cxe5!? still needs to be tested) 13...♘bd7 14 ♕d2 b6 15 ♘h4 g6 16 f4 with unclear play, Petursson-Adamski, Oslo 1983.

b) 11...0-0 12 cxd6 cxd6 13 a3 (planning to gain more space on the queenside with b4 has proven a better plan than 13 ♘e1 or 13 ♘h4) and now:

b1) 13...♘a6 (this does not prevent b4, but it is the most natural square for the knight in this variation) 14 b4 ♗d7 15 ♕b3 axb4 16 axb4 ♗b5 17 ♖fc1 ♖fc8 18 ♗h3 ♖c7?! (Black is reluctant to hand over the c-file to White, but 18...♖xc1+ 19 ♖xc1 ♕d8 intending ...♕b6 would nevertheless have been fine for Black) 19 ♘h4 g6 and now the very strong move 20 ♖e1! ensures White a small advantage, Ki.Georgiev-Cebalo, Sofia 1986. His bishop on h3 stops Black doubling rooks on the c-file, so White can peacefully avoid exchanges and instead switch his attention to the kingside. It is not easy for Black to find better places for his pieces, and so it is all up to White, who can also consider a positional plan with ♘g2-e3. Note also that ...♗d7 is almost always met by ♗f1.

b2) 13...a4! 14 ♘e1 ♗d7 15 ♘d3 ♗b5 16 ♕f3 ♘a6 17 ♖fc1 ♘d7! (much better than 17...♗xd3 18 ♕xd3 ♘c5 19 ♕b5 ± Beliavsky-Rashkovsky, Lvov 1981) 18 ♗h3 ♘dc5 19 ♘xc5 ♘xc5 20 ♖c3 ♕g5 = Naumkin-Lysenko, USSR 1983.

11...0-0

This is the most logical continuation but Black can also play:

a) 11...♘a6 normally transposes to lines considered later after 12 ♘d3, but Lautier-Shaked, Tilburg 1997 continued independently with 12 ♕b3 (in fact the move-order was 11 ♕b3 0-0 12 ♘e1 ♘a6) 12...0-0 13 ♕c3 ♘c5 14 b3 c6 15 ♘c2 cxd5?! (Ftačnik recommends 15...♗d7 followed by ...♖fc8) 16 exd5 ♗f5 17 ♖fe1 ♕c7 18 h3 ♗g6 19 ♖e3 ♕b6 20 a3 and now 20...♖fc8 would have more or less equalized.

b) 11...h5!? is a sharp move avoiding stereotyped positions. Then there is a wide choice for White:

b1) 12 ♘d3 h4 13 ♕e2 (13 f4 hxg3 14 hxg3 ♘g4 15 ♕e2 ♘h2 leads to an unclear position, according to Ilinčić) 13...♘a6 14 b3 hxg3 15 hxg3 ♘b4 (15...♗g4!? 16 f3 ♗d7 intending ...♘h5 is interesting) 16 ♘xb4 axb4 17 a3 bxa3 18 ♖a2 ♗h3 19 ♗xh3 ♖xh3 20 ♖fa1 ♕d7 21 ♖xa3 ♖xa3 22 ♖xa3 ♖h6 23 ♖a8+ ♔e7 24 ♖a7 ♕h3 25 ♕f3 ♘g4! = D.Ippolito-Yermolinsky, Reno 1996.

b2) 12 h3 h4 13 g4 (White has a large space advantage, but all his pawns are on light squares, which makes most endings in Black's favour) 13...♘bd7 14 ♘d3 g5 (preventing White from breaking with f4 and also ensuring an eventual outpost on f4; Ivanchuk-Ro.Hernandez, Lucerne Wcht 1989 instead saw 14...b6 15 ♕c2 ♘c5 16 ♘xc5 bxc5 17 f4 ♘d7 18 f5 and White was better) and now:

b21) 15 ♖e1 (intending ♘f1-e3) 15...♘c5 16 ♘xc5 dxc5 17 ♘f1 ♔d8!? 18 b3 ♘e8 19 ♘e3 ♖h6!? 20 ♕d2 (20 ♘f5 ♗xf5 21 exf5 is probably slightly better for White) 20...♖b6 21 ♖ab1 a4 22 ♕c3 f6 = Lein-Henley, Hastings 1982/3.

b22) 15 ♕a4 ♘h7?! (White should not be allowed to advance so far and so quickly on the queenside, and so 15...♔d8!? is worth considering) 16 b4 ♘hf8 17 c5 ♘g6 18 ♘c4 and White is better, J.Horvath-Chandler, Manila OL 1992.

b23) 15 b3 and then:

b231) 15...♘c5 16 ♘e1! ♗d7 17 a3 followed by b4 was better for White in Zilberberg-Sloth, corr. 1992.

b232) 15...♘f8 16 a3 ♘g6 17 ♖e1 0-0 18 b4 ♗d7 19 f3 b6 20 ♕c2 c5 = Piket-Shaked, Tilburg 1997.

b3) 12 ♘c2 h4 13 ♘e3 g6 14 b3 ♘a6 15 a3 ♔f8 16 b4 ♔g7 17 ♘b3 b6 18 ♘c1 (Black obtains some compensation if White takes on a5: 18 bxa5 bxa5 19 ♘xa5 ♘c5 20 ♘c6 ♕e8 21 f3 ♗d7 22 ♘b4 hxg3 23 hxg3 ♘h5) 18...♗d7 19 ♘d3 ♖h7 with an unclear game, Meduna-Rashkovsky, Lvov 1981.

b4) 12 h4 0-0 13 ♘d3 ♘a6 (both sides have weakened their respective king's positions but Black has gained control of g4, which should make White more reluctant to push his pawn to f4) 14 a3 ♗g4 15 ♕e1!? (Finkel also considers 15 f3 ♗d7 16 b4 c6!? 17 bxa5 cxd5 18 exd5 ♗f5 19 ♘e4 ♘d7 20 ♖b1 ♘dc5 21 ♖b5! ♗xe4 22 fxe4 g6, with unclear play) 15...a4! 16 ♕e3 c6 17 ♖ac1 ♖fc8!? (intending 18...cxd5; if the immediate 17...cxd5 then 18 exd5 and now 18...♖fc8 can be met by 19 f4!) 18 c5!? ♘xc5 19 ♘xc5 dxc5 20 ♘c4! ♘d7 with an unclear position, Bykhovsky-Finkel, Israel 1994.

b5) The switchback 12 ♘ef3! *(D)* is currently regarded as White's best option:

B

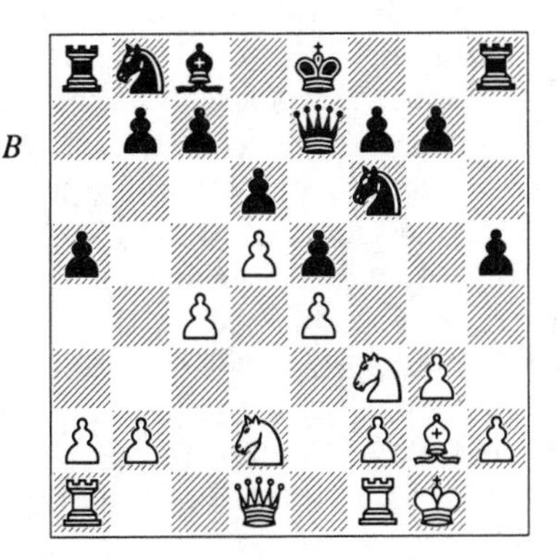

b51) 12...♗g4 13 ♕b3! b6 14 c5 (White should probably prefer 14 ♕e3 ♗xf3 15 ♘xf3 ♘bd7 16 ♘h4! ♘g4 17 ♕e2 g6 18 ♗h3 ♘df6 19 f3 ♘h6 20 ♕d2! ± Ilinčić-Arkell, Bratislava 1996) 14...dxc5 (the only move) 15 ♘xe5! ♕xe5 16 ♘c4 a4! (White's queen must be forced away from b3; in a few moves it becomes clear why) 17 ♕c2 (17 ♕b5+ is met by 17...♗d7) 17...♕g5 18 f4 ♕h6 19 e5 and now Black can play:

b511) 19...♘fd7 20 h3 h4 21 hxg4 hxg3 22 ♖f3 is better for White.

b512) 19...♘g8 20 d6 gives White a great attack.

b513) 19...♘xd5?! 20 ♗xd5 ♖a7 21 ♖ae1!? (threatening 22 e6, but Tukmakov also considered 21 f5 h4 22 ♖f4!?) 21...♗e6! 22 ♗g2 (22 ♘e3!?) 22...g6 23 ♘e3 ♘d7 24 ♕e4 and White has good compensation, Tukmakov-K.Arkell, Reykjavik 1990.

b514) 19...♘h7! (the validity of White's sacrifice is tested for real after this move) 20 d6 ♖a7 21 dxc7 ♖xc7 (here we see why it was essential to force White's queen away from b3 at move 16; with the queen on b3, White could now have taken on b6) 22 ♘d6+ ♔e7 23 f5 h4 and it is Black who seems to have the more dangerous attack, Maiwald-De Boer, Groningen 1991.

b52) 12...♘bd7 13 ♘h4 g6 14 ♕e1 ♘c5 15 ♕e3 ♗d7 16 ♖ae1 0-0 17 h3 ♘h7! 18 ♔h2 b5 19 b3 bxc4 20 ♘xc4 ♗b5 with counterplay, Pelletier-Izeta, Ubeda 1998.

12 ♘d3 *(D)*

12...♗g4

Black wishes to provoke the move f3 before dropping the bishop back to d7. As d7 is a good square for the bishop in any case, this does not constitute a loss of time.

Alternatively Black can continue 12...♘a6:

a) 13 b3 ♗g4 14 f3 ♗d7 15 ♕e2 c6 16 ♖fc1 cxd5 17 cxd5 b5 = Danielsen-Ruban, Nørresundby 1992.

B

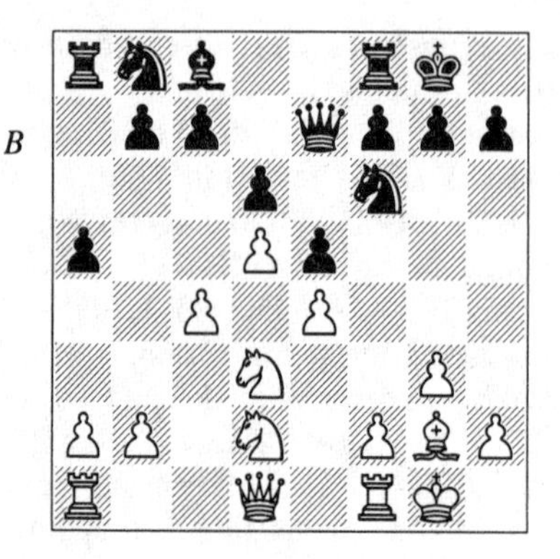

b) 13 a3 ♗g4 (Black might also try 13...♘c5!? or 13...c6!?) 14 f3 ♗d7 and then:

b1) 15 f4 was played in Cosma-Certić, Belgrade 1995 (but via the move-order 13...♗d7 14 f4 so in fact the move-numbers were decreased by one): 15...♗g4 16 ♗f3 (Certić considered 16 ♕e1 to be stronger, for example 16...exf4 17 gxf4 ♖ae8 18 ♕e3 c6 19 dxc6 bxc6 20 c5! and White is better) 16...♗xf3 17 ♕xf3 ♘d7 18 b4 (18 b3!?) 18...c6 19 ♕e3 (19 f5!?) 19...exf4! 20 gxf4 cxd5 21 cxd5 axb4 22 axb4 ♘c7 23 ♕d4 ♘f6 and Black stood well.

b2) 15 b4. Now to avoid getting squeezed on the queenside Black should break up White's advance by playing ...c6. He can do so either before or after exchanging on b4:

b21) 15...c6 with a further branch:

b211) 16 ♕b3?! cxd5 17 cxd5 (in view of what follows, White might try 17 exd5 axb4 18 axb4 b5 19 f4!?) 17...axb4 18 axb4 ♘c7 (Black has obtained fine control of the queenside and intends to centralize his knight with ...♘b5-d4) 19 ♕b2?! ♗b5 20 ♖a3 ♖xa3 21 ♕xa3 ♗a6! with a slight advantage for Black, Skembris-Beliavsky, Yugoslav Cht (Igalo) 1994.

b212) 16 dxc6 bxc6 17 ♘b3 (17 ♕b3!? is better) 17...axb4 18 axb4 d5 19 c5 dxe4 20 fxe4 ♗e6 and Black has a good position, Van der Sterren-Douven, Amsterdam 1989.

b213) 16 bxa5 (anti-positional, but arguing that Black should have exchanged on b4 before playing ...c6) 16...cxd5 (after 16...♕d8!?, 17 ♘b3 cxd5 18 cxd5 ♗a4 is a little annoying for White but he could try 17 f4!?) 17 cxd5 ♗b5 18 ♕b3 ♘c7 19 ♘c4! (19 a4 ♗xd3 20 ♕xd3 ♖xa5 21 ♖fb1 ♘d7 22 ♕c3 ♖c5 23 ♕b4 b5 24 axb5 ♖xb5 = Beliavsky) 19...♗a6?! (better is 19...♗xc4 20 ♕xc4 ♖xa5 21 ♖fb1 b5, with only an edge for White) 20 a4 and White is better, Notkin-Karpeshov, Russian Cht (Briansk) 1995.

b22) 15...axb4 16 axb4 c6 17 dxc6 bxc6 18 ♕c2 (18 ♕b3!?) 18...d5 19 c5?! (19 b5?! ♘b4 20 ♘xb4 ♕xb4 21 bxc6 ♕c5+ 22 ♔h1 ♗xc6 is also good for Black, but Yusupov recommends 19 ♕c3!? ♗e6 20 ♖a5 as a superior possibility for White) 19...♗e6?! (according to Yusupov, 19...dxe4 20 ♘xe4 ♘d5 21 ♕d2 ♗f5 is a better option for Black) 20 ♖a4! dxe4 21 fxe4 (21 ♘xe4 ♘d5 22 ♕d2 =) 21...♘g4! 22 ♖fa1 ♘c7 23 ♖xa8 ♘xa8! = Seirawan-Yusupov, Belgrade 1991.

c) 13 f4 ♘d7 and now:

c1) 14 f5 c6?! (14...f6 15 a3 ♘dc5 is better) 15 a3! ♘ac5 (here Black would have a rather cramped position after 15...f6 16 b4) 16 ♘xc5 ♘xc5 17 f6! gxf6 18 ♕h5 with a promising attack, Servat-Milos, São Luis 1995.

c2) 14 ♕f3 ♘dc5 (14...♘ac5 is best met by 15 ♘f2!) 15 ♘xc5 ♘xc5 16 f5 ♗d7 17 ♕e3 (planning 18 f6 gxf6 19 ♕h6 with an attack; the direct 17 f6?! can be answered by 17...♕xf6 18 ♕xf6 gxf6 19 ♖xf6 ♔g7 20 ♖af1 b5! with counterplay) 17...f6 *(D)* is a position reached twice in the Mecking-Seirawan match in 1992. White has, as usual, a space advantage, but it seems that Black has reasonable counterplay:

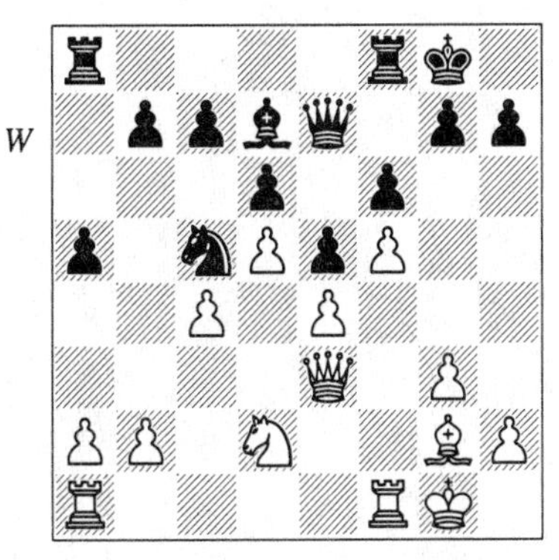

c21) 18 ♗f3 g5 (18...g6! is recommended by Seirawan, with the idea 19 g4 g5!, which is fine for Black, but White should play 19 ♗e2) 19 h4! gxh4 20 gxh4 ♔h8 21 ♔h2 ♖g8 22 ♖g1 and White has the better prospects, Mecking-Seirawan, São Paulo (2) 1992.

c22) 18 b3! (it is not clear that White can break through on the kingside, so instead he prepares to expand on the queenside) 18...b5 (this may not be the right pawn break; I would prefer 18...c6) 19 cxb5 ♗xb5 20 ♖fc1 c6 21 dxc6 ♕c7 Mecking-Seirawan, São Paulo (6) 1992 and now Seirawan considers 22 ♘c4 to be White's best, and after 22...♗xc4 23 ♖xc4 ♕xc6 a dynamically equal middlegame arises.

Returning to the position after 12...♗g4 *(D)*:

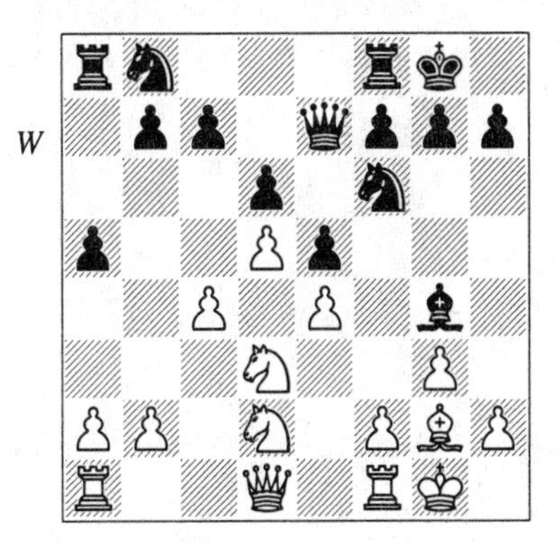

13 ♕e1

Or 13 f3 (avoiding a loss of time but weakening the dark squares and decreasing the scope of the g2-bishop) 13...♗d7 14 ♕b3 ♘a6:

a) 15 f4 ♘g4 16 ♖ae1 b6 17 h3 ♘h6 18 fxe5 dxe5 19 ♖f2 f6 = Speelman-Seirawan, Brussels 1988.

b) 15 ♕c3 b6 16 b3 ♘c5 17 a3 ♘h5 (preparing counterplay with ...♕g5 and ...f5) 18 ♘b2!? ♕g5 19 b4 ♘a6 20 ♖ae1 (capturing the a-pawn would allow Black's queen to penetrate: 20 bxa5 bxa5 21 ♕xa5 ♕e3+ 22 ♖f2 ♖fb8 with good compensation) 20...f5 (20...g6!?) 21 exf5 ♗xf5 22 ♘e4 ♕h6 23 ♘d3 ♘b8 24 c5 ± Adianto-Benjamin, New York 1991.

13...♘a6 14 ♕e3

The queen is placed more actively, but perhaps 14 f4!? is even stronger, intending to trap the bishop with f5. 14...exf4 (on 14...♗d7, Volkov intended 15 fxe5 dxe5 16 ♘f3 ♘b4 17 ♘fxe5 ♘c2 18 ♕c3 ♘xa1 19 ♖xa1 with compensation, although I believe Black ought to go for this) 15 gxf4 ♖fe8 16 a3 a4 17 ♕e3 ♗d7 18 ♖ae1 and White is better, S.Volkov-Loginov, Kstovo 1997.

14...♗d7 15 f4

According to Van Wely, 15 a3, with the point 15...c6 16 ♕b6, is better.

15...♘b4 16 ♘e1 c6 17 a3 exf4 18 gxf4 ♘a6 19 ♕d4

Since the queen is undefended on e3, there is unfortunately no time to bring the knight into the game with 19 ♘d3, owing to 19...cxd5 20 cxd5 ♘xd5.

19...cxd5 20 cxd5 ♘c5 21 e5 ♘g4 22 ♘ef3 ♗b5 23 ♖fc1 ♘d3

The position is complicated, Van Wely-Adams, New York Open 1996.

6 4 ♗d2: The Aggressive 4...c5

1 d4 ♘f6 2 c4 e6 3 ♘f3 ♗b4+ 4 ♗d2 c5 *(D)*

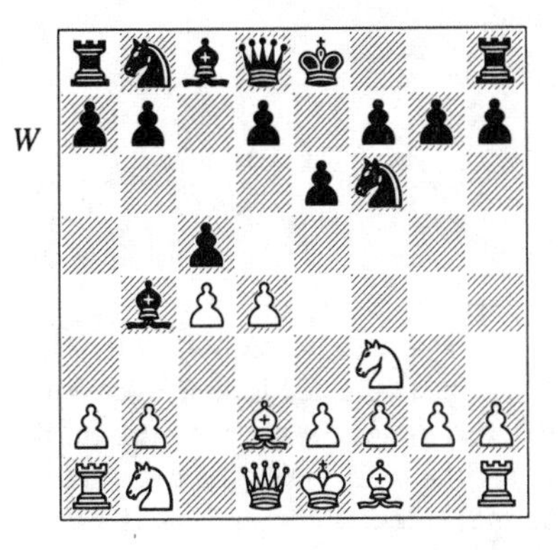

This strange-looking move is an attempt to liven up the Bogo-Indian, and appeals to players who are willing to experiment and are looking for an interesting strategic battle. Black is willing to accept doubled b-pawns, but in return hopes to create pressure on the c-file or, with the help of the central advance ...e6-e5, to provoke White into moving his d-pawn and so give Black a strong-point on c5.

The move 4...c5 was regarded as somewhat off-beat up to its use by Korchnoi to gain a winning position against Kasparov in 1986. Thereafter it became part of the respectable main-line theory of the Bogo.

Typical Pawn Structures

The following position resembles a typical example of Black having implemented a basic part of his strategy. The ...e5 thrust has been made, to which White has replied by moving the d-pawn one step forward. Thereby Black has gained good control of the c5-square and has possibilities of creating pressure down the c-file.

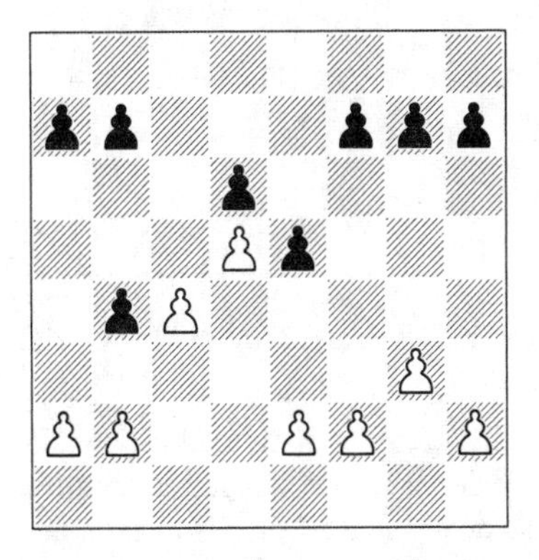

In the next diagram White has decided to get rid of the irritating pawn on b4 and has opened the a-file by playing a3. Black has again carried out the ...e5 advance but this time White has chosen to ignore it. By supporting his d-pawn with e3, White refuses to concede the important c5-square.

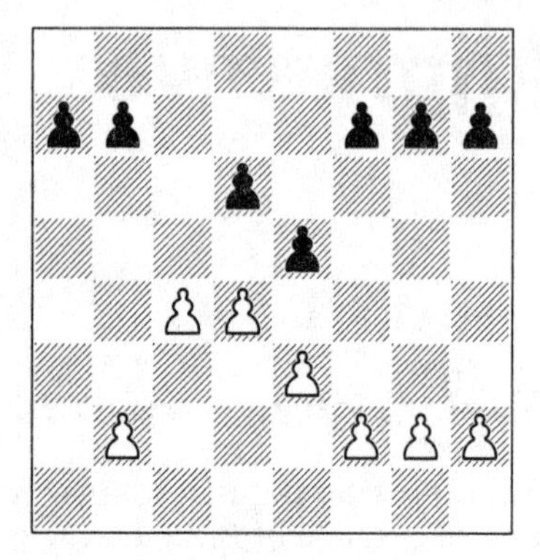

Planning for White

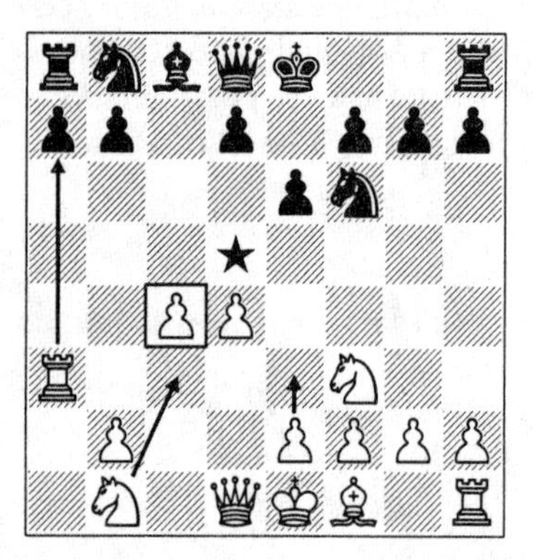

Black's far-advanced b-pawn does hinder White's normal development, so a very logical plan is to exchange it off by the move a3. This is what has happened in the above diagram. The semi-open a-file may help White to generate some play there but, more importantly, sensible development with ♘c3, e3, etc., is now feasible. As we shall soon find out, a frequent plan for Black is to advance by ...d6 and ...e5, and thus White may well try to make use of the d5-square. Developing with e3, contrary to the fianchetto, has the advantage that the slightly vulnerable c-pawn is protected.

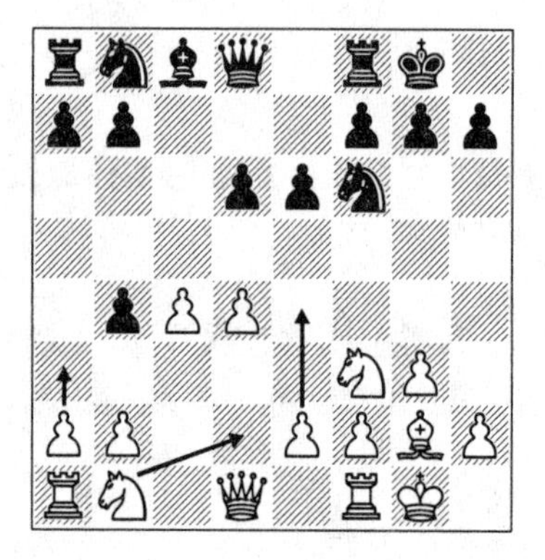

An even more popular plan for White is a kingside fianchetto, hoping to exert considerable pressure on the long diagonal h1-a8. However, this diagonal often becomes closed. White retains the possibility of opening the queenside by a3 but awaits the course of events. Sometimes it may be worth arguing that with one more central pawn there is no reason for White to open the queenside. A fairly standard way to develop is to play ♘bd2 and e4, to which Black often reacts by playing ...d6 and preparing ...e5 in some way (often by ...♘c6 or ...♖e8). When Black has played the ...e5 advance, one idea for White is to close the centre with d5 and play for a space advantage by opening up the queenside by a3. This has the obvious disadvantage of giving up the c5-square, but White is able to fight to regain control of it by bringing a knight to d3.

Planning for Black

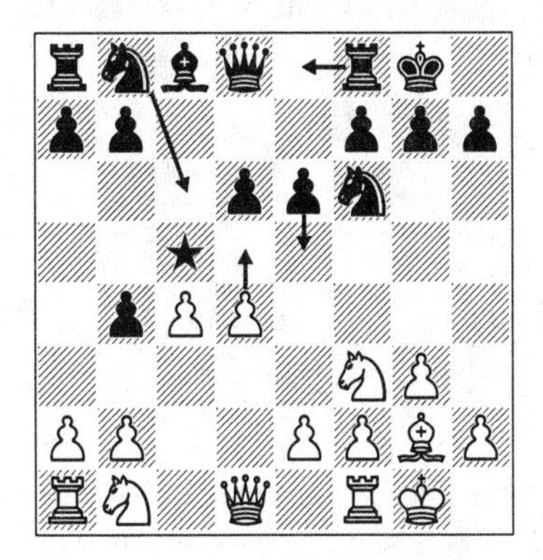

Here we have the same starting point as in the previous diagram. We already know that White wants to play ♘bd2 followed by e4. A common way to counter this is to play ...♘c6 and ...e5. Preparing ...e5 by ...♖e8 is also seen once in a while, but often Black will need his knight on c6 anyway. The idea behind ...e5 is either to dissolve the tension in the centre or to provoke d5, which gives White a small space advantage but also abandons control of the key c5-square.

Quick Summary

5 ♗xb4 is without doubt the most popular move, but players who are not keen on the strategic elements arising after this have seemed to favour the immediate fianchetto 5 g3 (Line A). Then Black's sharpest continuation, 5...♕b6, has been the most popular. After 6 ♗g2 ♘c6 Black increases the pressure on the d4-pawn and virtually forces White to sacrifice it with 7 d5. Nonetheless this is a dangerous sacrifice and Black must be careful, but practice has shown that his defensive resources after 7...exd5 8 cxd5 ♘xd5 9 0-0 ♘de7 10 e4 d6! are adequate.

The main line is 5 ♗xb4 cxb4, when White has chosen between several different set-ups. The quiet 6 e3 (Line B1) should cause Black no real worries. He has the choice between a queenside fianchetto, and traditional development based on ...0-0, ...d6 and ...♘c6. 6 a3 (Line B2) is more dangerous. Here White opens the a-file and in some cases hopes to exert even more pressure by advancing his b-pawn. Again Black can develop traditionally or choose a queenside fianchetto. Line B3, 6 g3, is the most common. By developing the bishop to g2 immediately, White attempts to make the fianchetto less attractive for Black, who may thus choose to play 6...0-0 7 ♗g2 d6. With 8 ♘bd2 (Line B31) White intends to bring this knight to e3. Then if Black plays ...e5 at some stage White has better control of the d5- and f5-squares. The drawback of this is that it is rather time-consuming and it is more often seen that White chooses the simple 8 0-0 (Line B32). Then 8...♖e8 (Line B321) and 8...♘c6 (Line B322) involve the same idea, namely to play ...e5. After 8...♖e8, Black still needs to play ...♘c6 to be able to force ...e5, and the line 9 a3 ♘c6 10 d5! exd5 11 cxd5 ♘e7 12 axb4 ♘exd5 13 b5 has proved quite good for White. Therefore attention is focused on 8...♘c6.

The Theory of 4 ♗d2 c5

1 d4 ♘f6 2 c4 e6 3 ♘f3 ♗b4+ 4 ♗d2 c5

We shall now investigate two main continuations for White:

Others can be dismissed fairly quickly. For example, 5 a3 is rather innocuous, despite having been tried by a few strong players. 5...♗xd2+ 6 ♕xd2 cxd4 7 ♘xd4 0-0 8 ♘c3 d5! and then:

a) 9 cxd5 ♘xd5 10 e3 ♘xc3 11 ♕xc3 ♗d7 12 ♗e2 ♘c6 13 ♖d1 ♕g5! 14 ♘f3 ♕e7 15 b4 a6 = Oll-Kengis, Sydney 1991.

b) 9 e3 with a further branch:

b1) 9...dxc4 10 ♗xc4 a6 11 a4 ♗d7 12 0-0 ♘c6 13 ♘xc6 ♗xc6 14 ♕xd8 ♖fxd8 = H.Gretarsson-Petursson, Reykjavik 1996.

b2) 9...a6 10 cxd5 ♘xd5 11 ♗d3 ♘xc3?! 12 ♕xc3 b5 13 ♗e4! ♖a7 14 ♖c1 e5 15 ♘f3 f6 16 ♕c5 ♖e7 17 0-0 ♘d7 18 ♕c2 g6 19 ♖fd1 ± H.Gretarsson-Kosashvili, Reykjavik 1996.

b3) 9...e5!? (much more ambitious, but also more risky) 10 ♘f3 e4 11 ♘d4 dxc4 12 ♗xc4 ♕c7 13 ♗e2 ♕e5 14 ♘db5! ♘c6 15 ♕d6 ♖d8 16 ♕xe5 ♘xe5 with roughly equal chances, Miles-Korchnoi, Biel 1992.

A)

5 g3 *(D)*

5...♕b6

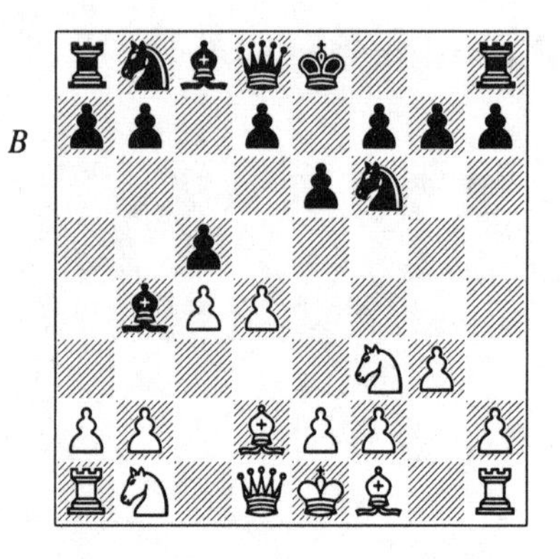
B

This aggressive move is clearly Black's most popular option. He may not really be threatening to win a pawn, but exerts a lot of pressure on White's queenside and d-pawn. The disadvantage is that Black is somewhat neglecting his development. Alternatives:

a) 5...0-0 6 ♗g2 ♘c6 7 0-0 d6 (or 7...♗xd2 8 ♕xd2 d6 9 ♘c3 ♕e7 10 d5 ♘a5 11 b3 e5 12 e4 a6 with an unclear game, Dlugy-Garcia Martinez, Havana 1985) 8 ♗e3 ♕e7 9 d5 exd5 10 cxd5 ♘e5 11 ♘xe5 ♕xe5 12 ♘c3 ♗xc3 13 ♗f4 ♕h5 14 bxc3 ♗h3 15 ♗xh3 ♕xh3 16 f3 ♕d7 17 a4 ♘h5 18 ♗d2 ♖ae8 19 ♖a2 ♘f6 with approximately equal chances, Lputian-Vyzhmanavin, Jurmala 1983.

b) 5...♗xd2+ and then:

b1) 6 ♘bxd2 cxd4 7 ♘xd4 ♕b6 and now:

b11) 8 ♘2b3 was analysed by Yudasin, but doesn't seem to promise anything for White after 8...d5 9 c5 ♕b4+ 10 ♕d2 ♕xd2+ 11 ♘xd2 ♗d7 with equality.

b12) 8 ♘4b3 (also analysed by Yudasin) 8...♕c6 9 e4 ♘xe4 10 ♘d4 ♘c3 (for some reason Yudasin does not take into account the possibility

10...♘xf2, perhaps because he thought that Black's queen is in danger of becoming trapped after something like 11 ♔xf2 ♕xh1 12 ♕h5 ♘c6 13 ♘4f3 b6 14 ♖e1 followed by ♗g2) 11 ♘xc6 ♘xd1 12 ♘xb8 ♘xb2 13 a4 d5! 14 cxd5 exd5 15 ♖a2 ♘c4 16 ♘a6! bxa6 17 ♘xc4 dxc4 18 ♗xc4 =.

b13) 8 ♘b5!? a6 9 ♘c3 ♕c6 (or 9...♕xb2 10 ♘a4 intending ♗g2, ♖b1 and c5 gives Black difficulties getting the bishop out) 10 e4 d6 11 ♗g2 0-0 12 0-0 ♕c7 13 ♔h1!? ♘c6 14 ♖c1 ♗d7 15 f4 ♖ac8 16 g4! h6 17 ♘b3! and White has a promising position, Yudasin-Izeta, Dos Hermanas 1993.

b2) After 6 ♕xd2 ♘e4 it has not really been established where White should put his queen:

b21) 7 ♕d3 ♕a5+ 8 ♘fd2 ♘xd2 9 ♘xd2 cxd4 10 ♕xd4 0-0 11 ♗g2 ♘c6 12 ♕d3 (12 ♕d6!?) 12...♘e5 13 ♕c2 ♖b8 14 0-0 ♕c7 15 ♖ac1 b6 16 ♖fd1 f5 ½-½ Stohl-Hulak, Slovakia-Croatia match, Piestany 1996.

b22) 7 ♕e3 ♕a5+ 8 ♘bd2 ♘xd2 9 ♘xd2 0-0 (9...cxd4 10 ♕xd4 transposes to 'b21') 10 dxc5 ♘a6 11 ♗g2 ♕xc5 12 ♕xc5 ♘xc5 13 0-0-0 a5 14 ♘b1 ♖d8 15 ♖d6 ♖a6 16 ♖hd1 and White is clearly better, as Black will have great difficulties getting his bishop out without losing too much material, Kramnik-P.Nikolić, Munich rpd 1994.

b23) 7 ♕c2 ♕a5+ 8 ♘bd2 ♘xd2 9 ♕xd2 ♕xd2+ 10 ♔xd2 is not a terrifying ending for Black. Black will presumably have to put up with a backward d-pawn, but this will not be difficult to defend, and instead he will be able to generate counterplay on a semi-open b- or c-file.

b231) 10...b6!? 11 ♗g2 ♗b7 12 dxc5 bxc5 13 ♘e1 ♗xg2 14 ♘xg2 ♔e7 15 ♖hd1 d6 16 ♔c3 ♘d7 17 ♘e3 g5!? 18 f3 h5 ∓ Skembris-P.Nikolić, Portorož/Rogaška 1993. Black's d-pawn is not a problem, as the only way White can attack it is by doubling rooks on the d-file, whilst Black can easily defend it by ...♖b8-b6. Meanwhile Black has possibilities practically all over the board. Even pushing the d-pawn may in some cases be feasible.

b232) 10...cxd4 11 ♘xd4 ♘c6 12 e3 (12 ♘b5 is not really dangerous in view of 12...♔e7) 12...d6 13 ♗g2 ♗d7 14 ♖ac1 ♔e7 15 ♖hd1 ♖ac8 16 b3 a6 17 f4 h6 18 h4 ½-½ Yudasin-Karpov, Leon 1993. White has a little more space but Black's position is rock-solid.

6 ♗g2

There are some other possibilities, but none of them promise much:

a) 6 d5 (an unconvincing pawn sacrifice) 6...exd5 7 cxd5 ♘xd5 8 ♗g2 ♘f6 9 0-0 d5 10 ♗g5 0-0 11 ♘c3 ♗xc3 12 bxc3 ♘bd7 and White has nothing to show for his material deficit, Shvidler-Korchnoi, Beersheba 1987.

b) 6 ♕b3 ♘c6 7 dxc5 ♗xc5 (Bareev gave two other ways to equalize: 7...♗xd2+ 8 ♘bxd2 ♕xc5 followed by ...b6 =, or 7...♕xc5 8 ♗xb4 ♕xb4+ 9 ♕xb4 ♘xb4 10 ♘a3 ♔e7 with an equal ending) 8 ♕xb6 axb6! (8...♗xb6 9 ♘c3 is slightly better for White, as the dark-squared bishops are still on the board) 9 ♘c3 d5 10 cxd5 exd5!

(this damages Black's pawn structure, but 10...♘xd5 11 a3 is simply good for White, and activity does count for something too!) 11 ♗g2 0-0 12 0-0 d4! 13 ♘b5, Bareev-Razuvaev, Sochi 1987, and now Bareev suggested 13...♗e6! 14 b4 ♘xb4 15 ♘fxd4 ♗xa2 =.

c) 6 ♘c3 cxd4 7 ♘b5 ♗xd2+ 8 ♕xd2 ♘c6 9 ♘d6+? (White holds the balance, but nothing more, with 9 ♘fxd4) 9...♔e7 10 ♖c1 ♕c5 11 ♘xc8+ ♖axc8 12 a3 ♕a5 13 ♗g2 ♕xd2+ 14 ♘xd2 d6 ∓ Pelts-Petursson, Philadelphia 1989.

6...♘c6

Black's play is based on attacking d4, but note that interpolating an exchange on d2 is inaccurate: 6...♗xd2+?! 7 ♕xd2 ♘c6 8 d5! exd5 9 cxd5 ♘xd5 10 ♕xd5 ♕xb2 11 0-0 ♕xa1 12 ♘bd2! ♕f6 13 ♘e4 with a great attack for White, Barlov-Steinbacher, Biel 1988.

7 d5 exd5 8 cxd5 ♘xd5 *(D)*

W

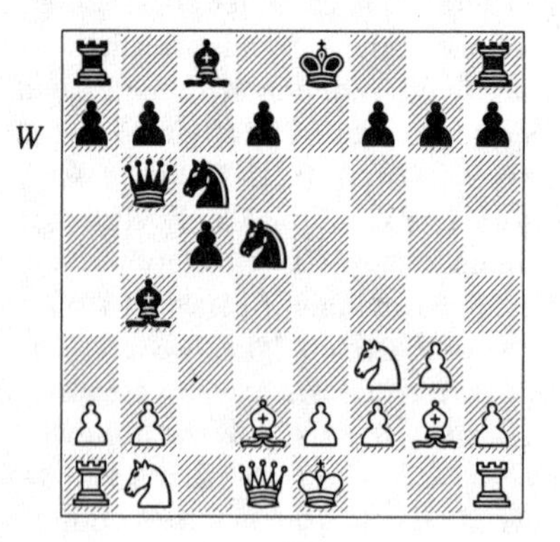

9 0-0

At the cost of a pawn, White has obtained a slight lead in development, and Black will also face some difficulties coordinating his pieces. 9 0-0 does seem like the most logical move, but 9 a3!? is also possible. Then Black has continued 9...♗a5 (9...♗xd2+?! is dubious, as after 10 ♘bxd2 White is threatening ♘c4, and 10...♕xb2 11 ♘c4 ♕c3+ 12 ♘fd2 gives White excellent compensation) 10 ♗xa5 ♕xa5+ 11 ♘fd2 ♘f6 12 ♘c3 d5 (White was threatening ♘c4, and 12...0-0?! 13 ♘c4 ♕c7 14 0-0 intending ♘d6 yields White good compensation) 13 ♘b3 (not 13 ♘xd5? ♘xd5 14 ♗xd5 ♗h3, when White is denied the possibility of castling, and Black is simply threatening ...0-0-0 or ...♖d8) 13...♕b6 14 ♘a4 ♕b5 15 ♘bxc5 (15 ♘c3 ♕b6 is just a repetition) 15...0-0 16 ♕d3 (White has won back the pawn and now happily offers an exchange of queens, which Black can hardly avoid, because 16...♕a5+ 17 b4 is very good for White) 16...♕xd3 17 ♘xd3 and now:

a) 17...♘d4 18 ♖d1! ♗f5 19 e3 ♘b3 20 0-0 ± Barlov-Cebalo, Yugoslav Ch 1989.

b) 17...♗g4 18 h3 ♗f5 19 0-0 (19 ♖d1 is a possible improvement for White) 19...♘d4 20 ♘b4 ♘xe2+ 21 ♔h2 b5 22 ♘c5 ♖ac8 23 ♘b7 ♖c7 24 ♘d6 ♘d4 25 ♖fd1 ♖d8 = Bellon-Schüssler, Haifa Echt 1989.

9...♘de7 10 e4 d6!

An accurate move, as after 10...0-0 11 ♗e3 Black has development difficulties, which cannot be solved tactically by 11...d5 12 exd5 ♖d8, owing to 13 ♘g5! – Kasparov.

11 ♗e3

Borges-Dizdar, Lucerne Wcht 1997 deviated with 11 ♗c3 ♗xc3 12 ♘xc3 ♗g4 13 ♕xd6 ♗xf3 14 ♗xf3 ♖d8 15 ♕f4 ♕xb2 16 ♖fc1 b6, and Black was clearly better.

11...♕c7 12 a3 ♗a5 13 ♘bd2!?

Kasparov-Korchnoi, Brussels 1986 continued with the inferior 13 ♗f4?! ♘e5 14 b4?! cxb4 15 axb4 ♗xb4 16 ♕a4+ ♘7c6 17 ♘d4, and Black should now have played 17...♗c5, when White does not have enough compensation.

13...♗xd2

Black exchanges his bad bishop for a potentially very active knight. This seems to be the only move tried in practice, but Vaisman also gives the possibilities 13...♗e6 14 ♘g5 and 13...♗g4 14 ♖c1, in both cases with compensation for White.

14 ♕xd2

In the game Chiburdanidze-Chandler, Haninge 1988, White stubbornly attempted to bring a knight to c4, and following 14 ♘xd2!? ♗e6 15 f4 f6 16 ♖c1 a5 17 ♕h5+ ♗f7 18 ♕g4 0-0 19 h4 she had some compensation.

14...0-0?!

14...♗g4, as suggested by Vaisman, is more accurate. White should then continue playing for the initiative with 15 b4!.

15 ♖fd1 ♖d8 16 ♗f4 ♗g4 17 ♗xd6 ♕c8! 18 ♕g5 ♕e6 19 ♗xc5 ♖xd1+ 20 ♖xd1

Now 20...♘g6? 21 ♕e3! ♘ge5 22 ♖d5 left White in control in Vaisman-Wirthensohn, Auxerre tt 1987. However, Black can improve on this by 20...♕b3, creating some complications.

B)

5 ♗xb4 cxb4 *(D)*

W

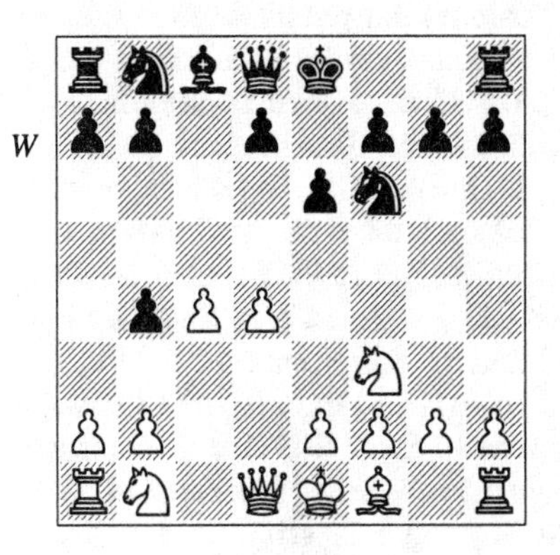

This is the basic position of the so-called Vikoni Variation. White has taken up the challenge and doubled Black's b-pawns, but the very best way to continue after this still needs to be established.

B1: 6 e3	120
B2: 6 a3	122
B3: 6 g3	124

A few other possibilities for White:

a) 6 ♕c2 d6 7 e4 e5 8 c5 0-0 9 cxd6 exd4 10 ♘bd2 ½-½ Timman-P.Nikolić, Tilburg 1987.

b) 6 ♕d3!? is a completely new move, and deserves much more attention; I am actually surprised that no one has come up with the idea before. As in line 'a', White intends to strengthen his centre with e4 but does not allow the counter-thrust ...e5. 6...d6 (6...d5 7 ♘bd2 0-0 8 e3 b6 9 ♗e2 ♗b7 10 0-0 ± Ilinčić) 7 e4 0-0 8 ♘bd2 a5 9 e5 dxe5 10 ♘xe5 ♘fd7 11 ♘df3 (a very sensible continuation but Ilinčić thinks that

11 f4 is even stronger, e.g. 11...♘xe5 12 fxe5 f6 13 exf6 ♕xf6 14 ♘f3 ♘c6 15 ♕e4! followed by ♗d3) 11...♘xe5 12 ♘xe5 ♘c6 13 ♖d1 ♗d7 14 ♗e2 ♘xe5 15 dxe5 ♗c6 16 ♕e3 ♕c7 17 ♖d6 ± Ilinčić-Draško, Pale 1997.

c) 6 ♘bd2 0-0 7 e4 d6 and now:

c1) 8 ♗d3 e5 (8...♕c7 9 0-0 ♘bd7 10 c5 dxc5 11 e5 ♘d5 12 ♗xh7+ ♔xh7 13 ♘g5+ ♔g6 14 ♕g4 f5 15 ♕g3 f4, Quinteros-Seirawan, Biel IZ 1985, 16 ♕g4 ♘7f6 17 exf6 ♘xf6 18 ♘xe6+ ♘xg4 19 ♘xc7 ♖b8 20 dxc5 is clearly better for White) 9 0-0 ♘bd7 (9...♖e8 10 ♖e1 ♗g4 11 ♕b3 ♗xf3 12 ♘xf3 exd4 13 c5!? ♘c6 14 ♘g5 ♖e7 15 f4 led to a rather unclear position in Muse-Schönthier, W.German Ch 1987) 10 a3 bxa3 11 ♖xa3 exd4 12 ♘xd4 ♕b6 13 ♘b5 ♘e5 14 ♗c2 ♗e6 15 b3 ♖fe8 16 ♕a1 a6 17 h3 ♘c6 18 ♖c1 ♕c5 = Karpman-Vitolinš, USSR 1976.

c2) 8 ♕c2 ♘c6 (or 8...♘fd7 9 g3 e5 10 ♗g2 ♘c6 11 d5 ♘cb8 12 a3 ♘a6 with a roughly equal position, Tukmakov-P.Nikolić, Leningrad 1987) 9 ♗d3 ♘d7 10 0-0 e5 11 d5 ♘cb8 12 a3 ♘a6 13 ♘b3 ♕b6 14 axb4 ♘xb4 15 ♕c3 a5 16 ♗b1 ♕c7 17 ♖a3 b6 = Tukmakov-Vitolinš, Jurmala 1985.

c3) 8 ♗e2 ♕c7 (8...♘bd7 9 ♕b3 a5 10 a3 bxa3 11 ♕xa3 ♕c7 12 0-0 b6 13 ♗d1! and now 13...e5?! 14 ♗a4 ♖d8 15 ♖ac1 exd4 16 ♘xd4 was very good for White in Chandler-Kneževič, Keszthely 1981 but 13...♗b7 is more circumspect) 9 0-0 e5 10 c5!? dxc5 11 dxe5 ♘g4 12 ♘h4 ♘xe5 13 f4 ♘ec6 14 e5 ♖d8 15 ♕e1 ♘d4 16 ♗d3 ♘bc6 17 ♘e4 c4 with an unclear position, Ehlvest-Hulak, Zagreb IZ 1987.

B1)

6 e3 *(D)*

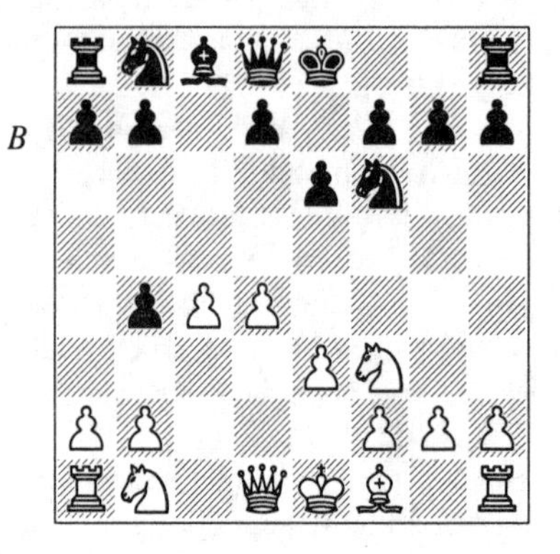

6...0-0

The immediate fianchetto, 6...b6 7 ♗d3 ♗b7, is an important alternative for Black:

a) 8 0-0 0-0 9 a3 bxa3 10 ♘xa3 d6 11 ♖e1 ♘c6 12 ♘c2 e5 13 ♗f1 ♗c8 14 b4 ♗f5 15 b5 ♘a5 16 ♘b4 ♕c7 17 ♖c1 ♖ac8 18 d5! and White is better, Lukacs-Tal, Sochi 1984.

b) 8 ♘bd2 0-0 9 0-0 d6 and here White has tried a variety of ideas:

b1) 10 a3 bxa3 11 bxa3!? ♘bd7 (the knight is committed a little too early; I would prefer 11...♖e8) 12 ♕b1 e5 13 ♘g5 h6 14 ♘ge4 exd4 15 exd4 d5 16 ♘d6 ♗c6 17 ♖e1 dxc4 18 ♘2xc4 ± H.Gretarsson-Vidarsson, Reykjavik 1994.

b2) 10 e4 ♘c6 11 ♖e1 ♘d7 12 ♗f1 e5 13 d5 ♘cb8 14 a3 bxa3 15 b4 a5 16 ♖xa3 ♘a6 17 bxa5 bxa5 with a good position for Black, Orr-Petursson, Manila OL 1992.

b3) 10 ♕b3 a5 11 a3 ♘a6 12 ♖ad1 ♕c7 13 ♗b1!? e5 (13...h6!?) 14 ♘g5

♖fe8 15 ♕c2 looks promising for White, Naumkin-Verat, Paris 1993.

7 ♗e2

White puts no energy into fighting for the e4-square and merely attempts to develop smoothly.

An important alternative is 7 ♗d3 d6 (7...b6 transposes to the previous note) and then:

a) 8 ♕c2 ♘c6 9 ♘bd2 h6 10 0-0 ♕e7 11 ♖fd1 ♗d7 12 ♖ac1 ♖fc8 13 ♕b1 ♘a5 14 ♘e1 b6 15 ♘c2 ♘c6 16 ♘e4 a5 = Portisch-Timman, Tilburg 1988.

b) 8 0-0 ♖e8 9 h3 b6 (of course Black is not quite ready to play ...e5, due to 9...e5? 10 dxe5 dxe5 11 ♘xe5! ♖xe5 12 ♗xh7+) 10 ♘bd2 ♗b7 11 ♘g5 ♘bd7 12 ♖c1 ♖c8 13 ♕b3 a5 14 ♘ge4 ♕c7 15 a3 bxa3 16 ♕xa3 ♗xe4 17 ♘xe4 ♘xe4 18 ♗xe4 ♘b8! = Speelman-P.Nikolić, Brussels 1988.

7...b6

Alternatively there is 7...d6 8 0-0 and now:

a) 8...♘c6 9 ♕b3 (9 a3 bxa3 10 ♖xa3 transposes to Line B2) 9...♕a5!? 10 a3 ♗d7 11 ♖c1 ♖fc8 12 h3 ♖c7 13 ♖d1 b6 14 axb4 ½-½ Gavrikov-Salov, USSR Ch (Moscow) 1988. Gavrikov and Itkis give the variation 14...♕xb4! 15 ♕xb4 ♘xb4 16 ♘c3 =.

b) 8...a5 9 a3 ♘a6 10 ♘bd2 b6 11 ♘e1 e5! (Black wants to develop the bishop to f5, as 11...♗b7 12 ♘d3 bxa3 13 bxa3 is slightly better for White) 12 ♘d3 ♗f5?! (according to Kramnik this is inaccurate, and Black should have played 12...bxa3 13 bxa3 ♖e8 with a fairly even game; after the text-move White liquidates to a slightly better position) 13 dxe5 ♗xd3 14 exf6 ♗xe2 15 ♕xe2 ♕xf6 16 ♘f3 ♖fd8 17 ♖ad1! bxa3 18 bxa3 ± Kramnik-Mokry, Salzburg 1993.

8 0-0 ♗b7 9 ♘bd2 *(D)*

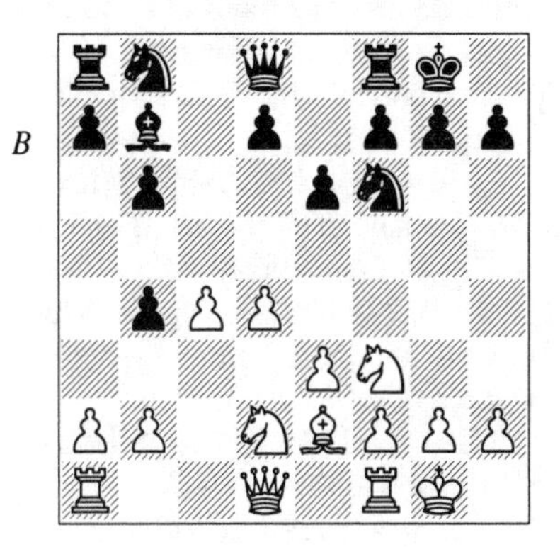

9...d6

The alternative, 9...a5, leads to similar positions, but there is a slight difference in the move-order. 10 a3 ♘a6 11 ♘e1! shows a typical plan for White in the Bogo-Indian; the knight is transferred to d3, from where it pressurizes the b4-pawn and controls some important central squares. Furthermore, White intends to exchange off the bishops. Now:

a) 11...d5?! 12 cxd5 ♘xd5 13 a4! ♘ac7 14 ♘ef3 ♘e7 15 ♘e5 ♖c8 16 ♖e1 ♘cd5 17 ♗f1 ♖c7 18 ♘dc4 was very good for White in the game Ehlvest-Ki.Georgiev, Vršac 1987.

b) 11...♕e7 is suggested by Ehlvest: 12 ♗f3 d6 13 ♘d3 bxa3 14 bxa3 ♗xf3 15 ♕xf3 e5 16 ♘e4 exd4 17 ♘xf6+ ♕xf6 18 ♕xf6 gxf6 19 exd4, when White has a slight advantage in the endgame.

10 ♘e1 ♕e7

Or 10...e5 11 ♘d3 exd4 12 exd4 a5 13 a3 bxa3 14 bxa3 ♘c6 15 ♘f3 ♖e8 16 ♖e1 ± Piket-Schmittdiel, Wijk aan Zee 1993.

11 ♘d3 a5 12 a3 bxa3 13 bxa3 e5!

This prevents the exchange of bishops and solves all Black's opening problems.

13...♘bd7 14 ♗f3 ♖ab8 15 ♗xb7 ♖xb7 16 ♖b1 ♖c8 17 e4 e5 18 d5 ♖cb8 19 ♕e2 ♕d8 20 g3 ♘c5 21 ♘c1 ♖e7 22 ♘a2 ♕d7 23 ♘c3 gave White a tiny advantage in Kramnik-Kosten, Oviedo rpd 1992.

14 ♖b1 ♘bd7 15 ♖e1 ♖fc8 16 ♗f1 ♖c7 17 ♘b2 ♖b8

Black has equalized, Cvitan-Arlandi, Geneva 1997.

B2)

6 a3 *(D)*

B

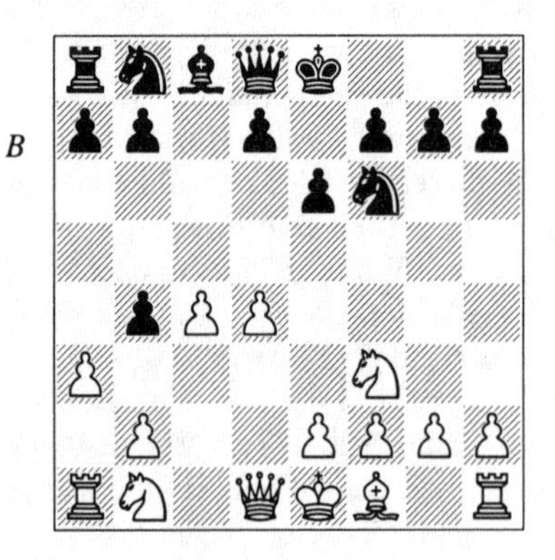

6...bxa3

6...♕e7 is a largely neglected alternative. In my opinion White should simply continue 7 e3. I am not quite sure what the queen on e7 adds to Black's position, whilst 7 e3 is a normal way to develop. However, in some games White has felt provoked by Black's queen move and has continued 7 c5!? bxa3 8 ♘xa3 0-0 9 ♘c4 ♘c6 10 e3 ♖b8. White has a very active position but it all depends on whether he can maintain the pawn on c5. Now:

a) 11 b4!? ♘xb4 12 ♖xa7 ♘e4 (12...♘c6 13 ♖a1 b5 is an idea) 13 ♗d3 (naturally, White is keen on completing his development, but 13 ♕b1! is much stronger) 13...♘xc5! (Black grabs the first opportunity to seize the initiative) 14 dxc5 ♕xc5 15 ♖a5? (a fatal error; White should have continued 15 ♖a1 d5 16 ♘a3 e5 17 ♗b5!, when matters are rather unclear) 15...♘xd3+ 16 ♕xd3 ♕b4+ 17 ♘fd2 b5! –+ Meduna-Knežević, Prague 1985.

b) 11 ♗e2 (much safer, but also not active enough) 11...b6 12 cxb6 axb6 13 0-0 d6 14 ♕b3 ♗d7 15 ♖fc1 = Bany-Draško, Polanica Zdroj 1988.

7 ♖xa3

White reserves the possibility of developing the knight to c3, and may even have some slight hopes of doing something on the semi-open a-file.

7 ♘xa3 is a major alternative. After 7...0-0 (7...d6 8 b4!? 0-0 9 e3 transposes to 'b2') we have:

a) 8 g3 ♘c6 9 ♗g2 and then:

a1) 9...d5!? 10 0-0 b6!? 11 ♘e5 ♗b7 (Gligorić-Hulak, Palma de Mallorca 1989) 12 ♘xc6 ♗xc6 13 b4! ±.

a2) 9...♕a5+ 10 ♕d2 ♕xd2+ 11 ♔xd2 d5 12 ♖hd1 ♖d8 13 ♔e1 b6 14 ♘e5 ♘b4 15 ♖dc1 ♗b7 16 ♘c2

♘xc2+ 17 ♖xc2 ± Gostiša-Grosar, Bled/Rogaška Slatina 1991.

b) 8 e3 and now:

b1) 8...b6 9 ♗e2 ♗b7 (9...♘c6 transposes to 'b3') 10 0-0 ♘c6 11 ♘e5 d5 12 ♘xc6 ♗xc6 13 ♗f3 ♕e7 14 ♖c1 ♖fc8 15 c5 bxc5 16 ♖xc5 ♘d7 17 ♖c3 ♘b6 18 ♗e2 ♕b7 19 b3 = Beliavsky-Timman, Tilburg 1993.

b2) 8...d6 9 b4!? (this did in fact occur via the move-order 7...d6 8 b4!?) 9...a6 (Beliavsky also considered 9...a5!? 10 ♘c2 b6 followed by ...♗b7) 10 ♗e2 b6 11 0-0 ♖a7?! (this is probably a little too creative; the simple 11...♗b7 12 ♕b3 ♘bd7 followed by ...♕e7 and ...♖fc8 is better – Beliavsky) 12 ♕b3 ♖c7 13 ♘b1 ♗b7 14 ♘c3 ♕e7 15 ♘d2 ♖fc8 16 ♖ac1 e5 17 d5 e4 18 ♕b1 ♖e8 19 ♘b3 ♕e5 20 ♘d4 ♗c8 21 b5! ± Beliavsky-Gostiša, Skofja Loka 1995.

b3) 8...♘c6 9 ♗e2 b6 10 0-0 d6 (this is a very sensible set-up, and Black has probably already equalized) 11 ♕b1?! (11 ♘c2 is better) 11...a5 12 ♖d1 ♗a6 13 ♘c2 d5 14 b3 ♘e4 15 ♕b2 f5 with a good position for Black, Beliavsky-Salov, Szirak IZ 1987.

7...0-0 *(D)*

Another possibility is 7...b6, which attempts to stop White setting up a broad pawn-centre with ♘c3 and e4. 8 ♘c3 ♗b7 9 e3 (9 d5 0-0 10 e4 with a slight advantage for White has been suggested by Christiansen) 9...0-0 10 ♗d3 and now:

a) 10...d5 11 cxd5 ♘xd5 12 0-0 ♘c6 13 ♕b1 ♘f6 14 ♘e4 (14 b4 is a sensible alternative) 14...h6 15 ♘xf6+ ♕xf6 16 ♗h7+ ♔h8 17 ♗e4 ♕e7 18 ♖c1 ♖fc8 19 ♖ac3 ♘b4 20 ♘e5 ± Christiansen-Timman, Linares 1985.

b) 10...d6 11 ♕b1 (11 b4!?) 11...a5 12 b4 axb4 13 ♖xa8 ♗xa8 14 ♕xb4 e5 15 d5 ♘a6 with approximately equal chances, Petursson-Korchnoi, Reykjavik 1987.

W

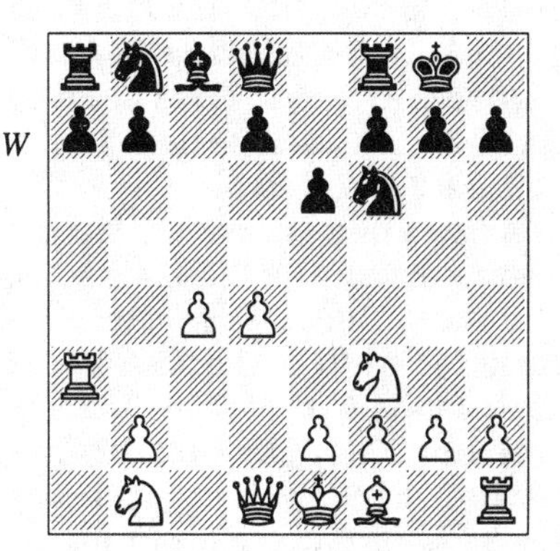

8 e3

White embarks on a smooth scheme of development, and simply wants to get his pieces out. Other options:

a) 8 ♘c3 d6 9 e4 (this is the most aggressive, but also often the kind of position that Black is hoping for; 9 e3 transposes to the main line) 9...♘c6 10 ♗e2 e5 11 d5 ♘b4 12 0-0 ♗g4 13 ♘e1 ♗xe2 14 ♕xe2 a5 15 ♘b5 ♕b6 (15...♖c8!?) 16 ♔h1 ♖ac8 17 ♖g3 g6, with unclear play, Gligorić-Hébert, Saint John 1988.

b) 8 g3!? and then:

b1) 8...d5 9 cxd5 exd5 10 ♗g2 ♘c6 11 0-0 ♖e8 12 ♘c3 ♗g4 13 h3 ♗xf3 14 ♗xf3 ♕d7 15 ♔g2 h5 16 h4 g6 17 e3 with a slight advantage for White, who has possibilities of exerting pressure against Black's a- and d-pawns, K.Arkell-Motwani, London 1988.

b2) 8...d6 9 ♗g2 ♘c6 (9...♕c7 is maybe more accurate; Zaltsman-Arnason, New York 1989 then continued 10 b3 ♘c6 11 0-0 ♘b4 12 ♕d2 a5 13 ♘c3 ♖d8 14 ♖aa1 ♗d7 15 ♖fd1 ♖ac8 16 ♖ac1 ♕b8 =) 10 0-0 e5 11 h3 ♖e8 12 ♘c3 ♗f5 13 ♘h4 ♗g6 14 ♘xg6 hxg6 15 dxe5 dxe5 16 ♕xd8 ♖exd8 17 ♖d1 ± Braga-Gulko, Rome 1988.

8...d6 9 ♗e2 ♘c6

Again a queenside fianchetto is a viable alternative for Black, e.g. 9...b6 10 0-0 a5 (10...♘c6 is maybe more accurate) 11 b4 ♘c6 12 bxa5 ♘xa5 13 ♘c3 ♗a6 14 ♘d2 e5 15 d5! ♗c8 16 ♕b1 ♗d7 17 ♖a2 ♕c7 18 ♖b2 ♖fb8 19 ♖c1, and White is better, Beliavsky-Seirawan, Montpellier Ct 1985.

10 ♘c3 e5 *(D)*

Black attempts to gain some more space. In Granda-P.Nikolić, Havana 1987, Black indeed suffered through lack of space after 10...a5 11 0-0 ♘b4 12 e4! ♘d7 13 ♘b5! ♕e7 14 ♕d2 b6 15 ♕g5!? (the offer of a queen exchange increases the significance of the weakness on d6) 15...♕xg5 16 ♘xg5 h6 17 ♘f3 d5 18 cxd5 exd5 19 e5 and White was better.

11 0-0 ♗g4 12 h3

12 ♘xe5 does not lead to anything, e.g. 12...dxe5 13 ♗xg4 exd4 14 exd4 ♕xd4 15 ♕xd4 ♘xd4 16 h3 h5 17 ♗d1 a6 = Disler-Barbero, Bern 1989.

12...♗h5 13 ♕d2 ♕b6!?

13...♖e8 14 ♖d1 h6 15 ♖aa1 b6 16 ♕c2 ♕e7 17 ♕a4 ♖ec8 18 ♖ac1 ± Wilder-Chandler, London 1988.

14 ♘d5

W

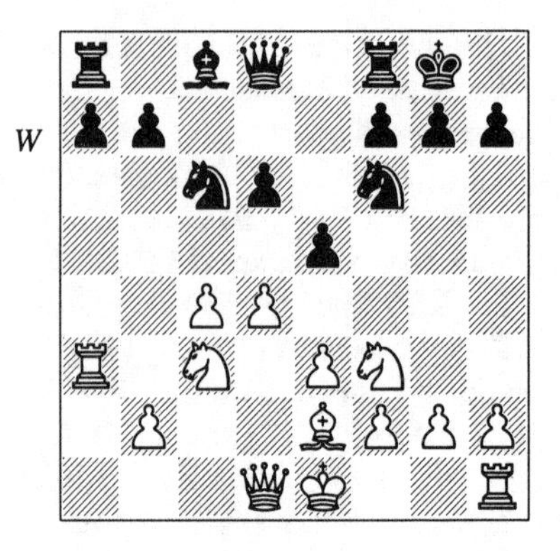

White opts for the most forcing continuation. 14 ♖d1 is a sensible alternative.

14...♘xd5 15 cxd5 ♗xf3 16 ♗xf3 ♘b4 17 dxe5 dxe5 18 d6 ♖ad8 19 ♖d1 ♖d7 20 ♖c3 a5 21 ♖c4 g6

The position is level, Meduna-Spiridonov, Baile Herculane Z 1982.

B3)

6 g3 *(D)*

B

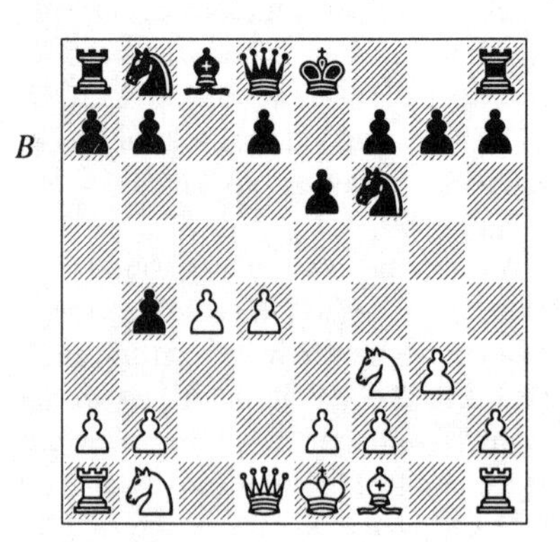

6...0-0

A sound alternative is 6...b6 intending to neutralize the pressure on the h1-a8 diagonal. After 7 ♗g2 ♗b7 8 0-0 0-0 White can attempt to break up the queenside immediately or try to provoke ...a5 first:

a) 9 ♘bd2 d6 10 ♖e1 (10 ♕b3 a5 11 a3 ♘a6 transposes to 'b' below) 10...♖e8 11 e4 (in Eingorn-Lerner, USSR 1985 White hit on a wrong plan with 11 ♕a4?! a5 12 ♘g5 ♗xg2 13 ♔xg2, and after 13...♕c7 14 ♘ge4 ♘bd7 15 a3 ♘xe4 16 ♘xe4 e5! 17 axb4 exd4 Black was already a little better) 11...e5 12 d5 a5 13 ♘h4 ± Lerner.

b) 9 ♕b3 a5 10 a3 ♘a6 (Black must try to keep control of b4; the careless 10...bxa3 would be met by 11 bxa3!, whereafter the b6-pawn is too weak) 11 ♘bd2 d6 12 ♖fd1. White plans to exchange bishops with ♘e1, and in practice Black has not found a way to obtain full equality:

b1) 12...♕e7 13 ♘e1 ♗xg2 14 ♘xg2 ♖fd8 15 ♘e3 ♕e8 16 ♕d3 ± Karpov-Korchnoi, Amsterdam 1987.

b2) 12...♖c8 13 ♘e1 ♗xg2 14 ♘xg2 ♕c7 15 ♘e3 e5?! 16 ♕d3! bxa3 17 bxa3 exd4 18 ♕xd4 and White is better, Salov-Seirawan, Barcelona 1989.

c) 9 a3 bxa3 10 b4!? (White will find it harder to set his b-pawn in motion after 10 ♖xa3 ♘c6 – Hort-Arnason, Oslo 1984 continued interestingly 11 ♘c3 ♘a5 12 c5!? d6 13 ♕a1 dxc5 14 dxc5 ♕e7 15 ♖c1 {Black would have a fine position after 15 cxb6 axb6, so White attempts to complicate matters with a pawn sacrifice} 15...♕xc5 16 ♘e4 ♕e7 17 ♘xf6+ ♕xf6 18 b4 ♕xa1 19 ♖cxa1 ♘c6 20 ♘e5 ♖ac8 21 ♗xc6 ♗xc6 22 ♖xa7 ±) 10...♘c6 11 ♘e5 ♕c7 12 ♘xc6 ♗xc6 13 ♘xa3 ♗xg2 14 ♔xg2 a5 and Black has comfortably equalized, Van Wely-Piket, Monaco (6) 1997.

7 ♗g2 d6 *(D)*

Black prepares the ...e5 advance, which will gain a little more space and make it possible to develop the bishop. Alternatives mainly involve a queenside fianchetto:

a) 7...♕c7 8 ♘bd2 d6 is Line B31, but Sosonko-Timman, Dutch Ch 1997 continued 8...b6 with similar play to the note to Black's 6th move: 9 a3 bxa3 10 ♖xa3 ♗b7 11 0-0 d6 12 b4 ♘c6 13 b5 ♘a5 14 ♕a1 ♖fc8 15 ♖c1 ½-½.

b) 7...d5 8 ♘bd2 ♘c6 9 0-0 b6 10 ♖c1 ♗b7 11 e3 ♕d6 12 ♕a4 ♖fc8 13 ♖c2 ♖c7 14 ♖fc1 ♖ac8 15 cxd5 exd5 16 ♗h3 and White took control of the c-file in Ivanchuk-Gulko, New York Open 1988.

W

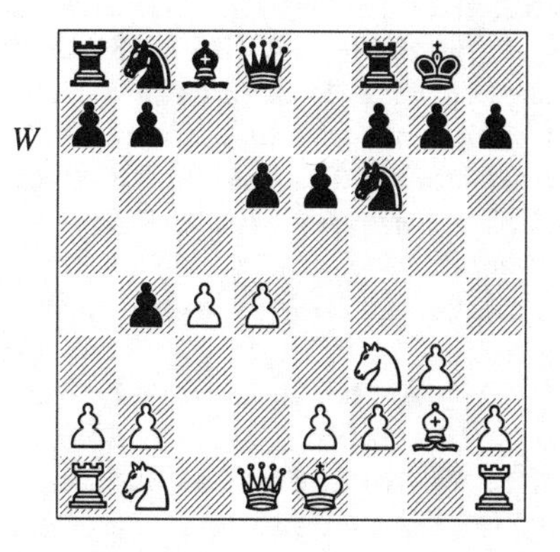

Now we examine two continuations:

B31: 8 ♘bd2 126
B32: 8 0-0 127

After 8 a3, Korchnoi-Christiansen, San Francisco 1995 continued 8...♘a6? 9 0-0 ♕e7?! 10 ♕b3! bxa3 11 ♕xa3 ♗d7 12 ♘fd2 ♖fb8 13 ♘c3 ♘c7 14 e4 ±, but Black should play 8...bxa3, whereafter 9 ♖xa3 transposes to Line B2, note 'b2' to White's 8th move.

B31)

8 ♘bd2 ♘c6

As against 8 0-0, this seems to be the best continuation for Black, but there are a couple of other options:

a) 8...♕c7 prevents White's intended plan, and after 9 0-0 the game transposes to note 'b2' in Line B32.

b) 8...♖e8 9 ♘f1 and then:

b1) 9...♕a5 10 ♘3d2 (even permitting Black to execute his plan would be slightly better for White: 10 ♘e3!? b3+ 11 ♕d2 ♕xd2+ 12 ♘xd2 bxa2 13 ♖xa2 ♘c6 14 ♗xc6! ± Razuvaev) 10...e5 11 ♘b3 ♕c7 12 ♘e3 a5 13 dxe5 dxe5 14 0-0 a4 15 ♘d2 ♘c6 16 ♘d5 ♕d8 17 ♘e4 ♘xe4 18 ♗xe4 ♗g4! (18...f5 19 ♗g2 e4 20 ♕d2 is also better for White according to Razuvaev) 19 ♖e1 ♘d4 20 ♕d3 f5 21 ♗g2 ± Razuvaev-Mandl, Dortmund 1993.

b2) 9...a5 10 ♘e3 with a further branch:

b21) 10...b6 11 a3 bxa3 12 bxa3 ♗a6 13 0-0 ♘bd7 14 ♕b3 ♖c8 15 ♖fc1 ♕e7 16 ♖c2 ♖c7 17 ♖ac1 ♖ec8 18 ♘d2 with a small advantage for White, Portisch-Chandler, Reykjavik 1991.

b22) 10...♘a6 11 0-0 ♗d7 12 ♘d2 (or 12 a3 ♖c8 13 ♘d2 ♗c6! 14 ♗xc6 bxc6 15 axb4 ♘xb4 16 ♕a4 ♖a8 17 ♘b3 e5 18 ♖fc1 exd4 19 ♘xd4 ♕b6 with a slight edge for Black, Gurieli-Petursson, Katerini 1993) 12...♖b8 13 ♖c1 ♕e7 14 ♘b3 b6 15 ♕d3 ♘c7 16 ♘d2 ♖ec8 17 ♖fd1 h6 18 a3 bxa3 19 ♕xa3 ♘a6 = Schandorff-Petursson, Manila OL 1992.

9 ♘f1

9 0-0 transposes to Line B322.

9...e5

Other options:

a) 9...♗d7!? 10 ♘e3 ♘e7 (Black takes measures against a possible d5 from White; 10...a5 11 d5 ±) 11 0-0 a5 12 ♕d3 ♖c8 (12...b5 13 cxb5 ♕b8 is a clearer way to equality) 13 a3 ♕b6 14 axb4 ♕xb4 15 ♕d2?! (the wrong square to offer the exchange on; better is 15 ♕a3 ♕xa3 16 bxa3 with an edge) 15...♕xd2 16 ♘xd2 a4! = Khalifman-Christiansen, Las Palmas 1993.

b) 9...♕a5!? 10 ♘e3 b3+ (Black has, in various different variations, tried to make this idea work, but it seems like White always comes out on top) 11 ♕d2 ♕xd2+ 12 ♘xd2 and now:

b1) 12...♘xd4 13 ♘xb3 ♘xb3 14 axb3 and White has the advantage, Dokhoian-Ionov, Klaipeda 1988.

b2) 12...bxa2 13 ♗xc6! (it is of course not very tempting to play 13 ♘c2, but the exchange on c6 is in fact very good – White's knights will be quite successful in restricting the scope of Black's bishop) 13...bxc6 14 ♖xa2 ♖d8 15 f3! (not permitting 15 0-0?! e5 with counterplay) 15...♖d7 16 ♔d1 ♖e7 17 ♖a5! ♖b7 18 ♔c2 ♖ab8 19 b3 ♔f8 20 ♖ha1 ♖a8 21 ♔c3 ± Dokhoian-Arnason, Sochi 1988.

10 ♘e3 ♘g4

10...e4?! 11 ♘d2 ♖e8 12 d5 ♘b8 13 0-0 a5 14 a3 ♘a6 15 axb4 ♘xb4 16 h3 ♗d7 17 ♘b3 b6 18 ♘d4 ♖c8 19 b3 was clearly better for White in Dgebuadze-Maherramzade, Ubeda 1998.

11 ♘c2

White should certainly avoid the exchange of knights, but this is not the only way to do it. 11 ♘d5 was seen in Kengis-Khalifman, Manila OL 1992. Black got a fine game by redeploying the knight to f5: 11...♘h6 12 0-0 ♘f5 13 e3 ♗e6 14 ♕d2 a5 15 a3 ♖e8 16 ♖fd1 bxa3 17 bxa3 exd4 18 exd4 b5 19 cxb5 ½-½.

11...a5 12 0-0 ♗f5 13 ♘fe1 ♗xc2 14 ♘xc2 ♘f6 15 ♕d2 ♖e8 16 ♖fe1 ♕b6

The game is equal, Vyzhmanavin-Mokry, Tilburg 1994.

B32)

8 0-0 *(D)*

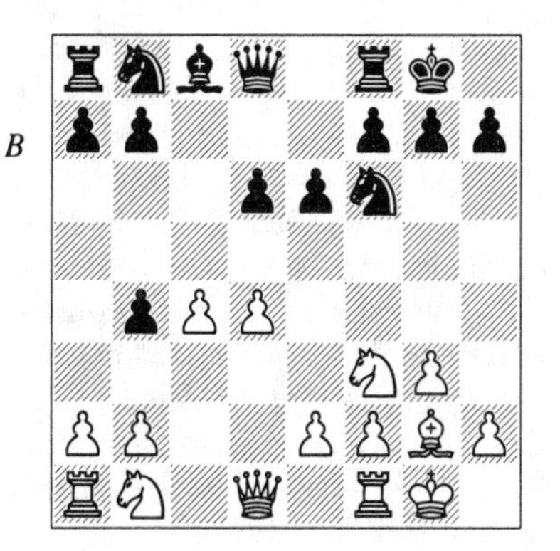

Now we have the following continuations:

B321: 8...♖e8 128
B322: 8...♘c6 130

Some other possibilities:

a) 8...♕e7 (I am a little suspicious about this move, as the queen is often needed on the queenside, mostly on b6) 9 a3 bxa3 10 ♖xa3 (the simplest, but 10 b4!? may be good enough for an advantage too, e.g. 10...b6 11 ♖xa3 ♗b7 12 ♘bd2 ♘c6 13 ♕b3 a5 14 bxa5 ♖xa5 15 ♖xa5 bxa5 16 ♕b6 ± Goldin-Lautier, Sochi 1989) 10...e5 (or 10...♘c6 11 ♘c3 ♘b4? 12 ♕d2 b6 13 ♘a4 ♘a6 14 ♖fa1 and White already has a very clear advantage, Fedorowicz-Gomez Jurado, Candas 1992) 11 ♘c3 ♗g4 12 h3 ♗xf3 13 ♗xf3 ♘c6 14 ♗xc6!? (14 e3 is more solid) 14...bxc6 15 d5 ♖fc8 16 b3 ♕d7 17 ♔h2 ± Gleizerov-Kiselev, Cheliabinsk 1993.

b) 8...♕c7 is better than the other queen move, but again, I think, commits the queen a little prematurely. White may decide to protect his c4-pawn in three ways:

b1) 9 ♕d3 b6 10 a3 ♘a6 11 ♕b3 bxa3 12 ♕xa3 ♗b7 13 ♘c3 ♖fd8 14 e4 ♘e8 15 e5 dxe5 16 ♘xe5 ♗xg2 17 ♔xg2 ♕b7+ 18 ♔g1 ♘b8 with approximately equal chances, A.Shneider-Komarov, Cattolica 1993.

b2) 9 ♘bd2 b6 (9...a5 is probably better) 10 d5 (Hjartarson recommends 10 a3! bxa3 11 ♖xa3 ♗b7 12 b4 with advantage to White) 10...♗b7 11 dxe6 fxe6 12 ♘d4 ♗xg2 13 ♔xg2 e5 14 ♘f5 ♘c6 15 ♘f3 ♖ad8 16 ♘e3 ± Portisch-Hjartarson, Reykjavik 1988.

b3) 9 ♕b3 a5 10 a3 ♘a6 11 axb4 ♘xb4 12 ♘c3 ♗d7 13 e4 e5 14 ♖fd1 b6 15 ♖d2 ♖ac8 16 ♕d1! ♗g4 17 b3 with a slight advantage for White,

P.Nikolić-Grosar, Portorož/Rogaška 1993.

c) 8...a5 and now:

c1) 9 a3 (usually a very good strategy for White, but perhaps not the best now that Black has played ...a5, and is able to cover the b4-pawn conveniently with ...♘a6) 9...♘a6 10 ♘bd2 with a choice for Black:

c11) 10...♖e8 11 ♘e1! e5 12 ♘c2 ♕b6 (12...bxa3 13 ♖xa3 ♕c7 14 ♕a1 is a little better for White) 13 c5!? dxc5 14 dxe5 ♘g4 15 ♘c4 ♕c7 16 f4 ♗e6 17 ♘d6 b3 18 ♘e1 ♘e3 19 ♕d2! ♘xf1 20 ♔xf1 ♖ed8 21 ♘f3 with compensation for White, Tregubov-Zoler, Berlin 1995.

c12) 10...♕c7 11 ♕c2 (this time the knight manoeuvre to c2 is less effective, because after 11 ♘e1 e5 12 ♘c2 Black can simply develop with 12...♗d7, obtaining a roughly equal position) 11...♗d7 12 ♖ac1 ♖ac8 13 ♕b1 ♕b8 14 ♘g5 h6 15 ♘ge4 ♘e8 16 ♘f3 e5 17 dxe5 dxe5 18 ♖fd1 ♗f5 and Black has equalized, Cifuentes-Granda, Termas del Rio Hondo 1987.

c2) 9 ♘bd2 ♘bd7 10 a3 bxa3 11 ♖xa3 ♕c7 12 ♘e1 e5 = Van der Sterren-Seirawan, Wijk aan Zee 1986.

c3) 9 ♕d3! (as Black has spent time solidifying his queenside, White decides to play in the centre) 9...♘bd7 10 ♘bd2 e5 11 ♖fe1 ♖e8 12 ♘g5 ♖a6!? 13 ♖ad1 h6 14 ♘ge4 ♘xe4 15 ♗xe4 ♘f6 16 ♗g2 ♕e7 17 e4 ± Pinter-P.Nikolić, Reggio Emilia 1987/8.

B321)

8...♖e8 *(D)*

9 a3

W

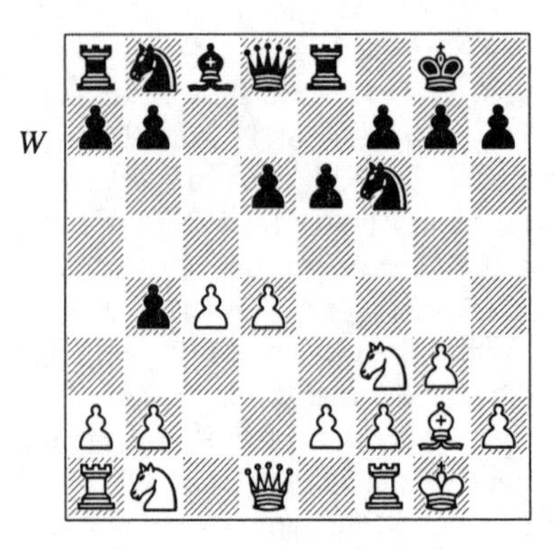

9 ♘bd2 a5 (9...♘c6 transposes to Line B322) 10 e4 e5 11 a3 ♘a6 12 h3 b6 13 ♖e1 ♗b7 14 ♕c2 ♖c8 15 ♕d3 ♘d7 was about equal in Pinter-Granda, Zagreb IZ 1987

9...♘c6

Black has several other options:

a) 9...♘a6 is probably best met by 10 ♘bd2, when the knight is somewhat out of play on a6.

b) 9...bxa3 10 b4!? (10 ♖xa3 ♕c7 11 b3 a5 12 ♘c3 ♗d7 13 ♕d2 ♘a6 14 e4 ♗c6!? 15 e5 dxe5 16 ♘xe5 ♗xg2 17 ♘b5 ♕e7 18 ♔xg2 b6! was unclear in Pushkov-Obukhov, Sochi 1993) 10...♘c6 11 b5 ♘a5 12 ♘xa3 (White has built up a large space advantage and the assessment depends on whether Black can find a well-timed counterstroke in the centre) 12...♕c7 13 ♘d2 ♖b8 (13...e5!?) 14 ♖c1 b6 15 ♘b3 ♘xb3 16 ♕xb3 e5 17 ♘c2 ± Avrukh-Obukhov, Kurgan 1994.

c) 9...♕b6 (this was Korchnoi's attempt to rehabilitate the variation with 8...♖e8) 10 axb4! (10 ♕b3 ♘c6 11 d5 ♘a5 is good for Black) 10...♕xb4 11 ♘a3! (White is hoping to jump further to b5, whereafter Black's queen could easily find itself in trouble, being almost alone in enemy territory) 11...♘a6 (the lines 11...♕xb2 12 ♘b5 and 11...♘c6 12 ♘b5 ♖d8 13 ♖a4 ♕xb2 14 ♘e1, followed by ♘d3, are simply losing for Black, but he could also try to retreat the queen to b6) 12 ♘e1! (12 ♘b5 ♗d7 13 ♖a4 ♕xb2 is not completely clear as after 14 ♕d3 Black will play 14...d5!) 12...♕b6 (certainly not 12...♕xb2 13 ♘b5 followed by ♘d3, and White wins) 13 c5! ♕d8 (the only move; 13...dxc5 14 ♘c4 ♕b4 15 ♖a4 ♕b5 16 ♘d6 +–) 14 cxd6! ♕xd6 15 ♘c4 ♕c7 16 ♕b3 ♘d5 17 ♘d3 ± Chernin-Korchnoi, Beersheba 1993.

10 d5! *(D)*

This move is currently giving Black some problems. Alternatives are less dangerous:

a) 10 axb4 ♘xb4 11 ♘c3 ♗d7! and then:

a1) 12 e4 ♗c6 13 ♖e1 e5 14 ♕d2 a5 15 ♖ad1 ♕c7 (15...♕b8!?) 16 ♖c1 ♖ad8 17 h3 ♕b8 18 ♘h4 ♗d7 19 ♔h2 ♘c6 20 ♘f3 ♗c8 21 ♖e3!? ± Dydyshko-Arlandi, Pula Echt 1997.

a2) 12 ♕b3 a5 13 ♖fd1 (13 ♘d2 ♕b6 14 ♘de4 ♘xe4 15 ♘xe4 ♗c6 16 c5 dxc5 17 dxc5 ♕c7 = Vyzhmanavin-Kengis, Barnaul 1988) and now:

a21) 13...♕b8 14 ♘d2 ♖a7 (an interesting idea, but a little slow; Black would like to play ...b6, ...♖c7 and then somehow exert pressure on c4) 15 ♘f1! b6 16 ♘e3 ♖c7 17 ♘a2! (a normal idea for White is to try to trade off Black's well-placed knight on b4) 17...♘a6 (17...♘xa2 18 ♖xa2 would also be a little better for White) 18 ♕a3 and White is better, Meyer-Hellsten, Gistrup 1996.

a22) 13...♕c7 14 ♘d2 (Skembris-Gostiša, Portorož/Rogaška 1993 varied with 14 ♖ac1 ♖ac8 15 ♘a2 ♘xa2 16 ♕xa2 b6 17 ♕a3 h6 18 h3 e5 =) 14...♖ac8 15 ♘a2!? ♘c6!? 16 e3 a4? (this turns out to be a fatal weakness; 16...b6 is more prudent) 17 ♕a3 ♘a5 18 ♗f1 e5 19 dxe5 ♖xe5 20 ♘c3 ± Vokač-Draško, Stary Smokovec 1988.

a3) 12 ♕d2 a5 13 e4 e5 14 ♖fe1 ♖c8 15 b3 b5! (a strong temporary pawn sacrifice) 16 cxb5 ♕b6 (Black will win back the pawn since 17 ♗f1?! is strongly met by 17...♗g4!) Gligorić-Cebalo, Yugoslavia 1987 instead continued 17 ♖ac1 ♗xb5 18 ♘xb5 ♖xc1 19 ♕xc1 ♕xb5 =.

b) 10 ♘bd2 a5 11 e4 bxa3 12 ♖xa3 e5 13 d5 ♘b4 was fine for Black in Pinter-Cebalo, Smederevska Palanka tt 1987.

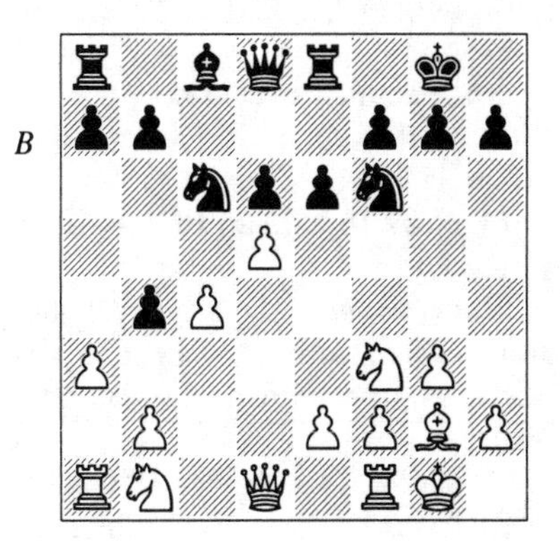

10...exd5 11 cxd5 ♘e7 12 axb4

Black has no problems after 12 ♘e1 bxa3 13 ♖xa3 b5!. P.Nikolić-Korchnoi, Zagreb IZ 1987 continued

14 b4 (Nikolić also analysed the knight journey 14 ♘c2?! a5 15 ♘b4 ♗d7 16 ♘c6, but Black has a good position after 16...♕b6) 14...a5 15 bxa5 b4! (accurate play; 15...♖xa5 16 ♕d2 ♖xa3 17 ♘xa3 ♕b6 18 ♘ec2, intending ♘b4, is slightly better for White) 16 ♖a4 ♖xa5 17 ♖xb4 ♘exd5 18 ♖b2 ♗f5 19 ♘f3 ♗e4 20 ♕d4 with equality.

12...♘exd5

12...♕b6? is an attempt to be clever, but fails after 13 ♘c3 ♕xb4 14 ♕d4! (simple and strong) 14...♕xd4 15 ♘xd4, when White has a large advantage, Ulybin-Gostiša, Moscow OL 1994.

13 b5 ♕b6

Another possibility is 13...♗d7 14 ♘d4 ♕b6 15 e3 ♖ac8 (15...♗xb5? 16 ♘xb5 ♕xb5 17 ♘a3 is too dangerous for Black) 16 ♕a4 a6 17 ♕b3 ♗xb5 18 ♖d1!? and White has good compensation for the pawn, Garcia Padron-Korchnoi, Las Palmas 1991.

14 ♘a3

White could also consider 14 ♘d4, whereafter 14...♗d7 15 e3 transposes to Garcia Padron-Korchnoi above.

14...♗d7 15 ♕d3 a6 16 ♘d4 ♖ac8 17 ♖fc1

White seems to be slightly better around here. The bishop on g2, in particular, is stronger than its counterpart on d7.

17...♖c5!? 18 ♘c4 ♕c7 19 ♘b3

19 ♗xd5 ♘xd5 20 ♘b3 is perhaps better.

19...axb5 20 ♘xc5 bxc4 21 ♕xc4

The last chance for an advantage for White is 21 ♘xd7! cxd3 22 ♘xf6+ gxf6 23 ♖xc7 ♘xc7 24 exd3.

21...♕xc5 22 ♕xc5 dxc5 23 ♖xc5 ♗c6

Black has equalized, P.Nikolić-Gostiša, Portorož/Rogaška 1993.

B322)

8...♘c6 *(D)*

As with 8...♖e8, Black prepares to free his position with ...e5.

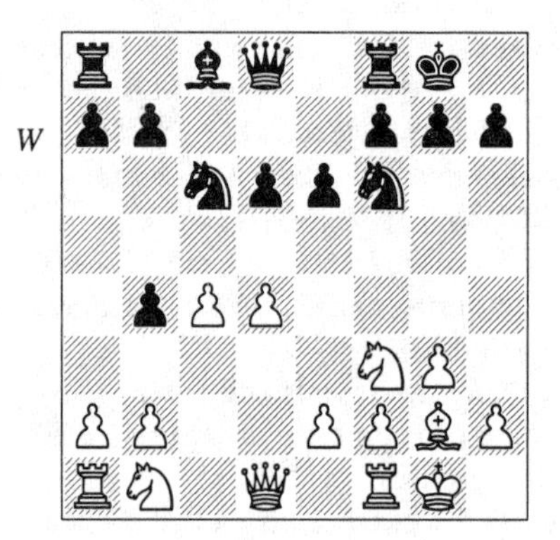

9 ♘bd2

This is the solid approach, but White has other options too:

a) 9 d5 exd5 10 cxd5 ♘e7. It makes sense to compare this position with the one that can arise from 8...♖e8. In the 8...♖e8 line Black's rook is on e8 (of course), and White has a pawn on a3. Therefore it is reasonable to say that Black faces fewer problems here, as the b4-pawn is in no danger, whilst Black threatens to win the d5-pawn. White has now chosen between:

a1) 11 ♕d4 ♘exd5 12 e4 ♘e7 13 ♕xb4 ♘c6 14 ♕a4 d5 (an interesting alternative is 14...♕b6!? 15 ♘bd2 ♕xb2! 16 ♘c4 b5 17 ♘xb2 bxa4 18 ♖fe1 ♘b4 19 ♖ad1 ♗b7 20 ♖xd6

♘xe4 21 ♖d4 ♘xa2 = Korchnoi) 15 e5 ♘e4 16 ♘c3 ♘xc3 17 bxc3 ♗e6 with about equal play, Van der Sterren-Korchnoi, Wijk aan Zee 1987.

a2) 11 ♘e1 ♕b6 12 ♘c2 ♖e8 13 ♘e3 ♘f5 14 ♘c4 ♕c7 15 ♕d3 ♘d7 16 b3 ♘c5 17 ♕d1 b5 18 ♘cd2 ♕e7 with equality, Polugaevsky-Arnason, Akureyri 1988.

b) 9 a3 bxa3 (9...♖e8 transposes to Line B321) 10 ♖xa3 (Black has no problems after 10 ♘xa3 e5! 11 ♘b5 a6 12 dxe5 dxe5 13 c5, when the stunning 13...♗h3!! equalizes; then, in Van der Sterren-Petursson, Reykjavik 1994, Black even managed to seize the initiative after 14 ♗xh3 axb5 15 ♖xa8 ♕xa8 16 e3 ♕a2 17 ♕e2 ♕d5 18 ♖c1 ♖d8) 10...e5 11 e3 and now:

b1) 11...♖e8 12 ♕b3! exd4 13 ♘xd4 ♘xd4 14 exd4 ♕c7 15 ♘c3 ♗e6!? 16 ♖a4 (it is not quite clear what happens if White grabs the pawn on b7: 16 ♕xb7 ♕xb7 17 ♗xb7 ♖ab8, and then either 18 ♗c6 ♖ec8 19 d5 ♗d7 20 ♗xd7 ♘xd7 21 ♖xa7 ♘e5 or 18 ♖xa7 ♖e7 19 ♖fa1! ♗xc4, but Black seems to have some counterplay in both lines) 16...♖ec8!? 17 ♕xb7 ♖ab8! 18 ♕xa7 ♕xa7 19 ♖xa7, Dzhandzhgava-Bogdanovski, Moscow OL 1994, 19...♖xc4! gives Black counterplay – Dzhandzhgava.

b2) 11...♗g4!? and now:

b21) 12 h3 ♗h5 (Petursson recommends 12...♗xf3! 13 ♗xf3 exd4 14 exd4 ♕b6 15 ♖b3 ♕xd4 16 ♖xb7 ♘e5! 17 b3 ♖ab8 with an equal game) 13 g4 ♗g6 14 ♘c3 h6 15 ♕a4 a5 16 dxe5 dxe5 17 ♖d1 ♕b8 18 ♕b5 ± Hort-Kindermann, Biel 1988.

b22) 12 ♕b3 ♕e7 (worse is 12...♕b6?! 13 ♕xb6 axb6 14 d5 ♘e7 15 ♖xa8 ♖xa8 16 ♘c3, when White has the advantage due to his better pawn structure, Van Wely-Petursson, Akureyri 1994) 13 ♘bd2 ♖fc8 14 d5 ♘b8 15 e4 ♕c7 16 ♖fa1 b6 17 ♘e1 a5!? 18 ♕e3 ♘a6 19 ♘d3 ♖ab8 20 b3 ♗d7 = I.Sokolov-Petursson, Akureyri 1994.

Returning to the position after 9 ♘bd2 *(D)*:

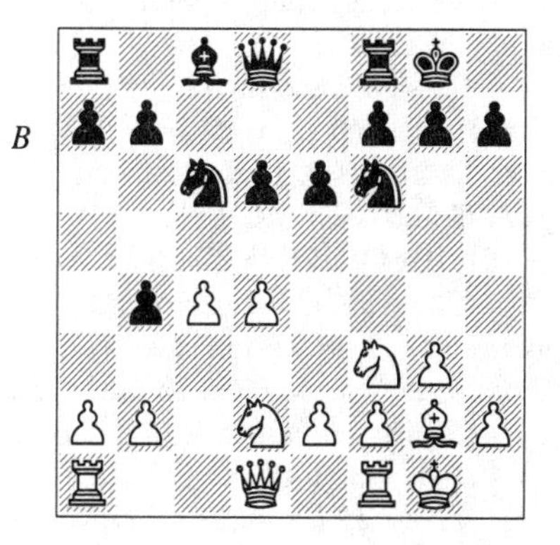

9...e5

This is the most consistent approach and leads to an interesting strategic fight. Other options:

a) 9...♕b6 10 e3 ♗d7 11 h3!? (11 ♕e2 is a natural move, but here White intends first to gain a little more space on the kingside) 11...♖ac8 12 g4 h6 13 ♕e2 a5 14 ♖fc1 ♘e7 15 a3 bxa3?! (this is dubious, as White will now make use of the semi-open b-file; instead Black should prefer 15...♘g6!? intending to recapture with the queen if White plays 16 axb4) 16 bxa3 ♕a6 17 ♖ab1 ♘g6 18 ♖c2 ♗c6 19 ♖cb2 and White has the advantage, Piket-I.Sokolov, Antwerp 1997.

b) 9...♕e7 (as stated earlier, the queen does not really belong here) 10 e4 a5 (the standard reply would be 10...e5 but after 11 d5 ♘b8 12 a3 White is better, as Black's queen is misplaced on e7) 11 d5! ♘b8 12 dxe6! ♗xe6 13 ♘d4 (White is slightly better owing to his good central control and Black's isolated pawn on d6) 13...♘a6 14 ♖e1 ♘c5 15 ♕c2 ♕c7?! 16 ♘f1 ♗d7 17 ♘e3 ± Dautov-Goldin, Leningrad Cht 1989.

c) 9...♖e8!? and then:

c1) 10 e3 e5 11 dxe5 dxe5 12 ♕c2 ♗g4 is fine for Black, Dzhandzhgava-Gelfand, USSR 1988.

c2) 10 e4 e5 11 d5 ♘b8 12 ♘e1 a5 (12...♘a6 13 ♘d3 transposes to the main line) 13 ♘d3 ♘a6 14 a3 bxa3 15 ♖xa3 ♘d7 (15...♗g4!?) 16 ♕a1!? b6 17 f4 (Stoica recommends 17 b4! axb4 18 ♘xb4 ♘dc5 19 ♕b2!? ♗b7 20 ♖fa1 ♘xb4 21 ♖xa8 ♗xa8 22 ♕xb4 ♕c7 23 ♕a3! with a slight advantage for White) 17...♖b8! = Cosma-Stoica, Romanian Cht 1994.

c3) 10 ♕c2!? e5 11 d5 ♘b8 12 ♘g5!? ♘a6 (12...a5) 13 a3 h6 14 ♘ge4 ♘xe4 15 ♗xe4 ♕b6 16 ♖fc1 ♗g4 (Black has good control of the key c5-square, so White decides to solve this problem with a pawn sacrifice) 17 c5!? dxc5 18 ♘c4 ♕d8 19 d6 ♖b8 20 axb4 ♘xb4 21 ♕d2 Hebden-Kosten, London 1990. White has good compensation: a7 is hanging and White has the potential plan of ♘e3 as well.

c4) 10 ♕b3 (with the idea of d5) 10...♕b6 (playable is also 10...a5!? 11 d5 exd5 12 cxd5 ♘e7 13 ♘d4 ♘f5 = Olafsson-J.Arnason, Reykjavik 1989) 11 e3 (interesting but as yet untested is 11 c5!? dxc5 12 ♘c4 ♕a6 13 dxc5 ♘e4 14 ♖fc1!? ♘xc5 15 ♕e3 ♘d7 16 a3!? with good compensation for White – Gelfand) 11...♗d7 (11...♘a5 12 ♕c2! ♗d7 13 b3 ♖ac8 14 ♕b2! ♕c7 15 ♖fc1 ♘c6 16 ♘e1 a5 17 ♘d3 was very pleasant for White in Pinter-Petursson, Tilburg 1993) 12 ♖ac1 (here 12 c5 dxc5 13 ♘c4 ♕a6 14 dxc5 is no problem for Black, in view of the reply 14...♘a5 =) 12...♘a5 13 ♕d3 ♖ac8 14 ♖fd1 h6! (preventing the manoeuvre ♘g5-e4, which would yield White a small advantage) 15 b3 (Gelfand recommends 15 ♗f1! ♖ed8 16 ♘e4 ±) 15...♕a6 16 ♗f1 e5 17 ♘e4 ♘xe4 18 ♕xe4, Karolyi-Gelfand, Amsterdam 1988, and now Black should play the aggressive 18...f5! 19 ♕h4 e4 20 c5 b5 with an equal game.

10 d5 *(D)*

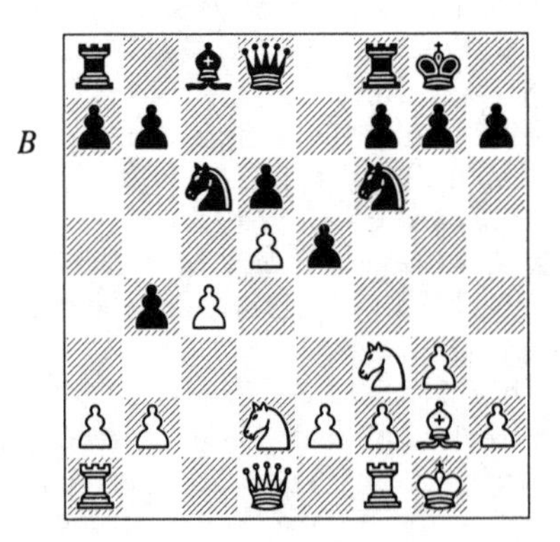

10...♘b8

It is by far the most common to retreat the knight to b8, from where it is able to go to a6 controlling the c5-square. However, Mokry has recently experimented with 10...♘e7!? 11 ♘e1 a5 12 a3 bxa3 13 ♖xa3:

a) 13...b6 14 ♘d3 ♗b7 15 ♕b1!? ♕c7 16 b4 axb4 17 ♕xb4 ♖xa3 18 ♕xa3 ♖a8 19 ♕b2 ♘d7 20 ♖b1 ± Kiselev-Mokry, Pardubice 1994.

b) 13...b5!? (this is much sharper, and perhaps also better) 14 ♘c2 ♕b6 15 cxb5 ♕xb5 16 e4 ♗d7 17 b3 ♕c5 18 ♘c4 a4, and although Black lost very quickly in Buturin-Mokry, Pardubice 1995, this position should be all right for him.

11 a3

In the game Hebden-S.Pedersen, Gausdal 1992, White continued less aggressively: 11 ♘e1 ♘a6 12 ♘d3 ♖e8 13 e4 ♗g4 14 f3 ♗d7 15 a3 bxa3 16 ♖xa3 ♕b6+ 17 ♖f2 ♘c5 18 ♘xc5 ♕xc5 19 ♗f1 a5, and Black had equalized.

11...♘a6

With this move Black decides to keep the tension on the queenside, but 11...bxa3 is a solid alternative, for example 12 ♖xa3 ♘a6 (in C.Horvath-Hulak, Makarska tt 1994, Black was able to hold the endgame after 12...♕b6 13 ♕b3 ♕xb3 14 ♖xb3 ♘bd7 15 ♖a1 a6 16 ♘e1 ♖e8 17 e4 ♔f8 18 ♘d3 ♔e7 19 ♖c3 b6 20 b4 although it seems to be clearly preferable for White) 13 ♕b3 h6 14 h3 ♘d7 15 ♘e1 ♘dc5 16 ♕c3 b5! (this is the only way to create counterplay) 17 b4 ♘a4 18 ♕b3 ♘b6 19 ♘d3 bxc4 20 ♘xc4 ♘xc4 21 ♕xc4 ♕b6 with a good position for Black, J.Horvath-Appleberry, Budapest 1994.

12 ♘e1 ♗g4

This is a rather common theme in the Bogo-Indian. Black exerts pressure on e2, and is not frightened of f3, which would decrease the scope of White's bishop and weaken the g1-a7 diagonal.

13 ♘d3 ♕b6 14 axb4

The alternatives look inferior:

a) 14 h3 ♗h5 15 ♖e1 bxa3 16 ♖xa3 ♗g6 17 e4 ♘d7 18 ♕b3 f5 = I.Farago-Korchnoi, Beersheba 1987.

b) 14 ♔h1 ♘c5 15 ♘xc5 ♕xc5 16 axb4 ♕xb4 17 f3 ♗d7 18 b3 a5 19 e4 b5, and Black is better, Naumkin-Stepanov, Budapest 1991.

14...♘xb4 15 c5 ♕b5 16 ♘xb4 ♕xb4 17 cxd6 ♖fd8!

Black should be able to hold the balance. Novikov-Lalev, Lvov 1988 instead continued 17...♕b5? 18 f3 ♗d7 19 e4 ♘e8 20 f4! and White was better.

7 The Catalan Bogo: 3 g3 ♗b4+

1 d4 ♘f6 2 c4 e6 3 g3 ♗b4+ *(D)*

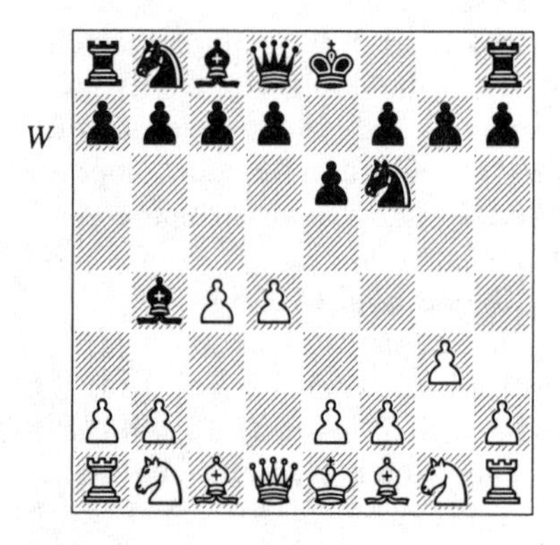

The Catalan Bogo may easily transpose to any of the previous chapters, but developing the bishop to g2 before moving the knight to f3 can be beneficial for White, who may utilize this distinction to employ the knight differently.

Nevertheless, the Catalan Bogo has its attractions for Black. Aside from the purely practical benefit of avoiding a mass of Catalan theory, the check is quite disruptive here too. Moreover, having played g3, White has fewer options about how to support his centre than in the standard Bogo – in particular Black's ...c5 advance will tend to liquidate the white d4-pawn.

Typical Pawn Structures

I am not sure whether we can say that there are any typical pawn structures throughout this chapter. Since there are a lot of transpositions to other chapters, the most usual pawn structures have already been dealt with. But one that we seem to come across on several occasions in this chapter is the following:

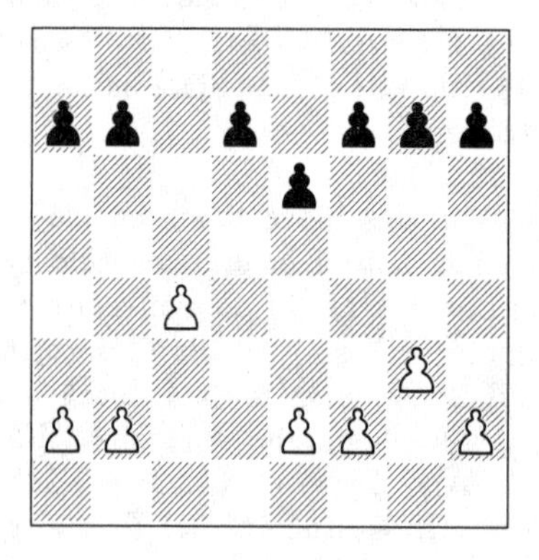

We can see that Black has played ...c5 and either Black has exchanged on d4 or White has taken the pawn on c5. A normal idea for Black is to play ...d5 to avoid being stuck with a backward d-pawn and to gain some space in the centre. However, he must take care not to get a weak isolated pawn.

Planning for White

White can try to utilize the fact that in many lines the bishop is developed to g2 before the knight has come out to f3. Let us take a brief look at a few examples in which this can be useful:

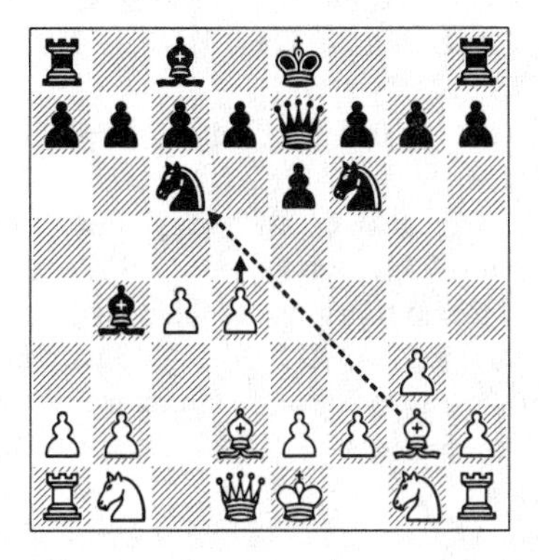

A rather normal position but White may exploit the fact that the g2-bishop is not hindered by a knight on f3 and play the aggressive d4-d5.

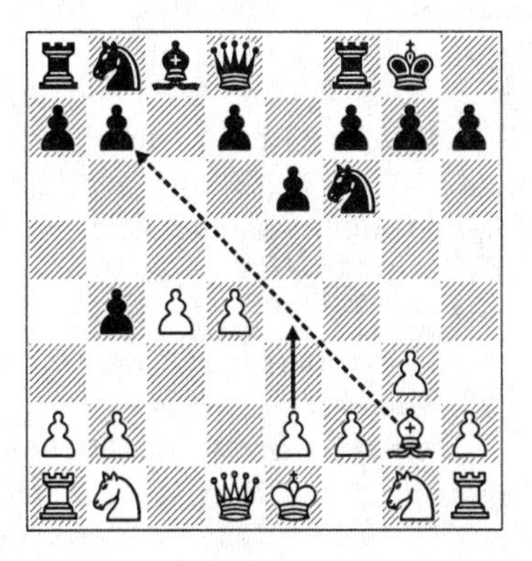

This is another example of how White can benefit from a slight change in the move-order. Here White can build up a broad centre with e2-e4.

Planning for Black

It is also quite difficult to come with a suggestion for a plan for Black, as it simply depends on which line one intends to play against a regular Bogo.

However, against 4 ♘d2 I suggest that Black goes for 4...c5!?, given that White has committed himself to a fianchetto very early.

Quick Summary

As already mentioned, there are a lot of transpositions to previous chapters. Line A (4 ♗d2 ♗xd2+) often transposes to Chapter 3, and this is indeed the case with the variation 5 ♕xd2 d5. Black can try 5...c5!? but White can decide whether he wants to transpose to Chapter 3 with 6 ♘f3, or play 6 ♗g2. Against 4...♕e7 (Line B) there is a little distinction compared to Chapter 5. In the line 5 ♗g2 ♘c6 White might try 6 d5!?. The little change in the move-order also benefits White if Black wants to play a 4...c5 Bogo. White can now play 5 ♗xb4 cxb4 6 ♗g2 and if Black does not play 6...d5 (which is normally not the choice of Black in this kind of position) White can play 7 e4!. This is dealt with in Line C. Last but not least we come to 4 ♘d2 (Line D). One thing that is worth noting here is that the move 4...b6, which is quite popular in a normal Bogo, is of course not very attractive here, and Black should instead go for 4...c5!?.

The Theory of the Catalan Bogo

1 d4 ♘f6 2 c4 e6 3 g3 ♗b4+

We shall now examine the following four variations:

Others just transpose to other lines:

a) 4 ♘c3 is a 4 g3 Nimzo-Indian and really outside the scope of this book.

b) 4 ♗d2 a5 5 ♗g2 d5 6 ♕c2 ♘c6 7 ♘f3 transposes to Chapter 4.

c) 4 ♗d2 ♗e7 5 ♗g2 d5 6 ♘f3 transposes to Chapter 2.

A)

4 ♗d2 ♗xd2+ *(D)*

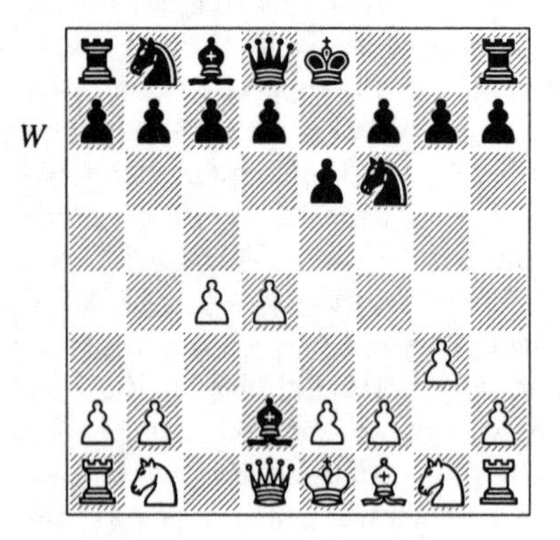

5 ♕xd2

5 ♘xd2 d6 (5...d5 6 ♗g2 0-0 7 ♘gf3 ♕e7 transposes to Line D11 in Chapter 5) 6 ♗g2 0-0 7 e3!? (7 ♘gf3 transposes to Chapter 3, note 'b' to White's 5th move) 7...c5 8 ♘e2 and now 8...cxd4 9 ♘xd4 ♕c7 10 0-0 ♘c6 11 ♘b5 ♕e7 12 ♖c1 ♖d8 13 ♕e2 ♗d7 14 ♖fd1 ♗e8 15 a3 was slightly better for White in Beliavsky-Andersson, Pula Echt 1997, but 8...♘c6 9 0-0 cxd4 10 ♘xd4 ♘xd4 11 exd4 ♕b6 12 ♘b3 ♗d7 should equalize.

5...c5!?

This is Black's sharpest approach. Other lines:

a) 5...0-0 6 ♗g2 and then both 6...d5 7 ♘f3 and 6...d6 7 ♘c3 e5 8 ♘f3 ♘c6 transpose to Chapter 3.

b) 5...d5 6 ♗g2 0-0 7 ♘f3 with another transposition to Chapter 3.

c) 5...d6 6 ♘c3 0-0 7 ♗g2 and then:

c1) 7...♘bd7 8 e4 e5 9 ♘ge2 ♖e8 10 0-0 c6 11 ♖ad1 ♕e7 12 f4 (Sveshnikov suggests the quiet 12 h3, with an edge) 12...♘b6 13 b3 ♗g4 14 ♖de1 ♗xe2 15 ♖xe2 ♘bd7 16 ♖d1 a6 17 ♕d3 ♖ad8 with approximately equal chances, Liebert-Malich, E.Germany 1973.

c2) 7...c5!? 8 ♘f3 ♕e7 9 0-0 b6!? 10 ♖ad1 ♗b7 11 dxc5 dxc5 12 ♕d6 ♘c6 13 ♘b5 ♖ae8 with a roughly equal position, Sosonko-Miles, Wijk aan Zee 1984.

6 ♗g2

6 ♘f3 transposes to Chapter 6.

6...cxd4

The other possibility, 6...0-0, looks promising for White: 7 dxc5 ♕c7 (7...♘a6 8 ♘c3 ♘xc5 9 b4 ♘a6 10 a3 gives White a pleasant space advantage) 8 ♕d6 ♕a5+ 9 ♘c3 ♘a6 (Vaganian-Adorjan, Thessaloniki OL 1984)

10 a3! ♕xc5 11 ♕xc5 ♘xc5 12 0-0-0 ± Vaganian.

7 ♘f3 ♘c6

7...♕c7 8 ♘xd4 ♕xc4 9 ♘a3 is clearly better for White – Vaganian, but a viable alternative is 7...d5 8 cxd5 (8 ♘xd4!? dxc4 9 ♘a3 0-0 {worse is 9...e5? 10 ♘db5 ♕xd2+ 11 ♔xd2 ♘a6 12 ♘xc4 ±} 10 ♘xc4 ♕e7 11 0-0 e5 12 ♘b3 ♖d8 13 ♕e3 gave White a slight advantage in Gleizerov-Sjöberg, Gothenburg 1997) 8...♕xd5 9 0-0 0-0 10 ♘xd4 ♕h5 with two promising options for White:

a) 11 ♘f3 e5 12 ♕g5 ♘c6 13 ♘c3 ♗g4 14 ♕xh5 ♗xh5 15 h3 ♗xf3 16 ♗xf3 ♖fd8 17 ♖fd1 ± Khalifman-A.Grosar, Bled/Rogaška Slatina 1991.

b) 11 ♖c1! (this seems even stronger, one finesse being 11...♖d8? 12 ♘xe6! ♖xd2 13 ♖xc8+) 11...♘bd7 12 ♘a3 ♘b6 13 ♘dc2!? e5 14 ♘e3 ♘g4 15 ♘xg4 ♗xg4 16 ♗xb7 ± Vaganian-A.Grosar, Bled/Rogaška Slatina 1991.

8 ♘xd4 ♕b6 9 e3 d5 10 cxd5 ♘xd4 11 ♕xd4 ♕xd4 12 exd4 ♘xd5

12...exd5 13 ♘c3 ♗e6 14 ♔d2 ♔d7 15 h3 h5 16 ♖he1 also yields White an edge according to Nogueiras and Estevez.

13 ♘c3 ♘xc3 14 bxc3 ♖b8 15 ♔d2

White is slightly better due to his more active position, Nogueiras-Lobron, Reggio Emilia 1985/6.

B)

4 ♗d2 ♕e7 *(D)*

5 ♗g2

Alternatives are less logical:

a) 5 a3 ♗xd2+ 6 ♘xd2 0-0 7 e4 e5 8 d5 d6 9 ♗g2 ♘bd7 10 ♘e2 a5 11 0-0 ♘h5 12 ♘c3 g6 13 h3 ♘c5 = Rosin-Klaeger, W.Germany 1967.

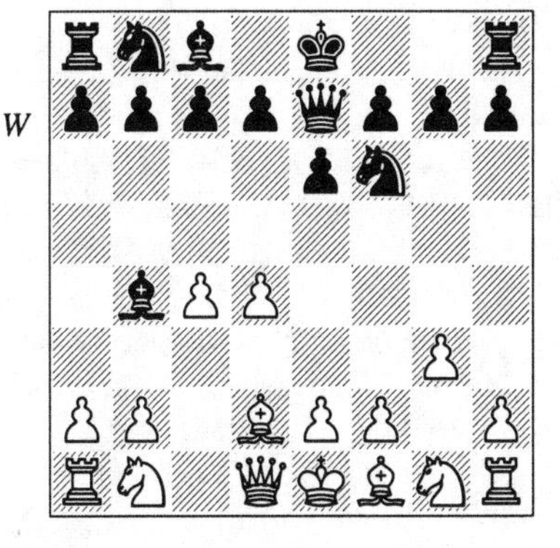

b) 5 ♘c3 ♗xc3 6 ♗xc3 ♘e4 7 ♕c2 ♘xc3 8 ♕xc3 0-0 9 ♗g2 d6 10 ♘f3 ♖e8 11 ♖d1 ♘d7 (11...e5!?) 12 0-0 e5 13 ♖fe1 e4 14 ♘d2 ♘f6 15 ♘f1 d5! = Seirawan-Benjamin, USA Ch 1987.

5...♘c6

As in Chapter 5 Black's most popular option is this eccentric knight move, but here White is able to harass it by advancing the d-pawn. Other options:

a) 5...0-0 6 ♘c3 (6 ♘f3 transposes to Chapter 5) 6...d6 7 a3 (7 e3 followed by ♘e2 is worth considering) 7...♗xc3 8 ♗xc3 e5! (better than 8...♘bd7 9 ♕c2 a5 10 ♘f3 ♖e8 11 0-0 e5 12 dxe5 dxe5 13 b4 with an edge for White, Karasev-Gaprindashvili, USSR 1977) 9 dxe5 dxe5 10 ♕c2 ♘c6 11 ♘f3 ♖d8 12 e3 (12 ♖d1 ♖xd1+ 13 ♕xd1 may be an improvement, but Black should have no worries) 12...♘d4! and Black has seized the initiative, Ward-Karlsson, Hillerød 1995.

b) 5...♗xd2+ 6 ♕xd2 d6 7 ♘c3 0-0 8 ♘f3 e5 transposes to Chapter 5.

6 d5!?

This is very consistent. 6 e3 is more cautious:

a) 6...e5 7 d5 ♗xd2+ (possible is also 7...♘b8 8 ♘e2 ♗xd2+ 9 ♕xd2 a5?! {9...d6 is better} 10 d6!? ♕xd6 11 ♕xd6 cxd6 12 ♘bc3 ♘a6 13 0-0 with excellent compensation, Nikolaidis-Loginov, Budapest 1994) 8 ♕xd2 ♘b8 9 ♘c3 d6 10 h3 a5 11 ♘ge2 ♘a6 12 g4!? ♘d7 13 ♘g3 ♘b6 14 b3 g6 15 0-0-0 ♘c5 16 f4 with an unclear game, G.Flear-Adams, Hastings 1996/7.

b) 6...0-0 7 ♘e2 e5 and then:

b1) 8 0-0 exd4 9 ♘xd4 ♕c5 (9...♗xd2 is probably better) 10 b3 ♘xd4?! 11 exd4 ♕xd4 12 ♗xb4 ♕xa1 13 ♗c3! ♕xa2 14 ♗xf6 gxf6 15 ♘c3 ♕b2 16 ♕g4+ ♔h8 17 ♕d4 with a strong attack, Burger-Keglević, corr. 1977.

b2) 8 d5 ♘b8 (8...♗xd2+ 9 ♕xd2 ♘b8 10 ♘bc3 d6 = Djurić) 9 ♘bc3 d6 10 a3 ♗xc3 11 ♘xc3 e4!? 12 ♕c2 ♖e8 13 h3 ♘bd7 14 0-0 ♘b6 15 b3, Hulak-Djurić, Bled/Rogaška Slatina 1991, and now 15...c6!? is Black's best, with an unclear game.

6...♘e5

6...exd5 7 cxd5 ♗xd2+ 8 ♘xd2 ♘e5 9 ♕c2 d6 10 ♖c1 is very good for White.

7 ♕b3 ♗xd2+

An interesting alternative is to preserve the bishop with 7...♗c5!?. S.Pedersen-Kiik, Oslo 1992 continued 8 ♘h3 0-0 9 0-0 d6 10 ♘c3 ♗b6 11 ♘a4 ♘g6 12 ♖fe1 e5 =.

8 ♘xd2 0-0

8...exd5 9 cxd5 c5 10 h3!? d6 11 f4 ♘g6 12 e4 0-0 13 ♘e2 b6 14 0-0 ♗a6 15 ♖fe1 was better for White in Fominykh-Totsky, Perm 1997.

9 ♘h3 d6 10 ♘f4 ♘g6 11 ♘d3 ♘g4 12 h3 ♘h6 13 dxe6 fxe6 14 e3 ♖b8 15 c5! d5 16 c6 b6 17 e4!

White is better, Ivanchuk-Epishin, Tallinn 1986.

C)

4 ♗d2 c5 *(D)*

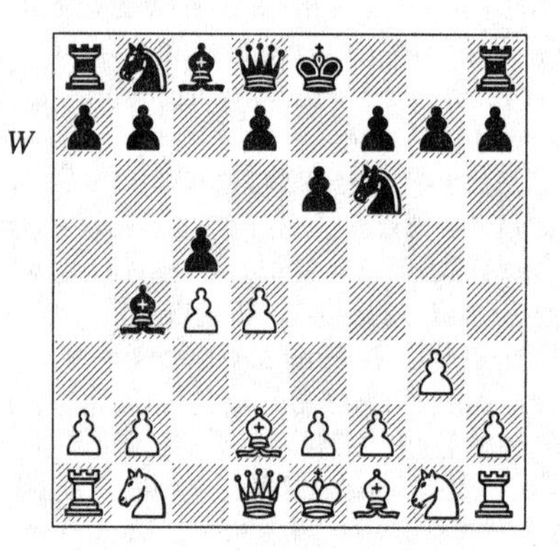

5 ♗xb4

5 ♗g2 is a major alternative:

a) 5...0-0 transposes to other lines – 6 ♗xb4 cxb4 is the main line, while 6 ♘f3 is dealt with in Chapter 6.

b) 5...♗xd2+ 6 ♕xd2 transposes to Line A.

c) 5...♘c6?! 6 ♗xb4 cxb4 7 d5 ♘e5 (7...exd5 8 cxd5 ♘e5 9 ♕d4 ±) 8 dxe6 fxe6 9 ♘d2 0-0 10 ♘gf3 with a pleasant game for White, Razuvaev-Dizdar, New York 1989.

d) 5...♕b6 6 d5! (compared to Line A in Chapter 6, this is not a sacrifice now) 6...exd5 7 cxd5 d6 (or 7...♗xd2+ 8 ♕xd2 0-0 9 ♘c3 d6 10 ♘f3 ♗g4 11 ♘h4!? ♘a6 12 h3 ♗d7 13 0-0 ♖fe8 14 b3 ± Volzhin-Emelin, St Petersburg 1998) 8 ♘c3 0-0 9 ♘f3 ♗g4 10 0-0 ♖e8 (Razuvaev-Kengis, Naberezhnye Chelny 1988) 11 h3 ♗xf3 12 ♗xf3 ♘bd7 ± Kengis.

e) 5...d5 6 cxd5 exd5 7 ♘f3 ♘c6 8 0-0 0-0 9 ♗e3?! (Korchnoi suggests 9 ♗f4 and 9 ♗xb4 cxb4 10 ♘bd2 ♖e8 11 ♕b3 '±' as possible improvements, but I am a little puzzled by this last line since there appears to be nothing wrong with 11...♖xe2, but of course White can play something like 11 e3 and only then ♕b3) 9...♖e8 10 a3 cxd4 11 ♗xd4 ♘xd4 12 ♘xd4 ♗c5 13 ♘c3 ♗g4 14 ♖c1 ♕d6 = Korchnoi-Morozevich, Madrid 1996.

5...cxb4 6 ♗g2 0-0

If Black wants to prevent 7 e4 then he should play 6...d5, when 7 ♘d2 ♘c6 8 ♘gf3 0-0 transposes to Chapter 6, whilst the more aggressive 8...♘e4!? featured in Atalik-Xu Jun, Beijing 1996, but after 9 ♘xe4 dxe4 10 ♘e5 ♕xd4 11 ♕xd4 ♘xd4 12 ♗xe4 f6 13 e3 fxe5 14 exd4 exd4 15 0-0-0 the d-pawn fell, and White was much better.

7 e4!

This shows an advantage of the knight not yet being on f3. Instead 7 ♘f3 transposes to Chapter 6.

7...d6

Or 7...d5 8 cxd5 exd5 9 e5 ♘e8 10 ♘e2 ♘c6 11 0-0 ±.

8 ♘e2 e5 9 0-0 ♘c6

This is certainly the most logical square for the knight, but recently Timman showed that 9...♘bd7 may not be such a bad idea, intending to exert pressure on the c4-pawn (by ...♘b6) rather than d4. 10 a3 bxa3 11 ♘xa3 ♕e7 12 ♘c2 ♘b6 13 ♘e3 ♘g4 14 ♘xg4 ♗xg4 15 f3 ♗d7 16 ♕d3 ♖fc8 17 b3 a5 with counterplay, Beliavsky-Timman, Frankfurt rpd 1998.

10 a3

10 d5 ♘b8 11 a3, as in Bönsch-Lutz, Graz Z 1993, should also be better for White.

10...bxa3 11 ♘xa3 a5 12 ♕d2 b6 13 ♖fd1 ♗a6 14 b3 ♖e8 15 ♘c2

White is slightly better, Beliavsky-A.Grosar, Portorož 1996.

D)

4 ♘d2 *(D)*

B

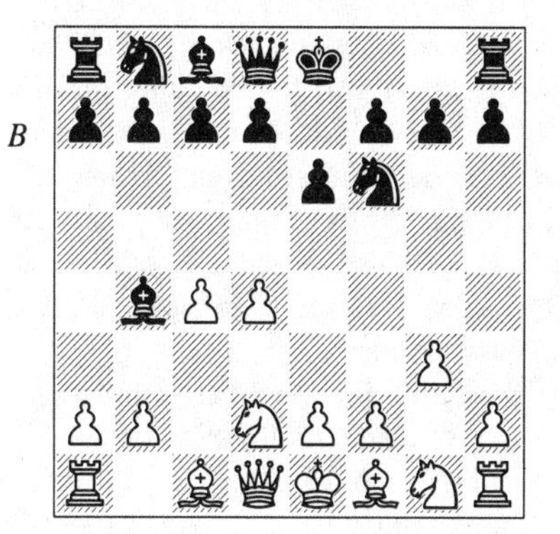

4...c5!?

In the regular 4 ♘bd2 Bogo (♘gf3 substituted for g3), the move 4...b6 is a common reply, but this is of course less attractive here. 4...c5 is, however, more logical here than in Chapter 1, since having played g3 White is not particularly keen on defending his centre with a later e3.

Instead after 4...0-0 5 ♗g2, 5...d6 6 ♘f3 transposes to Chapter 1, but possible is also 5...d5!? 6 ♕c2 c5!? 7 dxc5

♗xc5 8 ♘b3 ♗e7 9 ♘f3 ♘c6 = Shtyrenkov-Kubala, Pardubice 1997.

5 dxc5

Alternatives are:

a) 5 ♘f3 cxd4 6 ♘xd4 ♕b6 (6...♘c6 7 ♘c2 ♗e7 8 ♗g2 0-0 9 0-0 a6 10 b3 gave White a slight advantage in Alburt-Short, Foxboro (6) 1985) 7 a3 ♗xd2+ 8 ♕xd2 ♘c6 9 ♘b5!? (9 e3 0-0 10 b4 ♘xd4 11 ♕xd4 ♕c6 12 ♖g1 d6 13 ♗g2 ♕c7 is satisfactory for Black, Alburt-Adorjan, New York 1985) 9...0-0 (9...d5!? – Christiansen) 10 ♕e3! d5 11 ♕xb6 axb6 12 cxd5 ♘b4! (12...exd5 13 ♗e3 is pleasant for White) 13 ♖b1 ♘c2+ (a more solid move is 13...♘bxd5 but then White is just better) 14 ♔d1 exd5 and now 15 ♗g5? ♘g4! led to unclear play in D.Gurevich-Christiansen, USA Ch 1993, but White can improve with 15 f3! ♗d7 16 e3 ♖ac8 17 ♗d3!, e.g. 17...♖fe8 18 ♘d6 ♘xe3+ 19 ♔d2 ± D.Gurevich.

b) 5 a3!? ♗xd2+ 6 ♕xd2 and then:

b1) 6...cxd4 7 ♘f3 and now:

b11) 7...b6 8 ♗g2 ♗b7 9 0-0 ♕c8 (interesting is also 9...♗xf3!? 10 exf3 ♘c6 11 f4 0-0 12 b4 ♖c8 13 ♗b2 d5 14 ♖ac1 ♕d7 15 ♕d3 ♖fd8 16 c5 with unclear play, Gluckman-Zarnicki, Biel IZ 1993) 10 ♕xd4 ♘c6 11 ♕h4 ♘e7 = K.Urban-Eingorn, Swidnica 1997.

b12) 7...d5 8 cxd5 exd5 9 ♗g2 0-0 10 0-0 ♘c6 11 ♘xd4 ♖e8 12 ♘xc6 bxc6 13 ♕c2 ♗a6 14 ♖e1 ♕b6 15 ♗f4 ± Kožul-Kurajica, Bosnia 1998.

b13) 7...b5!? 8 cxb5 ♗b7 9 ♕xd4 ♕a5+ 10 ♕b4 ♕xb4+ 11 axb4 a6! 12 bxa6 ♘xa6 = Beliavsky-Makarychev, USSR Ch 1979.

b14) 7...♘c6 8 ♘xd4 ♘a5!? is an original and very interesting idea:

b141) 9 ♕b4 d5 10 ♘b5 (10 e4!? dxc4 11 ♘b5 ♘c6 12 ♕xc4 a6 13 ♘c3 ♘d4 14 ♕d3 e5 was fine for Black in Mikhalchishin-T.Karolyi, Kecskemet 1983) 10...♘c6! (much stronger than 10...♘xc4 11 b3 ± – Beliavsky) 11 ♕d6 ♕xd6 12 ♘xd6+ ♔e7 and Black is better due to his large lead in development, Birnboim-Finkel, Tel-Aviv 1993.

b142) 9 ♕d3!? d5 10 cxd5 ♕xd5 11 ♕b5+ ♕xb5 12 ♘xb5 0-0 13 ♗g2 ± Meins-Finkel, Groningen Open 1997.

b143) 9 e3 d5 10 cxd5 ♕xd5 11 f3 0-0 12 b4 e5 13 bxa5 exd4 14 ♗g2 dxe3 15 ♕xd5 ♘xd5 16 f4 ♖d8 17 0-0 ♗f5 18 ♖e1 ½-½ Fedorowicz-Short, Dortmund 1986.

b2) 6...♘c6 7 dxc5 ♘e4 8 ♕e3 ♕a5+ 9 ♗d2 ♘xd2 10 ♕xd2 ♕xc5 11 ♖c1 and now:

b21) 11...b6!? 12 ♗g2 ♗b7 13 ♘f3 ♘d4 14 b4 ♘xf3+ 15 ♗xf3 ♕c7 16 ♗xb7 ♕xb7 17 0-0 0-0 18 ♖fd1 ♖fd8 19 c5 bxc5 20 ♖xc5 with a slight initiative for White, Kaidanov-Chow, USA 1992.

b22) 11...a5 12 ♘f3 (12 ♗g2!? might be more accurate) 12...b5! 13 cxb5 ♕xb5 14 ♗g2 0-0 15 0-0 d5 16 ♖c2 ♗b7 17 ♖fc1 ♕b6 = Kaidanov-Rohde, Philadelphia 1992.

5...♗xc5

It is not essential to recapture the pawn immediately. 5...♘c6 6 ♗g2 0-0 7 ♘f3 ♗xc5 should transpose to the main line, but 5...♘a6 has also been tried. However, after 6 ♗g2 0-0 7 ♘f3

♘xc5 8 0-0 d5 9 cxd5 exd5 10 a3 ♗xd2 11 ♗xd2 ♖e8 12 ♗e3 ♘ce4 13 ♖c1 White was slightly better in the game Korchnoi-Andersson, Wijk aan Zee 1971.

6 ♗g2 ♘c6

Other options:

a) 6...♕b6 7 ♘h3!? 0-0 8 0-0 ♗e7 9 ♘f4 d6 10 b3 ± Chernin-Eingorn, Moscow 1990.

b) 6...♗e7 7 ♘gf3 ♕c7 8 0-0 0-0 9 b3 a6 10 ♗b2 d6 11 ♖c1 with a slight advantage for White, L.B.Hansen-Van der Wiel, Wijk aan Zee 1993.

c) 6...d5 7 ♘gf3 ♘c6 transposes to the main line.

7 ♘gf3 *(D)*

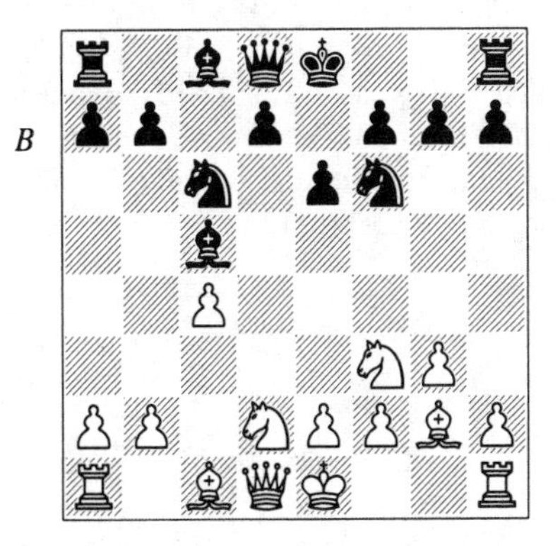

7...d5

Black has no desire to be left with a weak d-pawn and attempts to exchange it immediately. Other sensible approaches:

a) 7...0-0 8 0-0 b6 (a solid option is 8...♗e7!? 9 ♘b3 d6 10 h3 ♕c7 11 ♗e3 ♖d8 12 ♖c1 b6 = D.Gurevich-Dzindzichashvili, St Maarten 1990) 9 a3 a5 10 ♘b1 ♗a6 11 ♕a4 ♕e8!? 12 ♘c3 d5 13 cxd5 ♘xd5 14 ♘xd5 exd5 15 ♖e1 ♖d8 = Santos-Ivkov, Praia da Rocha 1978.

b) 7...b6 8 0-0 ♗b7 9 a3 0-0 (9...a5) 10 b4 ♗e7 11 ♗b2 ♖c8 12 ♕b1! h6 13 ♖d1 ♕c7 14 ♘e4 ♘xe4 15 ♕xe4 with a slight advantage to White, Smyslov-T.Petrosian, USSR 1967.

8 0-0 0-0 9 a3 a5 10 cxd5

In Kaidanov-Lobron, New York 1992 White varied with 10 ♕c2!? and after 10...♗a7?! 11 e4!? h6 12 b3 d4 13 ♘e1 ♘g4 14 ♘df3! ♘ge5 15 ♘xe5 ♘xe5 16 ♗f4 ♘g6 he should have played 17 ♘d3! with a slight advantage, e.g. 17...♘xf4 18 ♘xf4 e5 19 ♘d3 f5!? 20 exf5 ♗xf5 21 ♕e2! – Kaidanov, but Black would probably do better by retreating the bishop to e7 at move 10.

10...exd5

Black accepts an isolated pawn in return for active piece play.

11 ♘b3 ♗b6 12 ♘bd4 ♖e8 13 ♗e3 ♗g4!

With a roughly equal position, Alburt-Rohde, USA Ch 1991.

8 Transposition to the Nimzo-Indian: 4 ♘c3 b6

1 d4 ♘f6 2 c4 e6 3 ♘f3 ♗b4+ 4 ♘c3

For a Bogo player it is of course essential to have a line against 4 ♘c3 as well, even though this is strictly speaking a Nimzo-Indian. For this reason, the position is a little rare via the Bogo-Indian move-order, since if White wanted to face the Nimzo-Indian, he would generally have played 3 ♘c3.

4...b6 *(D)*

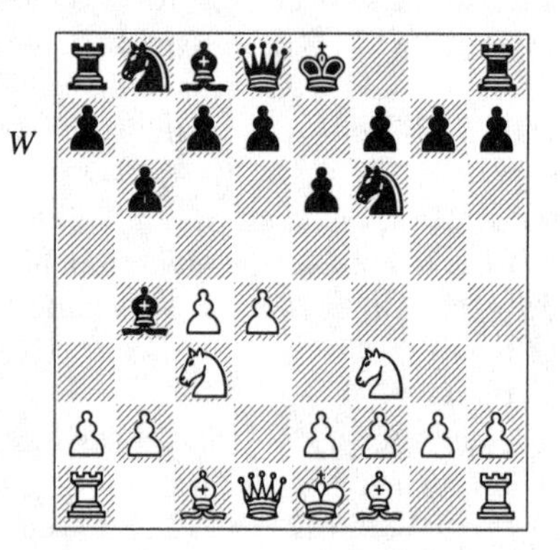

Of the numerous possibilities I have selected 4...b6, which I believe to be a sound and promising move. The game is now a Nimzo/Queen's Indian hybrid. This position can also occur via the move-order 3 ♘f3 b6 4 ♘c3 ♗b4 and so this chapter will also be of use to those who play 4 ♘c3 against the Queen's Indian.

Typical Pawn Structures

Below we have the most common pawn structure in this chapter. While Black has a structural plus in shape of White's doubled c-pawns, he has had to make a serious concession himself by advancing the g-pawn. This is often essential in order to unpin the knight on f6. In the long term the structure is in Black's favour (due to White's doubled c-pawns and isolated a-pawn), but White can try to create some middlegame disruption based on a d5-break or a c5-break.

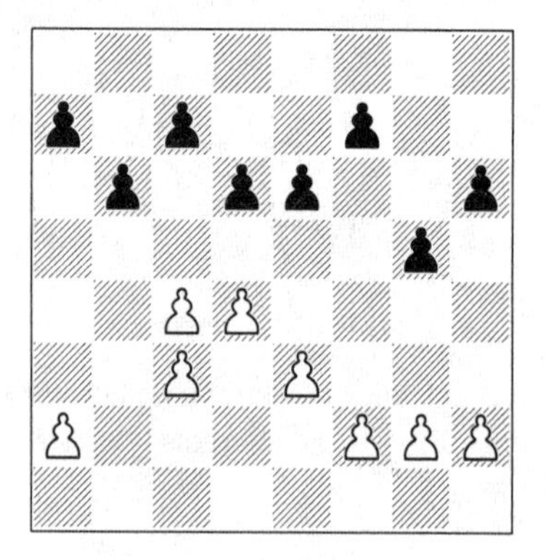

Planning for White

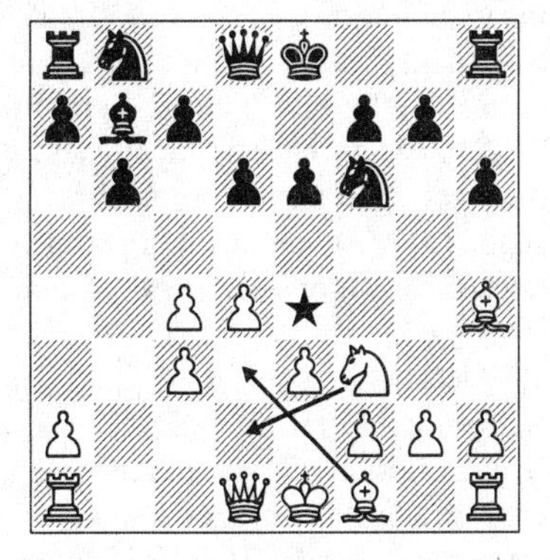

A key square in this line is e4. The ending is, as already explained, clearly favourable for Black if he manages to exchange a lot of pieces. Therefore White will attempt to minimize exchanges with the moves ♘d2, ♗d3 and f3.

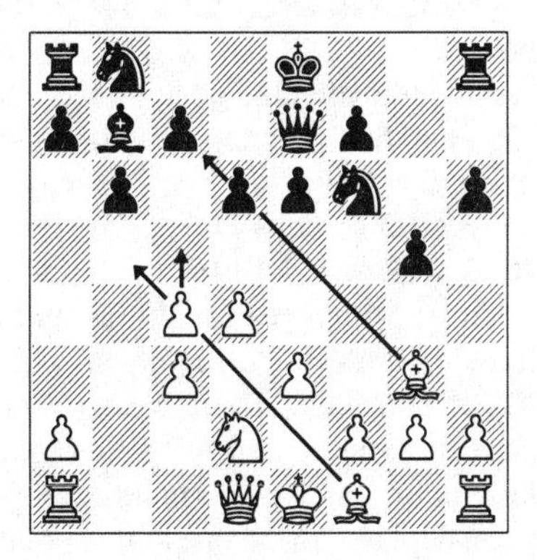

This is a very common position. White has a number of different plans to choose between, and a quite recent one is based on the c4-c5 thrust. Even though, in this exact position the move c4-c5 is completely new, the theme is well-known. White is prepared to sacrifice a pawn to open lines for his bishops. Let us assume that Black captures the pawn by ...dxc5. Apart from having increased the scope of the f1-bishop, suddenly its colleague on g3 wakes up too. If Black plays ...bxc5 the b-file is opened and White is well positioned to occupy it immediately with a rook.

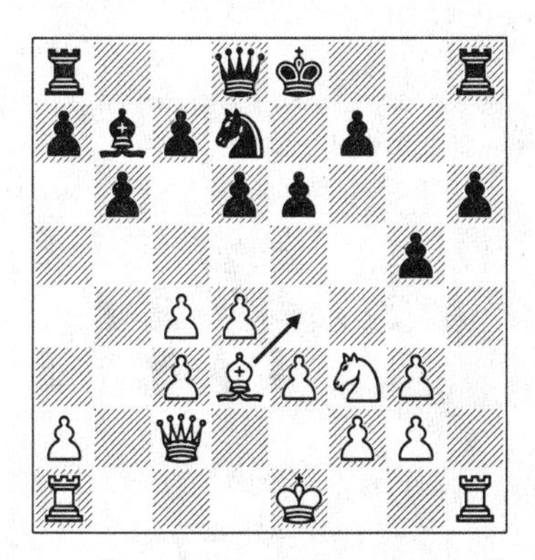

Another attractive strategy for White is to try to exchange the light-squared bishops. In the above diagram this can be achieved by the move ♗e4. After the exchange, c6 becomes a weak square, and White will no longer have to worry about Black's pressure on the long diagonal.

Planning for Black

As already explained a key square in this variation is e4. Therefore a logical plan for Black is to try to control e4 by occupying the square with a knight. Black is prepared to double the white

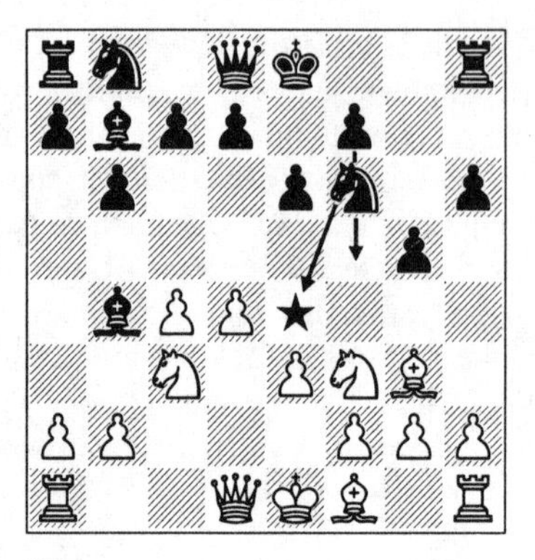

c-pawns by ...♗xc3 and the knight can be supported by the f-pawn.

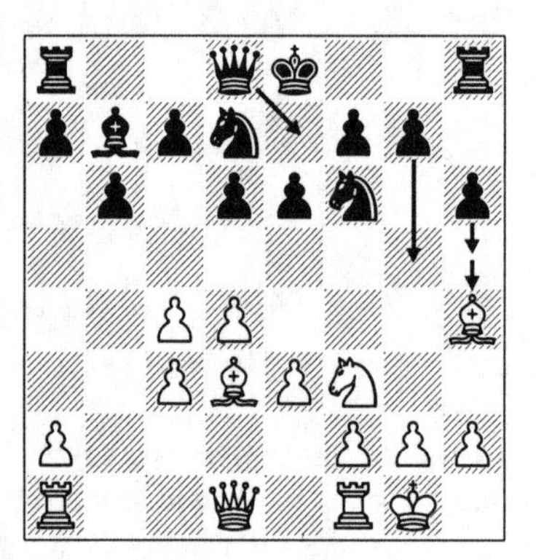

Another common plan is to control e4 from a distance and prepare a kingside attack by moving the queen to e7 followed by pushing the g- and h-pawns. This is a rather committal strategy and Black must be prepared for a battle with attacks on opposite wings.

Quick Summary

In my opinion, Seirawan's 5 ♕b3 (Line A) deserves more attention than it has got. The positions that arise are extremely interesting, particularly in the main line 5...c5 6 a3 ♗a5 7 ♗g5 h6 8 ♗h4 g5 9 ♗g3 g4, but it is worth noting that Seirawan himself preferred 7...♗b7 when he was faced with his own pet system. The main line is 5 ♗g5 (Line B) and also here some interesting positions occur, but of a more strategic kind. After 5...♗b7 6 e3 h6 7 ♗h4 Black has a choice of 7...g5 (Line B1) and the safer 7...♗xc3+ (Line B2). Following 7...g5 8 ♗g3 ♘e4 9 ♕c2 Black has another choice; here the move 9...♗xc3+ (Line B12) is again the safest, while after 9...d6 (Line B11) Black is currently looking for a water-proof reply to 10 ♗d3 ♗xc3+ 11 bxc3 f5 12 d5!.

The Theory of 4 ♘c3 b6

1 d4 ♘f6 2 c4 e6 3 ♘f3 ♗b4+ 4 ♘c3 b6

From the diagram position we shall examine the following two main variations for White:

A: 5 ♕b3 144
B: 5 ♗g5 149

Other 5th moves for White lead to lines of the Nimzo-Indian in which Black's fianchetto is viable and White has lost some flexibility by putting his knight on f3. Black should be OK here, but I am afraid that at this point I must draw the line and say "please see another book", for example *Easy Guide to the Nimzo-Indian* by John Emms.

A)

5 ♕b3 *(D)*

B

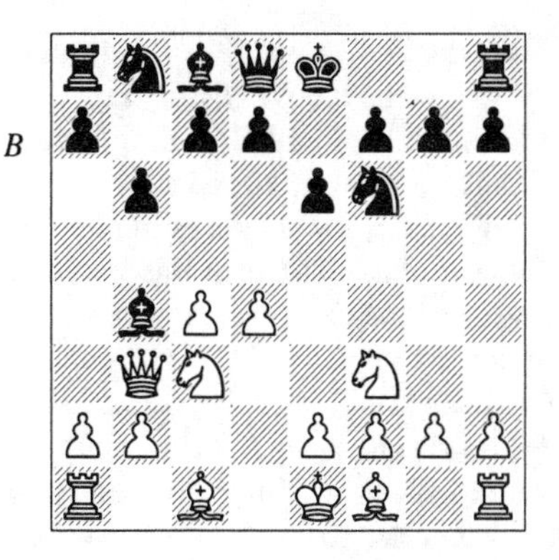

This is a long-time favourite of American grandmaster Yasser Seirawan. The early queen move intends to disturb Black's harmony and forces him to protect the bishop, since, bearing in mind the Nimzo-Indian line 1 d4 ♘f6 2 c4 e6 3 ♘c3 ♗b4 4 ♕c2 0-0 5 a3 (White spends a move forcing Black to exchange on c3), Black would not consider taking the knight on c3.

5...c5

Other options are less popular:

a) 5...♗a5 6 g3 ♗b7 7 ♗g2 0-0 8 0-0 ♗xc3 9 ♕xc3 d6 10 b3 ♘bd7 11 ♗b2 a5 12 ♖ad1 ♕e7 13 d5 with a slight advantage for White, Ubilava-Plaskett, Sochi 1984.

b) 5...♘a6 6 a3 ♗xc3+ 7 ♕xc3 c5 8 b4 0-0 9 dxc5 bxc5 10 b5 ♘c7 11 e3 ♘e4 12 ♕c2 ♗b7 13 ♗e2 f5 14 ♗b2 with an edge for White, Seirawan-I.Ivanov, USA Ch 1991.

c) 5...a5 and there may follow:

c1) 6 ♗g5 h6 7 ♗h4 ♗b7 8 e3 d6 9 ♗d3 ♘bd7 10 0-0-0 ♗xc3 11 ♕xc3 a4 with counterplay, Miles-Bischoff, Havana 1998.

c2) 6 g3 and now:

c21) 6...d5 7 cxd5 ♕xd5!? 8 ♕xd5 exd5 9 a3! ♗xc3+ 10 bxc3 ♗a6?! (Van Wely suggests 10...c5 instead) 11 ♗f4 ♘bd7 12 ♗h3 and White is slightly better, owing to his bishop-pair, Van Wely-Nijboer, Linares Z 1995.

c22) 6...♗b7 7 ♗g2 0-0 8 0-0 ♗xc3 9 ♕xc3 d6 10 b3 ♘bd7 11 ♗b2 ♘e4 12 ♕e3! ♕b8? (I do not see an idea behind this move; better is 12...♘ef6!) 13 d5! exd5 14 cxd5 ♗xd5, Dreev-Kiselev, Podolsk 1992, and now 15 ♘h4! ♖e8 16 ♗xg7!! ♔xg7 17 ♘f5+ ♔h8 18 ♕d4+ ♖e5 19 f4 c5 20 ♕b2 wins.

d) 5...♕e7 and now:

d1) 6 a3 ♗xc3+ 7 ♕xc3 ♗b7 8 e3 0-0 9 ♗e2 c5!? 10 0-0 ♖c8 11 dxc5 ♕xc5 12 b4 ♕e7 13 ♗b2 d5 14 ♕d4 dxc4 15 ♗xc4 a5 16 ♘e5 ♘c6 17 ♘xc6 ♖xc6 = I.Sokolov-Karpov, Groningen 1995.

d2) 6 ♗f4 d5!? 7 e3 0-0 8 a3 ♗xc3+ 9 ♕xc3 ♗a6 10 ♗g5 ♖c8 11 cxd5 ♗xf1 12 ♖xf1 exd5 13 ♖c1 ♕e6 14 ♗xf6 ♕xf6 15 ♔e2 c6 with an approximately equal game, Alterman-Hraček, Bad Homburg 1997.

6 a3 ♗a5

This remains the most popular, but 6...♗xc3+ is a fully viable alternative, e.g. 7 ♕xc3 0-0 and then:

a) 8 g3?! cxd4 9 ♕xd4 ♘c6 10 ♕h4 ♗b7 11 ♗g2 ♖c8 with a satisfactory position for Black, M.Gurevich-Kasparov, Linares 1991.

b) 8 dxc5 bxc5 9 ♗g5 is better, reaching a line from the ♕c2 Nimzo, i.e. 1 d4 ♘f6 2 c4 e6 3 ♘c3 ♗b4 4 ♕c2 0-0 5 a3 ♗xc3+ 6 ♕xc3 b6 7 ♗g5 c5 8 dxc5 bxc5 9 ♘f3. This position is outside the scope of this book, but here is one line: 9...♘c6 10 e3 d6 11 ♗h4 g5 12 ♗g3 ♘e4 13 ♕c2 f5 14 0-0-0 ♕f6 15 ♗d3 ♘xg3 16 hxg3 ♗b7 17 ♗e2 ♖ad8 with chances for both sides, Seirawan-Arnason, Manila OL 1992.

7 ♗g5 *(D)*

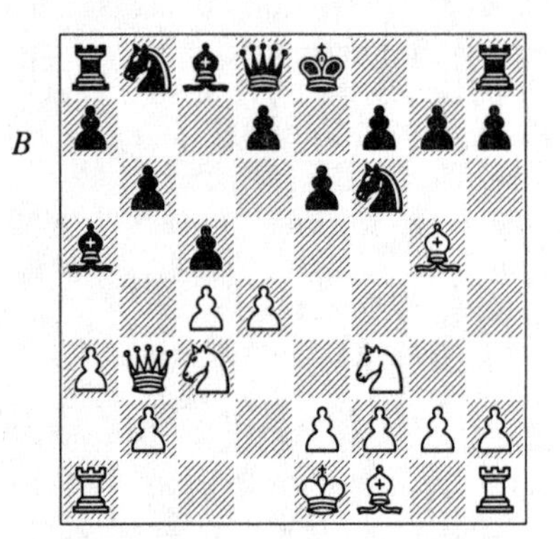

7...h6

Alternatives:

a) 7...♘c6 8 0-0-0 ♗xc3 9 d5! (this is the only way to fight for an advantage, because 9 ♕xc3 ♘e4 10 ♗xd8 ♘xc3 11 bxc3 ♘xd8 is very pleasant for Black) 9...♗e5! (Timman's recommendation after his encounter with Seirawan in Hilversum 1990; the 5th match game continued 9...exd5? 10 cxd5 ♗e5 11 dxc6 ♕e7 12 cxd7+ ♗xd7 13 e3 ♖d8 14 ♖xd7! ♖xd7 15 ♗b5 and White was clearly better) 10 dxc6 ♕c7? (10...♗c7 is much preferable; then Soppe-Debarnot, Buenos Aires 1991 went 11 e3 h6 12 ♗h4 ♕e7 13 ♕a4 d6 14 ♗d3 g5 15 ♗g3 ♘h5 with unclear play) 11 g3! ♗d6 (11...♕xc6 12 ♘xe5 ♕xh1 13 ♘f3 ♗b7 14 ♗h3 ♗xf3 15 ♖xh1 ♗xh1 16 f3 followed by ♕d1 wins for White) 12 ♗g2 dxc6 13 ♖xd6! ♕xd6 14 ♖d1 ± Seirawan-Zarnicki, Buenos Aires 1993.

b) 7...♗b7. It is interesting that the greatest of all experts in this line, Seirawan, chooses this move when faced by his own pet system. 8 e3 (8 dxc5?! ♘a6! 9 cxb6?! ♘c5 10 ♕c2 ♗e4 11 ♕d1 ♗xc3+ 12 bxc3 ♕xb6 clearly favoured Black in Van Wely-Seirawan, Wijk aan Zee 1995) 8...♗xf3!? 9 gxf3 cxd4 10 exd4 ♘c6 11 0-0-0 ♗xc3 12 ♕xc3 ♖c8 13 ♔b1, Korchnoi-Polugaevsky, Reykjavik 1987, and now Black should play 13...d5!? with unclear play.

8 ♗h4

An alternative is 8 ♗xf6 ♕xf6:

a) 9 d5 0-0 10 e3 d6 11 ♗d3 exd5 12 cxd5 a6 13 0-0 b5 14 ♘e4 ♕e7 15 ♕d1 ♗b7 16 ♗c2 ♘d7 17 ♖b1 ♘e5 with chances for both sides, Kamsky-de Firmian, New York 1991.

b) 9 e3 cxd4!? 10 exd4 0-0 11 ♗e2 ♗b7 12 0-0 ♗xc3 13 ♕xc3 d6 14 ♖ac1 ♘d7 15 ♘d2 ♖fc8 = H.Gretarsson-Hjartarson, Icelandic Ch (Reykjavik) 1995.

8...g5!?

An aggressive continuation typical of the entire system with 4...b6. Black aims to exploit the fact that White's dark-squared bishop has left its home on the queenside. Other options:

a) 8...♘c6?! 9 0-0-0! (threatening 10 d5 or 10 ♘b5) 9...♗xc3 10 ♕xc3 cxd4 11 ♘xd4 ♘e4 12 ♕h3! ± Seirawan-Timman, Hilversum (3) 1990.

b) 8...♗b7 9 0-0-0 ♗xf3 10 gxf3 ♘c6 was Fayard-Emms, Cappelle la

Grande 1991, and now Fayard recommends 11 ♘b5! ♘xd4 12 ♘xd4 cxd4 13 ♖xd4 ♖c8 14 ♔b1 ±.

9 ♗g3 g4

Very consistent, but probably not to everyone's taste, so here are some other options:

a) 9...♘c6 10 0-0-0 ♗xc3 11 ♕xc3 ♘e4 12 ♕c2 ♘xg3 13 hxg3 cxd4 14 ♘xd4 ♘xd4 15 ♖xd4 ♗b7 16 e3 ♕f6 17 ♔b1 ± Gheorghiu-Leuba, Suhr 1991.

b) 9...♘e4 10 e3 ♘c6 11 ♗d3 ♘xg3 12 hxg3 g4 13 d5! gxf3 (it is better to exchange on d5 first: 13...exd5! 14 cxd5 gxf3 15 dxc6 fxg2 16 ♖g1 ♕f6! 17 0-0-0 ♗xc3 18 cxd7+ ♗xd7 19 ♕xc3 ♕xc3+ 20 bxc3 ♗c6 21 e4 = Moran-Lerner, Berlin 1994) 14 dxc6 fxg2 15 ♖g1 ♕f6 (15...dxc6? 16 0-0-0 yields White plenty of compensation) 16 ♗e4! ♗xc3+ (an improvement on 16...d5? 17 cxd5 exd5 18 ♗xd5 ♗e6 19 ♗xe6 ♕xe6 20 ♕xe6+ fxe6 21 0-0-0 ♗xc3 22 bxc3 ♖d8 23 ♖xg2 ♖xd1+ 24 ♔xd1 ♔e7 25 ♖h2 ± Psakhis-Grünfeld, Israel 1991) 17 ♕xc3 ♕xc3+ 18 bxc3 d6! 19 0-0-0! (capturing on g2 leaves White a pawn up, but Black has enough counterplay against White's tripled c-pawns – therefore active play is needed; 19 c7 d5 20 cxd5 ♗b7 21 0-0-0 ♗xd5 22 ♗xd5 exd5 23 ♖xd5 ♖c8 24 ♖xg2 ♖xc7 25 ♖h2 ♖c6 results in an even ending – Lerner) 19...♗a6 20 ♖xd6 ♖d8 21 ♖xd8+ ♔xd8 22 ♖d1+ ♔c8 23 ♗xg2 ♖d8 24 ♖h1 ♗xc4 25 ♖xh6 ♔c7!, Yrjölä-Lerner, Helsinki 1992, and now White can generate some pressure with 26 ♖f6!? ♖f8 27 g4 ♔d6 28 g5 ♔e7 29 ♖f4.

10 ♘d2

10 0-0-0!? ♗xc3 11 ♕xc3 gxf3 12 d5! is given as clearly better for White by Psakhis but no one has yet had the courage to try it in practice; a convincing line is needed against 12...♖g8!.

10...cxd4 *(D)*

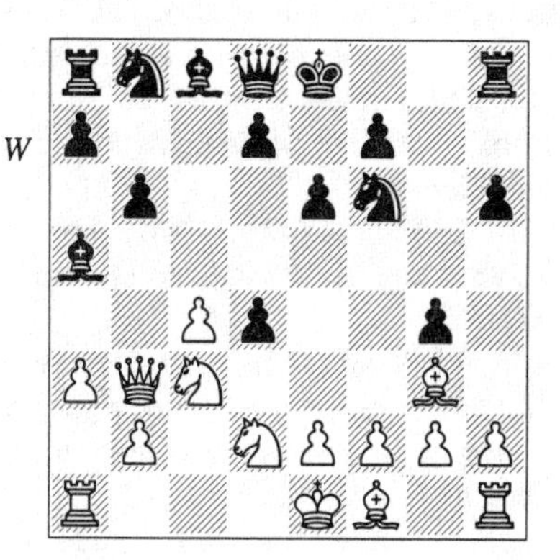

11 ♘b5!?

11 ♘cb1 is more passive but quite interesting too. Dreev-Kiselev, USSR Ch (Moscow) 1991 continued 11...♘e4 12 ♕d3 ♘xg3 (12...♘xd2 13 ♘xd2 ♗xd2+ 14 ♕xd2 ♘c6 15 h3 is very good for White according to Ftačnik) 13 ♕xd4!? ♗xd2+ 14 ♘xd2 ♘xh1 15 ♕xh8+ ♔e7 16 ♕xh6 ♗b7 17 ♕g5+ ♔e8 (17...f6 is an attempt to play for more than a draw, but this is extremely risky as Black's knight on h1 hardly has any chances of escaping; a possible continuation is 18 ♕g7+ ♔d6 19 ♖d1 ♔c7 20 ♕xg4 with unclear play) 18 ♕g8+ ♔e7 19 ♕g5+ ♔e8 20 ♕g8+ ♔e7 ½-½.

11...♗xd2+

Kiselev and Gagarin also analyse 11...♘e4, and if this proves sound then that may be an argument for choosing 11 Ncb1. Some sample variations, full of surprising tactical turns, begin after 12 Nc7+ Kf8, and then there are three choices for White:

a) 13 Nxa8 Bxd2+ 14 Kd1 Nc6 15 Qd3 f5 16 f3 (White may try to bring out the knight by 16 Nc7 but this results in a surprising turn-around after 16...Bf4! and Black wins) 16...Nxg3 17 hxg3 Be3 18 fxg4 Ne5 and Black should win.

b) 13 Qd3 Bxd2+ 14 Kd1 Bb7 15 Nxa8 Bxa8 16 Qxd4 Rg8 is clearly better for Black.

c) 13 0-0-0 seems to be the strongest continuation for White, whereby he avoids the loss of the knight on d2. Then there is:

c1) 13...Qg5 14 Qd3 Bxd2+ 15 Rxd2 Nxd2 (15...Nc5 16 Qc2 +–) 16 Qxd2 Qxd2+ 17 Kxd2 Bb7 18 Nxa8 Bxa8 19 Bxb8 +–.

c2) 13...Bxd2+ 14 Rxd2 Nxd2 (14...Qg5 15 Qd3 is 'c1' above) 15 Kxd2 Bb7 16 Nxa8 Bxa8 17 Bd6+ and now Black must decide where to move the king:

c21) 17...Kg7 permits 18 Be5+, and after 18...f6 19 Bxd4 Nc6 20 Qg3! Kh7 21 Bc3! White has the advantage on account of his bishop-pair.

c22) 17...Kg8! 18 Qg3 Nc6 19 h3 (19 Qxg4+ Qg5+ ∓) 19...f5!? (19...h5 20 hxg4 Qg5+ 21 Bf4 Qxg4 22 Rxh5! Qxg3 23 Rxh8+ Kxh8 24 Bxg3 results in a favourable ending for White) 20 hxg4 Qg5+ 21 Bf4 Qxg4 22 Qxg4+ fxg4 23 Rxh6 Rxh6 24 Bxh6 Kh7 with reasonable chances for Black, who, compared to the above line, is much more active here.

12 Kxd2 Ne4+ 13 Ke1 *(D)*

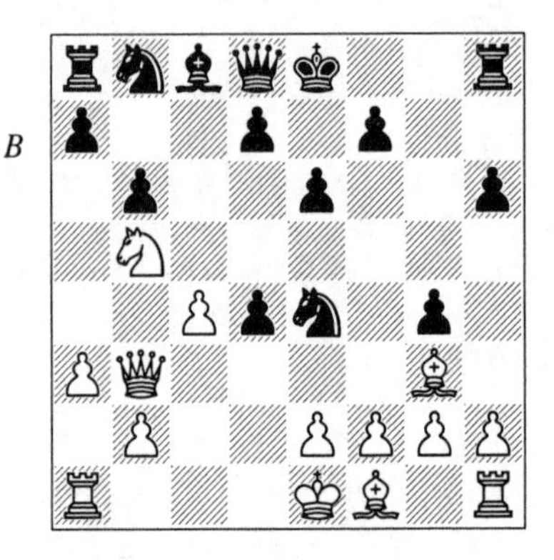

13...d6

Avoiding the knight fork and planning ...e5. Other possibilities for Black are:

a) 13...Nxg3 14 Qxg3 ±.

b) 13...0-0?! (experimental) 14 Nc7 f5 15 Nxa8 Bb7 16 f3 Nc5 17 Qc2 Qf6 18 Bd6 Bxa8 19 Bxf8 Kxf8 20 Rd1 +– Fraschini-Rodriguez, Montevideo 1994.

c) Some further analysis by Kiselev and Gagarin runs 13...Na6 14 Qd3 Nxg3, when White has several promising options:

c1) 15 Qxd4 Nxh1 16 Nd6+ (16 Qxh8+? Ke7 17 Qxh6 Qg8 is good for Black) 16...Ke7 17 Nf5+ exf5 18 Qe5+ with perpetual check.

c2) 15 Qxg3!? with the initiative.

c3) 15 hxg3 (best) 15...Qf6 16 Qe4! ±.

14 Qd3 Nxg3 15 Qxd4!

15 Qxg3 allows 15...e5!.

15...Nxh1

This is practically forced, as 15...e5 is not bearable, e.g. 16 ♘xd6+ ♔f8 17 ♕xe5 f6 18 ♕d5 +–.

16 ♕xh8+ ♔e7 17 ♕xh6 ♘d7 18 ♖d1 ♗a6

18...♕f8 19 ♕h4+ f6 20 ♘xd6 is also dangerous.

19 ♕f4

19 ♘xd6 is met by 19...♕h8!.

19...♗xb5 20 ♕xd6+ ♔e8 21 cxb5 g3

21...♕e7 22 ♕c6 ♖d8 23 g3 and White wins the knight on h1, with a clear advantage.

22 hxg3 ♖c8 23 ♕d4

White has excellent compensation, Malaniuk-Lendwai, Kecskemet 1991.

B)

5 ♗g5 ♗b7 6 e3 h6 7 ♗h4 *(D)*

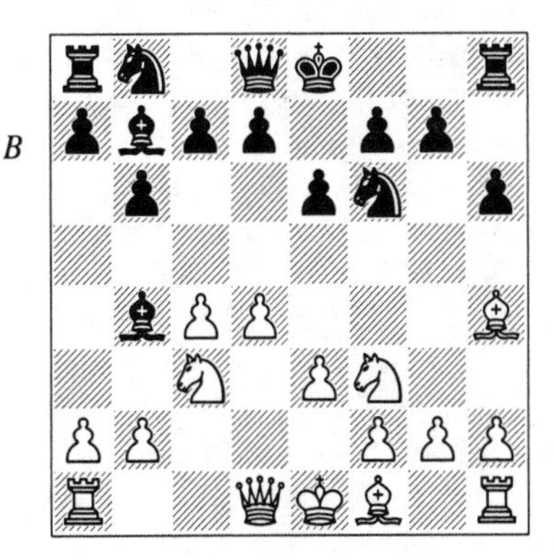

Now we shall consider the two main continuations for Black:

B1)

7...g5

This sharp approach used to be the most popular but nowadays the sounder 7...♗xc3+ is taking over.

8 ♗g3 ♘e4 9 ♕c2

The interesting gambit 9 ♘d2 is rarely seen, but may catch some opponents unaware. Black must decide whether to accept the sacrifice:

a) 9...♗xc3 10 bxc3 ♘xg3 and then:

a1) 11 fxg3?! ♕e7 12 e4 d6 13 ♗d3 ♘d7 14 ♕a4 0-0 15 0-0 (15 0-0-0!?) 15...♘f6 (15...e5 is perhaps more accurate, with the idea of blowing White's centre apart with ...exd4 followed by ...c5) 16 ♕d1 e5 = Lputian-Plaskett, Hastings 1986/7.

a2) 11 hxg3 d6 12 ♗d3?! (12 a4!? is better) 12...♘d7 (Black should not be afraid of taking on g2: 12...♗xg2!? 13 ♖h2 ♗b7 14 ♕c2 ♘d7 15 ♗e4 d5! ∓ Cebalo) 13 ♗e4 ♗xe4 14 ♘xe4 ♕e7 15 ♕a4 f5 16 ♕c6 ♔f7 17 ♘d2 ♘f6 = Iz.Jelen-Cebalo, Yugoslav Ch 1981.

b) 9...♘xg3 10 hxg3 ♗f8 (this replacement of the bishop is fairly logical as the h6-pawn needs protection; 10...♗xc3 transposes to 'a' above; 10...♘c6 11 ♕c2 ♗f8 12 a3 ♗g7 13 ♗e2 ♕e7 14 g4 0-0-0, Schüssler-Miles, Reykjavik 1986, 15 ♘f1 ±) 11 f4!? ♗g7 12 ♕a4 ♕e7 13 0-0-0 ♘c6 14 ♗e2 0-0-0 15 ♔b1 ♔b8 16 ♖c1 ♕b4 17 ♕d1 ± Kasparov-Miles, Dubai OL 1986.

c) 9...♘xc3 10 bxc3 ♗xc3 11 ♖c1 and now:

c1) 11...♗xd2+ 12 ♕xd2 d6 13 c5! dxc5 14 dxc5 (14 ♕b2!? cxd4 15 ♖xc7 ♗d5 16 ♗b5+ ♔f8 17 ♕xd4 f6 18 ♕c3 led to a quick win for White in

Colias-Kramer, Hammond 1989, but Black might be able to improve on move 14 or 15) 14...♕xd2+ 15 ♔xd2 ♗a6 16 ♗xc7 ♗xf1 17 ♖hxf1 and White is better, Smirin-Rozentalis, New York Open 1997.

c2) 11...♗b4 12 h4 with a further branch:

c21) 12...♘c6?! (understandably, this has only had a single outing) 13 d5 ♕e7!? (13...♘a5 14 hxg5 ♕xg5 15 ♗xc7 is clearly better for White) 14 dxc6 dxc6 15 ♗e5 0-0-0 16 ♗c3 ♗xc3 17 ♖xc3 c5 18 hxg5! hxg5 19 ♖xh8 ♖xh8 20 e4 and White is better, Schüssler-Arnason, Reykjavik 1986.

c22) 12...gxh4 13 ♖xh4! ♗d6 14 ♕g4 ♕e7 (14...♗xg3 15 ♕xg3 ♘c6 16 d5 ♘e7 17 ♗d3 d6 18 ♕g7 ♖g8 19 ♕h7! gave White excellent compensation in Kasparov-Timman, Hilversum (2) 1985) 15 ♗xd6 cxd6 16 ♕g3! f5 17 c5!? with unclear play, Agdestein-Hellers, Gausdal Z 1987.

c23) 12...♗d6 13 ♗xd6 cxd6 14 d5!? ♕f6?! 15 ♘e4 ♕e5 16 ♕d4! ♔e7 17 hxg5 ± Stocek-Röder, Budapest 1998.

Returning to the position after 9 ♕c2 *(D)*:

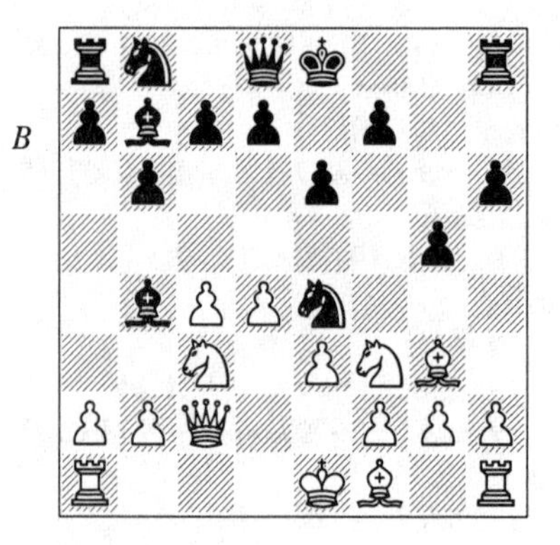
B

Play now branches into:

B11)

9...d6 10 ♗d3 ♗xc3+ 11 bxc3 f5

With this active continuation Black intends to keep his knight on e4.

12 d5!

This direct attack at Black's vulnerable centre was first discovered by Keres. Quiet play such as 12 0-0 ♘d7 13 ♘d2 ♘df6 14 ♘xe4 ♗xe4 15 ♗xe4 ♘xe4 16 f3 ♘xg3 17 hxg3 ♕d7 gives Black a satisfactory position, Gligorić-Taimanov, Zurich Ct 1953.

12...♘d7

Black has had surprising difficulties finding a reliable reply in this position, but currently this logical developing move stands the test. Other attempts:

a) 12...♘c5 and now:

a1) 13 ♘d4 ♕f6 14 0-0 (14 h4 causes no real problems for Black: 14...♘ba6 15 ♘xe6 ♘xe6 16 dxe6 ♔e7! 17 ♗xf5 ♘b4 18 ♕d2 ♕xf5 19 cxb4 ♗xg2 20 ♖g1 ♗f3 with equality, Ki.Georgiev-Kudrin, Amsterdam 1985) 14...♘ba6 15 ♘xe6 (15 f4 ♘xd3 16 fxg5 hxg5 17 ♘xe6 ♘ac5! 18 ♖xf5 ♕e7 ∓ Psakhis) 15...♘xe6 16 dxe6 0-0 17 f4 g4 18 e4 fxe4 19 ♗xe4 ♗xe4 20 ♕xe4 ♘c5 21 ♕c6 ♕xe6 22 f5 ♕f7 = Tukmakov-Ornstein, Thessaloniki OL 1984.

a2) 13 h4! (provoking ...g4 improves White's possibilities) 13...g4 14 ♘d4 ♕f6 15 0-0 *(D)* and there are now two main possibilities for Black:

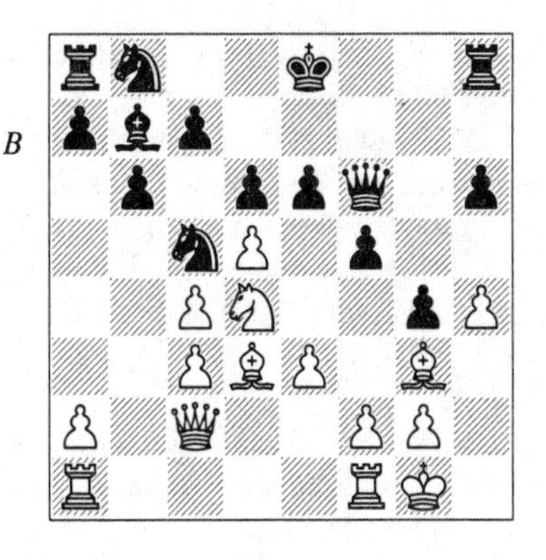

a21) 15...♘xd3 16 ♕xd3 e5 17 ♘xf5! (better than 17 ♕xf5 ♕xf5 18 ♘xf5 ♗c8) 17...♗c8 18 f4! (stronger than 18 ♘d4!? or 18 e4 ♗xf5 19 exf5 ♘d7 20 f4 gxf3 21 ♕xf3 0-0-0 22 a4 a5 with an unclear position, Miles-Timman, Cologne TV 1986) 18...♕xf5 (even worse is 18...♗xf5 19 e4 ♗h7 20 fxe5 or 18...gxf3 19 ♖xf3 ♗xf5 20 ♖xf5 ♕g7 21 ♗xe5!! dxe5 22 d6! +– Nunn) 19 e4 ♕h5 20 fxe5 dxe5 21 c5 ♔d8 22 d6 ♕e8 23 dxc7+ ♔xc7 24 ♕d5 ♘c6 25 ♖f7+ ♗d7 26 ♖af1 with a decisive attack, Miles-Beliavsky, Tilburg 1986.

a22) 15...♘ba6 (the tactical difficulties Black faces after 15...♘xd3 have made Black turn to this logical developing move, but also here Black must be prepared for a tough defence) 16 ♘xe6 ♘xe6 17 ♗xf5! (the only way to continue his attack; 17 dxe6 0-0 18 e7 ♖f7! is fine for Black) 17...♘g7 18 ♗g6+ ♔d7 19 f3 ♖af8 20 fxg4 ♕e7 21 e4. White has sufficient compensation: he already has three pawns for the piece, Black's king is still fighting to escape the centre and the g7-knight faces a rather cloudy future. Now:

a221) 21...♔c8 is a logical attempt to solve one problem at a time, but is probably too slow. 22 ♕d2! (hitting h6 in some lines) and then:

a2211) 22...♔b8 23 ♕d4! (23 ♖xf8+ ♖xf8 24 ♕xh6 ♗c8! is less clear, Kasparov-Timman, Hilversum (4) 1985) 23...♘e8 24 e5! (this dynamic central thrust is perhaps even better than 24 ♖f7!? ♖xf7 25 ♕xh8 ♖f8 26 ♕xh6 ♘c5 27 h5 ♘d7 28 ♗f5 ♗c8 29 ♖f1, with compensation, Salov-Timman, Saint John Ct (5) 1988) 24...dxe5 25 ♗xe5 ♖hg8 26 h5 ♘d6 27 ♖xf8+ ♖xf8 28 ♗g7 and White wins the h-pawn, again with plenty of compensation, Van der Linde-Duistermaat, Utrecht 1986.

a2212) 22...♘c5 23 ♖xf8+ ♖xf8 24 ♕xh6 ♕f6 25 ♗f5+! ♘xf5 26 ♕xf6 ♖xf6 27 exf5 ± Miles-Timman, Tilburg 1986.

a222) 21...♘c5! 22 ♕e2 ♔c8 23 e5 ♗a6 24 e6 with an unclear position, Ivanchuk-Anand, Monaco rpd 1993.

b) 12...exd5 13 cxd5 ♗xd5 is very risky for Black, who will soon face difficulties with his pawn on f5. 14 ♘d4 ♕f6 15 f3! ♘xg3 (worse is 15...♘c5 16 ♗xf5 ♘bd7 17 ♘b5 0-0-0 18 ♖d1! ♗e6? 19 ♗e4 ♔b8 20 ♖xd6! +– Ribli-Seirawan, Malta OL 1980) 16 hxg3 ♘d7 17 ♗xf5 0-0-0 (17...♘c5 again needs consideration, but Black will have long-term problems with his king: 18 ♘b5 ♕g7 19 ♗g6+ ♔d7 20 ♗f5+ ♗e6 21 ♗xe6+ ♘xe6 22 ♘d4 ± Tal-Dückstein, Zurich 1959) 18 ♕a4 a5 19 ♔f2 (19 g4!?

± Keres) 19...h5 20 Rab1 h4 21 e4 Bb7 22 gxh4 gxh4 23 Ne6 with a clear advantage for White, Keres-Taimanov, USSR Ch (Moscow) 1955.

c) 12...Qf6 *(D)*.

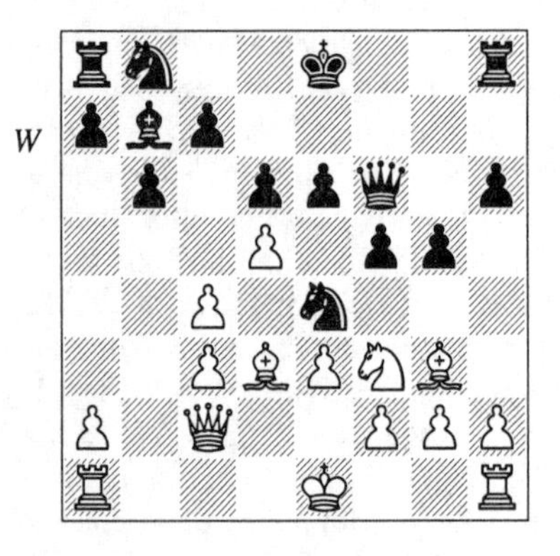

This subtle move is also a reasonable attempt for Black. Now 13 Nd4 exd5 14 cxd5 Bxd5 15 f3! transposes to line 'b', but Black can play 13...Nc5 transposing to 'a1', which seems OK for Black. Therefore White has recently searched for an advantage in the line 13 Bxe4 fxe4 14 Qxe4 Qxc3+ 15 Ke2 Qb2+ 16 Nd2 Qf6 17 h4 g4 18 h5 Nd7 (18...Qf5!? 19 Qxf5 exf5 20 e4 0-0 21 exf5 Nd7 22 Rh4 Rae8+ 23 Kd3 Nf6 gave Black some compensation in Izeta-Garcia Trobat, San Sebastian 1989) 19 Bh4 Qf5 20 Qxe6+ Qxe6 21 dxe6 Nc5 22 e7. This is the critical position for the assessment of 13 Bxe4. White has a real candidate for promotion on e7 but Black has sufficient control over the promotion square for this not to be an immediate concern. However, the pawn creates some disturbance and controls the f8-square, thereby limiting Black's counterplay. Now:

c1) 22...Bxg2? 23 Rhg1 Bh3 (this places the bishop somewhat off-side but attempts to keep the g-file closed) 24 Rg3! (with the simple idea of Rag1, Kd1 and f3) 24...Kd7 25 Rag1 Rhg8 26 Kd1! Ke6 27 f3 Kf5 28 Kc2! ±.

c2) 22...Kf7 23 f3 Rag8 24 Rhg1 gxf3+ (it may be worth considering Psakhis's suggestion 24...Rg7!? 25 Raf1 gxf3+ 26 gxf3 Rhg8 27 Rxg7+ Rxg7) 25 gxf3 Nd7?! 26 f4! ± Adianto-Timman, Amsterdam 1996.

c3) 22...Kd7 23 f3 Rag8 24 e4 gxf3+ 25 gxf3 Rg2+ 26 Ke3 Rhg8 27 Raf1 Ne6 28 Rf2 Rxf2 29 Kxf2 Nf4 30 Bf6 Bc6 with an unclear position, Salov-Timman, Saint John Ct (3) 1988.

13 Nd4

Of course, accepting the sacrifice needs a closer look: 13 Bxe4 fxe4 14 Qxe4 Qf6! (Black can afford to lose another pawn as he will easily round one of them up, whilst obtaining sufficient counterplay afterwards) 15 0-0 (15 Qxe6+ Qxe6 16 dxe6 Nc5 is fine for Black) 15...0-0-0 (15...Nc5?! is dubious in view of 16 Qd4! 0-0 17 e4 exd5 18 exd5 Qg6 19 Rfe1 Rae8 20 h4! ± Kharitonov-Vaiser, Barnaul 1984) 16 Qxe6 Qxe6 17 dxe6 Nc5 18 Nd4 Rde8 19 f3 Ba6 20 Nb5 Rxe6 21 e4 Kb8 (after 21...Na4!?, 22 Rac1 Kd7 23 Rc2 h5 was fine for Black in Ree-Taimanov, Hamburg 1965; Taimanov suggests 22 Nxa7+ as stronger and continues with 22...Kd7 23 Nb5 Bxb5 24 cxb5 Nxc3 25 a4 Ra8 26

♖a3!, but he must have overlooked 26...♘xb5!) and now:

a) 22 ♖ab1 g4 23 ♖fe1 gxf3 24 gxf3 h5 with equality, Hort-Bellin, Hastings 1975/6.

b) 22 ♖fd1 g4, Razuvaev-Salov, Moscow 1986, and now Tukmakov analyses 23 e5!? dxe5 24 ♖d5 gxf3 25 gxf3 ♖he8 26 ♖e1 with unclear play.

13...♘dc5 14 dxe6

14 ♘xe6 ♘xe6 15 dxe6 ♕f6 =.

14...♕f6!

14...♖f8 was featured in Kamsky-Salov, Moscow 1992 but after 15 ♗e2! ♕f6 16 ♗h5+ ♔e7 17 ♗f7! Black was in trouble, and in fact he chose to sacrifice the exchange for the bishop. One cute line showing Black's problems is 17...♘xg3?! 18 hxg3 ♗e4?? 19 ♕xe4! ♘xe4 20 ♘c6#.

15 f3 f4! 16 exf4

16 ♗xe4 ♗xe4 17 fxe4 fxg3 18 hxg3 0-0-0 is a funny variation analysed by Komarov – I do not think I have ever seen such a wrecked pawn structure!

16...♘xd3+ 17 ♕xd3 ♘c5 18 ♕e2 gxf4

Black is clearly better, Komarov-Mantovani, Reggio Emilia 1996/7.

B12)

9...♗xc3+ 10 bxc3 *(D)*

10...d6

Lately Black has tried to improve his move-order by 10...♘xg3, when White has the usual choice of how to recapture:

a) 11 hxg3 and now:

a1) 11...d6 12 ♗d3 transposes to the main line.

B

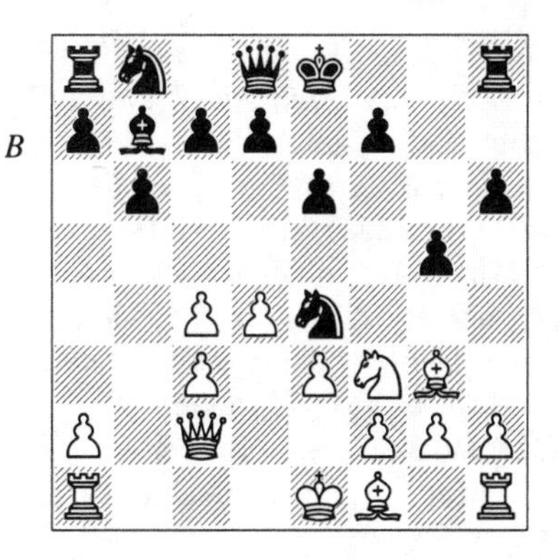

a2) 11...g4 12 ♘e5 ♕g5 13 ♖h4 f5 14 c5! ♘c6 15 ♘d3 ♘e7 16 ♘f4 ± Plachetka-Spasov, Nice OL 1974.

a3) 11...♕e7 12 ♗d3 ♘c6 13 ♖b1 0-0-0 14 c5 d6 15 cxb6 cxb6 16 c4 ♔b8 with unclear play, Karpov-Speelman, London 1982.

a4) 11...♘c6 12 ♖h5!? ♕f6 13 g4 ♘e7 14 ♘d2 c5 15 g3 ♕g7 (Kengis suggests 15...♔f8 followed by ...♔g7 with only a small advantage for White) 16 ♗e2 d5, Ionescu-Kengis, Timisoara 1987, 17 f4! ±.

b) 11 fxg3 g4 12 ♘h4 and now:

b1) 12...♘c6 13 ♗d3 ♕f6 is an interesting possibility, stopping White castling. Campos Moreno-M.Marin, Andorra 1997 continued 14 ♕e2 h5 15 a4 ♖h6 16 ♖b1 d6 17 ♗e4 0-0-0 18 ♗xc6 ♗xc6 19 a5 ♖g8 20 ♖a1 ♖g5 21 axb6 axb6 22 ♔d2 ♕g7 23 ♖a7 ♖f6 with unclear play.

b2) 12...♕g5. Leaving out ...d6 (compared with the main line) means that White does not have time to evacuate his king and is therefore forced to protect e3. 13 ♕f2 ♘c6 14 ♗d3 f5 15 e4!? (15 0-0 0-0 16 ♕e2 ♘e7 17 e4?!

fxe4 18 ♗xe4 ♗xe4 19 ♕xe4 ♖xf1+ 20 ♖xf1 ♖f8 gave Black a slightly better ending in Andreev-Tunik, St Petersburg 1996) 15...fxe4 16 0-0 exd3 (16...♘d8!? stops White's queen coming to f7 with check and protects e4, but it is difficult to see how Black's king is then going to escape) 17 ♕f7+ ♔d8 18 ♘g6 ♔c8 19 ♘xh8 ♗a6 and Black has pretty good compensation, Aseev-Tunik, St Petersburg 1996.

11 ♗d3

Alternatives:

a) 11 c5!? ♘d7 (11...bxc5 12 ♖b1 ♗c6 is perhaps better) 12 ♗b5 bxc5 13 ♖b1 ♘xg3 14 hxg3 ♔e7 15 0-0 with some compensation, Spassky-Matanović, Palma de Mallorca 1968.

b) 11 ♘d2 ♘xg3 12 hxg3 ♘d7 13 f3 (the problem with 11 ♘d2 is that White is forced to protect g2 in a rather awkward way before the bishop can be developed; the other way is 13 ♖h2, when 13...♕e7 14 ♗e2 0-0-0 15 ♗f3 f5 16 a4 a5 17 ♖b1 ♗xf3 18 gxf3 h5 with the idea of ...h4, led to unclear play in Miles-Etmans, Utrecht 1986) 13...♕e7 14 ♗d3 0-0-0 15 a4 a5 16 g4 e5 17 ♔f2 ♖de8 18 ♖ae1 ♘f6 = Matanović and Ugrinović.

11...♘xg3 *(D)*

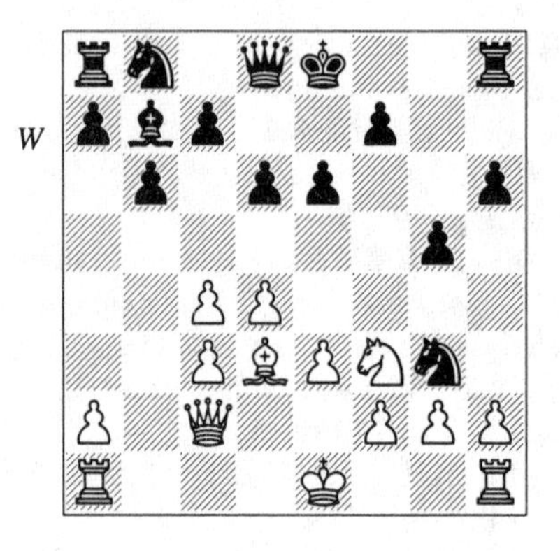

W

12 fxg3

This has a slightly better reputation than the other capture. White seeks play on the semi-open f-file, which appears more promising than having the h-file opened. After 12 hxg3 ♘d7 there is a choice for White:

a) 13 g4 ♔e7 14 e4 ♘f6 15 0-0-0 ♘xg4 16 ♕e2 ♕g8 17 e5 gave White some compensation in Goldin-Levin, USSR 1984, but no one has had the courage to repeat the idea.

b) 13 a4 ♔e7!? 14 a5 c5 15 d5 (15 a6 ♗xf3 16 gxf3 ♕c7 17 ♔e2 ♘f6 18 ♖h2 ♖ag8 was very promising for Black in Browne-Andersson, Buenos Aires 1980) 15...♘f6 16 e4 e5 17 ♘d2 ♗c8 18 ♔e2 ♗d7 and again only Black can play for a win, Farago-Langeweg, Malta OL 1980.

c) 13 ♗e4! (the exchange of the light-squared bishops is strategically very desirable for White, as it creates some holes in the black position and nullifies the pressure on the long diagonal) 13...♗xe4 14 ♕xe4 ♔e7 (in the game Christiansen-de Firmian, USA 1985 White obtained a very good position after 14...♘f6 15 ♕d3 g4 16 ♘d2 ♕e7 17 a4 a5 18 ♖b1 h5 19 ♖b5 ±) 15 ♞d2 ♘f6 16 ♕c6 (16 ♕d3!?) 16...♕d7 17 ♕xd7+ ♔xd7 18 ♔e2 h5 19 f3 ♖ab8 = Agzamov-Dorfman, USSR Ch 1981.

12...♘d7

12...g4 13 ♘h4 ♕g5 is less accurate here in view of 14 0-0! ♕xe3+ 15 ♔h1

♘d7 16 ♖f4! ± Spassky-Polugaevsky, Tel-Aviv OL 1964.

13 0-0 ♕e7 14 ♖f2

Other options:

a) 14 ♗e4 ♗xe4 15 ♕xe4 0-0 16 ♕c6 ♖ac8 17 ♘d2 a5 was about equal in S.Pedersen-Polak, Witley 1993.

b) 14 ♕a4 0-0 15 e4 e5 16 ♖ae1 ♔h8 17 ♕d1 ♖ae8 = Arencibia-Borges, Villa Clara Guillermo Garcia mem 1998.

c) 14 a4 a5 15 e4 (or 15 ♗e4 ♗xe4 16 ♕xe4 0-0 = Vaganian-Plaskett, London 1986) 15...0-0-0!? 16 ♘d2 g4 17 ♖f4 (17 ♖f2 is preferable) 17...h5 18 ♘f1 ♖dg8 19 ♘e3 ♕g5 20 ♕e2 f5! 21 exf5 e5 followed by ...h4 with an attack, Psakhis-Motwani, Troon 1984.

14...0-0-0

14...c5 15 ♖af1 0-0 was seen in Christiansen-Benjamin, USA Ch 1985. Then 16 g4 promises White a slight advantage.

15 ♗e4

The alternative is 15 ♖af1, but with the text-move White keeps more options open.

15...f5 16 ♗xb7+ ♔xb7 17 e4 ♖df8 18 a4 a5

18...♕h7!? may be a better try.

19 ♖e1 ♕h7 20 e5!

White is better, Timman-Miles, Tilburg 1985.

B2)

7...♗xc3+ 8 bxc3 d6 *(D)*

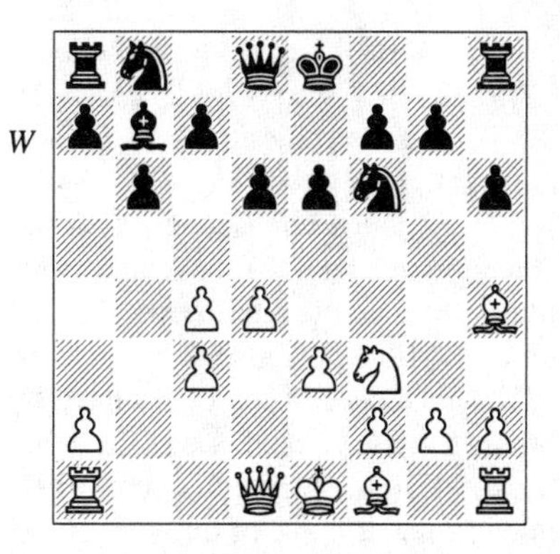

9 ♘d2

The most common move but 9 ♗d3 is an important alternative. Here White intends to castle and only then to move the knight to d2. This move-order is maybe a little more flexible as White is not committed to playing f3. After 9...♘bd7 10 0-0 Black has a choice:

a) 10...g5 11 ♗g3 ♘e4 12 ♘d2!? ♘xd2 (or 12...♘df6?! 13 ♘xe4 ♘xe4 14 ♗xe4 ♗xe4 15 d5! and White is better, Tolush-Taimanov, USSR Ch (Leningrad) 1956) 13 ♕xd2 f5 (interesting is 13...h5 14 f4 h4 15 ♗e1 gxf4 16 ♖xf4 h3 ½-½ S.Pedersen-J.O.Fries Nielsen, Gothenburg 1996) 14 f3 (14 f4 ♕e7 15 ♖ae1 also looks good for White, Larsen-Donner, Munich OL 1958) 14...0-0 15 a4 a5 16 ♖fb1 ± Ki.Georgiev-Ionescu, Sofia 1986.

b) 10...0-0 (this is generally considered too passive) 11 ♘d2 e5 12 f4 exf4 13 exf4 ♖e8 14 ♕c2 ♖e3 15 ♖fe1 ♖xe1+ 16 ♖xe1 ± Ristić-Gostiša, Yugoslav Ch 1990.

c) 10...♕e7 11 ♘d2 g5 12 ♗g3 and now:

c1) 12...0-0-0 is perhaps premature. White continues aggressively with 13 c5! (13 f3?! is too slow: 13...h5 14 h4 ♘h7! 15 ♕e1 ♖dg8 16 ♕f2 f5 and Black is better, S.Pedersen-Larsen, Danish Ch (Ålborg) 1994) 13...dxc5

14 Qa4 Kb8 15 Ba6 Ba8 16 Rab1 Nh5 17 Nc4 Nxg3 18 fxg3 f5 19 Bb5! with a strong attack, A.Greenfeld-Ambrož, Biel 1985.

c2) 12...h5 13 h4 (the most consistent approach but the more cautious 13 f3 is a fully viable alternative; then after 13...h4 14 Bf2 0-0-0 15 e4 Nh5 White take care of his own safety by 16 Re1 Nf4 17 Bf1 Rdg8 18 h3 ± Barsov-Eslon, Linares open 1997, rather than try the optimistic 16 c5 dxc5 17 Qa4 Nf4 18 Ba6 Nb8!, when the attack is repelled, Hjartarson-Stoica, Taflfelag-Politehnica 1987) 13...Rg8 14 f3 0-0-0 15 hxg5 Rxg5 16 Bh4 ± Petursson-A.Greenfeld, Hastings 1985/6.

9...g5

Black can also wait with this move, but in order to free his position it probably has to be played sooner or later.

9...Nbd7 10 f3 only seems to give White the additional possibility of retreating the bishop all the way to f2, for example:

a) 10...Qe7 11 e4 e5 12 Bd3 g5 13 Bf2 Nh5 14 Nf1 Nf4 15 Ne3 g4 16 0-0! (16 Bc2) 16...gxf3 17 Qxf3 and White is clearly better. Here are some sample variations to prove this, based on analysis by Khalifman in *Informator*:

a1) 17...Nxd3 18 Nf5 Qg5 19 Bh4 Qf4?! 20 Ng7+ Kf8 21 Ne6+ fxe6 22 Qxd3 +–.

a2) 17...Rg8 18 Bc2 0-0-0 19 Bg3 ±.

a3) 17...Qg5 18 Bc2 and again White is clearly better as he keeps his bishops.

a4) 17...exd4 18 Nd5! Nxd5 19 exd5 Ne5 20 Qe4 ± Khalifman-Emelin, St Petersburg Ch 1996.

b) 10...Nf8 11 Bd3 g5 12 Bf2 Rg8 13 Qa4+ Qd7 14 Qa3!? Ng6 15 0-0-0 Nh4 16 Rhg1 c5 17 e4 ± Gelfand-Salov, Dos Hermanas 1997.

10 Bg3 Qe7 *(D)*

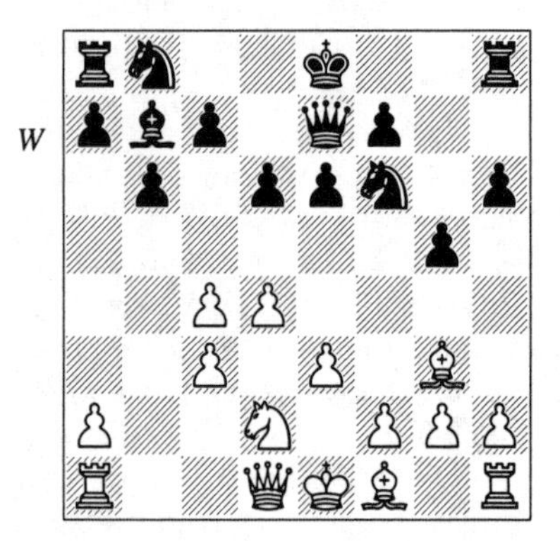

11 h4

By opening the h-file White not only stops a future expansion of Black's kingside pawns but also creates the possibility of exerting pressure by a later Rh6. There are, however, some very interesting alternatives:

a) 11 f3 is considered rather harmless in view of Vucić-Hjartarson, New York 1994, which continued 11...Nc6 12 Be2 0-0-0 13 0-0 Nh5 14 Bf2 f5 =.

b) 11 a4!? (trying to provoke ...a5, which would become a weakness if Black later decided to castle queenside) 11...Nc6! (11...a5 12 h4 Rg8 13 hxg5 hxg5 14 Qb3 Na6 15 Rb1 Kf8 16 Qd1 Bc6 17 Rh2 Kg7 18 c5! ± Kasparov-Karpov, London/Leningrad Wch (18) 1986) 12 Nb3 h5 (12...a5?!

13 c5! is very good for White) 13 f3 h4 14 ♗f2 a5 15 ♗e2 0-0-0 with an unclear game, Dokhoian-Lerner, Lvov Z 1990.

c) 11 c5!? is a new attempt by the young Russian star Zviagintsev, but some further tests are needed before a conclusion can be drawn. 11...dxc5 12 ♗b5+ ♔f8 (12...c6 13 ♗d3 is very unpleasant for Black owing to the weakness on d6, while 12...♗c6 13 ♕f3 ♘d5 14 ♗xc6+ ♘xc6 15 c4 ♘db4 16 a3 g4 17 ♕e4 f5 18 ♕b1 ♘a6 19 ♕b5 ♘ab8 20 d5 ♕f6 21 0-0 a6 22 ♕a4 exd5 23 cxd5 b5 24 ♕c2 reveals another point of White's interesting idea) 13 0-0 (intending f4) 13...h5 14 e4!? ♘xe4 15 ♘xe4 ♗xe4 16 ♖e1 ♗b7 17 h3 with an unclear position, Zviagintsev-Solozhenkin, Russian Ch 1995.

11...♖g8

11...g4 is met by 12 h5!.

12 hxg5 hxg5 *(D)*

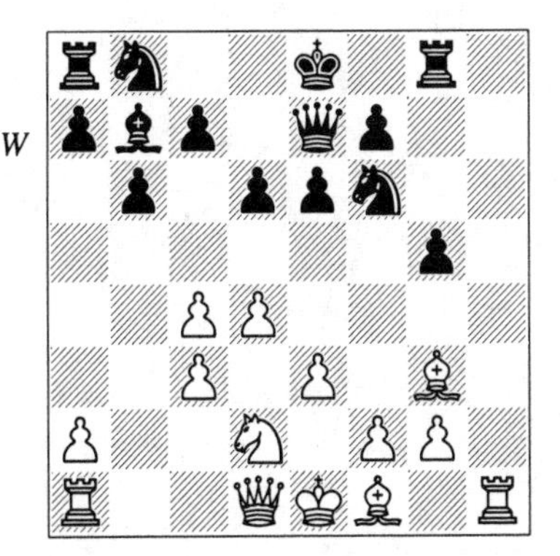

13 ♗e2

With this sensible developing move White intends to exchange the bishop with ♗f3. Fortunately, as we shall see, it is too dangerous for Black to capture the pawn on g2. Other options do not promise much:

a) 13 a4 ♘c6 14 ♕b1 0-0-0 15 ♘b3 ♖h8 is unclear, Piket-Lerner, Amsterdam 1988.

b) 13 ♖h6!? ♔f8!? 14 ♗e2 ♔g7 15 ♖h1 ♘c6 16 ♕c2 ♖h8 17 0-0-0 ♖xh1 18 ♖xh1 ♖h8 19 ♖xh8 ♔xh8 was roughly equal in Rogozenko-Kindermann, Moscow OL 1994.

c) 13 ♕c2 ♘c6 14 ♘b3 0-0-0 15 0-0-0 ♖h8 16 ♗e2 ♔b8 = A.Sokolov-Hjartarson, Copenhagen 1997.

d) 13 ♕a4+ ♕d7 14 ♕c2 ♘c6 15 ♗e2 0-0-0 16 ♖h6 ♕e7 17 0-0-0 ♖h8 18 ♖dh1 ♖xh6 19 ♖xh6 ♘g8 20 ♖h7 ♘f6 21 ♖h6 ♘g8 22 ♖h2 f5 = Lobron-Estremero Panos, Linares open 1998.

13...♘c6 *(D)*

13...♗xg2? 14 ♖h6 with the idea of ♗f3 is awkward for Black, e.g. 14...g4 15 ♗h4 ♘bd7 16 ♕a4 ♔f8 17 0-0-0 ♔g7 18 ♖h5 with an attack for White, Bareev-Dolmatov, USSR Ch 1987.

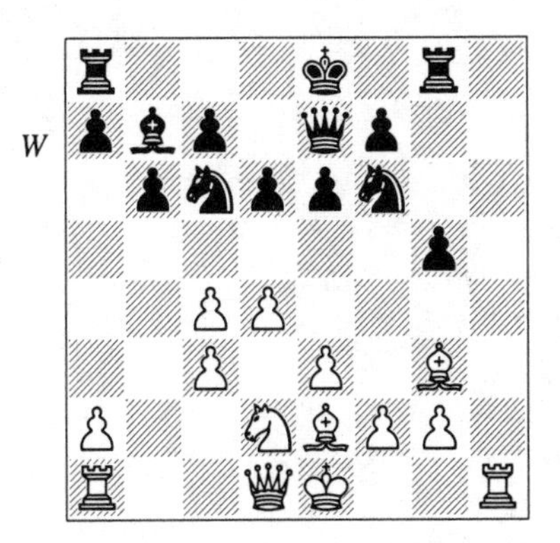

14 ♕a4

Kasparov-Psakhis, La Manga (2) 1990 went 14 ♕c2 0-0-0 15 0-0-0 ♖h8 16 e4 ♔b8 17 ♘b3 ♘d7 18 ♗d3 ♕f6 with a roughly equal game.

14...0-0-0 15 ♗f3 ♕d7 16 ♖h6 ♘a5 17 ♗xb7+ ♔xb7 18 ♕xd7

After 18 ♕d1 ♘e8 19 ♕f3+ ♔b8 20 ♖h7 ♖g7 21 ♖xg7 ♘xg7 22 ♕f6 ♘f5 23 ♕xg5 ♖h8 Black had good compensation in Thorsteins-Hjartarson, Eupen tt 1994, since White has difficulties finding a safe place for his king. In the game, 24 ♔e2 ran into 24...♘xc4!, while 24 0-0-0 would be met by 24...♕a4!.

18...♘xd7 19 ♔e2 ♖g7 20 ♖ah1 ♖dg8

The game is equal, Savchenko-Lerner, Simferopol 1988.

Index of Variations

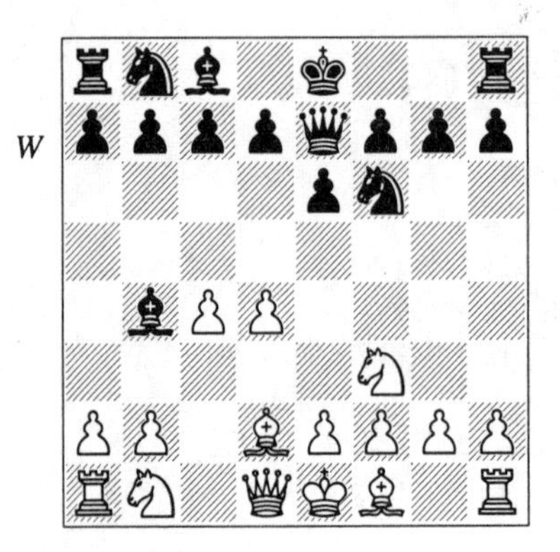

6: 4 ♗d2: The Aggressive 4...c5

7: The Catalan Bogo: 3 g3 ♗b4+

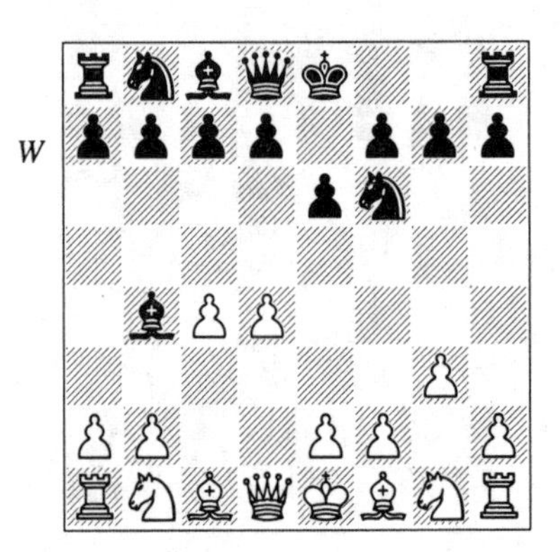

8: Transposition to the Nimzo-Indian: 4 ♘c3 b6